The Mutiny on H.M.S. *Bounty*

The Mutiny on H.M.S. *Bounty*

A Guide to Nonfiction, Fiction, Poetry, Films, Articles, and Music

DONALD A. MAXTON

Foreword by Sven Wahlroos

McFarland & Company, Inc., Publishers
Jefferson, North Carolina, and London

LIBRARY OF CONGRESS CATALOGUING-IN-PUBLICATION DATA

Maxton, Donald A., 1951–
The mutiny on H.M.S. Bounty : a guide to nonfiction, fiction, poetry, films, articles, and music / Donald A. Maxton ; foreword by Sven Wahlroos.
    p.   cm.
Includes bibliographical references and index.

ISBN 978-0-7864-3064-2
softcover : 50# alkaline paper ∞

1. Bounty Mutiny, 1789 — Bibliography. 2. Bounty Mutiny, 1789, in literature — Bibliography. 3. Bounty Mutiny, 1789 — Film catalogs. 4. Bounty Mutiny, 1789 — Songs and music — Bibliography. I. Title
Z4008.B68M395   2008   016.9104'5 — dc22   2008008588

British Library cataloguing data are available

©2008 Donald A. Maxton. All rights reserved

No part of this book may be reproduced or transmitted in any form or by any means, electronic or mechanical, including photocopying or recording, or by any information storage and retrieval system, without permission in writing from the publisher.

On the cover: *Bounty Prepares to Depart Tahitie* by John Hagan (courtesy Pitcairn Islands Study Center)

Manufactured in the United States of America

McFarland & Company, Inc., Publishers
Box 611, Jefferson, North Carolina 28640
www.mcfarlandpub.com

To Elizabeth Huberman, Bob Maxton and Margaret Schley,
with gratitude for their teaching and guidance
— and to the memory of Sven Wahlroos,
whose *Mutiny and Romance in the South Seas*
and love of the *Bounty* Saga were inspirational.

Acknowledgments

Thanks to Director Herbert Ford, Curator Gary Shearer and System Administrator Patrick Benner for their gracious assistance during many pleasant hours of research at the Pitcairn Islands Study Center, Pacific Union College. I owe a special debt of gratitude to Herb, who carefully reviewed the manuscript and made suggestions, and to Gary, who generously shared the fruit of many years of bibliographic research, particularly on articles published in the *Australasian Record, Pacific Union Recorder, Pacific Islands Monthly, Pitcairn Log, Review & Herald* and *UK Log*. Thanks to Patrick for his expert technical assistance.

Many thanks to Glynn Christian, Ron Edwards of the Pitcairn Islands Study Group and Dr. Sven Wahlroos, who reviewed the manuscript and made perceptive comments; my wife, Marie Moss Maxton, for her assistance and companionship during many hours of library research and travel; Carol Halebian, Gregory Suriano, June Ackerman, Marion Maxton, and Lisa and Henry Moss for their support and encouragement; John Chodes and Richard Crane, who kindly provided information and pictures from, respectively, *The Longboat* and *Mutiny on the Bounty—A Sea-Faring Show*; Cheryl Cole, Emily Cooke and Michele Bird, Orion Publishing Group; David Essex; Douglas N. Harding Rare Books; Tessa Hodgson and the late Brian Roylance, Genesis Publications Limited; Elizabeth Huberman; Dr. Richard P. Kennedy, Highgate School; Joseph W. Lawrence, Jack London Foundation, Inc.; Shelagh Phillips, Oxford University Press; Jackie Sarkies, Melbourne University Press; David Smith, The New York Public Library; Judy Taylor Hough; Adrian Webb, United Kingdom Hydrographic Office; and to "Sam," my faithful feline friend.

The collections of the following institutions were a rich source of material and information: Archibald S. Alexander Library, Rutgers University, New Brunswick, New Jersey; Beinecke Rare Book and Manuscript Library, Yale University, New Haven, Connecticut; G. W. Blunt White Library, Mystic Seaport, Mystic, Connecticut; The British Library, London; Caird Library, National Maritime Museum, Greenwich, England; Carl A. Kroch Library, Cornell University, Ithaca, New York; Doe and Moffitt Libraries, University of California, Berkeley; Hesburgh Library, Department of Special Collections, University of Notre Dame, Notre Dame, Indiana; McLaughlin Library, Seton Hall University, South Orange, New Jersey; The Newark Public Library, Newark, New Jersey; The New York Public Library, New York City, New York; Henry Ransom Humanities Research Center, The University of Texas at Austin; Pitcairn Islands Study Center, Pacific Union College, Angwin, California; and Sterling Memorial Library, Yale University, New Haven, Connecticut.

Table of Contents

Acknowledgments	vii
Foreword by Sven Wahlroos	1
Preface	5
1. 18TH CENTURY NONFICTION	7
Major Works	7
Additional Works	19
Supplemental Bibliography	21
2. 19TH CENTURY NONFICTION	23
Major Works	24
Additional Works	46
Supplemental Bibliography	51
3. 20TH AND 21ST CENTURY NONFICTION	55
Major Works	56
Additional Works	97
Supplemental Bibliography	105
4. FICTION, POETRY AND PLAYS	129
Major Works	130
Additional Works	157
Supplemental Bibliography	164
5. ILLUSTRATED BOOKS	167
Major Works	169
Additional Works	197
Supplemental Bibliography	201

6. FILMS, MAGAZINES AND MUSIC 203
    Major Works 204
    Additional Works 225
    Supplemental Bibliography 228

Appendix I: Selected Documentaries 231
Appendix II: Selected Web Sites 233
References 235
Index 239

Foreword
by Sven Wahlroos

The story of the *Bounty* mutiny is an inexhaustible goldmine for readers, authors, artists and film producers. And for anyone interested in adventure, drama and mystery, the mutiny can become a mother lode.

This fascination with a relatively unimportant mutiny on the small ship *Bounty* has continued since the event became known in England in 1790. Since then, the *Bounty* story has not only retained its allure; it has spread all over the western world, becoming the most famous mutiny in maritime history.

The insignificance of the loss of a small Royal Navy transport vessel stands in stark contrast to the overwhelmingly large number of publications on the subject and the millions of readers it has attracted over the last two centuries. The total number of major English-language works and noteworthy publications has now reached nearly 2,000, a number that does not include manuscripts, articles in newspapers and popular magazines, book reviews and works in other languages.

It would seem to be an impossible task to trace the history of such an enormous amount of literature and the reactions, emotions and opinions that it has generated in the reading public over the years. But the author of this work has accomplished it!

Donald A. Maxton has not only found and examined an extremely large number of publications dealing with the mutiny and its protagonists; he has provided the reader with a handbook, based on a magnificent annotated and illustrated bibliography.

Mr. Maxton's impeccable scholarship and immense knowledge of the *Bounty* history and literature is evident. He has selected a wide sampling of works that have played a role in reflecting—and sometimes forming—the reading public's perception of the mutiny and its protagonists over the past 200 years. His choice of books ranges from rare and highly expensive volumes (for example, the works published by the Golden Cockerel Press) to a 15-cent children's version.

His keen insight and analytical skill make for a captivating work, unique in the *Bounty* literature. Its main feature is the excellent, informative annotation of works concerning the *Bounty* story and also the important events on Pitcairn Island, without which the story would not be complete. Mr. Maxton masterfully turns a number of these annotations into "mini-articles," some of which could stand by themselves, and which provide a larger background and setting for the content of the annotated work.

The commentaries do not follow any prescribed pattern other than the date of publication: they are independent and tailor-made for the subject of the work described and its special interest. At times, one work is compared or contrasted with another, which gives further depth to the evaluation. The annotations are relevant and to the point, providing readers with a superb guide to the nature and quality of the work evaluated and what they can expect when reading it.

Mr. Maxton also quotes liberally from these works. For example, in commenting on Lieutenant J. Shillibeer's *A Narrative of the Briton's Voyage to Pitcairn's Island* (1817), he not only describes Shillibeer's meeting with the sons of Fletcher Christian and Edward Young, but also includes an important sample of their conversation.

He gives us a clear history of the polemical battle between "pro-Bligh" and "pro-Christian" readers. The debates — sometimes heated — continue to this day. Bligh, who was greeted with admiration and acclaim when he returned from the open boat voyage, was met with disdain and scorn when he came back from his successful second breadfruit expedition. Mr. Maxton gives us a clear picture of why the public's view of the mutiny has swayed so markedly over the years.

His text provides some surprises, even for *Bounty* enthusiasts. Many readers will be surprised to learn that Mark Twain was interested in the *Bounty*/Pitcairn Saga, and even wrote a short story about the Pitcairners' opposition to Joshua Hill's dictatorial rule on the island ("The Great Revolution in Pitcairn," 1882). And Jules Verne wrote an account of the mutiny ("Les révoltés de la Bounty," 1880), which was translated into English with the uninformative title "The Ship and the Island" (1899). Louis Becke and Walter Jeffery wrote a novel entitled "The Mutineer: A Romance of Pitcairn" (1898) and Jack London fans will probably know one of his best short stories, "The Seed of McCoy" (1911). This dramatic tale is based on an actual voyage, and the hero is a descendant of able-bodied seaman William McCoy, one of the mutineers on Pitcairn.

Mr. Maxton has been extremely thorough in his investigation of how the *Bounty* Saga has influenced more current popular literature as well. For example, Captain Peter Heywood (once midshipman on H.M.S. *Bounty*, convicted of mutiny but pardoned) makes a cameo appearance in *Desolation Island*, one of Patrick O'Brian's highly popular Aubrey/Maturin novels. At one point, O'Brian casts Heywood as visiting Captain Jack Aubrey and Surgeon Stephen Maturin on Aubrey's ship. Heywood is asked to give his opinion of Bligh, and it is interesting to read what O'Brian has Heywood say about his old commander:

> He (Heywood) did not wish to say anything against Captain Bligh — a capital navigator — very touchy himself, but had no notion of how he offended others — would give you the lie in front of all hands one day and invite you to dinner the next — you never knew where you were with him — led Christian, the master's mate, a sad life of it, yet probably liked him in his own strange way — never knew where he was with *Bounty*'s people — no idea at all — was amazed when they turned on him — an odd, whimsical man: had gone to great pains to teach Heywood how to work his lunar observations, yet had sworn his life away with a most inveterate malice....

What O'Brian has Heywood say may be of only peripheral interest or importance, but the very fact that Heywood is mentioned at all in a book by a modern, highly popular author shows how much the story of the *Bounty* mutiny still influences our culture.

Both in his text and in the books he has chosen for annotation, Mr. Maxton pays proper attention to the last home of the mutineers: Pitcairn Island. He stresses the highly important influence of the Polynesians on the Pitcairn settlement and its subsequent history — and rightly points out that the prominent role of the Polynesian women on this island has not received the emphasis it deserves. After all, with the diminishing number of white men and certainly with the death of the last mutineer, John Adams, Pitcairn society gradually developed into a matriarchy that lasted some decades and exacted significant influence that extended beyond the first generation of children.

It is a tragedy that no one bothered to interview the mutineers' female consorts who, after all, could speak passable English by the time of the first contact with the outer world in 1807. The only recorded interviews are with Teehuteatuaonoa (nicknamed Jenny), the consort of mutineer Isaac Martin.

Illustrations are an important part of this book, including dust jackets and title pages, artwork that depicts scenes from the works discussed, advertisements, posters and pictures of stage performances. In the captions, Mr. Maxton discusses their significance, artistic quality and how well they illuminate both fiction and nonfiction works connected with the *Bounty* mutiny.

Mr. Maxton annotates four of the five feature-length *Bounty* movies produced to date. The fifth is a silent film from 1916, which has deteriorated to such an extent that it cannot be shown. Nevertheless, he gives us all of the available data. His annotations of the extant feature films are objective, realistic, and stress the differences between artistry and historical accuracy.

Mr. Maxton briefly comments on the content and quality of several recent documentary films and includes — last but not least — a list of Web sites. Some of them will be of importance to "newcomers" and others will appeal to most *Bounty* enthusiasts.

This work is a landmark in *Bounty* history, and is bound to become a must-have resource for all *Bounty* researchers and maritime historians. It will help them immensely when they wish to publish a book or article on this or a related subject. I certainly wish this book had been available when I wrote my own book on the *Bounty* Saga.

The book also is likely to be a page-turner for those who are already *Bounty* fans. I am honored to present Mr. Maxton's work to the reading public.

May the *Bounty* sail forever!
Sven Wahlroos, Granada Hills, California, September 2006

The late Sven Wahlroos, Ph.D, noted psychologist, author and sailor, became fascinated with the mutiny on the Bounty *as a boy in Finland. He studied the literature all his life and spent time on Pitcairn and Norfolk Islands. He wrote* Mutiny and Romance in the South Seas: A Companion to the Bounty Adventure, *several journal articles on the* Bounty *mutiny, and the* English-Tahitian, Tahitian-English Dictionary.

Preface

The mutiny that occurred on His Majesty's Ship *Bounty* during the early morning hours of April 28, 1789 — the most famous insurrection in naval history — has commanded the attention of people for more than 200 years. The *Bounty* voyage was initiated by the scientist, Sir Joseph Banks, at the behest of English planters who were eager to transport shoots of the breadfruit plant from Tahiti to the West Indies, where they would be grown as a cheap, nourishing food for their slaves. Banks, who served as President of the Royal Society, was influential in naval circles and at court, and King George III granted his request. Banks suggested that Lieutenant William Bligh be appointed commander of the expedition.

When H.M.S. *Bounty* set sail on December 23, 1787, its mission was of little interest to the Royal Navy or the general public. The voyage would have become a minor footnote in history were it not for the mutiny, which engendered an astonishing sequence of events that I will refer to in this book as the "*Bounty* Saga." Its high drama and the remarkable personalities involved continue to inspire interest as well as controversy.

The *Bounty* Saga includes the ten-month voyage to Tahiti in a dangerously small, cramped vessel, with no Royal Marines on board to maintain discipline; the idyllic interlude the crew spent on this island paradise; the clash between former friends Lieutenant Bligh and Master's Mate Fletcher Christian, followed by the mutiny; the perilous, heroic journey of Bligh and his loyal men to safety in a small, open boat, perhaps the most remarkable voyage of its kind in history; the mutineers' fruitless attempt to settle among South Pacific islanders on Tubuai; Captain Edward Edwards' dogged pursuit of the mutineers in H.M.S. *Pandora*, a mission ending in shipwreck; the suspense-filled court-martial of ten captured mutineers, with their lives hanging in the balance; and a determined campaign to destroy Bligh's reputation that has influenced our opinion of him for more than two centuries.

Remarkably, the mutiny itself was a bloodless affair, but ultimately it lead to the loss of many lives. The story of Pitcairn Island, an integral part of the *Bounty* Saga, is bittersweet. Christian and his party of mutineers, along with their native companions, struggled to build a refuge on Pitcairn, only to have it end in jealousy, interracial strife, alcohol abuse and murder. Providentially, this tale has a happy ending. The survivors of these bloody events ultimately fashioned a peaceful, religious society that became a model and inspiration for the rest of the world. The public continues to be intrigued by this remarkable community.

People never tire of pondering the mutiny, asking such questions as "Who was to blame?" "What exactly provoked the mutiny?" "Was Bligh a cruel tyrant, or did he take better care of his crew than most commanders?" The reputations of Bligh and Christian, the two primary antagonists, have fallen and risen over time, and the discussion has shown no sign of abating since Bligh published the first account of the mutiny in 1790.

Since that date, the literature surrounding H.M.S. *Bounty* has grown to include thousands of works. In addition to non-fiction books and articles — both popular and scholarly — the *Bounty* Saga has inspired novels, short stories, children's books, poems, stage and radio dramas, musical plays, and even comic books. There have been five film treatments and numerous documentaries, and a growing number of Web sites devoted to the subject.

The sheer volume of this information is overwhelming. This book is designed to serve as a roadmap and reference guide for anyone interested in the *Bounty* Saga — from people whose interest has been whetted, perhaps, by viewing one of the films — to the maritime history specialist approaching this topic for the first time. It covers the most important *Bounty* material published from 1790 to 2006, selected for its historic, scholarly, literary, artistic or popular significance. More than 1,700 books, articles and other material are included, spanning the entire breadth of the *Bounty* Saga.

To keep the book to a reasonable length, I have excluded, with a few exceptions, manuscripts held by major libraries, museums or in private collections; newspaper articles; works in foreign languages; and audio recordings of individual books.

In each chapter, descriptive, analytical discussions of the major works are presented in chronological, rather than alphabetical order, allowing readers to consider and compare them in the cultural or scholarly context of their period — and perhaps identify new topics for study. The name of the author begins each entry, followed by the title and information as it is presented on the title page of that work. If the work was published anonymously, or under a pseudonym, the author's name is given in parentheses. Similarly, if there was no stated date of publication but the date has been confirmed, that date is given in parentheses. These discussions are followed by an annotated bibliography of selected works.

The supplemental bibliographic listings that close each chapter offer an even broader sampling of *Bounty*/Pitcairn literature, with subjects ranging from the *Pandora* wreck excavations and contemporary life on Pitcairn Island, to the controversy over James Morrison's *Journal* and the history of the Seventh-day Adventist church in the Pacific. They include new, illustrated, children's and paperback editions of important books, articles in popular and specialist periodicals, and some interesting anthologies that feature retellings of the *Bounty* Saga. A handbook of this literature is long overdue, and I hope that all H.M.S. *Bounty* and Pitcairn Island enthusiasts find this volume useful and enjoyable.

1

18th Century Nonfiction

The immense bibliography of material associated with the *Bounty* Saga begins with William Bligh's *A Narrative of the Mutiny on Board His Majesty's Ship* Bounty, a slender, 88-page volume published in 1790, one year after the mutiny. This merely stimulated the public's appetite for the full story, which Bligh provided in 1792 — from his own perspective, of course — in *A Voyage to the South Sea*.

During the next three decades, these two books were translated, reprinted and rehashed in various compilations, notably *Dangerous Voyage of Captain Bligh, in an Open Boat, over 1200 Leagues of the Ocean, in the Year 1789*, which appeared in 1817, 1820, 1822 and 1824. In more recent years, *A Narrative of the Mutiny* and *A Voyage to the South Sea* have appeared in many forms, from inexpensive paperbacks to facsimiles and lavish fine press editions.

Unfortunately, some of the earliest primary material is difficult to locate outside of a major research library. The important accounts of Captain Edward Edwards of *Pandora* and *Pandora*'s surgeon George Hamilton were published together in 1915, but this volume has become very scarce. Hamilton's *A Voyage Round the World in His Majesty's Frigate Pandora* has been reprinted twice in recent years, but only in limited editions that tend to be both elusive and expensive.

A portion of the *Bounty* court-martial may be consulted in an inexpensive paperback, but the rest of the document, published in 1931 and never reprinted, is a collector's item. James Morrison's *Journal* and other important documents by Bligh and John Fryer, the *Bounty*'s Master, have never appeared as inexpensive editions. It would be a boon for *Bounty* Saga enthusiasts and scholars if an enterprising publisher decided to make affordable editions of these books more widely available.

Major Works

WILLIAM BLIGH: *A Narrative of the Mutiny on Board His Majesty's Ship* Bounty; *and the Subsequent Voyage of Part of the Crew, in the Ship's Boat, from Tofoa, One of the Friendly Islands, to Timor, a Dutch Settlement in the East Indies.* Written by Lieutenant William Bligh. Illustrated with charts. London: Printed for George Nicol, Bookseller to His Majesty, Pall-Mall, MDCCXC (1790). *A Narrative of the Mutiny on Board His Majesty's Ship* Bounty. Philadelphia: William Spotswood, 1790. First American edition.

"I sailed from Otaheite on the 4th of April 1789, having on board 1015 fine bread-fruit plants, besides many other valuable fruits of that country, which, with unremitting attention, we had been collecting for three and twenty weeks, and which were now in the highest state of perfection."

This is how William Bligh chose to begin *A Narrative of the Mutiny on Board His Majesty's Ship* Bounty, the first published account of history's most famous mutiny — not from the beginning of *Bounty*'s voyage on December 23, 1787 as one might expect, but on April 28, 1789, the day of the mutiny.

Bligh had reasons to begin the story *in medias res*, and alludes to them in the book's "Advertisement:" "This part of the voyage is not first in the order of time, yet the circumstances are so distinct from that by which it was preceded, that it appears unnecessary to delay giving as much early information as possible concerning so extraordinary an event."

Bligh's return to England in March 1790 and the news of his remarkable open-boat voyage immediately galvanized the public. Newspapers published stories about the *Bounty* mutiny within days of Bligh's return, and a play, *The Pirates: Or, The Calamities of Capt. Bligh*, quickly opened at the Royalty Theatre. Bligh planned to publish a complete account of *Bounty*'s voyage, but he recognized the importance of getting his account of the mutiny quickly into print. Bligh biographer Gavin Kennedy discusses Bligh's motivations in the article "Turning Mutiny into a Legend," written for the National Maritime Museum's *Bounty* Bicentenary exhibition in 1989:

> In journalistic terms, Bligh had a story to tell, especially after surviving the rigours of the open boat voyage, but he also had another motive: to explain why a mutiny had occurred on his ship, and why he was unable to prevent it, or having failed to prevent it, why he, or some of the loyal men in the crew, were unable to put it down. His career, if not his pride, depended on how convincing was the explanation he gave to the Admiralty and to the wider public.

The Admiralty court-martialed and acquitted Bligh for the loss of the *Bounty*. Readers were anxious to learn more, but in the near term, *A Narrative of the Mutiny* would have to suffice. It was published in June 1790, just three months after Bligh's return. It quickly became a best-seller, with editions appearing in America, Ireland and Holland. This stirring account of the mutiny and open-boat voyage confirmed Bligh's reputation as a national hero — for the time being.

Most of *A Narrative of the Mutiny* is devoted to the open-boat voyage. Bligh's prose style is surprisingly objective, considering how much he suffered through the terrible events he describes: "Just before sun-rising, Mr. Christian, with the master at arms, gunner's mate, and Thomas Burket, seaman, came into my cabin while I was asleep, and seizing me, tied my hands with a cord behind my back, and threatened me with instant death, if I spoke or made the least noise."

Here, for the first time in print, Bligh takes the position that the mutiny had nothing to do with his relationship with *Bounty*'s officers and crew, but with their desire to return to the idyllic lives they enjoyed on Tahiti: "It will very naturally be asked, what could be the reason for such a revolt? In answer to which, I can only conjecture that the mutineers had assured themselves of a more happy life among the Otaheiteans, than they could possibly have in England; which, joined to some female connections, have most probably been the principal cause of the whole transaction."

Bligh didn't acknowledge it in print, but there were more reasons for the mutiny than the crew's desire to return to Tahiti. As George Mackaness writes in his introduction to *A Book of the "Bounty,"* "Many of the petty officers had been a great trial to him, and their gen-

A
NARRATIVE
OF THE
MUTINY,
ON BOARD

HIS MAJESTY's SHIP *BOUNTY*;

AND THE

SUBSEQUENT VOYAGE OF PART OF THE CREW,

IN THE SHIP's BOAT,

From TOFOA, one of the Friendly Islands,

To TIMOR, a Dutch Settlement in the East Indies.

Written by LIEUTENANT WILLIAM BLIGH.

ILLUSTRATED WITH CHARTS.

LONDON:
PRINTED FOR GEORGE NICOL, BOOKSELLER TO HIS MAJESTY, PALL-MALL.
M DCC XC.

Title page of the first edition of William Bligh's *A Narrative of the Mutiny on Board His Majesty's Ship* Bounty. Published in 1790, this was the first published account of the mutiny. Bligh's more extensive account, covering the mutiny and the rest of *Bounty*'s voyage, appeared two years later.

eral inefficiency and continual neglect of duty had often sorely tried his temper." For example, Master John Fryer and Boatswain William Cole failed to air out the spare set of sails, which became mildewed. This kind of carelessness could mean disaster for a vessel at sea. Mackaness continues, "Nevertheless, in the hour of trial most of them remained loyal to him." The most important exception was Fletcher Christian, ringleader of the mutiny.

Bligh never mentions the abuse he directed at Christian in the days leading up to the mutiny. Instead, he writes, "Christian, in particular, I was on the most friendly terms with; that very day he was engaged to have dined with me; and the preceding night he excused himself from supping with me, on pretence of being unwell; for which I felt concerned, having no suspicions of his integrity and honour."

Bligh and Christian had been on friendly terms at the beginning of the voyage, but not on the way home. He invited Christian to supper directly after shaming him before the entire crew for taking a few coconuts, an incident that the general public would not learn about until well after the court-martial. Boatswain's Mate James Morrison and Able Seaman John Adams report this unpleasant incident, which proved to be the last straw for Christian.

One reason for the popularity of *A Narrative of the Mutiny* is Bligh's storytelling gifts. His description of the mutiny is all the more compelling for its dispassionate tone, and the tale of the open boat voyage is one of the great narratives of the sea. He creates vivid pictures for the reader, such as his observation of Christian during the mutiny: "As for Christian, he seemed meditating instant destruction on himself and every one.... The remembrance of past kindnesses produced some signs of remorse in Christian. When they were forcing me out of the ship, I asked him, if this treatment was a proper return for the many instances he had received of my friendship? He appeared disturbed at my question, and answered, with much emotion, 'That,—captain Bligh,—that is the thing—I am in hell—I am in hell.'"

Readers anxiously awaited Bligh's promised narrative of the entire *Bounty* voyage. They would have to wait for two years.

WILLIAM BLIGH: *A Voyage to the South Sea, Undertaken by Command of His Majesty, for the Purpose of Conveying the Bread-fruit Tree to the West Indies in His Majesty's Ship The Bounty, Commanded by Lieutenant William Bligh. Including an Account of the Mutiny on Board the Said Ship and the subsequent Voyage of Part of the Crew in the Ship's Boat from Tofoa, One of the Friendly Islands, to Timor, a Dutch Settlement in the East Indies. The Whole Illustrated with Charts, &c.* Published by the Permission of the Lords Commissioners of the Admiralty. London: Printed for George Nicol, Bookseller to His Majesty, Pall-Mall, MDCCXII (1792).

When William Bligh published *A Narrative of the Mutiny on Board His Majesty's Ship* Bounty in 1790, he promised to publish a more complete account of *Bounty*'s voyage in the book's "Advertisement:" "The rest will be laid before the Public as soon as it can be got ready; and it is intended to publish it in such a manner, as, with the present Narrative, will make the account of the voyage compleat."

Bligh kept his promise, and *A Voyage to the South Sea*, one of the most important and famous books of Pacific voyages, appeared in 1792. It incorporates the text of *A Narrative of the Mutiny*, with corrections and revisions, and adds nearly 200 pages of material based on Bligh's private journal.

In 1791, the Admiralty commissioned Bligh to command H.M.S. *Providence* on a second breadfruit voyage, so he was not able to prepare the book for publication himself. Captain James Burney, who had sailed with Captain Cook, edited Bligh's journal and prepared it for press, with the assistance of Sir Joseph Banks.

A Voyage to the South Sea tells the story of *Bounty*'s outward voyage, including such compelling events as Bligh's attempt to round Cape Horn. He was at his finest during this struggle, although he ultimately failed. In addition to describing the horrific sailing conditions, he demonstrates his concern for the crew of the cramped vessel, where a great deal of space had been devoted to accommodating the breadfruit plants they would gather in Tahiti:

> At six in the morning the storm exceeded what I had ever met with before; and the sea, from the frequent shifting of the wind, running in contrary directions, broke exceeding high.... The gale continued, with severe squalls of hail and sleet, the remainder of this, and all the next day.... The ship now began to complain, and required to be pumped every hour; which was no more than we had reason to expect from such a continuance of gales of wind and high seas. The decks also became so leaky, that I was obliged to allot the great cabin, of which I made little use, except in fine weather, to those people who had wet berths, to hang their hammocks in; and by this means the between decks were less crowded.

Once the *Bounty* reached Tahiti, Bligh was a keen observer of local customs and natural history during his stay, and his reports of the island and its people are a highlight of *A Voyage to the South Sea*. For example, he describes in detail the various fishing techniques employed by the Tahitians: "Their fishing is mostly in the night, when they make strong lights on the reefs, which attract the fish to them. Sometimes, in fine weather, the canoes are out in such numbers, that the whole sea appears illuminated.... Their hooks being bright, are used without bait, in the manner of our artificial flies."

In the sections of *A Voyage to the South Sea* devoted to the open boat voyage, we can observe the qualities that enabled Bligh to bring his loyal crew to a safe haven against tremendous odds. In addition to his courage, peerless navigational skills, and ability to bond the crew in a common mission, he reveals character traits that shielded him, and the crew, from desperation.

For a good part of the voyage, each man was rationed to 1/25 lb. of "bread" (ship's biscuit), given twice a day. Eating more would have quickly depleted their meager food supply. Bligh writes: "To make the bread a little savoury, most of the people frequently dipped it in salt water; but I generally broke mine into small pieces, and eat it in my allowance of water, out of a cocoa-nut shell, with a spoon; economically avoiding to take too large a piece at a time, so that I was as long at dinner as if it had been a much more plentiful meal." Bligh and his loyal crew probably would never have been heard of again if he had not risen to the challenge with such discipline, leadership and imagination.

The first editions of *A Narrative of the Mutiny on Board His Majesty's Ship* Bounty and *A Voyage to the South Sea* are rare, expensive and essential pieces of Bountiana. Fortunately, both have been reprinted in less expensive formats, including facsimile and illustrated editions. The most accessible ones are *A Book of the 'Bounty'* (Everyman's Library, 1938, 1981), which includes both books, along with additional material; and *The* Bounty *Mutiny* (Penguin Putnam, 2001), which omits *A Voyage to the South Sea* but collects a variety of other rare publications.

(STEVEN BARNEY AND EDWARD CHRISTIAN): *Minutes of the Proceedings of the Court-Martial Held at Portsmouth, August 12, 1792 On Ten Persons Charged with Mutiny on Board His Majesty's Ship the Bounty With an Appendix, Containing a Full Account of the Real Causes and Circumstances of that Unhappy Transaction, the Most Material of Which Have Hitherto Been Withheld from the Public.* London: Printed for J. Deighton, Opposite Gray's-Inn, Holborn, MDCCXCIV (1794).

WILLIAM BLIGH: *An Answer to Certain Assertions Contained in the Appendix to a Pamphlet Entitled Minutes Of The Proceedings Of The Court-Martial held at Portsmouth August 12,*

1792 on Ten Persons Charged With Mutiny on Board his Majesty's Ship the Bounty. By Captain William Bligh. London: Printed for G. Nicol, Bookseller to his Majesty, Pall-Mall, 1794.

EDWARD CHRISTIAN: *A Short Reply to Capt. William Bligh's Answer.* London: Printed for J. Deighton, Opposite Gray's-Inn, Holborn, 1795.

When William Bligh returned to England in August 1793 from his voyage on H.M.S. *Providence*, he had every reason to think that he would be welcomed and praised for successfully completing his second mission to transport breadfruit plants to Jamaica. Although he received a gift of 1,000 guineas from Jamaica's House Assembly, his reception at home was quite different. Bligh's fellow captains avoided him, and Nathaniel Portlock, his lieutenant on *Providence*, was granted an audience at the Admiralty, while he was not.

Bligh had hoped to publish an account of the *Providence* voyage upon his return, but the Admiralty was no longer interested. In fact, the Royal Navy did not offer him a new command, but placed him on half pay. Three years earlier he had been lauded as a hero, "Breadfruit Bligh," but during his absence from England on *Providence*, he acquired a new sobriquet: "That Bounty Bastard."

He then entered a mostly unsuccessful struggle to rebuild his reputation, which the influential families of Fletcher Christian, and Peter Heywood — who had been condemned as a mutineer but pardoned by King George III — severely tarnished with the publication of Stephen Barney's *Minutes of the Proceedings of the Court-Martial Held at Portsmouth, August 12, 1792 on Ten Persons Charged with Mutiny on Board His Majesty's Ship the Bounty*. This volume included the evidence for the prosecution, followed by an Appendix written by Edward Christian, a professor of law and one of Fletcher Christian's brothers.

Edward Christian and the Heywood family collaborated on the Appendix in an effort to reach two specific goals: mitigate Fletcher Christian's guilt by revealing that Bligh's behavior drove him to mutiny, possibly providing him some protection if he was ever captured; and ensure that Peter Heywood's naval career would not suffer from his being convicted of mutiny. Heywood set the stage by writing to Edward Christian shortly after he received the King's Pardon and then meeting with him. He wrote, "Your

A post–mutiny portrait of William Bligh graces the frontispiece of *A Voyage to the South Sea*, published by George Nicol in 1792. The *Bounty*'s launch is pictured in the background. Perennially popular, this volume has appeared in paperback as well as deluxe, limited and illustrated editions for collectors.

The* Bounty *Mutiny, a Penguin Classic, reprints several rare 18th- and 19th-century books, pamphlets and articles in an inexpensive paperback format. The second printing was issued with new cover art: "Bligh Is Cast Adrift," by John Hagan. Reprinted by permission of Penguin Group (USA) Inc.

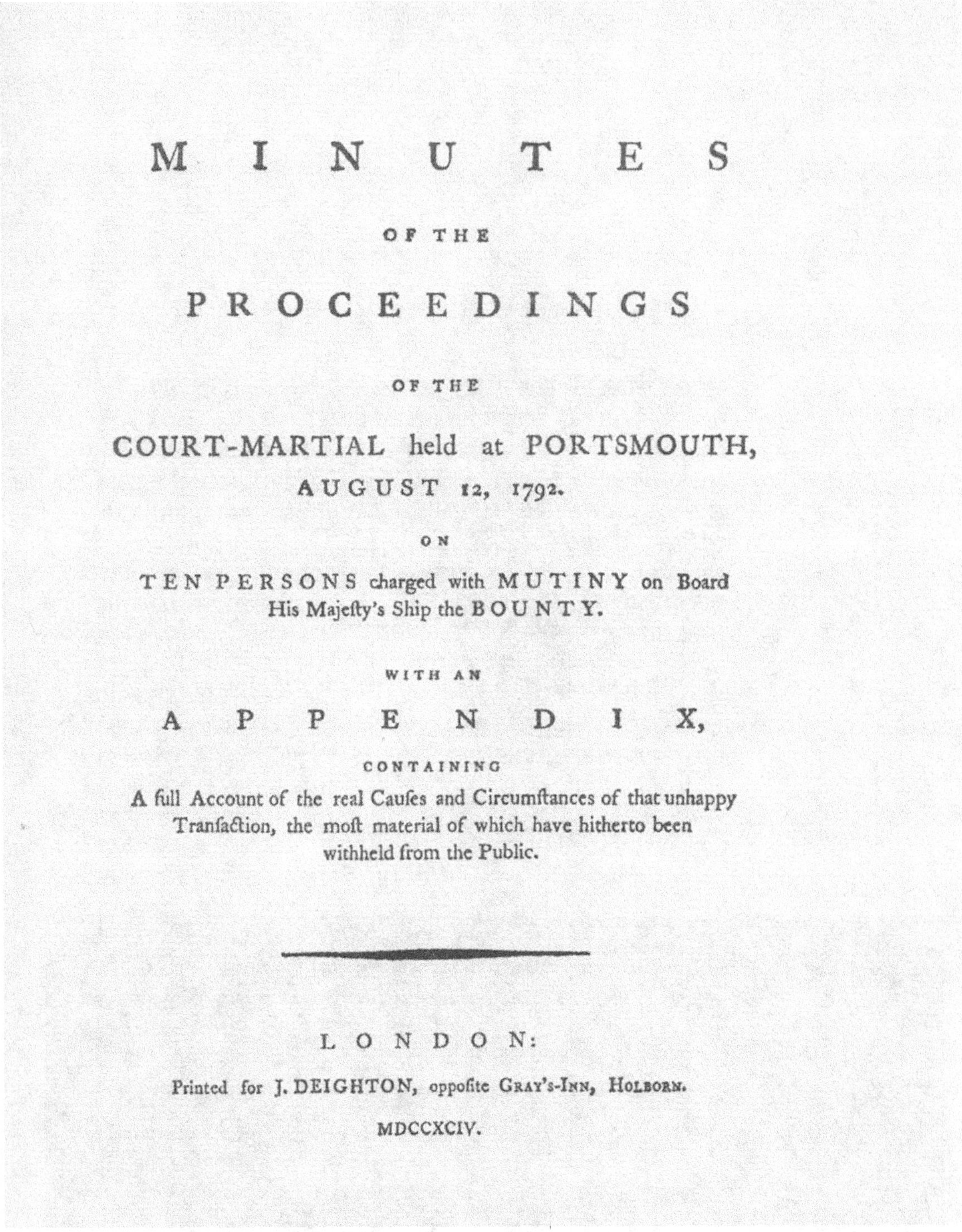

MINUTES

OF THE

PROCEEDINGS

OF THE

COURT-MARTIAL held at PORTSMOUTH,
AUGUST 12, 1792.

ON

TEN PERSONS charged with MUTINY on Board
His Majesty's Ship the BOUNTY.

WITH AN

APPENDIX,

CONTAINING

A full Account of the real Causes and Circumstances of that unhappy
Transaction, the most material of which have hitherto been
withheld from the Public.

LONDON:

Printed for J. DEIGHTON, opposite GRAY's-INN, HOLBORN.

MDCCXCIV.

Title page of *Minutes of the Proceedings of the Court-Martial Held at Portsmouth, August 12, 1792 on Ten Persons Charged with Mutiny on Board His Majesty's Ship the Bounty with an Appendix ...* by Steven Barney and Edward Christian, Fletcher Christian's brother. Christian wrote the Appendix to this volume in an effort to damage William Bligh's reputation and present his brother in a more positive light. He succeeded by drawing attention to Bligh's irascibility.

brother was not that vile wretch void of all gratitude, which the world had the unkindness to think him: but, on the contrary, a most worthy character ruined only by having the misfortune, if it can be so called, of being a young man of strict honour, and adorned with every virtue, and beloved by all (except one, whose ill report is his greatest praise) who had the pleasure of his acquaintance."

The "one whose ill report is his greatest praise" surely refers to Bligh. Heywood wrote a letter expressing similar sentiments to a newspaper in Cumberland, Fletcher Christian's home county. Edward Christian declares his reasons for publishing the Appendix in a preface to the pamphlet:

> The Circumstances Communicated in this Appendix have been collected by a person nearly related to Christian: and it is far from his intention or wish to insinuate a vindication of the crime which has been committed... The publication of the trial, and of these extraordinary facts, it is presumed, will in no degree impede the pursuit of justice, yet it will administer some consolation to the broken hearts, which this melancholy transaction has occasioned.

Edward Christian explains that he obtained important information following the court-martial, "Information as surprized him greatly, and in consequence of which, he resolved to make every possible enquiry into this unhappy affair." The Appendix summarizes the information he gathered during a series of meetings at the Crown and Sceptre Inn, Greenwich, with some of *Bounty*'s crew and officers, including Heywood, John Fryer, William Purcell, Thomas Hayward and Lawrence Lebogue. Using their words, he then proceeds to attack William Bligh's character and fitness as a commander: "They declare that Captain Bligh used to call his officers 'scoundrels, damned rascals, hounds, hell-hounds, beasts, and infamous wretches'; that he frequently threatened them, that when the ship arrived at Endeavour Straits, 'he would kill one half of the people, make the officers jump overboard, and would make them eat grass like cows.'"

Edward Christian argues that Bligh's unprofessional behavior drove his brother to desperation and mutiny, summarizing how Bligh accused Fletcher Christian of stealing his coconuts; disgraced him in front of his Tahitian friends; shook his hands in Fletcher's face, and many other abusive incidents that depict Bligh as a foul-mouthed tyrant. He vouches for the authenticity of the Appendix by listing "The gentlemen who were present at different conversations with the persons just mentioned." Although this impressive list includes clerics, attorneys and naval officers, he fails to mention that all of them are either good friends with, or under some obligation to, the Heywood and Christian families.

By and large, the Appendix achieved its mission of blackening Bligh's name. Gavin Kennedy, in his introduction to *A Book of the 'Bounty,'* states that "Edward Christian intended to provoke Bligh into a libel suit... Bligh would have been sucked into a confused and expensive case which, even if he emerged victorious, would have ruined him unless he got exceptional damages."

Although his future in the Royal Navy and ability to support his wife and children were at risk, Bligh did not pursue the matter in the courts. He tried to contain the damage by publishing a pamphlet entitled *An Answer to Certain Assertions Contained in the Appendix to a Pamphlet Entitled Minutes of The Proceedings of the Court-Martial held at Portsmouth August 12, 1792 on Ten Persons Charged With Mutiny on Board his Majesty's Ship the Bounty*.

In *An Answer to Certain Assertions*, Bligh writes, "This Appendix is the work of Mr Edward Christian, the brother of Fletcher Christian, who headed the mutineers of the *Bounty*, written apparently for the purpose of vindicating his brother's conduct at my expense." He then provides a "List of Proofs"—15 letters, testimonials, and affidavits, many provided by *Bounty*'s crew—that reflect or attest to his fitness as a commander. Here is a sample:

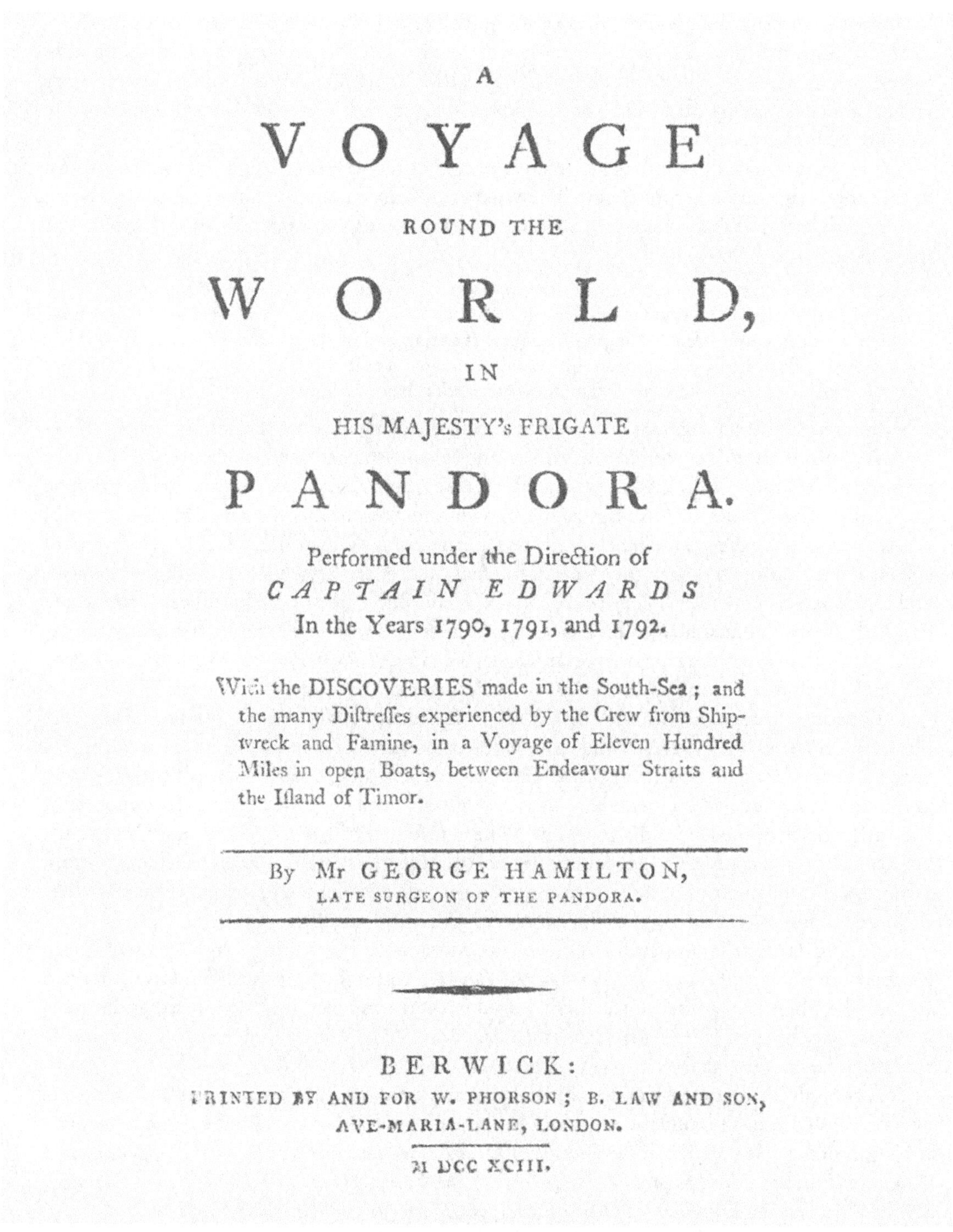

A

VOYAGE

ROUND THE

WORLD,

IN

HIS MAJESTY's FRIGATE

PANDORA.

Performed under the Direction of
CAPTAIN EDWARDS
In the Years 1790, 1791, and 1792.

With the DISCOVERIES made in the South-Sea; and the many Diftreſſes experienced by the Crew from Shipwreck and Famine, in a Voyage of Eleven Hundred Miles in open Boats, between Endeavour Straits and the Iſland of Timor.

By Mr GEORGE HAMILTON,
LATE SURGEON OF THE PANDORA.

BERWICK:
PRINTED BY AND FOR W. PHORSON; B. LAW AND SON,
AVE-MARIA-LANE, LONDON.
M DCC XCIII.

Title page of the first edition of George Hamilton's *A Voyage Round the World in His Majesty's Frigate Pandora*. Hamilton, who served as Ship's Surgeon during *Pandora*'s mission to capture the *Bounty* mutineers, wrote a highly descriptive, entertaining account of this ill-fated voyage. His vigorous writing style stands in marked contrast to the work of *Pandora*'s commander, Captain Edward Edwards.

I never heard the captain damn the officers, and call them names, and threaten to make them jump overboard, kill half of them, and make them eat grass like cows. I never heard any such a thing [John Smith].

Captain Bligh made no distinction, every officer was obliged to do his duty, and he showed no more favour to one man than another. I was sure every person in the *Providence* would speak well of Captain Bligh — he was a father to every person [Lawrence Lebogue, who also sailed with Bligh on *Providence*].

I never saw Captain Bligh shake his hand in Christian's face [Joseph Coleman].

I never remember to have heard Captain Bligh make use of such illiberal epithets and menaces as the Appendix attributes to him [Lieutenant John Hallett].

An Answer to Certain Assertions failed to undo the damage inflicted by Edward Christian's Appendix. Kennedy writes, "It is not really a proper answer — it presents material which could form the basis of an answer." Bligh may have intended to expand it into a legal brief, but this never occurred. In the meantime, Edward Christian quickly published a response, entitled *A Short Reply to Capt. William Bligh's Answer*, in which he defends the Appendix, arguing that Bligh's "Proofs" are "Little more than insinuations that the statements, which I thought it my duty to lay before the public, have been unfairly obtained, or unfairly represented."

A portrait of George Hamilton, Surgeon, Royal Navy. His pocket watch and some of the medical equipment and medicines he used on Pandora were retrieved after the ship's wreck was discovered in 1977. Little is known about Hamilton's subsequent career, but he lost an arm on a later voyage and vanishes from the official records in 1796 — the probable year of his death.

Edward Christian explains how his investigations into the mutiny were sparked through conversations with Peter Heywood and John Fryer, and that the "statements" he gathered for the Appendix are accurate and verified as truth by the *Bounty* people he interviewed. A careful lawyer, he closes *A Short Reply* by stating that he is not trying to defend his brother's actions, but to demonstrate how a promising young seaman had been mercilessly driven to throw away his life.

These three pamphlets were printed in very small numbers, and are far more difficult to find than Bligh's *A Narrative of the Mutiny* or *A Voyage to the South Sea*. *The Hill Collection of Pacific Voyages* states that *Minutes of the Proceedings* was "Printed for distribution among the author's friends, and Ministers of State." Only three copies of *A Short Reply to Capt. William Bligh's Answer* are known to exist.

Fortunately, they are available in an inexpensive Penguin Classics edition, entitled *The Bounty Mutiny* (2001). They also were reproduced in a facsimile edition, limited to 1,000 copies, by Georgian House, Melbourne (1952). *Minutes of the Proceedings of the Court-Martial* and Edward Christian's Appendix was reprinted in *A Book of the 'Bounty'* (1938, 1981).

GEORGE HAMILTON: *A Voyage Round the World in His Majesty's Frigate Pandora Performed Under the Direction of Captain Edwards In the Years 1790, 1791 and 1792.* Berwick: Printed by and for B. Law and Son, Ave-Maria-Lane, London, 1793.

George Hamilton's account of the vessel dispatched by the Admiralty in November 1790 to capture the *Bounty* mutineers, under the command of Captain Edward Edwards, is a valuable, entertaining supplement to Edwards' prosaic record.

As Ship's Surgeon, Hamilton had a unique perspective as well as an engaging personality, and he tells the story of H.M.S. *Pandora* in a lively fashion. On the other hand, Edwards' account "Compares in style and colour with a log-book," as Basil Thomson states in his introduction to *Voyage of H.M.S. 'Pandora'* (1915), which printed Edwards' reports to the Admiralty for the first time. Thomson describes Edwards as "A cold, hard man," and Hamilton as "rollicking" and "irresponsible."

Sir John Barrow, author of *The Eventful History of the Mutiny and Piratical Seizure of H.M.S. Bounty: Its Causes and Consequences*, was less kind to Hamilton, writing that his narrative is the work of "A coarse, vulgar, and illiterate man, more disposed to relate licentious scenes and adventures, in which he and his companions were engaged, than to give any information of proceedings and occurrences connected with the main object of the voyage."

Barrow is somewhat justified in his opinion, since Hamilton does not devote a great deal of space to the events that interest us most, such as the plight of the prisoners confined in "Pandora's Box," and the details of the open boat voyage following *Pandora*'s shipwreck. Hamilton's language is frank, colorful and sometimes coarse, all characteristics of much 18th century prose and poetry. His description of a "Hæva," or ceremonial dance, is a good example of this style:

> Two ladies, pretty fancifully dressed, as described in Captain Cook's Voyages, were introduced after a little ceremony. Something resembling a turkey cock's tail, and stuck on their rumps in a fan kind of fashion, about five feet in diameter, had a very good effect while the ladies kept their faces to us; but when in a bending attitude, they presented their rumps, to shew the wonderful agility of their loins; the effect is better conceived than described ... the piece concluded by the ladies exposing that which is better felt than seen; and, in that state of nature, walked from the bottom of the theatre to the top where we were sitting on the grass.

Hamilton's writing can be highly descriptive, such as his account of Tahitians mourning *Pandora*'s departure: "Every canoe almost in the island was hovering round the ship; and they began to mourn, as is customary for the death of a near relation. They bared their bodies, cut their heads with shells, and smeared their breasts and shoulders with the warm blood, as it streamed down; and as the blood ceased flowing, they renewed their wounds in the head, attended with a dismal yell." One of these mourners, Midshipman George Stewart's wife, "Peggy," died several months later, apparently from grief.

Edwards, who had few interests during the voyage beyond his duty and the job at hand, sticks to writing about day-to-day events on *Pandora*. Hamilton provides a window—as James Morrison's journal would when published much later—into the lives of the South Sea islanders during the late 18th century, from their religion and social customs to agricultural and sexual practices.

Hamilton also demonstrates a considerable amount of empathy for the natives, whose lives and culture were being dramatically influenced by European contact, a process that began when Captain Samuel Wallis arrived on H.M.S. *Dolphin* in 1767: "Happy would it have been for those people had they never been visited by Europeans; for, to our shame be it spoken, disease and gunpowder is all the benefit they have received from us, in return for their hospitality and kindness."

The *Bounty* mutineers who chose to remain on Tahiti introduced firearms to the native population, making their frequent local wars much more deadly. The Europeans also carried measles, pneumonia, and venereal disease, which began ravaging the population. In turn, the natives transmitted gonorrhea and other diseases to the crews of *Bounty* and *Pandora*.

Some time after *Pandora* left the island, Hamilton wrote, with his characteristic sense of humor, "We now began to discover, that the ladies of Otaheite had left us many warm tokens of their affection." The ivory syringe that Hamilton must have used when he treated the crew with mercury and other compounds has actually been recovered from the wreck site, along with his watch and other possessions. (See Peter Gesner's *Pandora: An Archaeological Perspective* [2000]).

It is regrettable that copies of Hamilton's *Voyage* are so elusive, because it deserves a wider audience. It has been reprinted twice in limited editions, but publication of Hamilton's *Voyage* in a more accessible and affordable format is long overdue.

Additional Works

Books

Bligh, William. *An Account of the Mutinous Seizure of the Bounty: with the Succeeding Hardships of the Crew. To which are Added Secret Anecdotes of the Otaheitian Females.* London: Robert Turner, 1790.

_____. *An Account of the Mutinous Seizure of the Bounty: with the Succeeding Hardships of the Crew. To which are Added Secret Anecdotes of the Otaheitian Females.* London: E. Bentley, n.d. (1792).

_____. *An Account of the Mutinous Seizure of the Bounty.* Introduction by Stephen Walters. Guildford: Genesis Publications, 1987.

An Account of the Mutinous Seizure of the Bounty was compiled from Bligh's *Narrative of the Mutiny*, supplemented by descriptions of Tahitian women from John Hawkesworth's *An Account of the Voyages Undertaken by the Order of His present Majesty for Making Discoveries in the Southern Hemisphere* (1773). The publishers undoubtedly hoped that additional information about the fabled women of the South Seas would attract book buyers.

In 1987, Genesis Publications used the texts of the 1790 and 1792 printings to produce a deluxe facsimile edition, limited to 150 copies bound in half leather.

_____. *The Log of H.M.S. Bounty, 1787–89.* Foreword by Lord Mountbatten. Guildford: Genesis Publications, 1975.

This impressive facsimile edition of Bligh's *Bounty* log, based on the manuscript held at the Public Record Office in London, was Genesis Publications' first book. It was limited to 500 numbered copies, 450 bound in half leather, with 50 bound in full leather signed by Lord Mountbatten. Reviewed by John C. Bower, Jr. in *American Neptune*, (January 1978): 71–72.

_____. *The Log of H.M.S. Providence, 1791–1793.* Foreword by the Earl Mountbatten of Burma. Introduction by Stephen Walters. Surrey: Genesis Publications, 1976.

This massive book of nearly 1,000 pages is a faithful facsimile of the handwritten log Bligh kept on H.M.S. *Providence* during his second, successful breadfruit voyage. Limited to 500 numbered copies, 450 bound in half leather, with 50 bound in full leather signed by the Earl Mountbatten of Burma. Based on Bligh's manuscript, held at the Public Record Office in London. Reviewed by John C. Bower, Jr. in *American Neptune*, (January 1978): 71–72.

_____. *Narrative of the Mutiny on Board His Majesty's Ship the Bounty.* Philadelphia: Franklin Court, 1977.

The Franklin Court Printshop and Bindery used the text of the first American edition of Bligh's *Narrative of the Mutiny* to produce this deluxe edition—illustrated with wood engravings—limited to 350 copies bound in quarter leather.

_____. *A Narrative of the Mutiny on Board His Majesty's Ship* Bounty. Sydney: The Library Shop, 1991.

Facsimile of the first British edition of Bligh's *Narrative of the Mutiny*, limited to 100 numbered copies. Published to coincide with the State Library of New South Wales *Mutiny on the Bounty* exhibition in March 1991.

_____. *A Narrative of the Mutiny on Board His Majesty's Ship* Bounty... *Minutes of the Court-Martial... Bligh's Answer to Certain Assertions... Edward Christian's Short Reply.* Melbourne: Georgian House, 1952, for The Australiana Society. Limited to 1,000 copies.

A handsome production that collects four of the most elusive *Bounty* books in a single volume.

_____, and James Burney. *A Voyage to The South Sea: Undertaken by command of His Majesty for the Purpose of Conveying the Bread-fruit Tree to the West Indies in His Majesty's Ship Bounty commanded by Lieutenant William Bligh including an account of the Mutiny on board the said ship and the subsequent voyage of part of the crew in the ship's boat from Tofoa, one of the Friendly Islands, to Timor, a Dutch Settlement in the East Indies* (bound with) Bligh, William, *A Narrative of the Mutiny on Board His Majesty's Ship* Bounty, *and the Subsequent Voyage of Part of the Crew in the Ship's Boat from Tofoa, One of the Friendly Islands, to Timor, A Dutch Settlement in the East Indies.* London: George Nicol, 1790.

Publisher George Nicol inserted the pages from the first edition of Bligh's *A Narrative of the Mutiny* into the text block of the just-printed *A Voyage to The South Sea* to make this special "advance" issue. Only a few copies are known to exist.

_____. *A Voyage to The South Sea.* Richmond: Hutchinson of Australia, 1979.

_____. *A Voyage to The South Sea.* Honolulu: Rare Books, n.d.

These two facsimile editions of Bligh's *A Voyage to the South Sea* are easier to find and less expensive than the first and deluxe limited editions.

_____. *A Voyage to the South Sea.* Edited by Robert Bowman. Gloucester: Alan Sutton Publishing, 1981.

The publisher released this reprint of Bligh's *A Voyage to the South Sea* in both hardcover and paperback editions. It includes a generous number of historic illustrations. In the epilogue, Robert Bowman concurs with Madge Darby that Edward Young may have instigated the mutiny, as well as the murders on Pitcairn Island.

_____, and Edward Christian. *The Bounty Mutiny.* Introduction by R. D. Madison. New York: Penguin Books, 2001. Reprinted in 2003 with new "Bounty Chronicles" cover artwork by John Hagan. Also published in a hardcover edition by The Traveler's Library.

Penguin Putnam performed a great service to *Bounty* Saga enthusiasts when they published *The Bounty Mutiny* in its popular "Penguin Classics" series. The only comparable collection is *A Book of the 'Bounty,'* which currently is out of print.

This inexpensive paperback makes accessible several extremely rare items, including Edward Christian's *Minutes of the Proceedings of the Court-Martial,* Bligh's *A Narrative of the Mutiny* and his *Answer to Edward Christian's Assertions,* and Christian's *A Short Reply to Capt. William Bligh's Answer.* Its useful appendices include Lady Belcher's account of the *Pandora* voyage, Frederick W. Beechey's visit to Pitcairn Island, and several important 19th century articles from *The Quarterly Review* and *United Service Journal.*

Bowker, R. M., and William Bligh. *Mutiny!! Aboard H. M. Armed Transport* 'Bounty,' *in 1789.* Old Bosham, Sussex, England: Bowker and Bertram, 1978.

The title of this book is misleading. At first glance, it resembles many other reprints of Bligh's *A Narrative of the Mutiny* and *A Voyage to the South Sea.* Actually, this is the first affordable—albeit incomplete—printed version of Bligh's *Bounty* log. A compact, well-printed volume, it includes illustrations, charts, photographs and useful commentary from the editor, a knowledgeable seaman familiar with Bligh's nautical terminology.

R. M. Bowker writes in his introduction that Bligh's log is "a document from which it is possible, by reading between the lines, to discover the real causes of the mutiny." *Mutiny!!* provides readers the opportunity to read a good portion of Bligh's day-to-day log without the expense of purchasing the Golden Cockerel Press or Genesis Publications editions.

Christian, Fletcher. *Letters from Mr. Fletcher Christian.* London: H. D. Symonds, 1796, 1797.

_____. *The Voyages and Travels of Fletcher Christian.* London: H.D. Symonds, 1797.

_____. *The Voyages and Travels of Fletcher Christian, and a Narrative of the Mutiny on Board His Majesty's Ship Bounty at Otaheite.* London: H. Lemoine, 1798.

See Chapter 5 for a discussion of these titles.

Fryer, John. *The Voyage of the Bounty Launch: John Fryer's Narrative.* Introduction by Stephen Walters. Illustrated by Roy Williams. Guildford: Genesis Publications, 1979. Limited to 500 numbered copies signed by Stephen Walters.

Another handsome *Bounty* book from Genesis Publications. This is a facsimile of the original narrative in John Fryer's handwriting, held by the National Maritime Museum, Greenwich. The printed text previously was available only in the Golden Cockerel Press's *The Voyage of the Bounty's Launch as Related in William Bligh's Despatch to the Admiralty and the Journal of John Fryer.* (See Chapter 5 for a discussion of Fryer's *Journal*.)

Hamilton, George. *A Voyage Round the World in His Majesty's Frigate Pandora.* Edited by Geoffrey Kenihan. Adelaide: William Torrens Publishers, 1990. Limited to 250 copies.

_____. *A Voyage Round the World in His Majesty's Frigate Pandora.* Sydney. Hordern House and the Australian National Maritime Museum, 1998. Facsimile edition limited to 950 copies bound in quarter leather.

Following its first publication in 1793, George Hamilton's *A Voyage Round the World in His Majesty's Frigate Pandora* was not reprinted until 1915, in *Voyage of H.M.S. 'Pandora' Despatched to Arrest the Mutineers of the 'Bounty' in the South Seas, 1790–91. Being the Narratives of Captain Edward Edwards, R.N. the Commander and George Hamilton, the Surgeon.*

In 1990, William Torres Publishers of Adelaide, Australia, produced an expensive, commemorative edition of Hamilton's *Voyage*. Hordern House Rare Books of Sydney, Australia, published a facsimile edition in 1998, with an introductory essay by Peter Gesner, Curator of Maritime Archeology at the Queensland Museum. Gesner is the foremost expert on the continuing recovery of the *Pandora* wreck.

Articles

"Historical Chronicles." *The Gentleman's Magazine* (May 1790): 463–464.

A very early account of the *Bounty* mutiny and Bligh's open boat voyage.

"Extract of a Letter from Portsmouth, Dec. 23." *The London Chronicle*, December 25, 1787, p. 8.

This newspaper briefly reports the departure of "Bounty armed ship for the South Seas."

"Particulars of the Late Execution On Board the *Brunswick*." *The Gentleman's Magazine* (December 1792): 1097–1098.

This anonymous, contemporary account of the execution of *Bounty* mutineers Thomas Burkett, Thomas Ellison and John Millward on H.M.S. *Brunswick*, October 29, 1792, provides a vivid glimpse into the events of that day. It clearly was written to quell rumors that Peter Heywood and James Morrison were pardoned for mutiny because of their wealth or family influence.

The author, an officer on *Brunswick*, reports that the night before their execution, the mutineers were not at all solemn, but, "In the full possession and vigour of their health and spirits, as in a seeming ignorance of their approaching fate."

He also attended the court-martial, where he admired the verbal skills of Boatswain's Mate James Morrison, who "Stood his own counsel, questioned all the evidences, and in a manner so arranged and pertinent, that the spectators waited with impatience for his turn to call on them, and listened with attention and delight during the discussion."

Supplemental Bibliography

Books

Bligh, William. *A Narrative of the Mutiny on Board His Majesty's Ship* Bounty. Dublin: R. White, 1790.
First edition published in Ireland.

_____. *Narrative of the Mutiny on the Bounty, on a Voyage to the South Seas: To Which Are Added Particulars, and a Relation of the Subsequent Fate of the Mutineers, and of the Settlement in Pitcairn's Island*. London: William Smith, 1838.

_____. *A Voyage To The South Sea*. Dublin: P. Wogan, 1792. First edition published in Ireland.

Carteret, Philip. "An Account of a Voyage Round the World 1766–1769," in *Hawkesworth's "Voyages."* London: W. Strahan and T. Cadell, 1773.

(Haweis, Thomas, Ed.) "Curious tradition, among the inhabitants of Otaheite." *Evangelical Magazine* 5 (January 1797): 23–25.

_____. *A Missionary Voyage to the Southern Pacific Ocean, Performed in the Years 1796, 1797, 1798, in the Ship* Duff, *Commanded by Captain James Wilson*. London: Gosnell for Chapman, 1799.

_____. "On the Otaheitian sacrifices." *Evangelical Magazine* 6 (March 1798): 110–112.

Mortimer, Lieut. George. *Observations and Remarks Made During a Voyage to the Islands of Teneriffe, Amsterdam, Maria's Islands near Van Dieman's Land, Otaheite, Sandwich Islands, Owhyhee, the Fox Islands on the Northeast Coast of America, Tinian, and from Thence to Canton, in the Brig Mercury, Commanded by John Henry Cox, Esq*. London: George Mortimer, 1791.

_____. *Observations and Remarks Made During a Voyage*. Fairfield: Ye Galleon Press, 1988. Facsimile reprint, limited to 220 copies.

_____. *Observations and Remarks Made During a Voyage*. New York: Da Capo Press, 1975.

"Voyage of Captain Bligh, to the South Sea, for the Purpose of Conveying the Breadfruit Tree to the West Indies," in William Mayor's *Celebrated Voyages, Travels, and Discoveries, from the Time of Columbus, to the Present Period*. London: E. Newbery, 1797. American publisher Samuel F. Bradford, Philadelphia, printed editions in 1802 and 1803.

Wilson, William. *A Missionary Voyage to the Southern Pacific Ocean, Performed in the Years 1796, 1797, 1798, in the Ship* Duff, *Commanded by Captain James Wilson*. London: Gosnell for Chapman, 1799.

Articles

"Account of the Miraculous Escape of *Captain Bligh*, of the *Bounty* Sloop." *The Annual Register, or a View of the History, Politics, and Literature, for the Year 1790*. London: J. Dodsley, 1793: 252–254.

"Authentic Particulars, Relative to the Loss of the Pandora Frigate." *American Apollo*, August 31, 1792.

"Narrative of the Adventures of the Mutineers on Board his Majesty's Ship the Bounty After Their Separation from Captain Bligh." *Edinburgh Magazine* (June 1796; July 1796): 431–440; 9–16.

Review of "William Bligh's Narrative of the Mutiny on board His Majesty's Ship *Bounty*." *The Gentleman's Magazine* 60, no. 6 (December 1790): 1123–1124.

"William Bligh's Narrative of the Mutiny on board His Majesty's Ship *Bounty*." *The Gentleman's Magazine* (December 1790): 1123–1124.

2

19th Century Nonfiction

The only volume that rivals the staying power of William Bligh's books is Sir John Barrow's *The Eventful History of the Mutiny and Piratical Seizure of H.M.S.* Bounty, which has been printed in innumerable formats since its first publication in 1831. Barrow, who had access to material unavailable to Bligh, including the papers of Peter Heywood and James Morrison, was able to provide a much fuller account of the *Bounty* Saga than Bligh, who died in 1816.

Between 1817 and 1831, the publication of books by John Shillibeer, Captain Frederick W. Beechey and Captain Amasa Delano — some including accounts of visits to Pitcairn Island — created a huge audience for news about the unique colony. Throughout the 19th century, articles about the *Bounty*, and especially Pitcairn Island, appeared regularly in popular publications like *The Illustrated London News, Harper's Weekly, The Friend, Harper's New Monthly* and *Sunday at Home*. Specialized journals, including *The Quarterly Review, The United Service Journal* and *Naval and Military Magazine* offered more specialized pieces about events in the *Bounty* Saga.

Captain Delano understood why people were fascinated with Pitcairn Island. In his 1817 *A Narrative of Voyages*, he called it "A subject, which has excited much interest in the public mind, and which is calculated to afford many valuable reflections upon human character ... the singular family which has been discovered on Pitcairn's Island, and which sprung from the mutineers of the English ship Bounty, and the Otaheitan women whom they carried with them."

Interest in Pitcairn Island and its people has not flagged in the nearly 200 years since Delano wrote these words. The very titles *Pitcairn: The Island, the People, and the Pastor: with a Short Account of the Mutiny of the Bounty*, by The Rev. Thos. Boyles Murray, and Lady Belcher's *The Mutineers of the* Bounty *and their Descendants in Pitcairn and Norfolk Islands*, make it clear that the general public often was more interested in the end results of the mutiny on Pitcairn Island than the mutiny itself. Nathan Welby Fiske's *The Story of Alec, or Pitcairn's Island: Being a True Account of a Very Singular and Interesting Colony* (1829) was a popular title for young readers. It was reprinted, with various titles, in 1848, 1854 and 1855.

During the mid- to late-19th century, book publishers also responded to popular interest in the *Bounty* Saga, producing volumes culled from the work of Bligh, Barrow and Belcher — such as David Herbert's *Great Historical Mutinies: Comprising the Story of the Mutiny of the Bounty, the Mutiny at Spithead, the Mutiny at the Nore, Mutinies in Highland Regiments and the Indian Mutiny, 1876,* which was published in a variety of formats. This particular volume made no claim to originality. Herbert states in the preface, "He [Herbert] makes no pretension to supply his readers with new facts. He is responsible only for choosing a subject of sufficient interest, culling as judiciously as he can from the ample materials at hand, and making such reflections during the course of the narrative as seem to be just and useful." Books were fairly expensive objects during the period, and titles such as *Great Historical Mutinies* packed a great deal of information into a single volume.

Toward the end of the century, a truly original book about Pitcairn Island did appear. The author was Rosalind Amelia Young, a "Native Daughter," as printed on the cover of her *Mutiny of the Bounty and Story of Pitcairn Island.* Pitcairn Island's first author, Young focused on what she knew best, which happened to be the topics of greatest interest to the public at this time: the history, religion and culture of Pitcairn Island. Several decades would pass before a higher degree of interest in the mutiny and personalities of Bligh and Christian would be rekindled.

Major Works

LIEUTENANT J. SHILLIBEER, R.M.: *A Narrative of the Briton's Voyage, to Pitcairn's Island; Including an Interesting Sketch of the Present State of the Brazils and of Spanish South America. Illustrated with Sixteen Etchings by the Author, From Drawings on the Spot.* London: Printed for Law and Whittaker, No. 13 Ave Maria Lane, Ludgate Street, 1817.

H.M.S. *Briton* and its consort H.M.S. *Tagus,* commanded respectively by Sir Thomas Staines and Captain Philip Pipon, paid an unforeseen visit to Pitcairn Island in 1814, during a mission to locate the *Essex,* an American frigate that had been attacking British whaling vessels. Six years earlier, on February 6, 1808, Captain Mayhew Folger of Nantucket, commander of the American sealing ship *Topaz,* arrived at Pitcairn Island, hoping that he might find seals there.

He thought that the island was uninhabited, but to his surprise, three young men canoed out to his ship and addressed him in perfect English. Folger was astonished to learn that he had discovered the whereabouts of the *Bounty* mutineers. *Topaz* was the first vessel to make contact with Pitcairn since the arrival of the *Bounty* in 1790. John Adams, the only surviving mutineer, invited Folger to land on Pitcairn, and told him about the early years of the mutineers' settlement. Although Folger recorded this information in his ship's log, he never had it published.

Unaware of Folger's discovery, Captain Staines and Captain Pipon were surprised, one evening, to sight an island where none was charted. According to their maps, Pitcairn was located 200 miles to the west. John Shillibeer, who was serving as Lieutenant of Royal Marines aboard the *Briton,* wrote and later published *A Narrative of the Briton's Voyage to Pitcairn's Island,* which provides a brief but fascinating glimpse of life on Pitcairn Island in 1814.

At daylight, the crews of *Briton* and *Tagus* were surprised to observe on the island, as Shillibeer reports, "Huts, cultivation, and people; of the latter, some were making signs, others launching their little canoes through the surf, into which they threw themselves with great dexterity, and pulled towards us.... For me to picture the wonder which was conspicuous in every countenance, at being hailed in perfect English ... would be impossible — our surprize can alone be conceived."

Fletcher Christian's son, Thursday October Christian, boarded the *Briton* accompanied by Edward Young's son, George (or possibly Daniel McKoy, son of William McKoy; the accounts differ). They asked Captain Pipon if he had ever heard of William Bligh, which made sense of the novelty of South Sea islanders speaking excellent English. Staines and Pipon knew, of course, that Captain Bligh had returned to England, and were eager to learn what had happened to Fletcher Christian. Shillibeer transcribed some of the crew's questions, along with the answers provided by Thursday October Christian and George Young:

Q: Christian you say was shot?
A: Yes he was.
Q: What cause do you assign for the murder?
A: I know no reason, except a jealousy which I have heard then existed between the people of Otaheite and the English — Christian was shot in the back while at work in his yam plantation.

Christian and Young also explained how John Adams survived the massacres after being wounded:

Q: How did Adams escape being murdered?
A: He hid himself in the wood, and the same night, the women enraged at the murder of the English, to whom they were more partial than their countrymen, rose and put every Tahitian to death in their sleep. This saved Adams, his wounds were soon healed, and although old, he now enjoys good health.

Like Folger, the captains went ashore and spent an entire day on Pitcairn. They saw the settlement that would later be named Adamstown, which *A Narrative of the Briton's Voyage* describes as "A picturesque little village, formed on an oblong square, with trees of various kinds irregularly interspersed. The houses small, but regular, convenient, and of unequalled cleanliness."

They also conversed with John Adams, and an account of this meeting exists in several forms, including a letter from Captain Staines to the Admiralty, an original manuscript by Captain Pipon, and an edited version of Pipon's manuscript that appeared in the *United Service Journal*. Adams' account of the mutineers' early years was inconsistent with the ones he provided Captain Folger and, later, to Captain F. W. Beechey of H.M.S. *Blossom*.

Pipon reported that they knew Adams was not being completely honest with them, at least about his role in the mutiny: "John Adams declared, as it was natural enough he should do, his abhorrence of the crime in which he was implicated, and said he was sick at the time in his hammock. This we understand is not true." John Adams also told them he was willing to return to his native England, even if it meant punishment for the crime of mutiny. His immediate family and the other islanders tearfully protested, and the two captains, deeply moved, saw no need to return him to England.

Their actions reassured Adams that he would never have to stand trial for mutiny. In *Mutiny and Romance in the South Seas: A Companion to the Bounty Adventure*, Dr. Sven Wahlroos states, "Luckily for Adams, both Staines and Pipon were compassionate, cultured, and reasonable men who could immediately see that Adams was important for the community and had accomplished a great deal in raising its children to fine human beings."

Although Shillibeer did not venture ashore, he and other members of *Briton*'s crew shared breakfast with the Islanders who came on board. They were intensely curious about everything they saw, including a dog and a cow. At the table, Shillibeer was startled by their pious behavior: "Before they began to eat; on their knees, and with hands uplifted did they implore permission to partake in peace what was set before them, and when they had eaten heartily, resuming their former attitude, offered a fervent prayer of thanksgiving for the indulgence they had just experienced. Our omission of this ceremony did not escape their notice for Christian asked me whether it was not customary with us also... I was both embarrassed and wholly at a loss for a sound reply." This memorable scene is a high point of *A Narrative of the Briton's Voyage to Pitcairn's Island*.

The prominence of "Pitcairn" in the title might lead one to believe that this is its primary subject, but most of the book consists of Shillibeer's colorful, opinionated descriptions of the ports and cities visited by *Briton* and *Tagus*—such as Rio de Janeiro, where, "The houses are generally well built, some of the streets are good, and all exceedingly filthy," and the "gloomy" Galapagos Islands, where he finds a 370-pound tortoise that "Soon lost its natural shyness, became much petted among the crew ... and was in regular attendance in the galley at the hours of meals."

A primitive etching by John J. Shillibeer, Lieutenant of H.M.S. *Briton*, is the only known portrait of Thursday October Christian, Fletcher Christian's son. *Briton* and H.M.S. *Tagus*, commanded by Sir Thomas Staines and Captain Philip Pipon, visited Pitcairn Island in 1814. Shillibeer entitled this print "Friday Fletcher October Christian," but the subject's name eventually became "Thursday October Christian" when the islanders realized that the *Bounty* crossed the International Date Line — thereby confusing their calendar — on its journey to Pitcairn. Christian's hat is decorated with feathers of the domestic fowl.

A Narrative of the Briton's Voyage to Pitcairn's Island is a charming narrative, and it is unfortunate that Shillibeer did not go ashore at Pitcairn; his observations probably would have been well worth reading. He writes, "No one but the Captains went ashore, which will be a source of lasting regret to me, for I would rather have seen the simplicity of that little village, than all the splendour and magnificence of a city."

AMASA DELANO: *A Narrative of Voyages and Travels In the Northern and Southern Hemispheres: Comprising Three Voyages Round the World; Together with a Voyage of Survey and Discovery, in the Pacific Ocean and Oriental Islands.* Boston: Printed by E. G. House, for the Author, 1817.

It is fortunate that Captain Amasa Delano shared a mutual interest in the *Bounty* mutiny and Pitcairn Island with his friend, Captain Mayhew Folger. Captain Delano incorporated an account of Folger's unpublished 1808 visit to Pitcairn Island in *A Narrative of Voyages and Travels*. This was the first book to be published in America with an account of the *Bounty* mutineers on Pitcairn Island.

Delano's interest in the *Bounty* probably dates to 1792, when he arrived in Timor on the ship *Massachusetts*, just a few months after the

The title page spread of Amasa Delano's *A Narrative of Voyages and Travels* features a frontispiece portrait of the author. Famous for its account of Captain Mayhew Folger's visit to Pitcairn Island in 1808, this volume also is noted for Delano's report of a slave revolt on the Spanish ship *Tryal* in 1805. Herman Melville based one of his greatest short stories, "Benito Cereno," on this event.

departure of Captain Edward Edwards of H.M.S. *Pandora*. Delano writes, "At Timor I found in the possession of Governor Vanjon, a manuscript history of the cruise of *Pandora*, written by Captain Edwards himself, who was sent out by the English government in search of *Bounty* and the mutineers. This manuscript I copied, and shall present the substance of it to the reader."

Delano discusses the mutiny and discovery of the Pitcairn Island settlement in Chapters V and VI of *A Narrative of Voyages and Travels*, quoting from various sources and weaving them into a coherent narrative: his own conversations with Folger; William Bligh's *A Voyage to the South Sea*; his own incomplete transcription of Edwards' manuscript; and an article from the *Quarterly Review* that discusses the interviews with John Adams conducted by Folger, Sir Thomas Staines and Captain Philip Pipon.

Delano makes note of the various discrepancies in these reports, especially those concerning the fate of Fletcher Christian. For example, Adams told Staines and Pipon that Christian behaved like a tyrant on Pitcairn, inciting the wrath of the Tahitian men by stealing one of their wives, which led to his murder. On the other hand, Adams told Folger that Christian was a benevolent leader and died a natural death.

In an attempt to clarify such issues, Delano recalls the many times he discussed H.M.S.

Bounty with Folger, who he met in 1800. Experienced seamen, they were particularly interested in what happened to Christian, who seemed to have disappeared from the face of the earth. Delano writes, "We had both suffered many varieties of hardship and privation, and our feelings were perfectly alive to the anxieties and distresses of a mind under the circumstances of Christian, going from all he had known and loved, and seeking as his last refuge a spot unknown and uninhabited. The spirit of crime is only temporary in the human soul, but the spirit of sympathy is eternal."

Delano conversed with Folger again years later, after the voyage of *Topaz* and his friend's meeting with John Adams:

> Smith [John Adams] said, and upon this point Captain Folger was very explicit in his inquiry at the time as well as in his account of it to me, that they lived under Christian's government several years after they landed; that during the whole period they enjoyed tolerable harmony; that Christian became sick and died a natural death, and that it was after this the Tahitian men joined in a conspiracy and killed the English husbands of the Tahitian women, and were by widows killed in turn on the following night. Smith was thus the only man left upon the island.

Delano also reports that the second mate of *Topaz* later told Lieutenant William Fitzmaurice of the Royal Navy that "Christian became insane, and threw himself from the rocks into the sea." Delano trusted Folger and confidently states that his friend's account "Must be much more direct and worthy of confidence than that of the second mate or Fitzmaurice, or of the *Quarterly Review*."

In Chapter VI, Delano reflects on the behavior of both Christian and Adams, acknowledging the seriousness of their crimes but casting both of them in a positive light: Christian, he says, "Has given so many proofs of his benevolence and love of duty, that his representations ought not lightly to be set aside, even on the subject of the mutiny.... Smith ... with a number of pagan women from Tahiti, has succeeded, according to all accounts, in training up a community of males and females in perfect chastity, sincerity and honesty."

Delano performed a valuable service by preserving Folger's visit, Edwards' account of *Pandora*, and the *Quarterly Review* material in *A Narrative of Voyages and Travels*. Edwards' journal would not appear in its entirety until the publication, in 1915, of *Voyage of H.M.S. 'Pandora' Despatched to Arrest the Mutineers of the 'Bounty' in the South Seas, 1790-91*, edited by Basil Thomson.

F. W. BEECHEY, R.N.: *Narrative of a Voyage to the Pacific and Beerings Strait, to Cooperate with the Polar Expeditions: Performed in His Majesty's Ship Blossom, Under the Command of Captain F. W. Beechey, R.N. F.R.S. &c. In the Years 1825, 26, 27, 28. Published by Authority of the Lords Commissioners of the Admiralty in Two Volumes*. London: Henry Colburn and Richard Bentley, New Burlington Street, 1831. First U.S. edition published by Carey and Lea, Philadelphia, 1832.

When Captain F. W. Beechey, commander of the British man-of-war H.M.S. *Blossom*, landed at Pitcairn Island in late 1825, the British Admiralty had been aware for some time that it was the *Bounty* mutineers' refuge, thanks to the letters and reports of Captains Folger, Staines and Pipon. Although Beechey's primary mission was to rendezvous at Beering's Strait with two polar expeditions, commanded by John Franklin and Edward Parry, his Admiralty orders included numerous stops in the South Pacific.

Beechey was instructed to survey Ducie, Henderson (then called Elizabeth Island) and Pitcairn Islands. Chapters III and IV in Volume One of Beechey's *Narrative of a Voyage* describe *Blossom*'s extensive stay on Pitcairn. The crew eagerly anticipated landing on the island, revealing a fascination with the *Bounty* story that has continued for more than 200 years:

Major Works

The interest which was excited by the announcement of Pitcairn Island from the mast-head brought every person upon deck, and produced a train of reflections that momentarily increased our anxiety to communicate with its inhabitants; to see and partake of the pleasures of their little domestic circle; and to learn from them the particulars of every transaction connected with the fate of the *Bounty*.

Beechey's account of Pitcairn Island is thorough and richly detailed. He had sufficient time to fully explore the island, making observations of its topography and climate, examining the flora and fauna, and observing the unique life of the 66 Islanders. He noted their appearance, clothing and customs, shared in their meals, and attended their school and church services. He clearly admired their accomplishments and way of life:

> All which remains to be said of these excellent people is, that they appear to live together in perfect harmony and contentment; to be virtuous, religious, cheerful, and hospitable, beyond the limits of prudence; to be patterns of conjugal and parental affection; and to have very few vices. We remained with them many days, and their unreserved manners gave us the fullest opportunity of becoming acquainted with any faults they might have possessed.

Beechey's account of the mutiny and history of Pitcairn, as published in *Narrative of a Voyage*, is based on the conversations he had with John Adams in *Blossom*'s cabin, as well as with some other Islanders, and notes he took from Edward Young's diary (now lost).

By the time of *Blossom*'s visit, Adams, age 65, was confident that he would never be forced to return to England and stand trial for mutiny. It is plausible that he would have been more candid with Beechey than he was with the commanders of *Topaz*, *Briton* and *Tagus*. Adams even signed a written copy of his conversation, which was transcribed by Beechey's clerk.

This narrative is the most detailed version of events that we have, although many readers have pointed out inconsistencies — as early as 1831, with the publication of *The Eventful History of the Mutiny and Piratical Seizure of H.M.S. Bounty* by Sir John Barrow — who called it "incorrect in many parts."

Adams had given fresh information to Beechey, suggesting that tension began between Bligh and Christian well before the *Bounty* reached Tahiti. Apparently, Christian owed Bligh some money. Adams said that Christian, "Unfortunately was under

John Adams as drawn by Captain F. W. Beechey, commander of H.M.S. *Blossom*. Beechey was a skilled artist, and made good use of this talent during his stay on Pitcairn Island. Published in Beechey's *Narrative of a Voyage to the Pacific and Beerings Strait*.

some obligation to him of a pecuniary nature, of which Bligh frequently reminded him when any difference arose. Christian, excessively annoyed at the share of blame which repeatedly fell to his lot, in common with the rest of the officers, could ill endure the additional taunt of private obligations; and in a moment of excitation told his commander that sooner or later a day of reckoning would arrive."

Adams also told Beechey that after Christian was severely castigated by Bligh in a dispute over some missing coconuts, he planned to desert the *Bounty* on a jerry-built raft, but that "he was on the point of launching it, when a young officer, who afterwards perished in *Pandora*, to whom Christian communicated his intention, recommended him, rather than risk his life on so hazardous an expedition, to endeavour to take possession of the ship."

Although Beechey does not name this "young officer," Adams clearly was referring to Midshipman George Stewart. Caroline Alexander, in *The* Bounty: *The True Story of the Mutiny on the* Bounty writes that Beechey referred to the "young officer" as "Stewart" in his manuscript.

When *Narrative of a Voyage* was published, Barrow, who was Second Secretary of the Admiralty and a close friend of Captain Peter Heywood, sent Heywood Chapters III and IV. Heywood was alarmed by Adams' claim that Stewart had instigated the mutiny. He and Stewart had been good friends, and any allusion to mutinous behavior on the part of Stewart cast a shadow on his own reputation and standing in the Royal Navy.

Heywood immediately sent a letter to Beechey, dated April 5, 1830, in which he denies that Stewart played any part in the mutiny. He claimed that Adams' report of Stewart's conduct, "is entirely at variance with [Stewart's] whole character and conduct ... both before and after the mutiny; as well as with the assurance of Christian himself ... that the idea of attempting to take the ship had never entered his distracted mind, until the moment he relieved the deck, and found his mate and midshipman [Hayward and Hallet] asleep."

Barrow printed this letter in *The Eventful History of the Mutiny and Piratical Seizure of H.M.S. Bounty*, published two years after Beechey's *Narrative of a Voyage*, which helped support Heywood's claim that Adams had been mistaken about Stewart. Barrow shifted the blame to Edward Young, who Richard Hough, author of *Captain Bligh and Mr. Christian*, believes was Christian's "Iago." Barrow writes, "The story he told to Beechey respecting the advice stated to have been given by Mr. Stewart to Christian, 'to take possession of the ship,' is, as has been shown [by Heywood's letter] wholly false; but here his memory may have failed him. If any such advice was given, it is much more likely to have proceeded from Young."

Barrow also wrote that Adams was not completely credible, since he had downplayed his own role in the mutiny, and noted the strange discrepancy in Smith's description of Christian's behavior on Pitcairn Island. Adams said to Captains Staines and Pipon that Christian had behaved like a tyrant, to Beechey, that he set an excellent example for all of the others.

It is not surprising that Adams, even near the end of his life, would be tempted to minimize the extent of his mutinous behavior, especially to the commander of a British man-of-war. The other inconsistencies are more difficult to explain. Perhaps, as Caroline Alexander suggests, Adams gave some of the other *Blossom* officers a more truthful version of events when he conversed with them below decks. Lieutenant Edward Belcher wrote in the journal he kept while serving on *Blossom*, "I am inclined to think [Beechey] did not get as accurate an account as we did below."

(SIR JOHN BARROW): *The Eventful History of the Mutiny and Piratical Seizure of H.M.S. Bounty: Its Causes and Consequences. Illustrated by Six Etchings from Original Drawings by Lieut.-Colonel Batty.* London: John Murray, Albermarle-Street; and Thomas Tegg, Cheapside (1831).

First American edition published as *A Description of Pitcairn Island and its Inhabitants: With an Authentic Account of the Mutiny of the Ship Bounty,* by Harper and Brothers, New York, 1832.

In the introduction to his edition of Sir John Barrow's *The Eventful History of the Mutiny and Piratical Seizure of H.M.S. Bounty: Its Causes and Consequences,* Gavin Kennedy writes, "For a book to be in print 150 years after it was first published it must have some remarkable qualities."

As the first comprehensive account of virtually every chapter in the *Bounty* Saga, Barrow's compact volume is remarkable, and an essential item in any collection of Bountiana. Published anonymously by John Murray as No. 25 in his popular "Family Library," it has been reprinted countless times in a variety of formats, and even with different titles. *The Eventful History of the Mutiny and Piratical Seizure of H.M.S. Bounty,* which inspired Charles Nordhoff and James Norman Hall to create *The Bounty Trilogy,* remains the best introduction to this timeless tale.

Barrow's book was well received from the beginning. William Henry Smyth, one of his contemporaries, writes in an 1831 edition of *United Service Journal,* "The train of marvelous circumstances connected with the mutiny in that vessel, the open boat navigation, the wreck of the Pandora, and the unexpected discovery of the last of the mutineers, altogether form a story so romantic and of such intense interest, that we rejoiced in seeing them embodied in a volume of Murray's Family Library."

In the preface to the first edition, Barrow, the anonymous "Editor," states that he "has been induced to bring into one connected view what has hitherto appeared only in detached fragments [and some of these not generally accessible]—the historical narrative of an event which deeply interested the public at the time of its occurrence." As Second Secretary to the Admiralty, it was politically expedient for Barrow to retain anonymity, at least until the learned how the Royal Navy would respond to his book.

He does a superb job of weaving the many strands of the *Bounty/Pandora/*Pitcairn story into a coherent whole. Reading his book can be a revelation to those whose familiarity with the *Bounty* story has been limited to the motion pictures, which are not only inaccurate, but also incomplete. No film has yet depicted the voyage of *Pandora* or the full story of the mutineers' settlement on Pitcairn Island.

Barrow was exceptionally well qualified to write this account of H.M.S. *Bounty.* Before assuming his post at the Admiralty, he had voyaged to Greenland, China and South Africa, and published excellent accounts of these travels. He put his writing talent to good use in *The Eventful History of the Mutiny and Piratical Seizure of H.M.S. Bounty.* As Kennedy states, "Of the dozens of books written on the *Bounty*, none stands out like Barrow's. He was uniquely placed by temperament and position to write the classic account, which, because of its high literary qualities, comes closer than any other to the real story of what happened — and why."

Barrow enjoyed full access to all of the relevant material at the Admiralty, including Bligh's log, the court-martial records and other documents. He had a close relationship with the Heywood family, and examined Peter Heywood's papers, which included a copy of James Morrison's manuscript journal. Barrow presents a thorough, suspenseful account of Heywood's court-martial and pardon, supplementing it with family letters, particularly the voluminous correspondence between Heywood and his adoring sister, Nessy.

He was intensely interested in why the mutiny occurred. In Chapter III, which is devoted to the mutiny, he quotes at length from Bligh's *A Narrative of the Mutiny on Board His Majesty's Ship* Bounty. Acknowledging that Bligh's account does not tell the complete story, he fills in the gaps by turning to the unpublished journal of James Morrison — which very few people had seen until Barrow quoted from it.

Morrison had narrated several important events that are missing from *A Narrative of the Mutiny*, including the incident of the stolen cheeses, Bligh's insistence that the men eat decayed pumpkin, and his harsh treatment of Christian in the days preceding the mutiny — especially the day before the mutiny, when Bligh accused the officers of stealing some of his coconuts:

> On their [the officers] declaring that they had not seen any of the people touch them, he exclaimed, "Then you must have taken them yourselves"; and proceeded to inquire of them separately, how many they had purchased. On coming to Mr. Christian, that gentleman answered, "I do not know, Sir, but I hope you do not think me so mean as to be guilty of stealing yours." Mr. Bligh replied, "Yes, you d—d hound, I do — you must have stolen them from me, or you would be able to give a better account of them."

Based on his reading of Morrison's journal and other sources, Barrow refutes Bligh's conviction — a view that he maintained until the end of his life — that the mutiny had been a well-planned conspiracy: "Christian, as fiery and passionate a youth as his commander could well be, and with feelings too acute to bear the foul and opprobrious language constantly addressed to him, was the sole instigator of the mutiny."

Barrow is critical of Bligh, especially of his temper and foul language, but he holds a higher opinion of the man than Admiral Sir Cyprian Bridge, who wrote an introduction to the

"George Young & his Wife (Hannah Adams) of Pitcairns Island." The etched frontispiece to Sir John Barrow's ***The Eventful History of the Mutiny and Piratical Seizure of H.M.S. Bounty: Its Causes and Consequences*** is based on a sketch by Lieutenant Smith of H.M.S. ***Blossom***. Commanded by Captain F. W. Beechey, ***Blossom*** visited Pitcairn Island in December 1825. At that time, 36 men and 30 women were living on the island.

Oxford World's Classics edition of *The Eventful History of the Mutiny and Piratical Seizure of H.M.S. Bounty* (1914). This little volume was reprinted many times, and thousands of readers must have absorbed Bridge's judgment that Bligh was not only a foul-mouthed tyrant, but far below his rightful station in the Royal Navy: "In fact he was not a gentleman either by bringing up or by nature. To speak plainly, he was a bully, and not a truthful one. In the ordinary and unexciting or monotonous course of peace-service he proved himself quite unfitted for the command of men. He was a tyrant whose mode of asserting his rights was brutal."

Barrow is far more hostile to Captain Edwards of H.M.S. *Pandora*, who, as the vessel was sinking, waited until the last moment before ordering the release of his prisoners—resulting in the deaths of Henry Hillbrant, Richard Skinner, George Stewart and John Sumner, who drowned while still shackled in the infamous "Pandora's Box." Comparing the accounts of Captain Edwards, Lieutenant Corner, Surgeon George Hamilton, James Morrison and Peter Heywood, Barrow states that "Captain Edwards must have deserved the character, ascribed to him, of being altogether destitute of the common feelings of humanity."

A portrait of Sir John Barrow as a young man. In addition to his long tenure as Secretary of the Admiralty, the author of *The Eventful History of the Mutiny and Piratical Seizure of H.M.S. Bounty: Its Causes and Consequences* was a vigorous proponent of exploration and a noted biographer.

We have Barrow to thank for one of the most romantic elements of the *Bounty* Saga: Captain Heywood's memory of glimpsing a man in Plymouth who may have been Fletcher Christian. This brief anecdote has generated a great deal of interest, adding many books and articles to the *Bounty* bibliography.

After reading Barrow's book, Charles Nordhoff and James Norman Hall realized that three books were needed to tell the *Bounty* Saga as historical fiction. Barrow's research and writing skills enabled him to tell the full history in one entertaining volume.

EDWARD TAGART: *A Memoir of the Late Captain Peter Heywood, R.N. With Extracts from his Diaries and Correspondence.* London: Effingham Wilson, 1832.

Edward Tagart published *A Memoir of the Late Captain Peter Heywood, R.N.* in 1832, the year following the death of former *Bounty* Midshipman Peter Heywood. In the preface, Tagart acknowledges that when composing *A Memoir*, he made extensive use of Barrow's *Eventful History of the Mutiny and Piratical Seizure of H.M.S. Bounty*, John Marshall's "Peter Heywood, Esq.," in *Royal Naval Biography* and the "Sketch of the Career of the Late Captain Peter Heywood, RN," that appeared in the *United Service Journal*. Tagart also had access to "the family volume containing the transactions and correspondence which took place at the time of the trial."

Tagart, a Unitarian minister at the church Heywood attended late in his life, was well

versed in religion and philosophy — in 1855 he published a work on John Locke — but he lacked the naval and scientific background needed to adequately describe Heywood's considerable accomplishments during a long naval career. Half of *A Memoir* is simply a rehashing of the *Bounty* mutiny and court-martial — information familiar to many readers by 1832. Nevertheless, *A Memoir* is worth reading for the fascinating glimpses into Heywood's personality and later career revealed through his letters and diaries.

One memorable incident illuminates the lasting impact that Tahiti and its people had on the young Heywood. While stationed on board *Montagu* at Gibraltar in 1816, Captain Heywood met two Tahitian youths who had escaped from kidnappers, but could not find a passage back to their native island. Heywood warmly welcomed them on board *Montagu*, addressing them in fluent Tahitian: "I took each by the hand and told them, that if I lived they should be sent home to their country, and assured them, that in the mean time they should remain with me, and that I would be their countryman, their friend and protector. Poor fellows! they were quite overwhelmed — their tears flowed apace — and they wept the thankfulness they could not express."

The experience stirred Heywood's memories of his 18-month sojourn on Tahiti following the mutiny, when he became deeply absorbed in Tahitian life — mastering the language so well that he produced an English/Tahitian dictionary and was able to speak it 25 years later. Heywood's letter reveals the deep empathy he still felt for the island's culture and way of life: "Plenty and content are the portion of all, unalloyed by care, envy, or ambition — where labour is needless and want unknown. At least, such it was twenty-five years ago.... But if I go on this way you will say I am a *savage*, and so I believe I am, and ever shall be in *some* points."

Heywood expressed similar sentiments about Tahiti in a letter to his mother dated November 20, 1791: "Whilst we remained there we were used by our Friends [the natives] with a Friendship, Generosity, & Humanity almost unparalleled, being such as never was equalled by the People of any civilized Nations, to the Disgrace of all Christians." Following such an experience, it is not surprising that Heywood eventually was attracted to the Unitarian Church, which held a liberal, tolerant view toward other religions and was dedicated to social reform. This philosophy also appealed to Charles Dickens, who was friends with Tagart for many years. Dickens wrote that the minister possessed "that religion which has sympathy for men of every creed and ventures to pass judgment on none.... I have carried into effect an old idea of mine and joined the Unitarians, who would do something for human improvement if they could; and practice charity and toleration."

Tagart tells us that following nearly 30 years of distinguished service in the Royal Navy, where he rose to the rank of Post Captain, Heywood retired in 1816 and married Francis Simpson. He peacefully lived out the rest of his days in Highgate and Regent's Park, London. Tagart gives us a flavor of Heywood's last years: "His house was the resort of friends, who looked up to him with respect, and of young aspirants in the profession, who came to profit by his experience and advice. Observation, reading, and reflection, contributed to enrich the mind, which early adversity had strengthened."

Heywood's "early adversity" — including harsh imprisonment on *Pandora*, shipwreck and

Opposite: This Oxford World's Classics edition of Sir John Barrow's *The Eventful History of the Mutiny and Piratical Seizure of H.M.S. Bounty: Its Causes and Consequences* features a dust jacket illustration by Lynton Lamb, who originally created it for the Golden Cockerel Press edition of William Bligh's *The Log of the Bounty*. By permission of Oxford University Press.

the ordeal of being on trial for his life—must have taken a significant toll on Heywood's health, and he died of heart failure at the age of 58. He was buried in the public vault of Highgate Chapel.

"Mutiny of the Bounty." *Chronicles of the Sea: Or, Fateful Narratives of Shipwrecks, Fires, Famines, and Disasters*, 1, Nos. 24, 25 (Supplement) (May 26, 1838): 185-200. London: William Mark Clark, for M. Moore.

Nineteenth-century readers who enjoyed tales of ships and the sea must have eagerly anticipated each new issue of *Chronicles of the Sea*. This weekly periodical, published by subscription in more than 100 installments from 1838 to 1840, was priced at one penny. It presented a wide range of sea-related stories—shipwrecks, mutinies, capture and survival stories, etc.—illustrated with handsome wood engravings. A sampling of articles from 1838, when *Chronicles of the Sea* published the tales of the *Bounty* and the *Pandora*, includes, "Loss of the Kent Indiaman," destroyed by fire in the Bay of Biscay; "Capt. Ross' Voyage in Search of the Missing Whalers;" "Loss of the Mèduse," a French frigate; and "Loss of H.M.S. Wager."

The two-part account of the *Bounty* mutiny presented in *Chronicles of the Sea* is fairly straightforward, adhering closely to the published accounts of William Bligh and Sir John Barrow. The anonymous author relies heavily on Bligh's conspiracy theory of the mutiny: "Thus far the voyage had advanced in a course of uninterrupted prosperity; but a conspiracy had been formed, which was concerted with so much secresy and circumspection, that not the slightest suspicion was occasioned of the impending calamity."

At the conclusion of the first part of the article, the anonymous author briefly summarizes Bligh's conduct as reported in James Morrison's unpublished manuscript journal, which had been quoted thirteen years earlier in Marshall's "Peter Heywood, Esq.," in *Royal Naval Biography*, and in Barrow's *Eventful History of the Mutiny and Piratical Seizure of H.M.S. Bounty*. Without condoning the mutiny—"It is very evident that the conduct of the mutineers was in no way justifiable"—the author concludes that Bligh was to blame: "His language to his officers, on almost every occasion on which he choosed to find fault, was so totally unfit for a gentleman bearing his majesty's commission, that it could not fail to disgust and estrange the minds of every one from him."

The second installment of "Mutiny of the Bounty," presented as a "supplement to the first part," narrates the capture of the mutineers, *Pandora*'s ill-fated voyage, the court-martial, and the fate of Fletcher Christian's party on Pitcairn Island. It is a fairly objective, unbiased account with one glaring error—the author confuses the island of Toobouai, where Christian first attempted to make a settlement, with Pitcairn Island: "It appeared that after the departure of Captain Bligh in the launch, they [the mutineers] proceeded to Toobouai ... a solitary island discovered by Captain Cook in 1777, and which has since received the name of Pitcairn's Island."

In less than 16 pages, *Chronicles of the Sea* presents a full, but remarkably succinct, account of the entire *Bounty* Saga. It also is free of the moralizing tone that colored so many of the articles about the mutiny and Pitcairn Island in the 19th century.

REV. THOS. BOYLES MURRAY, M.A: *Pitcairn: The Island, the People, and the Pastor; with a Short Account of the Mutiny of the Bounty. By the Rev. Thos. Boyles Murray, M.A., Secretary to the Society for Promoting Christian Knowledge*. London: Society for Promoting Christian Knowledge, 1853.

The Rev. Thos. Boyles Murray's *Pitcairn: The Island, the People, and the Pastor; with a Short Account of the Mutiny of the Bounty* is one of the most enduring and popular books about the *Bounty* Saga. Between 1853 and 1860, approximately 30,000 copies were printed. A hand-

CHRONICLES OF THE SEA.

No. 25.] SUPPLEMENT.—PRICE ONE PENNY. [May 26, 1838.

MUTINY OF THE BOUNTY.

Mutiny of the Bounty—(continued.)

INDEPENDENT of the object of the preceding voyage being rendered abortive, so audacious and criminal an act of insubordination as that committed by Christian and his associates, could not pass unnoticed. Lieutenant Bligh was promoted to the rank of commander, and a second time sent out to transport the bread fruit to the West Indies, which he succeeded in accomplishing. The British government having resolved to adopt every possible means to apprehend the mutineers and bring them to punishment, and also to obtain a survey of Endeavour Straits, for the purpose of facilitating the passage to Botany Bay, sent out the Pandora frigate, of twenty-four guns, and one hundred and sixty men, under the command of Captain Edward Edwards; with orders to proceed, in the first instance, to Otaheite, and if he did not find the mutineers there, to visit the different groups of the Society and Friendly Islands, and others in the neighbouring parts of the Pacific; and to use his best endeavours to seize and bring home in confinement, the whole or such part of the delinquents as they might be able to discover.

In January, 1791, the Pandora passed the Straits of Magellan, and anchored in Matavai Bay the 23rd of March. Before the ship had anchored, Joseph Coleman, the armourer of the Bounty, attempted to come on board; and several questions were put to him about the Bounty and her people, to which he gave ready replies. Soon afterwards he was followed by Mr. Peter Heywood and Mr. Stewart, midshipmen, who were brought down into the cabin; when, after some conversation, Heywood asked if Mr. Hayward, midshipman of the Bounty, but then Lieutenant of the Pandora, was on board, and who was sent for. After further conversation, Captain Edwards called in the sentinel to take them into custody, and to put them in irons. Soon after this, four others arrived, and from them and some of

A wood engraving of *Pandora* sinking from the periodical *Chronicles of the Sea*. This issue is the second installment of an article covering the *Bounty* mutiny.

some, well-illustrated volume, it was presented to countless young people as school prizes, and as confirmation and graduation gifts, sometimes in deluxe bindings.

Although it has not enjoyed the same level of success as Sir John Barrow's landmark volume, *The Eventful History of the Mutiny and Piratical Seizure of H.M.S. Bounty*, it has gone through multiple editions in Britain and the United States, usually with updated information. It was reprinted as recently as 1982.

The first edition of *Pitcairn: The Island, the People, and the Pastor* was published in London by the Society for Promoting Christian Knowledge (SPCK), where Murray served as Secretary. This organization had been in contact with the Pitcairn Islanders for many years. In the United States, the book first appeared in 1854, under the title *The Home of the Mutineers*, an abridged version published by the American Sunday-School Union.

The Pitcairn Island story, which was common public knowledge by the mid-1850s, holds a special cultural appeal, as Harry L. Shapiro writes in *The Heritage of the Bounty: The Story of Pitcairn through Six Generations* (1936): "At this time Sunday schools throughout the United States were glutted with tracts in which the lesson of Pitcairn was neatly pointed. Murderers and cutthroats might found a modern Eden, ran the parable, evil might produce good, and the simple and primitive might harbor the true righteousness, if the voice of God were heeded as on Pitcairn."

The fact that this "parable" was just one part of the exciting, adventure-filled saga of H.M.S. *Bounty* made the moral and religious lessons of Pitcairn Island more palatable to young readers. Murray understood the appeal of the *Bounty*'s story, describing it in his Preface as "The eventful history which is connected to the place, and which proves that real life may be as romantic as fiction."

Murray narrates the story of H.M.S. *Bounty* in the first third of *Pitcairn: The Island, the People, and the Pastor*, covering the main events in a fashion similar to Barrow. Occasionally, he inserts some interesting new material, such as the story of *Bounty*'s chronometer and its roundabout "journey" from Pitcairn Island to London. When discussing the mutiny itself, he is less critical of Bligh than is Barrow, focusing more on the evil deeds of the mutineers than on their commander's character flaws: "Bligh was a well-trained and distinguished officer of a formal school. Notwithstanding the occasional ebullitions of anger and excitement, which appear to have been more prevalent in naval commanders in those days, and which the rough and uneducated character of their crews was likely to provoke, still it was Bligh's study to make his men, not only efficient, but comfortable and happy."

Like Barrow, he romanticizes the experience of Peter Heywood. Introducing a series of Heywood family letters from the period of the court-martial, Murray writes, "This little work would be incomplete without some further notice of one, who was enabled, by the good Providence of God, in whom he trusted, to live down the scandal and heavy imputations, which, in consequence of his position and circumstances, in relation to other and older men [read Fletcher Christian], had fallen upon him in his youth. The following letters, which are classed according to their dates, cannot be read without emotion."

The remainder of Murray's volume is essentially a history of the Pitcairn Island settlement, from the arrival of the mutineers in 1790 to 1853. He discusses such significant events as the Islanders' emigration to Tahiti in 1833, which resulted in the death of many of them by illness; their return to Pitcairn; and the later emigration of many Pitcairners to Norfolk Island, where their descendants live today.

He also presents at length the remarkable career of George Nobbs, who arrived on Pitcairn Island in 1828 and spent most of his life there. Nobbs returned to England in 1853 to

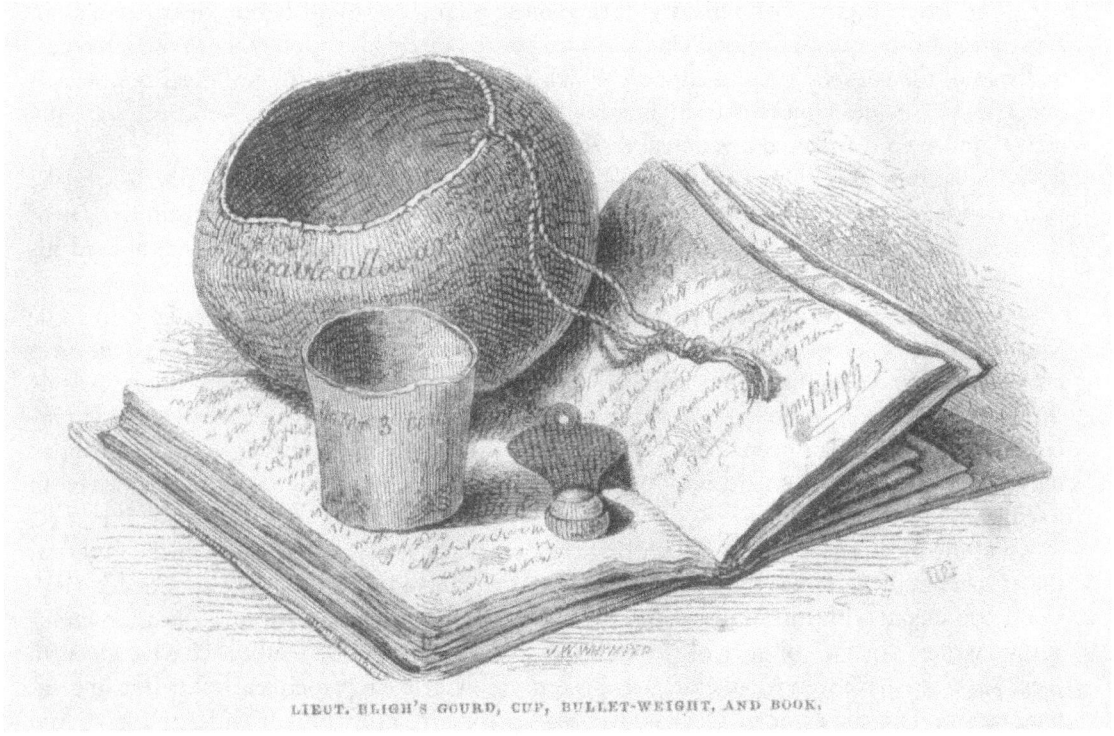

LIEUT. BLIGH'S GOURD, CUP, BULLET-WEIGHT, AND BOOK.

"Lieut. Bligh's Gourd, Cup, Bullet-Weight and Book," as pictured in Rev. Murray's *Pitcairn: The Island, the People, and the Pastor*. These precious items, which Bligh used during the open boat voyage, were auctioned by Christie's in 2002 as "The Bligh Relics," for £71,700.

be ordained as a chaplain and, on his return, served as Pitcairn's spiritual leader (the "Pastor" of the book's title), physician and schoolmaster for many years. His arrival, Murray writes, was "a providential occurrence for the well-being of the inhabitants."

He rounds off the volume with some of the sermons given by Rev. Nobbs, the island's Public Register, an account of Pitcairn's laws, a list of ships touching at Pitcairn and a selection of the Islanders' hymns. In its 300 pages, Murray provides a remarkable amount of material, making it an essential volume in any collection of Bountiana.

The Sailors' Magazine: Containing the Life of Peter Heywood, Midshipman of the Bounty. Also, a Sketch of the Principal Mutineers of the Bounty. Boston: American Seaman's Friend Society, n.d. (1865).

The Seaman's Friend Society, organized in 1825, was dedicated to improving the lives of sailors when they were on shore — primarily by discouraging them from using alcohol, visiting prostitutes or falling victim to confidence artists. Local branches provided decent lodging for sailors in boardinghouses (with libraries) and the Society provided Bibles and published reading material filled with inspirational stories, including *The Sailors' Magazine*.

The Society's founders were heavily influenced by the religious reform movement of the 19th century, and *The Sailors' Magazine* articles tend to be didactic and preachy. A 48-page "biography" of Peter Heywood, published by the magazine in the 1860s, is a good example. While it includes accurate information, it is laced with quotes from the scriptures, and facts are frequently ignored or distorted to express the Society's viewpoint and provide a moral lesson to the reader.

The article begins, "The history of the young man [Heywood] is very instructive as an illustration of the value of a good character, and of the care which God takes of the innocent, and also of the consolation and support which religion affords in a time of great temptation and trial." The anonymous author ignores the fact that on Tahiti, Heywood was sexually active, and even contracted a venereal disease.

The author also claims that Bligh's behavior toward Christian on the day before the mutiny was caused by alcohol: "On the afternoon of the 27th of April the Commander of the Bounty, under the *influence of intoxicating drink*, as is commonly supposed, abused his crew with oaths and threats which made them exceedingly angry with them."

Alcohol may have played a part in the mutiny — as suggested by Herbert Ford in "The Mutiny's Cause: A New Analysis," and by Caroline Alexander in *The* Bounty*: The True Story of the Mutiny on the* Bounty — but Fletcher Christian was probably drinking, not Bligh. Despite these inaccuracies, *The Sailors' Magazine* suggests a remarkably clear-cut motive for Christian's rebellion: "He had been stung by the recent insult, and having never learned to control his temper, he was now borne away by his passion as the ship without a rudder is driven in a tempest."

Following an account of William Bligh's open boat voyage and the story of the *Pandora*, the article briefly describes the court-martial, and reprints much of the correspondence Heywood conducted with his family at the time. Following Heywood's pardon, the anonymous author writes, "In the conduct of the excellent young man, whose history we have given in these pages, we have seen what a safeguard is found in Christian principle, in the time of great temptation. The character of Heywood raised up for him numerous friends, and gave him favor in the whole community." Luckily for Heywood, his family's "numerous friends" held influential positions in the Royal Navy, increasing the odds that he would receive the King's Pardon.

The article closes with an account of the settlement on Pitcairn Island, declaring that the violence of the early years stemmed from the mutineers' crime: "Though no human government took cognizance of their crime, God pursued them with his terrible judgment." And, like most 19th century articles about Pitcairn Island, *The Sailors' Magazine* points to John Adams' reformation as an example of Christian fortitude. The author drives the lesson home by comparing Heywood's experience with Adams': "This narrative illustrates the value of a Christian influence among Seamen. Young Heywood carried with him to sea principles which fortified him against temptation... By the same influence, John Adams, after a career of great wickedness was transformed into a useful man, and became 'a burning and shining light in the midst of the community in which he lived and died.'"

LADY BELCHER (DIANA JOLLIFFE): *The Mutineers of the Bounty and their Descendants in Pitcairn and Norfolk Islands. By Lady Belcher. With Map and Illustrations.* London: John Murray, 1870. First U.S. edition published by Harper and Brothers, New York, 1871.

Diana Jolliffe, born in 1806, became Captain Peter Heywood's stepdaughter after he married Francis Simpson in 1816, the year he retired from the Royal Navy. When Heywood died childless in 1831, Diana gained full access to his personal papers, which included at least one copy of James Morrison's manuscript journal. She maintained an interest in the *Bounty* Saga and in Pitcairn Island throughout her life. In his memoir, *Lady Belcher and Her Friends*, published one year after her death, the Rev. A.G. L'Estrange writes, "Miss Jolliffe was very loyal to her step-father, and said she was sorry that she ever heard she had any other father. In his will he called her his 'dear and affectionate stepdaughter.'"

In 1870, Lady Belcher published *The Mutineers of the Bounty and their Descendants in*

Pitcairn and Norfolk Islands, which covers much of the same ground that Sir John Barrow did nearly 40 years earlier in *The Eventful History of the Mutiny and Piratical Seizure of H.M.S. Bounty*. She brings the history of Pitcairn Island up to date and maintains, in the Preface, that Barrow's volume "did not contain all the information which might have been afforded ... the possession of a variety of private documents on the subject, have induced the writer to lay before the public what she ventures to believe will be found to be a more connected and impartial narrative."

Despite Lady Belcher's assertion, *The Mutineers of the Bounty* is anything but impartial. Throughout the book, she sentimentalizes Peter Heywood and blackens Bligh's already tarnished reputation. In *The Life of Vice-Admiral William Bligh*, George Mackaness calls her book "A ... partisan story based upon Morrison's Journal and intended principally as an exculpation of Peter Heywood," and that "The trivial complaints indulged in by Morrison are exaggerated into major grievances by Lady Belcher."

Lady Belcher's quotes from James Morrison's journal are from a manuscript copy that had been edited, most likely by Heywood himself, who changed or deleted anything that might cast a harsh light on himself or on his friend, George Stewart, who perished on *Pandora*. Caroline Alexander writes, Heywood had been "a zealous and watchful guardian of the *Bounty* Saga," who even provided a copy of Morrison's (edited) journal to his own biographer.

Mutineer John Adams told Captain F. W. Beechey that Stewart had encouraged Fletcher Christian to mutiny, a statement that was published in Beechey's *Narrative of a Voyage to the*

A ship sinking in a tempest-torn sea decorates this issue of *The Sailors' Magazine*, which features a biography of Peter Heywood. The young midshipman's physical and emotional sufferings served as inspirational material for this publication.

BOUNTY BAY, PITCAIRN ISLAND.

This engraving in Lady Belcher's *The Mutineers of the Bounty and their Descendants in Pitcairn and Norfolk Islands* is based on an illustration that appeared in F.W. Beechey's *Narrative of a Voyage to the Pacific and Beerings Strait.* It depicts Pitcairn longboats preparing to land in treacherous Bounty Bay. This remains a perilous exercise in seamanship, and the Pitcairners are among the finest handlers of small craft in the world. The Mitchell Library, State Library of New South Wales, Sydney, holds an unsigned oil painting of this scene.

Pacific and Beerings Strait. Barrow did Heywood a favor by including in his book a letter that Heywood had written to Beechey, refuting Adams' accusation. Lady Belcher further strengthened her stepfather's position on the matter by writing of Adams:

> On another point he was also singularly inaccurate; that of accusing young Stewart of advising Christian, his superior officer, to take the vessel. In the confusion which must have ensued on such an event, he could not have known what passed between Christian and Stewart when the latter went down to summon Christian to take the watch, and must either have forgotten, or never heard, that Christian had taken upon himself the blame of originating the mutiny; although, after the fatal step, so many had entered actively into the plan.

It is not surprising that Lady Belcher would want to preserve her stepfather's reputation, which he earned during a long and honorable naval career, but she did so at Bligh's expense. Although it never attained the popularity of Barrow's or Murray's books, *The Mutineers of the Bounty and their Descendants in Pitcairn and Norfolk Islands* played a significant role in solidifying Bligh's growing reputation as a merciless tyrant.

DR. ROBERT BROWN: "The Pitcairn Islanders, and the Mutiny of the *Bounty*." *Cassell's Family Magazine.* London, Paris and New York: Cassell, Petter, Galpin & Co., 1880. 212–216.

The 19th century was a veritable golden age of popular periodicals, such as *Blackwood's Edinburgh Magazine, Cassell's Family Magazine, The Friend, Harper's Weekly, The Illustrated London News, Once a Week* and many more. Family reading was a favorite form of entertainment, so publishers filled their magazines and newsletters with fiction and nonfiction that covered a wide range of interesting subjects, often accompanied by illustrations.

With its history of violence followed by religious redemption, the story of Pitcairn Island was a perennial favorite with readers of that era, and numerous retellings appeared in periodicals throughout the 19th century. *Bounty* scholars and enthusiasts surely would agree with Dr. Robert Brown, author of "The Pitcairn Islanders, and the Mutiny of the *Bounty*," who states, "The community settled in this lovely dot in the Pacific have a history all their own, which, though often told, yet seems never to lose its freshness for the world's ear."

Most articles about the *Bounty* mutiny and Pitcairn Island that appeared in the popular press, including "The Pitcairn Islanders, and the Mutiny of the *Bounty*," adopted a negative view of William Bligh. This is not surprising, since 19th century authors drew much of their content (often paraphrasing it) from Sir John Barrow's *Eventful History of the Mutiny and Piratical Seizure of H.M.S. Bounty*, and Lady Belcher's *The Mutineers of the Bounty and their Descendants in Pitcairn and Norfolk Islands*, both anti-Bligh.

Like the children's stories and books by Maria Hack, R. M. Ballantyne and "Peter Parley," many articles stressed the story's moral and religious implications. For example, one entitled "The Paradise in the Pacific," published in *Blackwood's Edinburgh Magazine*, reflects the usual view of Adams' character in 19th century periodicals: "Marvellous, indeed, was the change which reflection and merciful experience contributed to effect in his mind and character."

"The Pitcairn Islanders, and the Mutiny of the *Bounty*" presents a relatively balanced, objective view of the story — although Brown takes the usual anti-Bligh stance typical of the period: "Her commander, Lieutenant Bligh, was a good seaman, but a sullen martinet, of a type now extinct in the Royal Navy, but in those days of the triangle [on which soldiers were tied for flogging] and 'three dozen [lashes] all round for breakfast' only too common."

Dr. Brown gives Bligh due credit in his brief account of the mutiny and open boat voyage, but then casts a critical eye on the figure of John Adams, the mutineer commonly praised as the "Patriarch of Pitcairn Island." Adams, Brown says, "Was trying to be a changed character, and was trying to make amends for his former life by training up the young generation in the ways of virtue and honour ... of late doubts have not unnaturally been entertained of the strict truth of Adams' story."

Brown concedes the possibility that Adams' conversion from criminal to religious patriarch was genuine, but he maintains that such a radical transformation should not be taken at face value: "Adams, it must not be forgotten, was a desperate character when on board the *Bounty*, and it is well known that the tale he told of his share in the actual mutiny is utterly false." To make such a statement, Brown must have been familiar with Adams' conflicting accounts of the mutiny, as collected by Mayhew Folger, Amasa Delano, F.W. Beechey and other early visitors to Pitcairn Island.

Adams' conflicting accounts of Fletcher Christian's life on Pitcairn and the manner of his death leads Brown to discuss the intriguing rumors that Christian had returned to England in the early part of the 19th century, and that Captain Peter Heywood actually may have seen him in Plymouth. "The Pitcairn Islanders, and the Mutiny of the *Bounty*" also brings readers up to date on Pitcairn history, giving them a taste of island life — filling five pages of *Cassell's Family Magazine* with a wealth of edifying, entertaining information.

ROSALIND AMELIA YOUNG: *Mutiny of the Bounty and Story of Pitcairn Island, 1790-1894*. Oakland, CA., San Francisco, New York, and Kansas City: Pacific Press Publishing Company, 1894.

JOHN ADAMS' GRAVE.

Sunbeams illuminating the grave of John Adams imply the piety of the reformed mutineer in an illustration for the article, "The Pitcairn Islanders, and the Mutiny of the Bounty." The author of this story, which appeared in *Cassell's Family Magazine*, 1880, questions the sincerity of Adams' conversion.

Few 19th century books devoted to the *Bounty* Saga have remained in print for very long. The prime exceptions are Sir John Barrow's *The Eventful History of the Mutiny and Piratical Seizure of H.M.S. Bounty,* the Rev. Thos. Boyles Murray's *Pitcairn: The Island, the People, and the Pastor,* and Rosalind Amelia Young's *Mutiny of the Bounty and Story of Pitcairn Island.*

Young's charming volume, illustrated with photographs and line drawings, was the first book written by a Pitcairn Islander. It evolved from a brief article she wrote for *Scribners Monthly* entitled "The Mutineers of the '*Bounty*,'" published in October 1881. Young also wrote articles for *The Youth's Instructor* and the *Overland Monthly*, as well as the hymn "Pitcairn, Lone Rock of the Sea."

In the introduction to Young's book, E.H. Gates, a minister of the Seventh-day Adventist Church who spent more than 18 months on Pitcairn, remarks that Young was uniquely qualified to write a history of Pitcairn Island: "While her lifetime does not cover quite one-half of the time covered by the history of the island, she had access for many years to one at least who remembered events that occurred before the beginning of the present century." The person Gates refers to is Young's father, Simon Young, a grandson of John Adams and the second-oldest man on Pitcairn at the time of his death in September 1893. Young was serving as primary school teacher on the island when she wrote *Mutiny of the Bounty and Story of Pitcairn Island.*

Young covers H.M.S. *Bounty*'s voyage and mutiny in the first three chapters, devoting the rest of her book to both major and minor events in Pitcairn history. She provides detailed descriptions and fascinating glimpses of day-to-day life and customs in the late 19th century, from celebrating the Queen's birthday to sawing wood, egg hunting and making cloth from the bark of the tapa tree.

Mutiny of the Bounty and Story of Pitcairn Island is full of anecdotes and observations of events from the Pitcairners' point of view, such as the visit of F. W. Beechey on H.M.S. *Blossom* in 1825. Young writes, no doubt recalling the memories of her father, that "When the *Blossom* left the island, the tearful, affectionate farewells told how the hearts of all the islanders had been won to their visitors, whose pleasant stay and cheerful companionship had been such a bright spot in their quiet lives, and was to form ever after one of their most delightful and pleasing recollections."

The anecdotes are not always pleasant to read, for Young does not ignore the many hardships and accidents endured by the Pitcairners (which persist even to this day), such as the explosion of one of *Bounty*'s guns in 1853, when it was fired to salute the steamship *Virago*. This accident caused severe injuries in two young men and the death of Matthew McCoy. She describes how islanders sometimes died by accidents, and diseases such as tetanus and tuberculosis.

On an island as isolated as Pitcairn, the visit of a ship is an important event, and vessels stopped far more frequently during Young's lifetime than they do today. Occasionally there were accidents, such as the wreck of the *Cornwallis*, out of Liverpool, in 1875. The captain, who had a taste to see the refuge of the *Bounty* mutineers, drifted onto hidden rocks near Pitcairn's shore, completely wrecking his vessel. Young reports how the islanders, with their characteristic skill, courage and compassion, did everything in their power to help:

> The excitement that prevailed was great, and soon everybody was near the scene of the disaster. The other men that had been engaged about their several duties when the disaster took place, now returned from the fields, and, seeing what had happened, were quickly on the rocks near where the ship lay. Swimming off to the vessel, they were soon engaged with the others who had been before them in rendering what assistance they were able, and in a short time after the ship struck, all the crew had been safely landed.

The cover of the third edition of Rosalind Amelia Young's *Mutiny of the Bounty and Story of Pitcairn Island*. Young attracted many readers through her friendly writing style, and this title remains one of the most popular *Bounty*-related books.

Pitcairn often was a refuge to shipwrecked mariners, such those from another Liverpool ship, *Khandeish*, who were guests on the island for 51 days in late 1875. Young writes that at least one of the crew fell under Pitcairn's spell: "when, on the 19th of November, they left on the British ship *Ennerdale* for San Francisco, the parting on both sides was expressive of much sorrow. One of the men remained behind and was shortly afterwards married to a widow to whom he had become attached."

The islanders' generosity was repaid. The grateful crew, after arriving in San Francisco, arranged for the shipment of kitchen utensils, flour, fabric and finished clothing to Pitcairn. Young adds, "As a crowning gift to the whole, a beautifully-toned organ, of the Mason & Hamlin Organ Company, was sent." Once installed in Pitcairn's church, the Islanders rejoiced to hear its perfect tone.

Mutiny of the Bounty and Story of Pitcairn Island owes much of its appeal to anecdotes like this one, as well to Young's lucid, friendly writing style. Her book provides a special glimpse into Pitcairn's past that may be enjoyed as much today as it was when first published.

Additional Works

Books

(Barrow, Sir John). *The Mutiny and Piratical Seizure of H.M.S. Bounty*. Edited and with an introduction by Captain Stephen W. Roskill. London: Folio Society, 1976.

The Folio Society's illustrated, slipcased edition of Sir John Barrow's popular book has been reprinted several times. In his introduction, Captain Stephen W. Roskill provides a brief sketch of Barrow's career and a general discussion of events leading up to the mutiny. Folio Society titles are sold only to subscribers, but copies turn up frequently in the used book market, often for less than the original publication price.

_____. *The Mutiny and Piratical Seizure of H.M.S. Bounty.* Introduction by Admiral Sir Cyprian Bridge. London: Oxford University Press, 1914. Oxford World's Classics edition.

Reading a copy of this pocket-sized book inspired James Norman Hall to write *Mutiny on the Bounty* with Charles Nordhoff. This edition includes a rather dated essay by Admiral Sir Cyprian Bridge, where he describes Bligh as a low-class bully.

_____. *The Mutiny of the Bounty.* Edited by Gavin Kennedy. Boston: David R. Godine, 1980.

This beautifully printed, illustrated edition features an introduction by Gavin Kennedy, author of two excellent biographies of William Bligh and editor of *A Book of the "Bounty."*

_____. *The Mutiny of the "Bounty."* Illustrated by Nigel Lambourne. London and Glasgow: Blackie and Son, 1961.

See Chapter 5 for more details.

_____. *Mutiny! The Real History of the* H.M.S. Bounty. New York: Cooper Square Press, 2003.

The text of this unabridged, trade paperback reprint of *The Mutiny and Piratical Seizure of H.M.S. Bounty* appears to be photographed from the original plates. It includes an introduction by Edward E. Leslie, who provides a brief biography of Sir John Barrow and an account of the mutiny. He steers clear of the Bligh vs. Christian controversy, but clearly admires Bligh: "Give the devil his due; whatever Bligh's faults as a peacetime naval officer, he was a brave and resolute man and an extraordinary navigator. He was also one hell of a seaman." This quote reveals how much opinions about Bligh have evolved since Admiral Sir Cyprian Bridge wrote his introduction in the 1914 Oxford World's Classics edition.

Bennett, Frederick Debell. *Narrative of a Whaling Voyage Round the Globe From the Year 1833 to 1836.* London: Richard Bentley, 1840.

_____. *Narrative of a Whaling Voyage Round the Globe From the Year 1833 to 1836.* Amsterdam and New York: N. Israel and Da Capo Press, 1970. Facsimile edition.

Bennett's *Narrative of a Whaling Voyage Round the Globe From the Year 1833 to 1836* records his March 1834 visit to Pitcairn Island, when he learned that John Adams had died in 1829. Bennett discusses life on Pitcairn at the time and describes how Joshua Hill took over the administration of the island — an event that inspired Mark Twain to write "The Great Revolution in Pitcairn."

Brodie, Walter. *Pitcairn's Island and the Islanders in 1850.* London: Whittaker's and Co., 1851.

_____. *Pitcairn's Island and the Islanders in 1850.* New York: AMS Press, 1980. Facsimile edition.

Walter Brodie was stranded on Pitcairn Island with four fellow travelers for three weeks in March 1850. Later, he wrote this popular account, reprinted twice in the year of publication. He made excellent use of his time on Pitcairn, providing a vivid portrait of life there during the mid–19th century. Brodie states in the preface that he collected, "materials for an account of this virtuous and interesting community, which I feel myself bound to make public, in hope that it may draw attention, now more than ever needed, to their condition, and thus partially discharge the obligation which my fellow-passengers and myself have incurred."

Pitcairn's Island and the Islanders in 1850 includes an account of the *Bounty* mutineers' early life on Pitcairn, a description of the island's geography, the "Laws and Regulations of Pitcairn Island" and an account of the ships that called there between 1808 and 1850.

Delano, Amasa. *A Narrative of Voyages and Travels in the Northern and Southern Hemispheres.* Upper Saddle River, New Jersey: Gregg Press, 1970.

_____. *Delano's Voyages of Commerce and Discovery. Amasa Delano in China, the Pacific Islands, Australia, and South America, 1789–1807.* Stockbridge, Massachusetts: Berkshire House Publishers, 1994. Introduction by Eleanor Roosevelt Seagrave.

The first edition of Delano's *A Narrative of Voyages and Travels in the Northern and Southern Hemispheres* is a rarity, but Gregg Press produced a complete facsimile in 1994. Berkshire House Publishers published an edited, trade paperback version in 1994, with an introduction by Eleanor Roosevelt Seagrave. This edition includes Chapter VI, *Reflections on the History of the Bounty and Settlement on Pitcairn's Island.*

L'Estrange, Alfred Guy Kingan. *Lady Belcher and her Friends*. London: Hurst and Blackett, 1891.

    A.G.K. L'Estrange's memoir of the author of *The Mutineers of the Bounty and their Descendants in Pitcairn and Norfolk Islands* is well worth consulting for its account of the book's genesis, and the glimpses it provides into the life of Peter Heywood, the author's stepfather.

McFarland, Alfred. *Mutiny in the "Bounty" and Story of the Pitcairn Islanders*. Sydney: J. J. Moore, 1884.

    A good number of nonfiction titles about H.M.S. *Bounty* and Pitcairn Island were available by 1884, including the accounts of William Bligh, Sir John Barrow, Rev. Thos. Boyles Murray, Walter Brodie and Lady Belcher. Alfred McFarland was one of the first authors to use these books as source material. He also linked the *Bounty* Saga to the history of Australia and Norfolk Island, where many of the Pitcairn Islanders had emigrated earlier in the 19th century.

    McFarland pays lip service to Bligh's accomplishments, but he clearly is in the anti-Bligh camp, associating his behavior with the appalling acts of Captain Edward Edwards on *Pandora*: "Bligh—whose outrages, prior to it [the mutiny], were only surpassed by the later barbarities of Captain Edwards."

Murray, Hugh. "Mutiny of the Bounty, with Consequences Arising From it; Bligh's Voyage Through the Pacific in an Open Boat; Voyage and Shipwreck of the Pandora; Settlement and Present State of Pitcairn Island." In *Constable's Miscellany*, vol. 4: *Adventures of British Seamen in the Southern Ocean, Displaying the Striking Contrasts which the Human Character Exhibits in an Uncivilized State*. Edinburgh: Constable and Co., 1827.

    The *Bounty* story is told in four chapters here, much of it paraphrased from Barrow's *Eventful History of the Mutiny and Piratical Seizure of H.M.S. Bounty*.

Woodward, David. *The Narrative of Captain David Woodward and Four Seamen*. London: J. Johnson, 1805.

_____. *The Narrative of Captain David Woodward and Four Seamen*. London: Dawsons, 1969.

    Captain Woodward's *Narrative* includes two appendices of interest to *Bounty* scholars: Appendix V, 166–174, an account of Bligh's voyage in *Bounty*'s launch, and Appendix XI, 195–196, which describes the wreck of *Pandora*.

Articles

Belcher, Lady (Diana Jolliffe). "The Pitcairn Islanders." *Harper's New Monthly Magazine*, 42 (December—May 1871): 653–669.

    This popular journal condensed portions of Lady Belcher's *The Mutineers of the Bounty and their Descendants in Pitcairn and Norfolk Islands*, along with some of its illustrations, expanding the audience for her book.

Dillon, Captain Peter. "Pitcairn's Island—The Bounty's Crew." *United Service Journal* Part II (November 1829): 589–593.

    This is an important record of events in Pitcairn Island's early history, provided by Teehuteatuaonoa ("Jenny"), wife of mutineer Isaac Martin. Jenny returned to Tahiti from Pitcairn on the whaling ship *Sultan* in 1817. (See "Pitcairn's Island" by Samuel Topliff for a contemporary account of *Sultan*'s visit.)

    In *Mutiny and Romance in the South Seas*, Sven Wahlroos points out that Jenny's account appeared in the *Sydney Gazette*, July 17, 1819 and in *Bengal Hurkaru*, October 2, 1926. Dr. Wahlroos writes, "Teehuteatuaonoa's accounts are more reliable than those Adams gave, if for no other reason than that she had nothing to hide."

Folger, Mayhew. "Extract from the Log-book of Captain Folgar [sic] of the American Ship Topaz, of Boston." *Jersey Magazine, or Monthly Recorder* 1, no. 2 (August 1809): 79–80.

    One of the earliest published reports of Captain Mayhew Folger's discovery of Pitcairn Island in 1808. It focuses on Alexander Smith (he was not yet "John Adams"), his narrative of the mutiny and its aftermath. It also reports that Smith had presented *Bounty*'s chronometer to Captain Folger.

Marshall, John. "Peter Heywood, Esq.: One of the Survivors of the Mutiny on the Bounty." *Royal Navy Biography* vol. 2, part 2. London: Hurst, Rees, Orme, Brown, and Green, 1825: pp. 747–797.

_____. *Royal Navy Biography of Peter Heywood (Mutiny on the Bounty)*. New York: George R. Gorman, 1936. Reprint.

    This biography covers Peter Heywood's career up to 1816, when he retired from the Royal

AMERICAN CLASSICS™

Delano's Voyages of Commerce and Discovery

Amasa Delano in China, the Pacific Islands, Australia, and South America, 1789–1807

Edited by
ELEANOR ROOSEVELT SEAGRAVES
Foreword by William T. La Moy, *Peabody Essex Museum*

Delano's rare *A Narrative of Voyages and Travels* was reprinted in an edited, trade paperback format by Berkshire House Publishers in 1994, as *Delano's Voyages of Commerce and Discovery*. Delano is pictured on the cover. The Gregg Press reprinted the complete text in 1970.

Navy. The author clearly had access to James Morrison's journal, which was among Heywood's papers.

"Review of *Voyage de Dentrecasteaux*." *Quarterly Review* 3 (1810): 23–24.

A note attached to this article reports the discovery of Pitcairn Island by Captain Mayhew Folger. The *Quarterly Review* grudgingly acknowledged the truth of the discovery, even though it had been reported by, "Americans, with whom, we say it with regret, truth is not always considered as a moral obligation."

(Smyth, William Henry). "The Bounty Again!" *United Service Journal* part 3, no. 36 (November 1831): 305–314.

"The Bounty Again!" is William Henry Smyth's follow-up to "Sketch of the Career of the Late Captain Peter Heywood, R.N.," published in the April 1831 issue of *United Service Journal*. Smyth reiterates his harsh criticism of Bligh and continues to heap praise on Peter Heywood, who had passed away in February 1831. He claims that Bligh cruelly "mastheaded" Heywood at Cape Horn, forcing him to remain aloft for hours in an icy storm. Nordhoff and Hall used this incident—which may or may not have actually happened—in *Mutiny on the Bounty*. It also was dramatized in the 1935 MGM film based on that novel.

Smyth also comments on the recently published *Eventful History of the Mutiny and Piratical Seizure of H.M.S. Bounty* by Sir John Barrow.

_____. "Capt. Beechey's Narrative." *United Service Journal* no. 29 (April 1831): 527–531.

In this generally positive review of F.W. Beechey's *Narrative of a Voyage to the Pacific and Beerings Strait*, William Henry Smyth mentioned John Adams' important statement that the mutiny, "was incited by another whose name is not mentioned" (Midshipman George Stewart).

_____. "Letter to the Editor of the United Service Journal, signed 'X.Y.Z.'" *United Service Journal* no. 2 (1829): 366–367.

William Henry Smyth is "X.Y.Z.," who minces no words in this diatribe against William Bligh: "Now, though nothing can excuse mutiny, we all know that it can arise from but two causes, excessive folly or excessive tyranny.... Was not every act of Bligh's public life, after this event, stamped with an insolence, an inhumanity, and coarseness, which fully developed his character." Smyth used the same language in his "Sketch of the Career of the Late Capt. Peter Heywood, R.N."

_____. "Review of *A Memoir of the Late Captain Peter Heywood, R.N*. By Edward Tagart, 1832." *United Service Journal* no. 50 (January 1833): 92–93.

This is an extremely disparaging review of Edward Tagart's *A Memoir of the Late Captain Peter Heywood*. William Henry Smyth scores some valid points on Tagart's lack of nautical knowledge, but his main bone of contention seems to be that the author's motive in writing the *Memoir* "is to boast aloud that so excellent a man as Captain Heywood had swerved from the established religion of his country; and the author, editor or compiler of the pages which tell this, is a Unitarian preacher." Given Heywood's views of European civilization and religion in light of his experiences in Tahiti, the Unitarian Church may very well have been attractive to him in his later years.

_____. "Sketch of the Career of the Late Captain Peter Heywood, R.N." *United Service Journal* no. 29 (April 1831): 468–481.

This brief biography of Peter Heywood, published just two months after his death on February 10, 1831, is vehemently anti-Bligh and pro-Heywood. William Henry Smyth describes the *Bounty* mutiny, the mutineers' failed settlement at Tubuai, *Pandora*'s voyage, the *Bounty* courtmartial, and Heywood's later career in the Royal Navy, placing Heywood in a favorable light at every opportunity.

Topliff, Samuel. "Pitcairn's Island." *New-England Galaxy* 4 (January 12, 1821): 53–54. This article recounts the 1817 visit of *Sultan* to Pitcairn.

"The Transformed Island: A Story of the South Seas." *Sunday at Home Magazine: A Family Magazine for Sabbath Reading*. No. 1 (May 4 1854): 1–4; no. 2 (May 11 1854): 17–19; no. 3 (May 18 1854): 33–35; no. 4 (May 25 1854): 49–52.

This serial tells the story of Pitcairn Island up to the departure of the Rev. George H. Nobbs. "The Transformed Island" is characteristic of many 19th century articles about Pitcairn that employ its history as material for religious instruction. The article concludes, "We proposed to show the moral chemistry of God, extracting good out of evil; and all must admit that the narrative before us has most satisfactorily demonstrated this." Each chapter of "The Transformed Island" leads off with a charming illustration.

Supplemental Bibliography

Books

Adams, W. H. Davenport. "The Story of a Mutiny — The 'Bounty.'" Chapter 7 in *Famous Ships of the British Navy: or, Stories of Enterprise and Daring Collected from Our Naval Chronicles.* London: James Hogg and Sons, 1863.

Alexander, James M. *The Islands of the Pacific.* New York: American Tract Society, 1895.

Anonymous. *A Home on the Deep: Or, the Mariner's Trials on the Dark Blue Sea.* "By a Son of the Ocean." Boston: Higgins, Bradley and Dayton, 1857.

Barnard, Charles H. *A Narrative of the Sufferings and Adventures of Captain Charles H. Barnard, in a Voyage Around the World, During the Years 1812, 1813, 1814, 1815, and 1816; Embracing an Account of the Seizure of his Vessel at the Falkland Islands.* New York: J. Lindon, 1829.

Barrow, Sir John. *The Eventful History of the Mutiny of the Bounty. A Description of Pitcairn's Island and Its Inhabitants. With an Authentic Account of the Mutiny of the Ship Bounty, and of the Subsequent Fortunes of the Mutineers.* London: George Routledge and Sons, 1886. In Routledge's World Library.

_____. *The Eventful History of the Mutiny of the Bounty. A Description of Pitcairn's Island and Its Inhabitants. With an Authentic Account of the Mutiny of the Ship Bounty, and of the Subsequent Fortunes of the Mutineers.* New York: A.L. Fowle, 1900.

Beardsley, John E., Ed. *The Book of the Ocean and Life on the Sea.* Vol. 1. New York: Hurst and Co., n.d. (1860).

Bechervaise, John. *A First Fleet Family: A Hitherto Unpublished Narrative of Certain Remarkable Adventures Compiled From the Papers of Sergeant William Dew of the Marines.* London: T. Fisher Unwin, 1896.

_____. *Thirty-six Years of a Seafaring Life. By an Old Quarter Master.* Portsea: W. Woodward, 1839. The Standard Library. Includes Bligh's *Mutiny of the Bounty.*

Becke, Louis, and Walter Jeffery. *The Naval Pioneers of Australia.* London: John Murray, 1899.

Belcher, Sir Edward. *Narrative of the Voyage of H.M.S. Samarang, During the Years 1843–1846.* Two volumes. London: Reeve, Benham, and Reeve, 1848.

Bingley, Thomas. *Tales of Shipwrecks.* Chapter IV, "Uncle Thomas Tells About the Mutiny of the Bounty." Boston: Weeks, Jordan and Company, 1839.

Burke, Peter. *Celebrated Naval and Military Trials.* London: Wm. H. Allen and Co., 1866.

_____. *Celebrated Naval and Military Trials.* London: Wm. H. Allen and Co., 1866. Elibron Classics edition.

_____. *Pitcairn's Island: A Lecture Delivered at the Christchurch School-room, St. Pancras, January 12, 1853.* London: J. Whitaker, 1853.

Campbell, John. *Maritime Discovery and Christian Missions.* London: John Snow, 1840.

Campbell, Joseph. *Norfolk Island and its Inhabitants.* Sydney: Joseph Cook, 1879.

The Converted Mutineer and His Bible Class: Or, John Adams and the Children of the Mutineers. Boston: Massachusetts Sabbath School Society, 1855. Reprinted as *The Converted Mutineer and His Bible Class: Being a History of Pitcairn's Island* by the Congregational Publishing Society, Boston, 1875.

Conway, Shipley Esq., Lieut. R.N. *Sketches in the Pacific: The South Sea Islands Drawn from Nature and on Stone.* London: T. McLean, 1851.

Copy of Correspondence with the Government of New South Wales, in Reference to Pitcairn Islanders Settled in Norfolk Island. Great Britain: Colonial Office, 1863.

Dalyell, Sir John Graham. *Shipwrecks and Disasters at Sea.* Edinburgh: Archibald Constable, 1812.

Dick, William H. *The Mutiny of the Bounty and the Pitcairn Islanders.* N.p.: 1882.

Dilke, Charles Wentworth. *Greater Britain: A Record of Travel in English-Speaking Countries During 1866 and 1867.* New York: Harper and Brothers, 1869.

Fiske, Nathan Welby. *The Story of Aleck, or Pitcairn's Island. Being a True Account of a Very Singular and Interesting Colony.* Amherst, Mass: J. S. and C. Adams, 1829.

_____. *Aleck and the Mutineers of the Bounty: or, Thrilling Incidents of Life on the Ocean, Being the History of Pitcairn's Island.* Boston: John P. Jewett, 1854.

_____. *Aleck and the Mutineers of the Bounty: or Thrilling Incidents of Life on the Ocean, being the History of Pitcairn's Island and a Remarkable Illustration of the Influence of the Bible.* Boston: John P. Jewett and Co., 1855. New edition, revised and enlarged.

_____. *Aleck and the Mutineers of the Bounty: A Remarkable Illustration of the Influence of the Bible.* Boston: Massachusetts Sabbath School Society, n.d. (1855). New edition.

_____. *Aleck and the Mutineers of the Bounty: or Thrilling Incidents of Life on the Ocean, being the History of Pitcairn's Island and a Remarkable Illustration of the Influence of the Bible.* Cleveland: Jewett, Proctor and Worthington, 1855.

_____. *Aleck: the last of the mutineers: or, The History of Pitcairn's Island.* Amherst: J. S. and C. Adams, 1845. Second edition.

_____. *Aleck: the last of the mutineers: or, The History of Pitcairn's Island.* Philadelphia: E. C. Biddle, 1845.

_____. *The Last of the Mutineers: or The History of Pitcairn's Island.* Boston: Benjamin Perkins and Co., 1848. Third edition.

Francis, B. *The Isles of the Pacific: or, Sketches from the South Seas.* London: Cassell and Co., n.d. (1885).

Friday Christian; or, the First-Born on Pitcairn's Island. (By a poor member of Christ.) New York: D. Appleton and Co., 1849.

Herbert, David. *Great Historical Mutinies: Comprising the Story of the Mutiny of the Bounty, the Mutiny at Spithead, the Mutiny at the Nore, Mutinies in Highland Regiments and the Indian Mutiny.* London: William P. Nimmo, 1876.

_____. *The Story of The Good Ship Bounty and her Mutineers and Mutinies in Highland Regiments.* Edinburgh: W. P. Nimmo, Hay, and Mitchell, 1880.

_____. *The Mutiny of the Bounty.* Nimmo's Library of History, Travel & Adventure, 1883.

Heywood, Peter. *The Brazil Pilot: Or, Sailing Directions for the Coast and Harbours of Brazil; Also, Directions for the River Plate, by Capt. Peter Heywood, of H.M.S. Nereus.* London: W. Faden, 1818.

_____. *Directions for Sailing to and from the Coast of Brazil ... and Interesting Directions of Captain Heywood.* London: J.W. Norie, 1825.

_____. *Instructions for the Navigation of the Rio de la Plata, Presented to the Committee of Underwriters of Liverpool.* Baltimore: Franklin Press of H. Niles, 1816.

_____. *Piloting Directions for the East and West Coasts of South America.* London: J.W. Norie, 1826.

_____. *Piloting Directions for the Rio de La Plata, or River Plate: Compiled from Those of Captain P. Heywood.* London: J.W. Norie, 1826.

_____. *Remarks on, and Instructions for Navigating the River Plate.* London: W. Winchester and Son, 1813.

Hood, T. H. *Notes of a Cruise in H.M.S. Fawn in the Western Pacific in the Year 1862.* Edinburgh: Edmonston and Douglas, 1863.

Howe, Henry. *Life and Death on the Ocean: A Collection of Extraordinary Adventures, in the Form of Personal Narratives.* Cincinnati: Henry Howe, 1856.

Interesting Discoveries and Narratives: Containing an Account of the Ultimate Fate of the Mutineers of the Bounty. Shrewsbury: C. Hulbert, 1811.

Kingston, W. H. G., M. E. Shipley, Gertrude Crockford and Others. *The Burgomaster's Daughter and Other Stories.* London: John Hogg, 1899.

Lonsdale, Henry. *The Worthies of Cumberland.* London: Routledge, 1876.

The Loss of the Bounty: Proceedings of the Mutineers. London: C. Berger, 1833.

McFarland, Alfred. *The Case of Norfolk Island Stated.* Sydney: Gibbs, Shallard and Co., 1885.

Miles, Alfred H., ed. *Fifty-Two Stories of the British Navy, From Damme to Trafalgar.* London: Hutchinson, n.d. (1896).

Miller, F. B. *Tales of Travel Consisting of Narratives of Various Journeys Through Some of the Most Interesting Parts of the World.* London: Harvey and Darton, 1833.

Moresby, Sir Fairfax. *Pitcairn's Island.* Grantham: Bushby, n.d. (1852).

The Mutiny of the Bounty and Other Narratives. London and Edinburgh: W. and R. Chambers, 1888.

"The Mutiny of the Bounty; Or, the Marvellous Adventures of Christian and his Comrades." N.p.: "Cheerful Visitor Office," n.d. (1820).

Naval Anecdotes: Illustrating the Character of British Seamen. London: James Dundee, 1806.

Orlebar, J. *A Midshipman's Journal on Board H.M.S. Seringapatam, During the year, 1830: Containing Brief Observations on Pitcairn's Island and Other Islands in the South Sea.* London: Whittaker, Teacher, 1833.

"The Paradise in the Pacific." *Blackwood's Edinburgh Magazine*, 73, no. 452 (June 1853): 647–670.

Perils and Adventures on the Deep. Edinburgh: Thomas Nelson, 1843.

Pitcairn Island Correspondence: Condition of the Islanders, London, 1899.
Porter, David. *A Journal of a Cruise Made to the Pacific Ocean in the U.S. Frigate 'Essex' in the Years 1812, 1813 and 1814*. Philadelphia: Bradford and Inskeep, 1815.
Prior, Samuel. *All the Voyages Round the World from the First by Magellan to that of Freycinet in 1820*. Cooperstown, NY: H & E Phinney, 1841. First published in England in 1820.
Selwyn, Bishop George Augustus. *Notes of a Visit to Norfolk Island*. Auckland: William Atkin, 1872. Printed for private circulation.
(Sargent, Charles Lenox.) *The Life of Alexander Smith, Captain of the Island of Pitcairn: one of the Mutineers on Board His Majesty's Ship Bounty; Commanded by Lieut. Wm. Bligh. Written by Smith Himself, on the Above Island, and Bringing the Accounts from Pitcairn, Down to the Year 1815*. Boston: Sylvester T. Goss, 1819.
Shipwrecks and Disasters at Sea. London: H. G. Bohn, 1851.
Staines, Sir T., and P. Pipon. *Interesting Report on the Only Remaining Mutineer of His Majesty's Ship Bounty, Resident on Pitcairn's Island in the Pacific Ocean*. Sydney: Mitchell Library, 1940.
Statements of the Loss of His Majesty's New Ship the Bounty, W. Bligh, Esq. Commander, by a Conspiracy of the Crew: Including the Wonderful Escape of the Captain and about Twelve Men in an Open Pinnace: also, the Adventures of the Mutineers, as Communicated by Lieutenant Christian, the Ringleader, to a Relation in England. London: Thomas Tegg, n.d. (1809).
Stewart, Henry. *The Ocean Wave: Narratives of some of the Greatest Voyages, Seamen, Discoveries, Shipwrecks, and Mutinies of the World*. London: John Hogg, 1883.
Walker, G. H. *Adventures of British Seamen in Various Parts of the World*. Newcastle: W. Fordyce, 1841.
Wilkes, Charles. *The United States Exploring Expedition During the Years 1838–42*. Philadelphia: C. Sherman, 1844.

Articles

"Account of the Descendants of Christian and Other Mutineers of the Bounty." *Naval Chronicle* 33 (January-June 1815): 217–218.
Andre, Hattie. "Among the Pacific Islands." *Missionary Magazine* 10 (April 1898): 128–129.
_____. "Pitcairn Island Mission School." *Review and Herald* 70 (October 17, 1893): 648.
_____. "Uses of the Cocoanut Tree on Pitcairn Island." *The Youth's Instructor* 42 (October 25, 1894): 330.
"Another Account of the Descendants of Christian and Other Mutineers of the Bounty." *Naval Chronicle* 33 (January-June 1815): 3.
(Barrow, Sir John). "Pitcairn Island." *Quarterly Review* 13, no. 26 (July 1815): 374–383.
_____. "Recent Accounts of the Pitcairn Islanders." London: *Journal of the Royal Geographical Society* 3 (1833): 156–167.
Belden, V. "From Norfolk Island." *Review and Herald* 73 (December 22, 1896): 815–816.
Buffett, John. "Narrative of 20 Years' Residence on Pitcairn's Island." *The Friend* 4 (1846).
Christian, Fletcher. "Statements of the Loss of HM New Ship *Bounty*." *Mariner's Marvellous Magazine* 2 (1809).
Corliss, J. O. "The Pacific Islands As A Mission Field: A General Survey of the Region." *Review and Herald* 65 (March 6, 1888): 151.
Duncan, Archibald. "Narrative of the Loss of the Bounty Through a Conspiracy." *The Mariner's Chronicle* 4 (1811): 21–35.
_____. "Narrative of the Total Loss of his Majesty's Ship the Bounty." *The Mariner's Chronicle* 4 (1811): 49–62.
_____. "Loss of the Pandora Frigate." *The Mariner's Chronicle* 5 (1811): 271–273.
Fletcher, William. "Fletcher Christian and the Mutineers of the 'Bounty.'" *Transactions of the Cumberland Association for the Advancement of Literature and Science*, part 2 (1876–1877): 77–106.
Folger, Mayhew. "Letter to Amasa Delano." *Quarterly Review of Science and Arts* 1 (1819).
Gates, E. H. "Last Cruise of the 'Pitcairn.'" *Australasian Union Conference Record* 2 (July 12, 1899): 2–3.
_____. "News From the 'Pitcairn.'" *Review and Herald* 68 (March 3, 1891): 139–141.
_____. "Pitcairn Island." *Review and Herald* 69 (October 25, 1892): 662.
_____. "Report from the 'Pitcairn.'" *Missionary Magazine* 11 (June 1899): 261–262.
(Gifford, William.) "Review of Porter's *Journal of a Cruize*." *Quarterly Review* 13 (1815): 374–383.

Graham, John E. "Last Cruise of the 'Pitcairn.'" *General Conference Daily Bulletin* 1 (March 4, 1897): 241–244.

_____. "News From the 'Pitcairn.'" *Review and Herald* 73 (September 1, 1896): 564.

Greatheed, Samuel. (Nausistratus pseud.) "Authentic History of the Mutineers of the Bounty." *Sailor's Magazine and Naval Miscellany* 1, no. 10 (October 1820): 402–406; 1, no. 12 (December 1820): 449–456; 2, no. 1 (January 1821): 1–8.

Jones, C. H. "The Missionary Ship." *Review and Herald* 66 (April 2, 1889): 217.

_____. "Our Missionary Ship." *Review and Herald* 67 (August 19, 1890): 501.

"A Little World Awaiting the Advent." *Harper's Weekly*, April 14, 1894, p. 343.

"The Mission Schooner 'Pitcairn.'" *Review and Herald* 71 (January 30, 1894): 69.

"The Mutineers of the Bounty." *The Friend* 5 no. 4 (November 5, 1831): 25–26; no. 5 (November 12, 1831): 33–34; no. 6 (November 19, 1831): 41–42.

"Mutiny of the Bounty." *Chronicles of the Sea: Or, Fateful Narratives of Shipwrecks, Fires, Famines, and Disasters* 1, nos. 24–25 (Supplement) (May 26, 1838): 185–200.

"The Mutiny of the Bounty." *Missionary Chronicle*, January 1832.

Obituary, "Capt. P. Heywood, R.N. *The Gentleman's Magazine* 101, no. 6 (June 1831): 640–643.

P. A. L. (pseud). "Barker and Burford's Panoramas." *Notes and Queries* 4th Series, no. 7 (May 20, 1871): 432.

Pipon, Captain Philip. "The Descendants of the Bounty's Crew." *United Service Journal* part 1 (February 1834): 191–199.

"The Pitcairn in Port: Return of a Missionary Vessel From the Islands: Death of Captain Marsh." *San Francisco Morning Call*, October 9, 1892, p. 7.

"The Pitcairn Islanders." *The Friend*, 7, no. 31 (May 10, 1834): 241–242.

"The Pitcairn Islanders." *Illustrated London News*, February 15, 1879, 153–154.

"The Pitcairn Islanders." *Littell's Living Age* (Third Series) 9, no. 834 (May 26, 1860): 491–493.

"Pitcairn's Island from HMS Amphitrite." *Illustrated London News*, January 26, 1856, p. 92.

"Pitcairn's Island, South Pacific Ocean." *Illustrated London News* 50 (June 1867): 550.

Renouard, David T. "Pandora's Tender 1791." *United Service Magazine* part 3 (1842): 1–3.

"Review of the Mutiny on Board the Bounty." *United Service Journal* part 2, no. 7 (July 1829): 44–53.

"Review of *A Narrative of the Briton's Voyage to Pitcairn's Island... By Lieutenant J. Shillibeer, R.M.*" *The Gentleman's Magazine* 87, no. 4 (October 1817): 340–344.

"Review of Sir John Barrow's 'The Eventful History of the Mutiny and Piratical Seizure of H.M.S. Bounty: its Causes and Consequences.'" *The Gentleman's Magazine* 101, no. 6 (December 1831): 623–625.

"Tahiti and the Pitcairn Islanders." *Missionary Chronicle* (London Missionary Society). (1832).

Trood, Thomas. "Pitcairn and Norfolk Islands." *Sydney Quarterly Magazine* 9, no. 3 (September 1892): 191–196.

"T. W." Letter re: Review of *Lieutenant Shillibeer's A Narrative of the Briton's Voyage to Pitcairn's Island*. *The Gentleman's Magazine* 88, no. 1 (July 1818): 37–38.

"A Virtuous Colony." *Once a Week* 13 (July 29, 1865): 147–153.

"A Visit to Pitcairn's Island." *Leisure Hour*, May 4, 1867, p. 285–286.

Waldegrave, Captain. W. "Recent Accounts of the Pitcairn Islanders." *Royal Geographical Society Journal* 3 (1833).

Wilcox, F. M. "Pitcairn Island." *Review and Herald* 71 (February 27, 1894): 133.

Young, Roberta. "The Pitcairn Island School." *The Youth's Instructor* 42 (June 21, 1894): 195.

Young, Rosalind A. "From a Dot in the Sea, Pitcairn Island: 'Parting Song.'" *The Youth's Instructor* 42 (October 25, 1894): 330.

_____. "Letters from Pitcairn Island." *Overland Monthly* 18 (Second Series), no. 105 (September 1891): 294–308.

_____. "The Mutineers of the 'Bounty:' The Pitcairn Islanders from 1859–80." *Scribners Monthly* 22 (October 1881): 54–63.

_____. "The Object of True Education." *The Youth's Instructor* 42 (June 21, 1894): 194–195.

_____. "The Tent School-Room." *The Youth's Instructor* 42 (August 2, 1894): 242.

3

20th and 21st Century Nonfiction

A remarkable number of nonfiction books and articles related to the *Bounty* mutiny and Pitcairn Island were published throughout the 20th and into the 21st century. Rare, early classics such as William Bligh's *A Voyage to the South Sea* and Sir John Barrow's *Eventful History of the Mutiny and Piratical Seizure of H.M.S. Bounty* appeared in a number of inexpensive editions, making them accessible to millions of readers. Important primary documents came into print for the first time, including Bligh's *Log of the Bounty*, *The Journal of James Morrison* in the Golden Cockerel Press' beautifully illustrated "Bountiana" series. The journals of Captain Edward Edwards and Surgeon George Hamilton of *Pandora* were published in 1915 and the minutes of the *Bounty* court-martial in 1931.

This wealth of material has enabled general readers, as well as researchers, to examine the entire *Bounty* Saga in greater depth. A major reassessment of Bligh began with the appearance of no less than four major biographies between 1930 and 1938: Geoffrey Rawson's *Bligh of the 'Bounty,'* George Mackaness' *The Life of Vice-Admiral William Bligh*, Owen Rutter's *Turbulent Journey: A Life of William Bligh, Vice-Admiral of the Blue* and H.S. Montgomerie's *William Bligh of the "Bounty" in Fact and in Fable*. Additional biographies, of varying quality, appeared in the last quarter of the 20th century, including Kenneth S. Allen's *That Bounty Bastard*, Gavin Kennedy's *Bligh* and *Captain Bligh, the man and his mutinies* and Roy Schreiber's *The Fortunate Adversities of William Bligh*.

The inexpensive *A Book of the 'Bounty'* reprinted several collector's items, including *A Voyage to the South Sea* and the extremely rare *On Ten Persons Charged with Mutiny on Board His Majesty's Ship the Bounty With an Appendix Containing a Full Account of the Real Causes and Circumstances of that Unhappy Transaction, the Most Material of Which Have Hitherto Been Withheld from the Public*, by Stephen Barney and Edward Christian. *The Bligh Notebook* gave readers the thrill of following Bligh's daily notes and navigational observations, written under extreme conditions on *Bounty*'s launch. Three important letters written by Bligh after the open boat voyage appeared for the first time in *Awake, Bold Bligh!*

In 1936, Owen Rutter's *The True Story of the Mutiny in the "Bounty"* presented a fresh perspective on the dynamics of the mutiny. It was followed by a steady stream of books offering various interpretations, some of them controversial: Alexander McKee's *The Truth about the Mutiny on the Bounty*, Madge Darby's *Who Caused the Mutiny on the "Bounty?"* and Richard Hough's *Captain Bligh and Mr. Christian, The Men and the Mutiny*. In 1982, Glynn Christian's research for *Fragile Paradise, The Discovery of Fletcher Christian, Bounty Mutineer* revealed new clues that help explain Christian's actions.

Some of the most compelling *Bounty* and Pitcairn scholarship has appeared in such specialist publications and scholarly journals as *The Mariner's Mirror, American Neptune, Pacific Islands Monthly, Journal of the Polynesian Society, Australasian Record, Pitcairn Log, Adventist Heritage, UK Log, Pacific Record, Review and Herald, Maritime Life and Traditions* and *Journal of Pacific History*.

With the publication of *Studia Bountyana 1* in 1965, Rolf Du Rietz began blazing new trails in the pursuit of serious *Bounty* scholarship. In *Banksia 2*, a monograph on John Fryer, he disparaged popular writing that obsessively blames one party or the other for the mutiny: "This pursuit has become a kind of popular sport in pseudo-historical writing, resulting in countless commercially successful but scholarly more or less insignificant books." Du Rietz's monographs, so far available only in limited editions, deserve a much wider audience.

Interest in Pitcairn Island's early history and religious conversion was keen throughout the 19th century, and the public continues to be intrigued by this remarkable community. David Silverman, author of *Pitcairn Island*, emphasizes that Pitcairn history did not end in the early 1800s: "Sometimes it has been forgotten ... that the story did not end in the first quarter of the nineteenth century, but has continued to this day with the Pitcairn community still in being and still in danger ... life continues on the remote Pacific Island, where the progeny of the 'Bounty' mutineers arise, perchance, to dig yams, repair boats, or carve or weave a curio."

Pitcairn Island's history, anthropology, ethnology and culture have been closely examined in a number of major works, including Harry L. Shapiro's *The Heritage of the Bounty: the Story of Pitcairn through Six Generations*, Ian M. Ball's *Pitcairn: Children of Mutiny*, Trevor Lummis' *Pitcairn Island: Life and Death in Eden*, Herbert Ford's *Pitcairn-Port of Call* and Maurice Allward's *Pitcairn Island: Refuge of the Bounty Mutineers*.

A rich array of popular and scholarly material has not quenched the thirst of *Bounty* and Pitcairn Island buffs. The public's enthusiastic response to Caroline Alexander's *The* Bounty: *The True Story of the Mutiny on the* Bounty attests to our continuing fascination with all aspects of the *Bounty* Saga.

Major Works

Captain Edward Edwards, R.N., and George Hamilton: *Voyage of H.M.S. "Pandora" Despatched to Arrest the Mutineers of the "Bounty" in the South Seas, 1790–91. Being the Narratives of Captain Edward Edwards, R.N. the Commander and George Hamilton, the Surgeon*. With an Introduction and Notes by Basil Thomson. London: Francis Edwards, 83 High Street. Marylebone, 1915.

Thanks to the novels of Charles Nordhoff and James Norman Hall, and to popular cinema, the story of H.M.S. *Bounty* is so familiar that most people are acquainted with the phrase, "Mutiny on the *Bounty*" and the names, "Captain Bligh" and "Mr. Christian." The voyage of H.M.S. *Pandora* is familiar mostly to *Bounty* scholars and enthusiasts.

Antiquarian bookseller Francis Edwards made a significant contribution to *Bounty* literature when he published *Voyage of H.M.S. "Pandora,"* in 1915. This volume made more widely available two primary sources about the Admiralty's ill-fated attempt to capture the *Bounty* mutineers: More than 35 crewmembers and four of the captured mutineers died on the return voyage, when the ship foundered on Australia's Great Barrier Reef.

Captain Edward Edwards' reports to the Lords Commissioners of the Admiralty from

November 1790 to July 1792, published in full here for the first time; and George Hamilton's *A Voyage Round the World in His Majesty's Frigate Pandora*, first published in 1793. Edwards' dispatches make for dull reading compared to Hamilton's vibrant, often racy, language. In the introduction to *Voyage of H.M.S. 'Pandora,'* Basil Thomson characterizes Edwards as a "cold, hard man, devoid of sympathy and imagination, of every interest beyond the straitened limits of his profession. Edwards in the eye of posterity was almost the worst man that could have been chosen."

Thomson also notes that *Pandora* was plagued by ill luck from the beginning of her mission. On the voyage to Tahiti, a good portion of the crew suffered from fever, although conditions improved after rounding Cape Horn. Captain Edwards reports that on March 16, 1791, after reaching Ducie's Islands, Lord Hood's Island and Carysfort's Island, he sailed *Pandora* toward the north. It was an unlucky choice: if Edwards had sailed in a westerly direction, he surely would have sighted nearby Pitcairn Island and captured Christian and his party.

Edwards' reports become more compelling — albeit for their content more than for their style — when *Pandora* reaches Tahiti: "Before we anchored at Matavy Bay, Joseph Coleman, Armourer of the *Bounty*, and several of the natives came on board, from whom I learned that Christian the pirate had landed and left 16 of his men on the Island, some of whom were than at Matavy, and some had sailed from there the morning before our arrival [in *Resolution*, a schooner built by the mutineers] for Papara, a distant part of the Island, to join other of the pirates that were settled at that place."

Edwards blandly reports the capture of the remaining mutineers, who he imprisoned in "Pandora's Box," a structure far too small for humane confinement; his appropriation of *Resolution* as a tender; and *Pandora*'s ultimately fruitless search for Christian and the *Bounty*. His account of *Pandora*'s wreck on the Great Barrier Reef is compelling, but, as Thomson states, "Every reader must be struck by the fact that in his description of this disaster, Edwards never once speaks of the prisoners." Elsewhere in his reports, he consistently refers to them as "pirates," as if they had already been found guilty.

Hamilton writes that some of the prisoners were let out of "Pandora's Box" to help man the pumps and that an order was given for their release from irons just before the ship foundered. He also provides a more detailed report than Edwards' of the subsequent voyage in the ships' boats to Timor, paying far more attention to the survivors' sufferings from hunger and thirst. Thomson comments that "Edwards dismisses the boat voyage in very few words, though, in fact, it was a remarkable achievement to take four overloaded boats from the Barrier Reef to Timor without the loss of a single man."

Edwards and Hamilton's accounts complement each other well, especially as published here a single volume. Readers who wish to gain a fuller picture of *Pandora*'s voyage should consult the *Journal of James Morrison* and the letters of Peter Heywood — two of the "pirates" who left written records of their experiences. As Sir John Barrow states in *The Eventful History of the Mutiny and Piratical Seizure of H.M.S. Bounty: Its Causes and Consequences*, "Had it not been for the journal of Morrison, and a circumstantial letter of young Heywood to his mother, no record would have remained of the unfeeling conduct of this officer [Edwards] towards his unfortunate prisoners, who were treated with a rigour which could not be justified on any ground of necessity or prudence."

IDA LEE (MRS. CHARLES BRUCE MARRIOTT, F.R.G.S., HON. F.R.A.H.S.): *Captain Bligh's Second Voyage to the South Sea*. With Maps and Illustrations. London: Longmans, Green & Co., 1920.

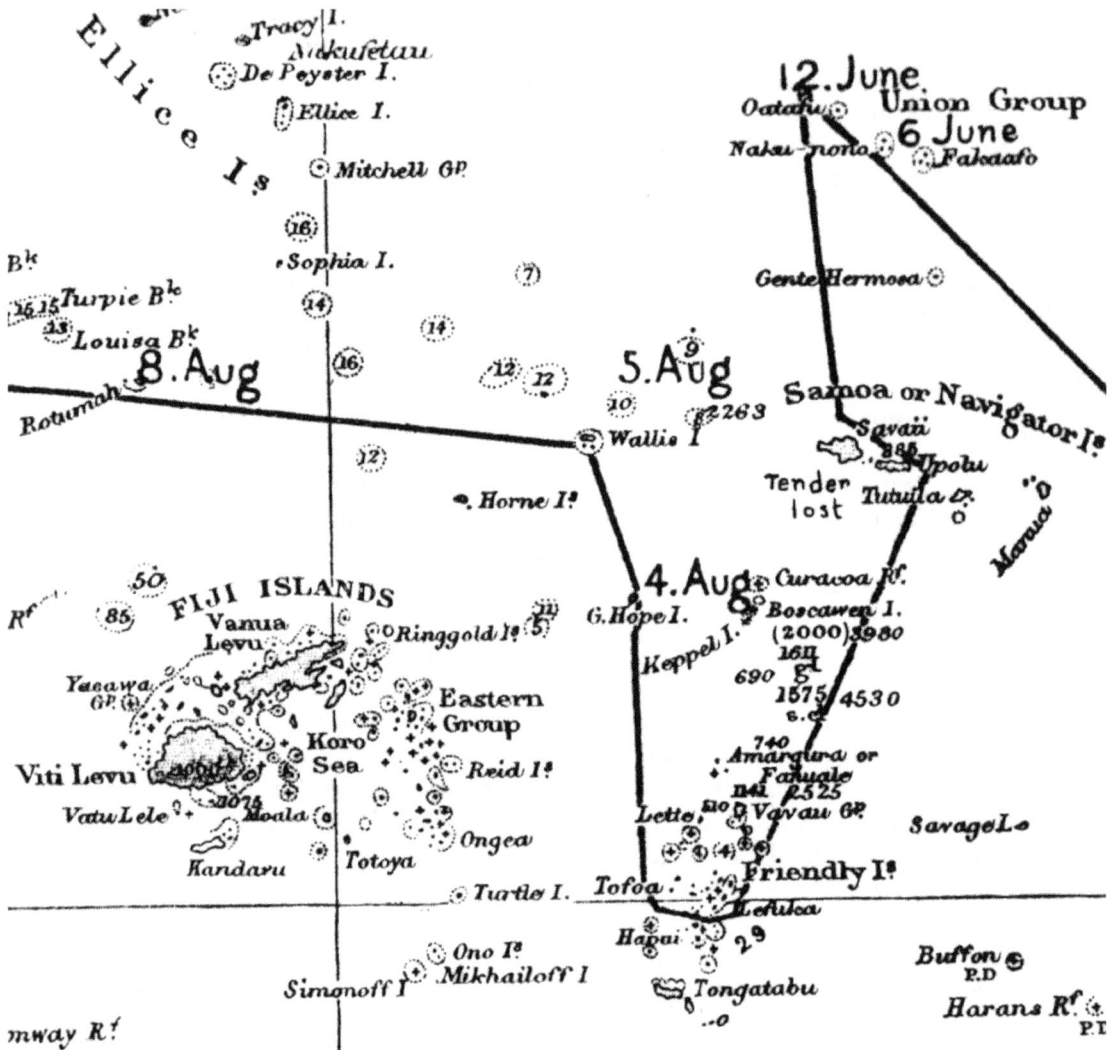

A map published in *Voyage of H.M.S. 'Pandora'* traces Captain Edward Edwards' fruitless search through the South Seas for Fletcher Christian and his party of mutineers. Ironically, Edwards passed fairly close to Pitcairn Island, Christian's refuge, on the voyage to Tahiti.

William Bligh's second, successful breadfruit voyage in H.M.S. *Providence*, the subject of Ida Lee's *Captain Bligh's Second Voyage to the South Sea*, is virtually unknown to the general public. The story of *Providence* and its tender, *Assistant*, might be more familiar if Bligh had published a record of the voyage. Bligh's correspondence reveals that he was planning to publish such an account, but it never reached print in his lifetime. The primary reason is that during the voyage, from 1791 to 1793, Bligh's reputation had been badly damaged by the machinations of the Christian and Heywood families. Bligh's official *Providence* logs were largely forgotten during the 19th century, and did not appear in print until the publication of Lee's book in 1920.

In the preface, Lee explains why the second breadfruit mission is virtually unknown, and also why it deserves to be published: "The second voyage contained no thrilling incidents, yet it also deserves a place in the history of exploration; not only because Bligh succeeded in carrying out the mission entrusted to him, but also because of the new and valuable information that he was able to give concerning the different places visited by the ships, and the various islands which lay in their track."

In Chapter VI, Lee provides a useful overview of the *Bounty* mutiny, but states that her primary intention in *Captain Bligh's Second Voyage to the South Sea* is not to "Make any comment upon the mutiny, or discuss Bligh's merits or his failings in connection with it. It is her aim to show the part played by Captain Bligh as a seaman and discoverer."

Bligh's achievements on the *Providence* are all the more remarkable when we consider that he suffered from terrible headaches and fever during a good part of the voyage — probably due to a case of recurring malaria, which he probably contracted at Batavia after the open boat voyage. At one point, he was totally incapacitated and had to place Nathaniel Portlock, who was on *Assistant*, in command of *Providence*. Bligh recorded in his journal on August 31, 1791, "I was extremely doubtfull how long I might survive, and therefore while I had power to think, I sent for Lieutenant Portlock to remain on board here, that I might give every necessary information and advice to Render the voyage successful."

Bligh was fortunate to have several outstanding officers on board *Providence*, including Portlock, who had sailed with Bligh on *Resolution* after Cook was killed (Lee includes part of Portlock's journal in Chapter XIX); George Tobin, a gifted artist, and Matthew Flinders, who went on to enjoy a distinguished career as Australia's foremost naval explorer. Their journals and artwork constitute a rich legacy of the second breadfruit voyage, which was filled with discoveries of considerable cultural, scientific and maritime interest.

Bligh and his officers mapped unknown parts of the Tasmanian coastline, discovered a number of uncharted islands in Fiji, made detailed observations of Tahitian culture, and, on the return journey, successfully navigated the notoriously dangerous Torres Strait, documenting a safer passage for future voyagers.

The *Providence* voyage may have been relatively uneventful, but it is of great interest to readers interested in the *Bounty* mutiny. Bligh embarked on this voyage before the return of Captain Edward Edwards and the mutineers captured by *Pandora*. It is fascinating to read of Bligh's arrival in Tahiti, especially his meeting with "Mary," the wife of Thomas McIntosh, who gave Bligh an eyewitness account of the mutineers' whereabouts and actions during 1789 and 1790. Bligh writes,

> This woman with several others had been with Christian to Tobooi: she related that they had stayed there two months with the 'Bounty.' Christian's intentions were to settle in that island ... Altercations ensued and war was declared ... Christian did not find it safe to remain ... and embarked with all his party and arrived two days later at Otaheite ... he determined to part with those of his men who were discontented, and immediately set to sail.... The "Bounty" then left Matavai with some natives on board, never to return again.

Mary also provided information about the lives of the loyalists and mutineers who remained on Tahiti after Christian's departure, including George Stewart and Peter Heywood, who, Bligh reports, "Were perfectly satisfied with their situation." Bligh, of course, was convinced that these two midshipmen had been active mutineers. After his return to England, Bligh learned that Heywood had been condemned but pardoned, and that Stewart had drowned when *Pandora* foundered off the Great Barrier Reef.

SIR CHARLES LUCAS, EDITOR: *The Pitcairn Island Register Book. Edited and with an Introduction by Sir Charles Lucas, K.C.B., K.C.M.G. Together with Map, Index and Appendices. With fold out "Chart The Truth about the Mutiny on the Bounty history of Pitcairn Island."* London: Society for Promoting Christian Knowledge, New York and Toronto: The Macmillan Co., 1929. Reprinted by the AMS Press, Inc., New York, 1977.

The Society for Promoting Christian Knowledge (SPCK), made its initial contact with the Pitcairn Islanders in 1819, and later published two important books focusing on their settlement: the Rev. Thomas Boyles Murray's *Pitcairn: the Island, the People, and the Pastor* and *The Pitcairn Island Register Book*, edited by Sir Charles Lucas. The latter volume, published in 1929 and reprinted in 1977, encompasses the history of Pitcairn from the destruction of the *Bounty* in January 1790 to February 1854, when the Pitcairners resettled on Norfolk Island. It is a complete transcription of the original, unique Register.

The Pitcairn Island Register Book has a venerable history. John Buffett, the first immigrant to the island, started a "Register" of important events in 1823. He eventually became schoolmaster and, with the help of John Adams, the island's religious leader. Buffet's Register ends in March 1839. When John Adams died in 1829, the Rev. George H. Nobbs continued and expanded the Register. He served as the leader of the Pitcairn community for many years, finally presenting the Register to the Rev. Murray in 1852.

Because more than one person had a hand in keeping the Register up to date, it varies in style and content. Primarily, it consists of births, marriages, baptisms, accidents, deaths and other important events in the life of the island community. The very early history of Pitcairn is sketchy, and Buffet's entries are rather brief. the Rev. Nobbs wrote more detailed descriptions of events than Buffett, such as the influenza epidemic in 1841 that reveals how the islanders had become increasingly dependent on passing ships:

> August 18th Arrived H.M. Ship *Curacao* Jenkin Jones Esq. Captain — (21 days from Callao) and a most opportune arrival it was, for there were at least twenty cases of influenza among the residents.— Immediately after arriving at the settlement Captain Jones with the Surgeon of the Ship (Dr Gunn) visited the sick; fortunately a small medicine chest had been fitted up on board for the use of the island and there being also a medicine chest on shore the surgeon was enabled to prescribe freely and beneficially.

Dr. Gunn cared for the sick for two days, but *Curacoa* departed Pitcairn on August 20, and the number of influenza cases grew. The Register reports that on September 5, Edward Quintall died from influenza and dysentery. On September 19, Isabella Christian, one of the oldest islanders and a living link with Pitcairn's early history, passed away: "Died Isabella (a native of Tahiti) relict (widow) of Fletcher Christian (of the *Bounty*) her age was not known, but she frequently said Captain Cook's first arrival at Tahiti was perfectly remembered by her." But amidst all of this illness and death, life on Pitcairn continued: "Peggy Christian was safely delivered of a male child," on September 9.

The Pitcairn Island Register Book lists nearly every ship that called at the island from 1823 to 1853. Many of them were American whale ships, such as *Phoenix* out of New Bedford, Massachusetts, carrying 350 barrels of spermaceti oil. It also includes yearly summaries of shipping activity, such as this entry for 1850: "American Whale ships 22. Merchant 7. British vessels of various classes from the Colonies bound for California 17. Hanoverian Merchant 1. Sum Total 47."

The Pitcairn Island Register Book describes more eventful ship visits in greater detail. The entry for December 18, 1849, reads: "Barque Pilgrim, London 30 days from Auckland. N.Z. bound for California. While off the island a number of passengers having got into one of the boats, previous to lowering, the davit gave way and precipitated them into the sea; a female child was rapidly disappearing when one of our people sprang from the tafferel and rescued her from a watery grave."

THE SHIP "SWIFT" OFF PITCAIRN'S ISLAND.

"The ship 'Swift' off Pitcairn's Island," an illustration from *The Gam: Being a Group of Whaling Stories*, by Charles Henry Robbins, published in 1899. It pictures a New Bedford whaling vessel that visited the island on January 5, 1840, as reported in *The Pitcairn Island Register Book*. A "gam" is a meeting of two or more whaling ships on the high seas.

Although it is difficult to find, *The Pitcairn Island Register Book* is a rich mine of information about life on the island for more than half of the 19th century. It gives the reader a genuine sense for the rhythm of life there during this period. Lucas includes a map of the Pacific Ocean, an index of people and places and three appendices: "The Pitcairn Island Fund Committee," compiled by Ethel Young; "The Whale ships at Pitcairn Island" by Sir Everard im Thurn; and a bibliography.

GEORGE MACKANESS: *The Life of Vice-Admiral William Bligh, RN, FRS*. Sydney: Angus & Robertson, 1931. Farrar and Rinehart, Inc. issued the first American edition as a single volume, circa 1936. In 1951, Angus and Robertson published a one-volume "new and revised edition."

Fresh Light on Bligh: Some Correspondence of Captain William Bligh, RN, with John and Francis Godolphin Bond, 1776–1811. Sydney: D. S. Ford, 1949. Limited to 140 copies. Reprinted as Australian Historical Monograph 5 (New Series), 1976.

Fresh Light on Bligh: Being Some Unpublished Correspondence of Captain William Bligh, RN, and Lieutenant Francis Godolphin Bond, RN, with Lieutenant Bond's Manuscript Notes Made on the Voyage of H.M.S. "Providence," 1791–1795. Sydney: D.S. Ford, 1953. Limited to 150 copies. Reprinted as Australian Historical Monograph 5 (New Series), 1976.

George Mackaness' massive, two-volume biography of William Bligh, first published in

Australia in 1931, is a touchstone of *Bounty* Saga literature. This definitive work is the first scholarly, impartial biography of a man whose post–*Bounty* career and achievements were largely unknown to the public for more than 100 years. *The Life of Vice-Admiral William Bligh* not only presented the first full picture of his life, but also sparked a rehabilitation of his reputation, which had been badly damaged during and after his lifetime.

Mackaness' treatment of the *Bounty* mutiny and its aftermath takes up approximately 50 percent of *The Life of Vice-Admiral William Bligh*. The rest of the book is devoted to Bligh's childhood and education; his early years in the naval and merchant services; the second breadfruit voyage on H.M.S. *Providence*; his participation in the Battle of Camperdown, mutiny of the Nore and other naval actions; and his role in the Rum Rebellion, which occurred while he was serving as Governor General of New South Wales.

In the preface, Mackaness points out that most people have a woefully incomplete picture view of Bligh: "His career was crowded with stirring incidents, yet to the modern world he is known only, and known but vaguely, as the central figure in two rebellions against constituted authority — the Mutiny of the Bounty and the New South Wales Rebellion of 1810. This book is an attempt to reconstruct the whole life-history of the man."

Mackaness based *The Life of Vice-Admiral William Bligh* on a wealth of unpublished manuscripts and other records held by the Mitchell Library in Sydney, Australia. His goal was to "Depict the man that Bligh really was," and he did a superlative job. Other excellent biographies of Bligh have appeared, including Owen Rutter's *Turbulent Journey: A Life of William Bligh, Vice-Admiral of the Blue* and Gavin Kennedy's *Bligh*, but none of them match the breadth and depth of *The Life of Vice-Admiral William Bligh*, which remains the standard biography.

In its review of the book, the *London Times* praised Mackaness' achievement and acknowledged that it gave readers the chance to reconsider the popular conception of Bligh as a tyrant: "By reinstating Bligh in our respect and admiration Dr. Mackaness ... [has] laid Britons under a deep obligation ... the result is what may be safely called a final biography."

Mackaness' analysis of the mutiny is required reading for *Bounty* Saga enthusiasts. He takes a rigorous, legalistic approach, devoting one chapter to "The Case for the Mutineers" and the next chapter to "The Case for Bligh." His arguments for each side are based on the available evidence, including Bligh's own accounts of the mutiny, *Bounty*'s logbook, the journal of James Morrison and other documents. Mackaness was a trailblazer, since a great deal of this material was unpublished while he was researching his book.

He stresses that many of the books published about the mutiny during the 18th and 19th centuries are unreliable because they were written by relatives or associates of the key players, including Edward Christian, Sir John Barrow and Lady Belcher: "Logic demands that the case for the mutineers should be based upon those extant and authentic documents that were written before the mutiny occurred, and not upon opinions expressed by relatives or partisan critics."

After considering all of the evidence, Mackaness agrees with Bligh's conclusion that the

Opposite: The first American edition of the two-volume *The Life of Vice-Admiral William Bligh, RN, FRS,* was published as a single volume. The second Australian edition also appeared as one volume. The dust jacket features Robert Dodd's familiar painting from 1790, *The Mutineers Turning Bligh and Part of the Officers and Crew Adrift from His Majesty's Ship the Bounty.* Dodd's painting has been reproduced in innumerable *Bounty*-related works, usually on the dust jacket. Jacket cover from *The Life of Vice-Admiral* William Bligh, R.N., F.R.S., revised edition, by George Mackaness. Farrar & Rinehart, Inc., 1951. Reprinted by permission of Henry Holt & Co., LLC.

crew's desire to return to Tahiti was the primary cause of the mutiny: "It is practically certain that the affair was due at bottom to contamination of the crew by their over-long association with the delights of Otaheite." The secondary and tertiary causes were, he writes, "the personal though temporary grievance of Christian against his commander; second, the unfortunate association in one watch of all the worst characters in the ship."

Not everyone agrees with Mackaness' conclusion, but he presents a compelling case. Most important perhaps, he convincingly presents Bligh as a demanding commander, but not one who, according to some of the earlier accounts, withheld food and mercilessly punished his crew: "His men, though warned time and again, committed serious misdemeanours, even to that of desertion. Bligh punished them according to naval regulations, and that was the end of it."

Mackaness made substantial contributions to Bligh scholarship throughout his life. In addition to editing *A Book of the 'Bounty,'* he wrote several privately printed scholarly monographs that are vital supplements to *The Life of Vice-Admiral William Bligh*.

In 1949, he edited and published *Fresh Light on Bligh: Some Unpublished Correspondence of Captain William Bligh, R.N., with John and Francis Godolphin Bond, 1776–1811*. This was followed by *Fresh Light on Bligh: Being Some Unpublished Correspondence of Captain William Bligh, R.N., and Lieutenant Francis Godolphin Bond, R.N., with Lieutenant Bond's Manuscript Notes Made on the Voyage of H.M.S. "Providence," 1791–1795* in 1953. In 1960, Mackaness authored "Extracts from a Log-book of H.M.S. Providence kept by Lieut. Francis Godolphin Bond," an article published in the *Journal and Proceedings of the Royal Australian Historical Society*. The first two volumes were limited to just 150 and 140 copies, respectively, but Review Publications Pty., Ltd. has reprinted them.

These letters, notes and journals were written by men who served under Bligh on H.M.S. *Providence* during the second breadfruit mission. They provide additional insights to Bligh's personality and style of command, and how that may have contributed to the mutiny on H.M.S. *Bounty*. They also stand as evidence that other seamen successfully adjusted to Bligh's style, even though they often found him to be haughty, overbearing and sometimes downright intolerable.

One of the key letters was written from Lieutenant Francis Godolphin Bond to his brother, Thomas Bond. Mackaness considers this letter to be "One of the most illuminating ever written concerning the character of Bligh:"

> Yes, Tom, our relation (Both were related to Bligh) had the credit of being a tyrant in his last expedition (on the *Bounty*) where his misfortunes and good fortune have elevated him to a situation he is incapable of supporting with decent modesty.... He has treated me (nay, all on board) with the insolence and arrogance of a Jacobs*; and notwithstanding his passion is partly to be attributed to a nervous fever, with which he has been attacked most of the voyage, the chief part of his conduct must have arisen from the fury of an ungovernable temper.... My time effectually taken up by Duty, that to keep peace I neglect all kind of study; yet the company of a set of well informed Messmates make my moments pass very agreeably, so that I am by no means in purgatory.

Gavin Kennedy, in his introduction to the revised *A Book of the 'Bounty,'* points out the importance of this letter, especially the last two sentences: "The significance of this letter lies in the fact that Francis Bond was at this time occupying roughly the same post, directly responsible to Bligh, that Fletcher Christian did on the *Bounty*." Kennedy remarks that the

---

*Mackaness was unable to trace this reference.

mutiny might not have occurred if Christian had "a set of well informed Messmates" like Bond, for company and counsel. Christian's messmates, Peter Heywood, George Stewart and Robert Tinkler, had little experience of life in the Royal Navy.

George Tobin, in a letter to Francis Godolphin Bond, acknowledges Bligh's infamous temper but also observes that he did have a milder side: "Yet, when all, in his opinion, went right, when could a man be more placid & interesting?... Once or twice indeed I felt the Unbridled licence of his power of speech, yet never without soon receiving something like an emollient plastaire to heal the wound." Tobin's statement makes one wonder if Bligh was planning to put the famous "coconut theft incident" to rest during dinner with Fletcher Christian on the evening before the mutiny—the dinner that Christian refused to attend.

Mackaness' biography of Bligh, along with these more recent collections, constitutes a monumental achievement in *Bounty* Saga scholarship that no enthusiast can afford to ignore.

OWEN RUTTER: *The True Story of the Mutiny in the "Bounty."* London: Newnes, n.d. (1936).

In addition to being a versatile writer, magistrate, district officer and planter in North Borneo, Owen Rutter was one of the most important and influential *Bounty* scholars working during the 1930s, a decade that in many ways became a renaissance of the subject.

Rutter's best-known, most significant contribution to *Bounty* scholarship was his editing of several titles for the Golden Cockerel Press, including the publication of John Fryer's *The Voyage of the* Bounty's *Launch* (1934) and *The Journal of James Morrison* (1935). He also wrote *Turbulent Journey* (1936), an excellent biography of William Bligh, edited *The Court-Martial of the "*Bounty*" Mutineers* (1931) and a novel about Fletcher Christian, *Cain's Birthday* (1930).

Less well known is *The True Story of the Mutiny in the "Bounty,"* published as part of Newnes' "Wide World Library" series of "True-life Travel and Adventure Books." This inexpensive volume gave thousands of readers the benefit of Rutter's considerable knowledge of the primary source material, which many people either did not have access to or could not afford to purchase from the Golden Cockerel Press. Rutter clearly states his objective in the Author's Note:

> One writer after another has perpetuated various errors and misconceptions by accepting what has appeared in print, instead of going to the original source. Moreover, most writers have shown a bias against Bligh, since sympathy is always apt to be with the underdog, who was Fletcher Christian. Therefore, to get at the true facts, it is necessary to go back to the beginning and examine the documents and records of the time.

The dust jacket flap copy repeats this statement but, ironically, also suggests that the purchaser, "Read the book and see the famous Metro-Goldwyn film 'Mutiny on the *Bounty*,' a triumph of film craft." While this film, starring Clark Gable as Fletcher Christian and Charles Laughton as William Bligh, provides excellent entertainment, it is riddled with inaccuracies and also helped reinforce the common image of Bligh as a sadistic commander. Those who read the book and saw the film surely must have been puzzled at these widely differing interpretations of the *Bounty* story.

Gavin Kennedy, in his introduction to the 1981 reissue of *A Book of the 'Bounty,'* comments on this dichotomy between the world of serious *Bounty* scholarship during the 1930s and what was going in the world of popular culture: "The ironic aspect of this activity was that as the historical records were published, giving a more generous view of the career of William Bligh than was common in the latter part of the nineteenth century, the popular cinema was presenting an entirely different characterization." Indeed, a more balanced cinematic

The artist who created this lovely dust jacket illustration for Owen Rutter's *The True Story of the Mutiny in the "Bounty"* is not credited. This volume presents a balanced view of the mutiny, characteristic of Rutter's scholarship. Reprinted from *The True Story of the Mutiny in the "Bounty,"* by Owen Rutter, copyright 1936. Reprinted by permission of Elsevier.

portrait of Bligh would not occur until 1983, with the release of The Bounty, starring Anthony Hopkins as Bligh.

Rutter's judicious, balanced view of the *Bounty* mutiny is an excellent example of responsible scholarship intended for a mass audience: "As I see it, the mutiny was caused by a clash of two irreconcilable temperaments... Had Bligh possessed enough imagination to realize that abuse will leave one man unmoved but goad another to rebellion, or had Christian been better schooled to accept hard words, however unjustified, from his superior officer, Bligh would not have been steering an open boat for Tofua on the morning of April 28, 1789, and Christian would not have been in command of the *Bounty*."

WILLIAM BLIGH AND OTHERS: *A Book of the 'Bounty' and Selections from Bligh's Writings*. Edited by George Mackaness, M.A., Litt.D. London: J. M. Dent & Sons Ltd., 1938. Decorated by Eric Ravilious. No. 950 of Everyman's Library.

A Book of the 'Bounty' Edited by George Mackaness. New introduction by Gavin Kennedy. London: J. M. Dent and Sons, 1981.

If a reader had shelf space for just one book about the *Bounty* mutiny, *A Book of the 'Bounty'* might be the ideal choice. This core collection of *Bounty*-related documents, edited by distinguished Australian scholar George Mackaness — at the personal request of publisher Hugh R. Dent — was first published by Everyman's Library in 1938. It collects Bligh's *A Voyage to the South Sea* and two extremely rare and significant items, making them available to a wide audience for the first time: Stephen Barney and Edward Christian's *On Ten Persons Charged with Mutiny on Board His Majesty's Ship the Bounty With an Appendix*, and *William Bligh's Answer to Edward Christian's Assertions*.

Mackaness edited a selection of Bligh's correspondence for *A Book of the 'Bounty,'* and included a selective bibliography. He would have liked to add *The Journal of James Morrison*, but this was not possible due to its length and Edward Christian's rare *A Short Reply to Capt. William Bligh's Answer*.

A second edition of this useful volume, edited and with a new introduction by Gavin Kennedy, appeared in 1981. Kennedy discusses the importance of the "Bligh-Bond Correspondence," prints extracts from these letters and updates the Selective Bibliography. Unfortunately, the second edition was printed on poor quality paper, which is rapidly deteriorating. The first edition of *A Book of the 'Bounty'* may well survive it.

C. S. WILKINSON: *The Wake of the Bounty*. London: Cassell & Company Ltd., 1953.

C. S. Wilkinson's *The Wake of the Bounty*, as described on the dust jacket, is "a delightful incursion into literary detection." This entertaining volume presents a full account of *Bounty*'s voyage and explores, in detail, the theory that Fletcher Christian survived the violent events on Pitcairn Island and returned safely to England — an idea that has captured the imagination of many readers since the publication of *Letters from Mr. Fletcher Christian* (London, 1796).

While *Letters from Mr. Fletcher Christian* quickly was proven to be a hoax, the possibility that Christian returned to England gained momentum after the publication of Sir John Barrow's *The Eventful History of the Mutiny and Piratical Seizure of H.M.S. Bounty*, where he writes:

> About the years 1808 and 1809, a very general opinion was prevalent in the neighbourhood of the lakes of Cumberland and Westmoreland, that Christian was in that part of the country, and made frequent private visits to an aunt who was living there... This, however, might be passed over as mere gossip, had not another circumstance happened just about the same time, for the truth of which the Editor does not hesitate to avouch.

Barrow recounts the experience of Captain Peter Heywood who, while walking on Fore-Street in Plymouth Dock, saw someone who looked exactly like Christian. Seeing Heywood, this man fled, eluding him on a chase through the streets. The experience had a profound and lasting effect on Heywood: "That Christian should be in England, Heywood considered as highly improbable, though not out of the scope of possibility ... his first thought was to

Noted wood engraver Eric Ravilious designed the artwork for the dust jacket of the first edition of George Mackaness' *A Book of the "Bounty."*

set about making some further enquiries, but on recollection of the pain and trouble such a discovery must occasion him, he considered it more prudent to let the matter drop, but the circumstance was frequently called to his memory for the remainder of his life."

Wilkinson not only develops the argument that Christian returned to England, but that he served as a model for the character of the "Ancient Mariner" in Samuel Taylor Coleridge's famous poem, "The Rime of the Ancyent Marinere." One piece of evidence is a tantalizing note that Coleridge jotted down in his notebook as a possible poetic topic, sometime in the mid–1790s: "Adventures of Christian the Mutineer." "The Rime of the Ancyent Marinere" was first published in *Lyrical Ballads, with a few other poems* (London, 1798). Coleridge and his close friend, the poet William Wordsworth, who had close connections to the Christian family, collaborated on this revolutionary volume of verse that heralded the birth of the Romantic movement in English literature.

Robert Southey, a popular poet in his day, wrote in a letter dated October 23, 1809, "I know too, or rather have every reason to believe that Fletcher C. was within these few years in England and at his fathers house — an interesting circumstance in such a history, and one which I hardly ought to mention — so do not you let it get abroad."

Wilkinson makes a convincing case that Fletcher Christian was the model for Coleridge's Mariner. He points out that John Livingstone Lowes, who analyzed Coleridge's creative process in *The Road to Xanadu: A Study in the Ways of the Imagination*, believed that "The Mariner's sense of guilt and remorse" may have been inspired by Christian's outbursts during the mutiny: "That — Captain Bligh — that is the thing. I am in hell — I am in hell." Lowes, who likens the Mariner's voyage to one "by Cook or Bligh," concludes that "The adventures of Christian the mutineer, as Coleridge conceived them, may well have been, like those of the guilt-haunted Mariner himself, the adventures of 'a soul in agony.'"

After outlining all of the available evidence and clues that support the theory — especially John Adams' contradictory accounts of Christian's fate and the close association of the Wordsworth and Christian families — Wilkinson comes to the conclusion that William Wordsworth must have heard the story of the *Bounty* voyage and mutiny from none other than Fletcher Christian himself. Later, Wordsworth would provide Coleridge this subject matter for "The Rime of the Ancyent Marinere": "Schoolmate, relative, and family friend of Fletcher Christian on the one hand, and on the other the collaborator with Coleridge in the planning, writing, and publication of the 'Ancient Mariner.'"

Wilkinson's statement that Fletcher Christian, "must, in fact, be the most famous of historical Englishmen of whom there is no full-length biography," evidently inspired Glynn Christian, one of Christian's descendants, to write *Fragile Paradise, The Discovery of Fletcher Christian*, Bounty *Mutineer. The Wake of the* Bounty remains a stimulating, entertaining contribution to *Bounty* literature.

ALEXANDER MCKEE: H.M.S. Bounty: *A True Account of the Famous Mutiny.* New York: William Morrow and Company, 1962. First published as a paperback by Mayflower Books, London, 1961. *H.M.S. Bounty: A True Account of the Notorious Mutiny.* London: Souvenir Press, 1969. Revised edition.

Alexander McKee's H.M.S. Bounty: *A True Account of the Famous Mutiny*, is one of several significant books on the *Bounty* mutiny published during the early to mid–1960s. This list includes Bengt Danielsson's *What Happened on the* Bounty: *A True Account of the Famous Mutiny* (London, 1962); Geoffrey Rawson's *Pandora's Last Voyage* (London and New York, 1963, 1964); Madge Darby's *Who Caused the Mutiny on the 'Bounty'?* (Sydney, 1965); and *Studia Bountyana* 1 and 2 (Uppsala, 1965, 1966), two scholarly monographs edited by the scholar Rolf Du Rietz.

THE WAKE OF THE BOUNTY

by C.S. WILKINSON

Was Fletcher Christian, the mutineer of Captain Bligh's "Bounty," the model for Coleridge's 'Ancient Mariner'?

Did he return to England from Pitcairn Island?

Did he tell his story to Wordsworth and did Wordsworth pass it on to his friend Coleridge?

The manuscript page reproduced here is from one of Coleridge's notebooks - one clue in this piece of literary detection

Du Rietz, one of the foremost authorities on the history of H.M.S. *Bounty*, praises McKee's straightforward account, calling it "One of the best books ever written on Mr. Bligh and the mutiny, because of its sound originality and its convincing treatment of some essential problems. It ranks among the pioneering works in the BOUNTY literature."

In *H.M.S. Bounty: A True Account of the Famous Mutiny*, McKee avoids discussing the many conflicting opinions about the *Bounty* mutiny reflected in myriad popular books, novels, magazine articles, films, and television programs. Du Rietz considers such polemics to be a waste of time, because in many cases the authors of these works are not qualified scholars. When McKee began writing his book, he was, as he states in a note to the revised edition, under pressure to complete it quickly, forcing him to consult "The printed documentary sources and, without preconceptions or taking much notice of what anyone else might have written (let alone a Hollywood scriptwriter!), set down what I found there."

McKee frequently refers to primary sources, including Bligh's log and the journals of James Morrison, John Fryer and George Hamilton, *Pandora*'s surgeon. His vigorous writing style and faithfulness to eyewitness accounts draw the reader directly into the tale of H.M.S. *Bounty*. He also provides accurate background information on shipboard conditions during the late 18th century to help the reader understand the events in context of the times. He is no fan of Bligh, whose abrasive behavior he clearly believes to be the cause of the mutiny, but he usually objective. For example, he praises Bligh's leadership during the failed attempt to round Cape Horn: "This was Bligh at his best, the ruthlessly efficient officer driving his sailing machine into the tempest of tortured waters round the Horn, and seeing to the comfort of his men before he saw to his own. In a brute struggle with the fury of the weather, or when hammering out hull-to-hull broadsides with an enemy in battle, Bligh was a captain to follow."

In 1969, Souvenir Press, Ltd., London, published a revised edition entitled *H.M.S. Bounty: A True Account of the Notorious Mutiny* that corrects some minor errors in the first edition.

BENGT DANIELSSON: *What Happened on the* Bounty. Translated from the Swedish by Alan Tapsell. London: George Allen & Unwin Ltd., 1962. Second (revised) edition published in 1963. This second edition also was published by Rand McNally and Company, Chicago, New York and San Francisco, 1963.

Bengt Danielsson was a distinguished ethnographer who sailed on Thor Heyerdahl's *Kon-Tiki* raft expedition, one of the most famous sea voyages of modern times. His intimate knowledge of the South Seas and Polynesian civilization (he made Tahiti his home in 1948), made him particularly well qualified to write an accurate book about H.M.S. *Bounty*. As Danielsson states in the Foreword, he strives "to give a true picture, based mainly on the studies and observations I have myself made during a fifteen-year sojourn in the South Seas."

Like many of the best books about the *Bounty* mutiny written in the 20th century, *What Happened on the* Bounty is soundly based on original material, including log books, letters and other documents — not, Danielsson writes in the Foreword, on "dry accounts in diary form, wildly partisan argumentation, and romanticised novels full of grotesque mistakes and

---

Opposite: The dust jacket of ***The Wake of the Bounty*** by C.S. Wilkinson reproduces the notebook page where Samuel Taylor Coleridge wrote, "Adventures of Christian, the mutineer..." These words inspired Wilkinson to speculate on the source of Coleridge's "Ancient Mariner." The publication of this book created a flurry of interest in periodicals and journals, with articles appearing in ***Illustrated London News*** and ***Dalhousie Review***.

The handsome dust jacket of the first American edition of Alexander McKee's *H.M.S. Bounty; A True Account of the Famous Mutiny*. The true first edition of McKee's popular work was an inexpensive, unattractive paperback.

flights of imagination." He tells the tale of the mutiny, Bligh's open boat voyage, *Pandora's* voyage, court-martial and Pitcairn Island in great depth. Danielsson also accomplishes the difficult task of presenting a balanced account, especially of the mutiny, which he recounts in riveting detail. He is objective and fair, especially in his common-sense evaluation of the infamous event leading up to the mutiny: Bligh's accusation that Christian stole some of his coconuts: "Admittedly, Bligh conducted himself very badly on this unfortunate day, but it is evident that Christian likewise entirely lost his sense of proportion as a result of what had happened. True, he had been very shabbily treated, but he should nevertheless have realized that Bligh was the victim of his own temper and that his bark was worse than his bite."

What Happened on the Bounty deserves its reputation as one of best volumes on the subject, although one wishes that the publisher had included an index. Other books by Danielsson of interest to *Bounty* enthusiasts include *Love in the South Seas* and *Forgotten Islands of the South Seas*.

GEOFFREY RAWSON: Pandora's *Last Voyage*. New York: Harcourt, Brace & World, 1964. First edition published in London: Longmans, Green and Co. Ltd., 1963.

The story of H.M.S. *Pandora*, dispatched by the British Admiralty in November 1790 to apprehend the *Bounty* mutineers and recapture the ship, is an epic in itself, "A great sea saga," as described on the dust jacket of Pandora's *Last Voyage* by Geoffrey Rawson.

Rawson's book is filled with enough action and drama to inspire a novel or film: *Pandora's* voyage from England to the South Seas; the capture and imprisonment of the *Bounty* crew members living in Tahiti and their imprisonment in "Pandora's Box;" Captain Edward Edwards' fruitless search for Fletcher Christian and *Bounty*; *Pandora's* shipwreck off Australia's Great Barrier Reef on the journey back to England; and the survivors' torturous open boat voyage to Batavia.

Rawson, who also wrote the first full-length biography of William Bligh, *Bligh of the 'Bounty'* (1930), weaves the key background facts of the *Bounty* mutiny into the tale of H.M.S. *Pandora*. He includes a detailed account of the loyalists and mutineers who did not follow Christian when he sailed for parts unknown in September 1789. The story of the 18 months they lived on Tahiti before H.M.S. *Pandora* arrived is a fascinating one, which includes James Morrison's construction of the schooner *Resolution*, the arrival of "John Brown," a villainous seaman left behind at Tahiti by the brig *Mercury* and the violent deaths of Charles Churchill and Matthew Thompson.

Other events associated with *Pandora's* voyage included in this volume are the fate of *Resolution* after Captain Edwards confiscated it for use as a tender—a mini-epic in itself—and of Mary Bryant and a group of fugitives from Botany Bay, who arrived in Batavia a few weeks ahead of *Pandora's* survivors.

Pandora's *Last Voyage* was a long overdue book-length account of this ship's mission, but it is not the final word on the subject. As *Bounty* scholar Rolf Du Rietz points out in the journal *Ethnos*, "There is very little to indicate that the author possesses even the slightest knowledge of relevant sources and publications brought to light or issued after 1938." He also berates Rawson for his "over-looking of William Henry Smyth's numerous writings on the *Bounty* and then *Pandora*, anonymously published in the United Service Journal."

One unusual aspect of the book is how Rawson supports Captain Edwards, whose behavior toward his captives and general abilities as a seaman have been subject to a great deal of discussion. Rawson, who served as a naval officer himself, generally defends Edwards against "armchair critics," citing Edwards' general orders from the Admiralty and the specific objectives of the voyage. However, he does acknowledge Edwards' culpability in the drowning of

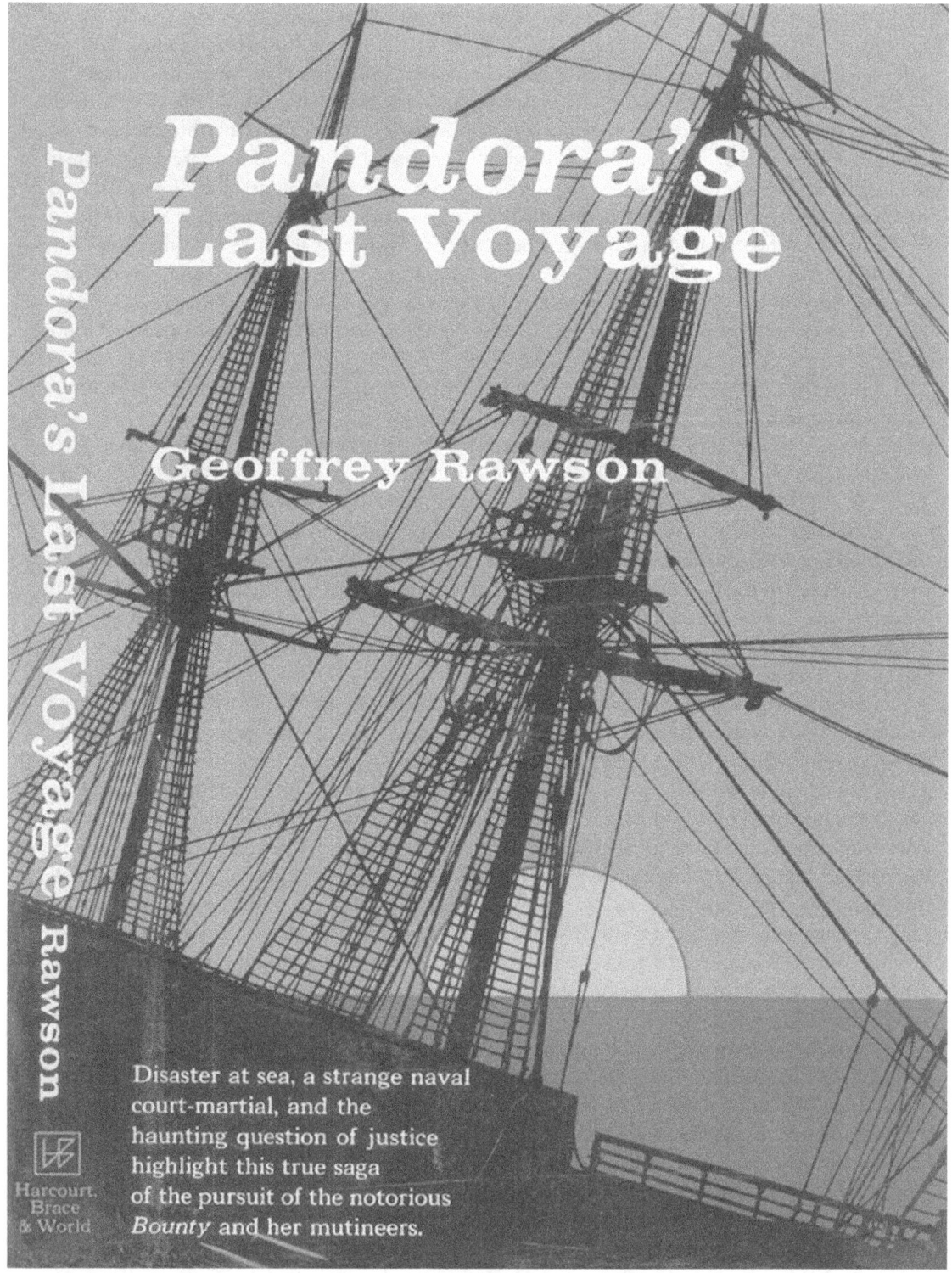

The dust jacket of the first American edition of Geoffrey Rawson's *Pandora's Last Voyage*, designed by Carl Smith, pictures the sinking vessel. Reprinted by permission of Harcourt Inc.

four prisoners, due to his failure to order their release from "Pandora's Box" as the ship was sinking: "This was atrocious behaviour on Edwards' part and cannot be condoned. There was absolutely no rhyme nor reason for it. It was, in modern parlance, sheer murder." Still, Rawson tends to shift the blame elsewhere: "It is surprising that none of the senior officers on board did not themselves take action to release the men." He does not acknowledge that Edwards may have viewed such an attempt as mutinous behavior. Rawson also calls the officers to task for not doing more to provision *Pandora*'s boats for the long open boat voyage ahead.

For many readers, the true hero of *Pandora* is Boatswain's Mate William Moulter who, as the ship was sinking, unbolted the hatch of "Pandora's Box," giving the prisoners a chance to escape.

Regardless of its defects, Rawson's book serves as a good introduction to the subject. While it may have some deficiencies, Du Rietz admits that Pandora's *Last Voyage* is a "vividly written little book."

MADGE DARBY: *Who Caused the Mutiny on the "Bounty?"* Sydney: Angus & Robertson Ltd., 1965.

ROLF DU RIETZ: *The Causes of the Bounty Mutiny: Some Comments on a Book by Madge Darby. Studia Bountyana,* Vol. 1. Uppsala: Dahlia Books, 1965. Limited edition of 500 copies. *The Causes of the Bounty Mutiny: A Short Reply to Mr. Rolf Du Rietz's Comments. Studia Bountyana,* Vol. 2. Uppsala: Appelbergs Boktryckeri, 1966. Limited edition of 500 copies

Madge Darby's succinct, stimulating account of the *Bounty* mutiny, *Who Caused the Mutiny on the 'Bounty'?* was inspired by the concept of using William Bligh's breadfruit voyage in *Providence* as a "control group," comparing it with the disastrous voyage of the *Bounty*. She takes the position that since the *Providence* voyage was a success, it is clear that something extraordinary must have taken place on H.M.S. *Bounty* to incite mutiny. Darby summarily rejects the notion that Bligh brought on the mutiny through tyrannical behavior: "While certain aspects of Bligh's character made him objectionable to many people in the Navy and explain some of the malice of the campaign that was conducted against him, they were not, for the most part, the sort of faults that were likely to drive a crew to mutiny."

Employing Freudian psychology to throw light upon the question of who is responsible for the mutiny, Darby arrives at some controversial conclusions that continue to be debated. She suggests that when the *Bounty* left Tahiti and Fletcher Christian had to part from his native paramour, he began to suffer from classic paranoid delusions. These were fueled by the forced celibacy of ship life, leading to a repressed homosexual desire for Bligh — his former friend — and ultimately a love/hate relationship.

Breaking down under Bligh's criticism, Christian indulged in suicidal fantasies of jumping overboard with Bligh, and finally decided to desert the *Bounty* on a jerrybuilt raft — which probably would have led to his death by drowning. Given Christian's distressed, highly emotional state, Darby theorizes that the mutiny would not have happened, or succeeded, without the cool, calm intervention of Midshipman Edward Young, who she calls "The Third Man:" "Up to the night before the event, Christian had not thought of mutiny.... It was generally believed by those involved that during the night someone persuaded him to take the ship."

Midshipman George Stewart is the usual suspect. He made a statement to Christian that has been interpreted both as a suggestion to plan a mutiny and as a warning that the crew might mutiny if Christian deserted the ship: "When you go, Christian, the people are ripe for any thing." Darby suggests that Young, the only officer to take Christian's side during the mutiny, was the prime instigator: "It is more likely that the third man was an officer, since none of the seamen would have dared to suggest mutiny to an officer. The only person who satisfied both conditions was Midshipman Young."

Darby also believes that Young also was the mastermind behind the plots and murders that later occurred on Pitcairn Island: "If the four plots are considered together, the mutiny, the massacre of the mutineers, the killing of the natives, and the murder of Quintal, it becomes clear that they have certain characteristics in common.... It is therefore reasonable to assume that they were all planned by the same brain. And Edward Young was the only person involved in all four."

Although Darby's theories are provocative, in *Who Caused the Mutiny on the 'Bounty'?* she cites no new references or sources, and her psychoanalysis of Christian is armchair psychology — as it has to be, since we lack the highly detailed information, such as a personal diary or journal — needed to validate a diagnosis such as paranoid or delusional behavior.

In 1965, following the publication of *Who Caused the Mutiny on the 'Bounty'?* Rolf Du Rietz issued a limited edition monograph entitled *Studia Bountyana* 1 (subtitled, "Some Comments on a Book by Madge Darby"), in which he critiques her methods and conclusions. Du Rietz invited Darby to respond, and he published her comments in *Studia Bountyana* 2 (subtitled "The causes of the *Bounty* mutiny, A Short Reply to Mr. Rolf Du Rietz's Comments"). In his concluding remarks, Du Rietz acknowledges their disagreement on the subject, but graciously states, "We should be grateful to Miss Darby for having introduced new and fresh aspects on the *Bounty* mutiny, and I think that her and my own efforts will not have been altogether in vain if they stimulate other scholars to further and deeper research into the fascinating story of the *Bounty*."

DAVID SILVERMAN: *Pitcairn Island*. With a foreword by Luis Marden. New York: The World Publishing Company, 1967

For many students of the *Bounty* Saga, the history of Pitcairn Island — especially from 1790 to 1808, when the islanders were totally cut off from the outside world — holds as much interest as the controversies surrounding the mutiny itself. One critical difference is that other than a brief journal by Edward Young (seen by Captain F.W. Beechey, but now lost), no written records survived those 18 dark years on Pitcairn. Silverman writes in the preface to *Pitcairn Island*:

> Whereas the voyage of the "*Bounty*" to Tahiti, the mutiny, the punitive expedition of the "*Pandora*," and the court-martial can be reconstructed from public records, logbooks, official correspondence, and other evidence admissible in a court of law, our knowledge of what happened in the first twenty years of the existence of the Pitcairn Colony rests almost entirely on hearsay, and contradictory hearsay at that.

In *Pitcairn Island*, Silverman gives a thorough account of *Bounty*'s voyage and of Pitcairn's early years, calling them, "The Pitcairn Mystery." An attorney, he is uniquely qualified to consider all of the evidence that has survived, including the accounts of Mayhew Folger, Amasa Delano, F.W. Beechey, and others.

He takes an interesting approach to the story by providing detailed background information (when available) on the mutineers and Polynesians, as if they were a cast of characters in a drama. Silverman then poses a series of questions: "What happened to those members of the cast missing when Mayhew Folger lifted the curtain in 1808, eighteen years after it had been pulled down?" Each question, including, "What Happened to Christian?" "Christian's Role on Pitcairn," "The Revolt of the Harem" and "What Happened to the *Bounty*?" is followed by a detailed exploration of the evidence.

Pitcairn Island is the most comprehensive scholarly book on the subject to appear since the publication of Harry L. Shapiro's *The Heritage of the* Bounty: *the Story of Pitcairn through*

Six Generations in 1936. Shapiro, an anthropologist, examined Pitcairn society as a unique, "unconscious and spontaneous" social experiment, discussing the blend of Polynesian and English bloodlines, culture, language and day-to-day life on the island.

Silverman treats these topics comprehensively, creating a rich, detailed picture of Pitcairn Island up to 1967. He tells the story of Pitcairn after 1808 on a subject by subject basis, such as "Education and Language," "The Pitcairn Economy," "Emigrants, Immigrants, and Visitors," "The Society of Pitcairn," and "The Population Problem."

Some readers may find Silverman's method tedious and repetitive, but *Pitcairn Island* has a special appeal to specialists on the subject, as Silverman intended: "This method serves the further purpose of making more readily available those aspects of the story which appeal to special interests, whether in the field of philology or philately." *Pitcairn Island* is best appreciated after learning the about Island's history through a more traditional, chronological approach.

RICHARD HOUGH: *Captain Bligh and Mr. Christian: The Men and the Mutiny*. London: Hutchinson & Co. Ltd., 1972. First American edition published by E. P. Dutton and Co., New York, 1973. Reissued with additions by Cassell Ltd., London, 1979. Reprinted by the Naval Institute Press, Annapolis, MD, 2000. Published as *The Bounty,* a paperback, movie tie-in edition by Penguin Books, Harmondsworth, 1984.

Captain Bligh and Mr. Christian: The Men and the Mutiny, by naval historian and biographer Richard Hough, is one of the more memorable books about the *Bounty* Saga published in recent years. It won the *Daily Express* Award for "The Best Non-Fiction Book of the Sea Published in the United Kingdom," for 1972. The book was so well received that E. P. Dutton and Co. released it as a paperback in 1974, while Cassell Ltd. reissued it with additional material six years after first publication.

Captain Bligh and Mr. Christian is a full account of the entire *Bounty* story, as well as the early history of Pitcairn Island. Hough's skillful "translation" of authentic language from the late 18th century, such as that recorded in the minutes of the court-martial, into lively dialogue provides a sense of immediacy to the reader.

The book is provocative in its conjecture, also proposed by Madge Darby in *Who Caused the Mutiny on the 'Bounty'?* that the mutiny was sparked, at least in part, by Christian's repressed homosexual desire for Bligh. Hough takes Darby's idea a step further by suggesting that there had been a consensual homosexual relationship between Bligh and Christian that fell apart after the long, sensual sojourn on Tahiti. If we accept Hough's premise that Bligh and Christian were lovers before arriving at Tahiti, the rest of his argument is convincing. He claims that Christian's relationships with the island's pliant women and Bligh's self-enforced celibacy generated a volatile mixture that ignited soon after *Bounty*'s mission on Tahiti was completed: "At Tahiti, the close relationship was broken, with Christian, ashore all the time, living a full-blooded heterosexual life with the native women, while Bligh, with Cook as an example, lived a sexually abstemious life."

As the *Bounty* prepared to leave Tahiti, Bligh became increasingly dissatisfied with the behavior of his seamen and officers, who had become slack and careless in their duties. Hough believes that at this point, Bligh tried to renew his intimate relationship with Christian but was rejected. As revenge, he directed the lion's share of his criticism and abuse at Christian.

Hough acknowledges that we probably will never know for certain if such a relationship actually existed, but that if it did, the mutiny is easily explained. He supports this theory by quoting from a letter that Peter Heywood wrote to Captain F.W. Beechey, dated April 5, 1830, which states that Christian, before sailing off into the unknown, revealed a secret to Hey-

The dust jacket of the first American edition of *Captain Bligh and Mr. Christian: The Men and the Mutiny*. The rough seas pictured on the front panel suggest the turbulence of the relationship between Bligh and Christian. Reprinted by permission of Dutton, a division of Penguin Group (USA) Inc.

wood: "At that last interview with Christian he also communicated to me, for the satisfaction of his relations, other circumstances connected with the unfortunate disaster, [the mutiny] which, after their deaths, may or may not be laid before the public."

Heywood never divulged Christian's message to the public, and Hough thinks that it may have concerned a homosexual relationship. Hough writes, "We only know that Christian confided something in secret to Peter Heywood before the two separated for the last time at Tahiti: that Heywood was asked to pass on a message to Christian's family.... Which might mitigate his crime in their eyes; that Heywood, after careful consideration, decided against saying anything, the secret of the message dying with him.... The most likely supposition is that Christian wanted at least his brother to know that he had been under unbearable pressure to renew an intimate relationship with his commander which had benefited him greatly in the past but which, after five months in the paradise of Tahiti, was no longer congenial."

Many *Bounty* scholars take issue with Hough's theory, emphasizing that sodomy was punishable by death

Richard Hough commissioned this drawing of Fletcher Christian, based on contemporary accounts of his appearance, from artist Larry Learmonth for *Captain Bligh and Mr. Christian: the Men and the Mutiny.* An authentic portrait of Fletcher Christian has never come to light. Reprinted by permission of Dutton, a division of Penguin Group (USA) Inc.

in the Royal Navy at this time, and that the officers and crew surely would have noticed and discussed such behavior in a vessel as small as the *Bounty*. In addition, the idea that a man as dedicated to his career in the Royal Navy as Bligh would have taken such a risk seems questionable. Nevertheless, Hough does present a persuasive case.

Hough also concurs with Darby that Edward Young, whose motives and behavior during the mutiny and on Pitcairn Island are so mysterious, was the "behind the scenes instigator of the mutiny," and that he also was the ringleader of the massacres on Pitcairn Island. Hough calls Young "The *Bounty*'s Iago," who pushed Christian toward mutiny, and Pitcairn's "dark progenitor of violence, mayhem and murder."

Recreating the first years of the Pitcairn settlement is a considerable challenge for any author, and Hough takes approach similar to that of Charles Nordhoff and James Norman Hall in their novel, *Pitcairn's Island*. Hough writes, "We can list the main events with their supposed dates; or we can create a compound of all the many stories originating from the islanders and their ancestors.... Highlighting what most evidence points to the truth, fitting the characters we now know well and allowing them to react, and to speak, as we believe they would have done."

Overall, *Captain Bligh and Mr. Christian* is decidedly "pro-Bligh," and provides a balanced interpretation of the mutiny that acknowledges each man's strengths and weaknesses. Hough believes that Bligh, for all of his faults, is a figure of greater stature than Christian:

> Bligh promoted above his ability this weak, moody, temperamental and sentimental young man. Christian was no leader. Where Bligh had moments of magnificence as a leader, Christian had none. Just as he destroyed the community of the *Bounty* with an explosion ignited by pent-up despair and shame, so he later brought about the destruction of the community he had founded on Pitcairn by a failure to rise to the responsibilities of leadership.

Yet, Hough does not deny that Christian must have had considerable charm, which "Was difficult to resist. So were his transparent kindness and his anxiety to please. Several times during the mutiny we can see him standing back in dismay at what he is doing. It is not only that he is putting the lives of all his shipmates in danger. He is making enemies. And to add to his anguish, he knows that it is too late."

Captain Bligh and Mr. Christian inspired director David Lean to create two films — *The Lawbreakers* and *The Long Arm* — that promised to be the most historically accurate *Bounty* motion pictures to date. *The Long Arm* would have told, for the first time on film, the full story of *Pandora*. Unfortunately, Lean was unable to bring these projects to fruition, but the script he commissioned from Robert Bolt was used as the basis for *The* Bounty, released in 1984. A paperback edition of *Captain Bligh and Mr. Christian*, entitled *The* Bounty, was issued to coincide with the release of the film, which was directed by Roger Donaldson.

IAN M. BALL: *Pitcairn: Children of Mutiny.* Boston: Little, Brown and Co., 1973.

Pitcairn: Children of Mutiny is an excellent introduction to Pitcairn Island, one that is especially appealing for its first-hand look at of life there in the late 20th century. Two-thirds of the book is devoted to contemporary Pitcairn, and is based on the experiences of journalist Ian M. Ball who, accompanied by his wife and three children, lived on Pitcairn Island for nearly a month conducting research.

Ball begins with an examination of the *Bounty* mutiny, focusing primarily on the Bligh/Christian controversy. He states in the Introduction, "A vindication of William Bligh ... is long overdue. Of the tens of millions of words that have been written this century and last about Bligh and the mutiny, a staggeringly high proportion is pure, easily detectable fiction."

After discussing the smearing of Bligh reputation following the *Bounty* court-martial — and how he began to be portrayed as a villain in print and on film — Ball demonstrates that most of the myths about Bligh are untrue, especially the accusations that he was a tyrant who constantly punished and starved his crew, and that the mutiny was a conspiracy. He also dismisses Richard Hough's theory that homosexuality played a role in the mutiny: "Bligh was certainly a passionate man, although hardly in the flesh sense. But confused? By no means. Bligh a bit of a gay, Christian his quarter-deck swish? Hardly. If there was anything unnatural about Bligh, it was his outright love for the navy and his infatuation with the missions it handed him."

Ball supports this position by quoting from Bligh's log for January 15, 1789, where he recalls meeting, "A person who, although I was certain he was a man, had great marks of effeminacy about him." Bligh learns that this individual is "of a class common in Otaheite

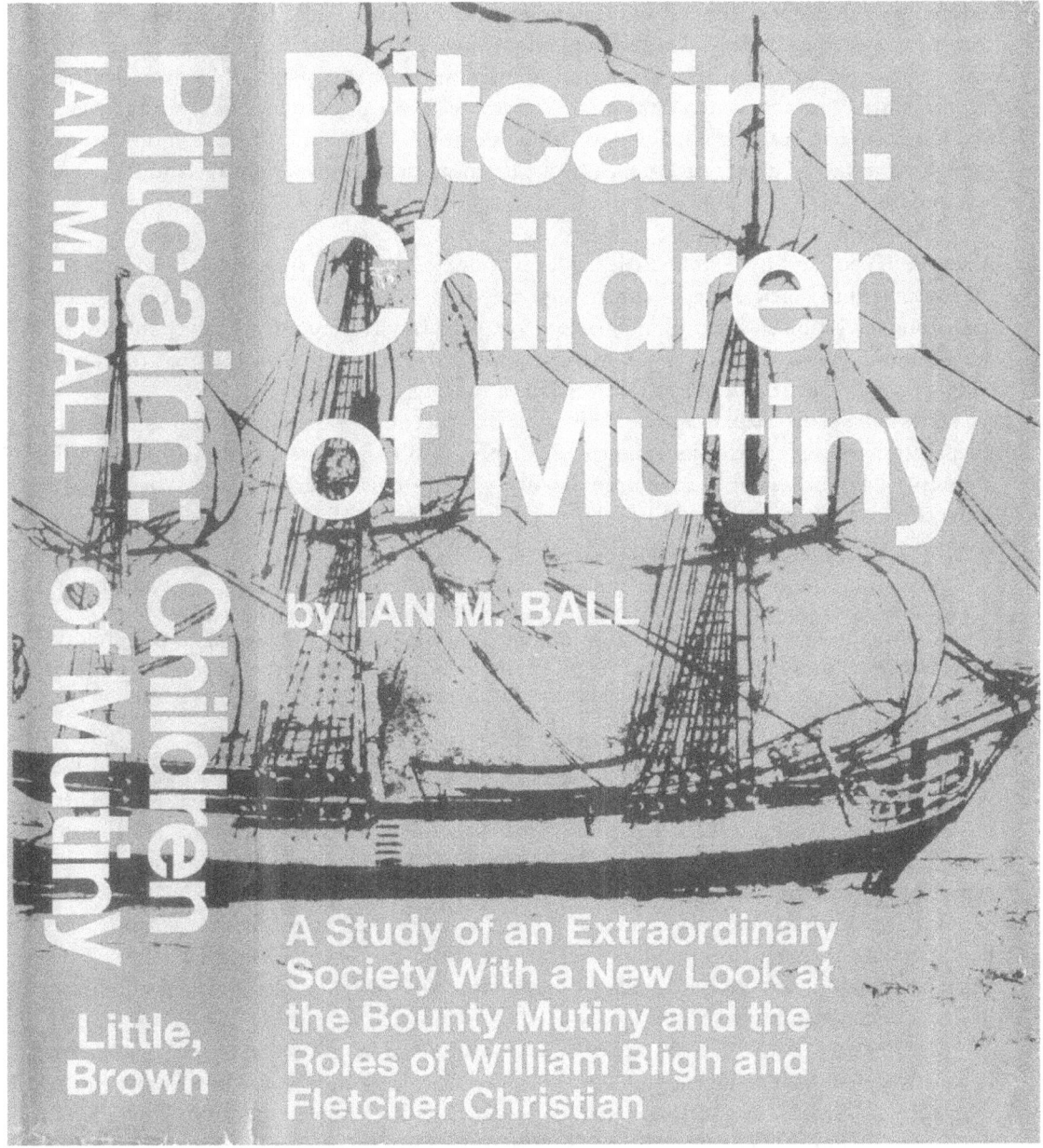

The dust jacket of Ian M. Ball's *Pitcairn: Children of Mutiny* features a drawing of H.M.S. *Bounty*. Reprinted by permission of Little, Brown and Company.

called Mahoo. That the men had frequent connections with him, and that he lived and observed the same ceremonies as the women did.... It is strange that in so prolific a country as this, man should be led into such sensual and beastly acts of gratification."

Ball devotes a considerable amount of space describing how Tahiti was a sexual paradise for *Bounty*'s crew, proposing that the most important factor leading to the mutiny was not, "the master's tyrannical regime at sea, nor by his insupportable nature, nor by his obsession the cat-o'-nine-tails, but by that old standby, sex." Six months of life on an idyllic island, indulging in fresh food, natural beauty and sensual pleasure, engendered what Ball calls "A crew predisposed to mutiny.... It required only a mental storm in Christian's brain to trigger what seems clearly to have been an unpremeditated insurrection." Ball thinks that Christian's "mental storm" was aggravated by alcohol: "We know from Laurence Lebogue, the Sail Maker, that Christian had been drinking with the ship's carpenter, William Purcell, at midnight, even though he was to be up at four o-clock in the morning to keep his watch. His mind certainly was disturbed."

The role of alcohol also is considered by Herbert Ford in "The Mutiny's Cause: A New Analysis" (1998) and by Caroline Alexander in *The* Bounty: *The True Story of the Mutiny on the* Bounty. Ford's article suggests that Bligh may have been a binge drinker, secretly imbibing strong navy rum in his cabin. This could explain Bligh's petulant rage over the loss of a few coconuts on the day before the mutiny. Like Ball, Alexander also feels that the alcohol was a factor in Christian's impulsive decision to mutiny.

The heart of *Pitcairn: Children of Mutiny* is Ball's account of his family's visit to the Island. He paints a vivid picture of just about every aspect of life there, beginning with his landing at Bounty Bay, a formidable experience that every visitor must reckon with. Ball describes the dangers and the great sailing skill of the Pitcairners:

> We shot in like an overpowered skiff, keeping nimbly ahead of the big swell the men had chosen... We skittered through the narrowest of channels, rocks visible below the foam just off each beam. The passageway seemed to be no broader than ten yards. And then came the moment of madness!... We were about to attempt a sharp turn to port! Somehow they did it, they accomplished the feat without swamping us and tearing Rosalind to pieces.... They were simply putting a vessel through a dangerous maneuver they had learned in boyhood and had practiced to perfection ever since.

Ball packed a considerable amount of activity into his family's month on Pitcairn Island, giving us the opportunity to experience, vicariously, many aspects of Island life, such as braving Bounty Bay's dangerous surf in a longboat, bringing fruit and curios to a visiting ship, sharing in the Pitcairners' generous meals, playing cricket and Christmas gift-giving. These activities and traditions are accompanied by a generous number of the author's photographs.

GLYNN CHRISTIAN: *Fragile Paradise: The Discovery of Fletcher Christian, Bounty Mutineer.* London: Hamish Hamilton, 1982. First American Edition published by Little, Brown and Company, Boston, 1982. Revised edition published in 1999, Doubleday, Sydney. Reprinted by Long Riders' Guild Press, 2005.

By the end of the 1930s, the life of William Bligh had been researched and documented in no fewer than four major biographies. But nearly two centuries would pass before the first biography of Bligh's antagonist and history's most famous mutineer appeared: Glynn Christian's *Fragile Paradise: The Discovery of Fletcher Christian.*

When Glynn Christian, a direct descendant of Fletcher Christian, was growing up in New Zealand, he was disappointed by the inaccurate film portrayals of his ancestor and the scant information available about his life in *Bounty* literature. *The Wake of the* Bounty, by C. S. Wilkinson was an exception. This book, which argues that Fletcher Christian may have escaped from Pitcairn Island and returned to England, motivated him to write *Fragile Paradise*. Glynn Christian writes, "Once I had read it my confusion was complete. Yet I was certain there must be some way of discovering the true fate of Fletcher Christian. It was not until 1975 that I realized there had never been a biography of him. I knew then I had somehow to unearth the truth about my ancestor and to write it."

Glynn Christian began a personal quest to learn as much as possible about his great-

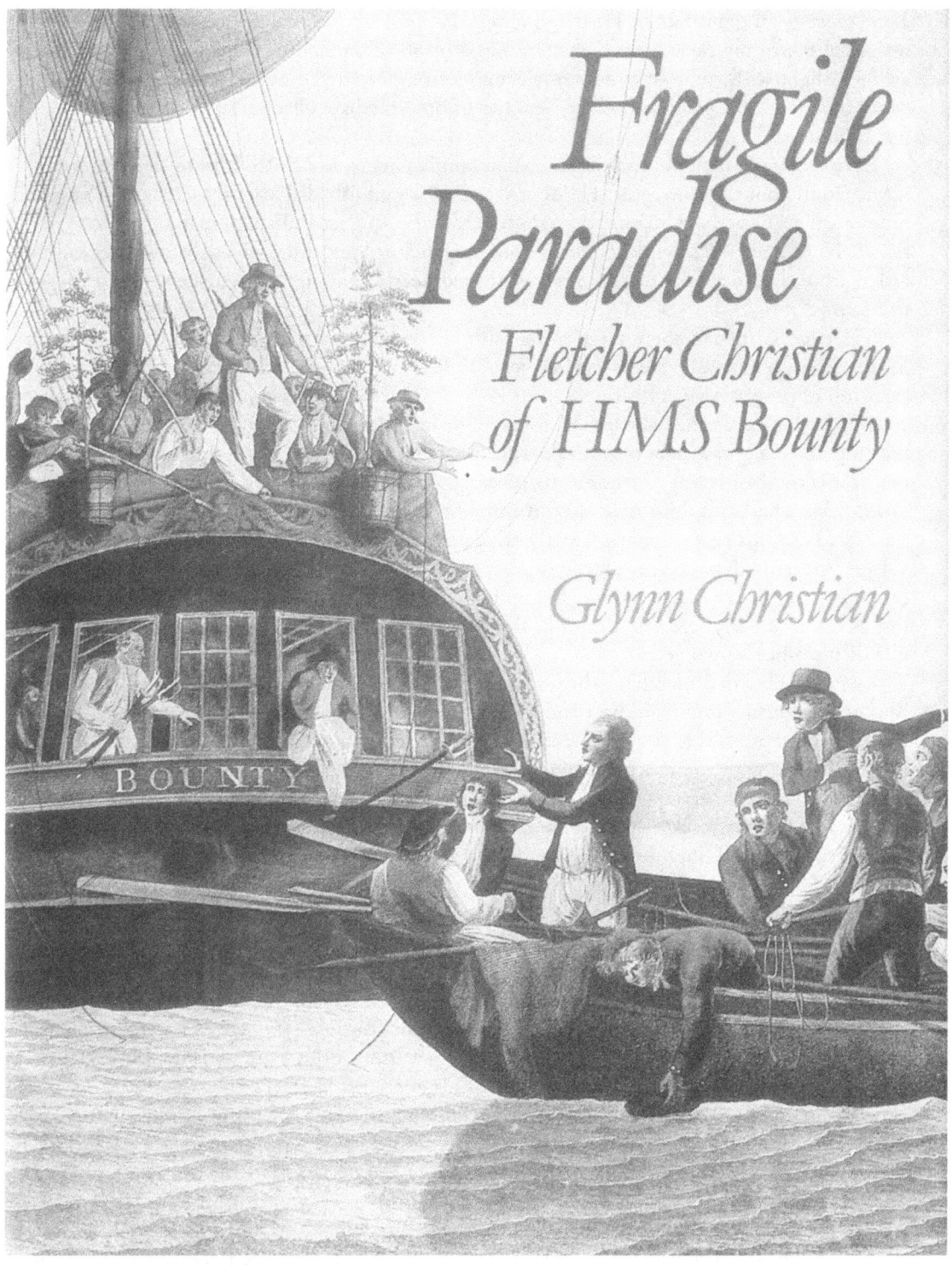

The dust jacket of the first American edition of Glynn Christian's *Fragile Paradise* reproduces part of Robert Dodd's *The Mutineers Turning Bligh and Part of the Officers and Crew Adrift from His Majesty's Ship the Bounty*. Reprinted by permission of Little, Brown and Company.

great-great-great grandfather. He based *Fragile Paradise* on the assumption that "There never was a mutiny of the *Bounty*. Rather there was a revolt of one man against another, Christian against Bligh, with some of the *Bounty*'s men joining in later. Logically that clash can only be understood if the passions and perversities of both men are chronicled. Until now this has not been done."

He examined the voluminous Christian family papers, which led him to significant new information about his ancestor. He discovered an unpublished diary by Fletcher Christian's older brother, Charles, who once served on *Middlesex*, an East India Company merchant vessel. In November 1787, while *Bounty*'s crew lingered at Spithead, anxiously awaiting sailing orders from the Admiralty, *Middlesex* was docked nearby, having just returned from a voyage to Madras.

Fletcher Christian spent an evening with his brother, who remembered the meeting in his diary, written in 1811. He praised Fletcher's physical strength and remarked that, "He was then full of professional Ambition and of Hope." Charles Christian also makes a tantalizing allusion to his experience aboard *Middlesex*: "When Men are cooped up for a long time in the Interior of a Ship, there oft prevails such a jarring Discordancy of Tempers and Conduct that it is enough on many Occasions by repeated Acts of Irritation and Offence to change the Disposition of a Lamb into that of an Animal fierce and resentful."

Charles Christian's remark, clearly triggered by unpleasant memories of the *Middlesex* voyage, spurred Glynn to consult the ship's log. He made a startling discovery in the log entry for September 5, 1787, two months before Fletcher Christian met with his brother: "Incredible as it may seem, there was a mutiny aboard *Middlesex*, and Charles Christian was cited as one of the officers involved."

Mutiny aboard a merchant ship was not a capital offense, and Charles Christian's punishment was suspension from East India Company service for two years. Although he left no written record of his role as a mutineer, it is more than likely that Charles Christian discussed the experience with his brother. Glynn Christian writes, "Fletcher's last conversations with his brother, then, must have been about mutiny. More than that, they were probably about the duty of officers towards their men and the actions that could be taken against captains who were cruel or thoughtless. No wonder Fletcher remained ashore all night — the conversation in Spithead must have been riveting."

It is plausible that his brother's actions aboard *Middlesex* were on Fletcher Christian's mind before he initiated the mutiny on H.M.S. *Bounty*. Glynn Christian believes that, "At some fatal moment he must have thought: 'Why should I go? Why shouldn't Bligh leave instead?' Put like this it did not even sound like mutiny. And had not Charles, his own brother, been forced to act against another captain for the same reasons?" We will never know for sure exactly what Christian was thinking, but future researchers surely must consider Glynn Christian's discovery in any future interpretation of his ancestor's motives.

Deciding that his research would be incomplete without spending some time on Pitcairn Island, Glynn Christian organized the Sir John Barrow Commemorative Expedition, which was officially approved by the Royal Geographical Society. He and his shipmates voyaged from Tahiti to Tubuai on the *Taiyo*, a modern, square-rigged brigantine.

On Tubuai, the site of Fletcher Christian's first settlement attempt, he located the battleground where the mutineers fought with the natives and mapped the remains of Fort George. On Pitcairn Island, he produced a definitive map for the Royal Geographical Society. With some help from Tom Christian, Glynn Christian pinpointed what he believes to be the unmarked graves of Fletcher Christian and Mauatua, his Tahitian consort.

Glynn Christian judges Bligh more harshly than the authors of the generally "pro-Bligh" biographies written during the 1930s, which did so much to rehabilitate Bligh's reputation. In the revised edition of *Fragile Paradise*, Glynn Christian examines more closely more recent theories about the mutiny and Christian's motivations. He thinks that the opinion of Sven Wahlroos, a practicing clinical and forensic psychologist, comes closest to the truth. Dr. Wahlroos hypothesizes that Fletcher may have had a borderline personality disorder, and that a brief psychotic episode led to the mutiny.

Revising *Fragile Paradise* also gave Glynn Christian an opportunity to highlight the important role of the Tahitian women in creating Pitcairn Island's unique culture. Once the Tahitian and English men were dead, the women, as natives of the South Seas, had the necessary skills for survival. Christian remarks, "Only they can have known how best to grow, tend and harvest crops and fish in this part of the world." Calling them "Pitcairn's Invisible Blood," he places them "Among the most extraordinary social pioneers of the late nineteenth century."

A notable achievement is that women on Pitcairn Island were voting before any other women in the world. Glynn Christian contends that this was the direct result of Fletcher Christian's philosophy when he established the rules of the Pitcairn settlement: that each person had a vote in the decision-making. If mutineers had only extended that right to include the Tahitian men, the first years of the island's history might have been peaceful ones.

WILLIAM BLIGH: *The Bligh Notebook. 'Rough account— Lieutenant Wm Bligh's voyage in the Bounty's Launch from the ship to Tofua & from thence to Timor.' 28 April to 14 June 1789.* With a draft list of the *Bounty* mutineers. Transcription and Facsimile. Edited by John Bach. North Sydney: This edition first published 1987 by Allen & Unwin in association with the National Library of Australia.

The National Library of Australia published *The Bligh Notebook* in 1986 as a boxed, two-volume set, limited to 500 copies. It includes a facsimile of the notebook that William Bligh kept during the voyage of *Bounty*'s launch and a transcription of the notebook. The Book of the Month Club issued a less expensive, two-volume set, and a trade printing that conveniently collects the facsimile and transcription in one volume appeared from Allen & Unwin in 1987.

Bligh wrote daily entries in this 108-page notebook throughout the dangerous voyage, using it, when weather permitted, as a reference to make more detailed entries in his official log and journal. Bligh recorded the notebook's provenance on the first leaf: "This account was kept in my bosom as a common memorandum of our time & transposed into my fair Journal every day when the Weather would admit with every material circumstance which passed. It happened that a Mr. Hayward had this Book with some Signals set down in it which appear in two Pages & I appropriated the blank leaves to this use."

This unique, precious volume, kept by Bligh's descendants for many years, was purchased at auction in 1976 by the National Library of Australia for $73,000, and is now one of the Library's most popular exhibits. Through the published facsimile editions, readers can leaf through its water stained pages and marvel that Bligh managed to keep such a detailed log and account of the voyage, filled with sketches, maps and complex nautical calculations.

Even during the brief intervals when the crew of the launch were not at sea, such as the two days they spent on Restoration Island inside Australia's Great Barrier Reef, Bligh used the notebook as a journal to record daily events and observations. It is clear that his natural curiosity never fails him as we read his entry for Friday, May 29 1789, after spending an exhausting, dangerous month at sea:

Variety of High & lowland Hills Woody

> Round Top Isld. a heep of Stones — left it — Got to Restoration Point ½ mile from it.—
> Only Oysters and Perrywinkles.—
> No Inhabitants but signs of having been here.— Saw two wigwams weather side only covered. Saw a Pointed Stick as at Adven Bay Weapons

Editor John Bach calls the notebook "An object for wonder, when one considers what it has been through." He writes in the introduction, "Given the violent motion of the small craft running before the trade winds, made worse by the occasional storm, and the frequent deluges of rain, it is surely a minor miracle that Bligh was able to maintain such a legible account, with so few signs of the inconvenience he was suffering." "Inconvenience" seems like an inadequate word to describe the physical and mental anguish experienced by Bligh and his loyal crew.

The Bligh Notebook is of special appeal to *Bounty* enthusiasts interested in the art of navigation. After providing a sound, balanced account of the mutiny, Bach describes in detail the techniques Bligh used to navigate the launch to Timor. He also reveals that Bligh inflated his admittedly formidable skills: "There is little doubt ... that Bligh tried to conceal from public knowledge the extent of his navigational equipment and it is only under the stress of making the daily calculations in the notebook that he occasionally leaves evidence of it, with his references to the Ramsden sextant and to Hamilton Moore's book" (*The Practical Navigator*).

In his official accounts of the voyage, Bligh fails to mentions that he had a sextant and reference book in the launch, implying that he sailed without this technical assistance. However, the journals of Boatswain's Mate James Morrison and Master John Fryer both document that Christian handed the sextant to Bligh as he boarded the launch. Bligh's motives in hiding this fact are unclear, but it is appears that he was trying to conceal what was, on Christian's part, an act of remorse, compassion or both.

Bligh's omissions in the *Notebook* do not take detract from his achievement, although they do provide an insight into his personality. Bach contends that Fryer, and perhaps Boatswain William Cole, had sufficient navigational skill to reach Timor in the launch, but maintains that neither man possessed the leadership qualities that Bligh displayed during this desperate ordeal. Reading the terse entries he writes as they near the end of their voyage can be a moving experience. On June 11 1789:

> People very weak.—
> Served Bread & Water for Supper.— No appearance of Land.—
> Gannet but no sight of Land
> Several pieces of Rock Weed
> Pleasant Wr.— Served Bread & Water.—
> Fine Wr. & Less Sea Very Hazy No signs Land — Bread & Water
> Distressed.

The Bligh Notebook is well illustrated, and includes a foldout plan of *Bounty*'s launch, a map and chronology of the voyage, contemporary engravings, photos of the type of navigational equipment that Bligh used, explanatory notes and a bibliography. It provides, according to Bach, "A rare look at Bligh the seaman, in the full and splendid practice of his profession, and as such he is beyond our criticism."

SVEN WAHLROOS: *Mutiny and Romance in the South Seas: A Companion to the Bounty Adventure.* Topsfield: Salem House Publishers, 1989. Revised edition published by iUniverse.com, Inc., Lincoln, 2001

Mutiny and Romance in the South Seas: A Companion to the Bounty Adventure by Dr. Sven Wahlroos is one of the most useful volumes about the *Bounty* Saga to appear since the publication of George Mackaness' *A Book of the 'Bounty' and Selections from Bligh's Writings* in 1938. Both are keystone books for *Bounty* enthusiasts, suitable for browsing or conducting serious research.

Dr. Wahlroos' book is not a collection of important primary documents like *A Book of the 'Bounty,'* but, as he writes in his introduction, a book "Intended for *Bounty* buffs, those in the making and those already 'hooked.' Although it can stand on its own (the story is told fully in Part I), it has been conceived primarily as a companion to reading about the *Bounty*."

Writing *Mutiny and Romance in the South Seas* clearly was a labor of love for Dr. Wahlroos, a practicing psychologist in California and enthusiastic student of the *Bounty* Saga. Although many armchair psychologists have speculated about the motives of William Bligh, Fletcher Christian, Edward Young and other participants in the mutiny, Dr. Wahlroos brings his professional expertise to bear on the subject. Noted *Bounty* scholar Rolf DuRietz writes in his foreword to *Mutiny and Romance in the South Seas*:

"Psychological writing is not an entirely new phenomenon in *Bounty* scholarship, but so far the results have not inspired confidence... The historian who specializes in *Bounty*-Pitcairn studies needs to know quite something of the human mind and of human behaviour in general, and no true *Bounty* enthusiast will be able to avoid a sense of exhilaration when balanced and responsible psychological scholarship is now beginning to be applied to the problems of the *Bounty*-Pitcairn drama."

One of the most commonly discussed issues in recent *Bounty* scholarship is the theory that repressed homosexual feelings or an actual intimate relationship was an integral element in the conflict between Bligh and Christian. Madge Darby first suggested it in *Who Caused the Mutiny on the* Bounty? and Richard Hough further developed the concept in *Captain Bligh and Mr. Christian: The Men and the Mutiny*. Dr. Wahlroos outlines his position on the subject in clear psychological terms. Addressing the breakdown of the men's' friendship, he writes:

> What had happened to their friendship that later caused it to deteriorate so badly? It is likely that Bligh had felt left out in Tahiti. He probably sensed that the Tahitians did not like him and resented Christian's deep involvement with them.... Considering Bligh's later hatred of Peter Heywood, he may have also resented Christian's close friendship with the young midshipman. But to read a homosexual conflict into the relationship ... goes against everything we know about Bligh and Christian. If there was any sexual element present at all (which is improbable), it is more likely that Bligh, unconsciously, was jealous of bachelor Christian's popularity with the Tahitian women when he himself felt bound by his marriage vows to stay chaste.

In Part I, Dr. Wahlroos tells the multi-faceted tale of H.M.S. *Bounty* chronologically, month by month, allowing the reader to easily follow the often-confusing array of events that constitute *Bounty*'s history. For example, in the entry for September 1789, we learn that while Bligh and his loyal crew were sailing on the schooner *Resource* for Batavia, Christian and his party were fighting the natives on Tubuai during their failed effort to settle there. In April 1791, when Bligh was appointed Commander of *Providence* and preparing to begin his second breadfruit mission, the crew of *Pandora*, in Tahiti, was constructing "Pandora's Box" to confine the prisoners.

Part I comprises approximately half of *Mutiny and Romance in the South Seas*, and concludes with the murder of Christian on Pitcairn Island in September 1793. A detailed "Encyclopedia" follows, with entries for the hundreds of people and events connected with *Bounty* Saga, from "Adams, John," the patriarch of Pitcairn Island, to "Young, Elizabeth," a descendant of John Mills and Matthew Quintal.

Rounding out the 500-page volume is "A Sample of Literature on the *Bounty* and Related

The dust jacket of Sven Wahlroos' *Mutiny and Romance in the South Seas: A Companion to the Bounty Adventure* features a photo of the *Bounty* replica constructed for the 1984 film, *The Bounty*. Reprinted by permission of Sven Wahlroos.

Subjects," a substantial bibliography listing more than 500 books and periodicals, followed by a comprehensive index. *Mutiny and Romance in the South Seas* also includes a map of Pitcairn Island and two detailed maps showing the maritime routes taken by Bligh and Christian. Dr. Wahlroos also incorporates the highly relevant history of Bligh's second breadfruit voyage on *Providence*, unfamiliar to many readers, which, provides a great deal of insight into Bligh's personality.

In an appendix to the revised edition of *Mutiny and Romance in the South Seas* (2001), Dr. Wahlroos deepens his psychological profile of Christian by emphasizing the importance of *honor*— over even life itself— to 18th-century men, especially to scions of prominent families like the Christians. He hypothesizes that Fletcher may have had a borderline personality disorder, and that a brief psychotic episode — triggered by being grossly humiliated by Bligh in front of the other officers and crew — led to the mutiny.

The breadth of information included in *Mutiny and Romance in the South Seas*, along with Dr. Wahlroos' insights as a trained psychologist, make it an essential reference tool and a significant contribution to the literature of the *Bounty* Saga.

HERBERT FORD: *Pitcairn — Port of Call*. Angwin: Hawser Titles, 1996.

In his introduction to *Pitcairn — Port of Call*, Herbert Ford poses a logical question: What has drawn thousands of ships, over the course of nearly 200 years, to approach this small, remote island in the vast Pacific Ocean? His answer: "The ships come because Pitcairn is the remnant of one of the world's great sea stories.... For many a captain the Island's colorful past has caused him to divert his ship scores, even hundreds of miles from its planned course. 'We'll give the crew a look-see,' he'll mutter, while it is his own look-see he's thinking most about."

The day-to-day life and survival of Pitcairn's population have always been linked to the ships that call there. In 1808, Captain Mayhew Folger's chance visit in the American sealer *Topaz* marked the beginning of the Islanders' contact with the outside world after 18 years of isolation. When the rest of the world learned about Pitcairn Island, whalers, clippers, ocean liners, cargo ships — virtually every type of seagoing vessel — began to anchor off the island, trading much needed manufactured goods for the islanders' fresh fruits and vegetables. Ford suggests that "The history of world shipping by type from the mid–1800s to the latter part of the 20th century may be rather precisely charted by the ships calling at Pitcairn Island."

Ford's summary of Pitcairn's history serves as prologue to his comprehensive list of every ship that has visited Pitcairn, from the *Bounty* on January 5, 1790 to ACT, a container ship out of Auckland, on December 25, 1990. Many of his succinct descriptions record relatively uneventful calls, such as the following entry for June 30 1952: "Wallarah Coal Company's ship Wallarah of Sydney, 1,448 tons, from Panama, bound for Sydney."

These brief vignettes, which Ford presents in a friendly informal, tone, provide a vivid impression of life on Pitcairn over the years. For example, on December 1876, the *Gareloch*, a British vessel sailing for England out of San Francisco, stopped at Pitcairn: "The captain reports that when passing Pitcairn Island, the ship is boarded by two boats from the Island. The Islanders report all is well, but that they are greatly in need of corn, as the rats had eaten all their crop of wheat. The *Gareloch* supplies them with a few necessities, including some flour."

Some visits were destined to have a lasting impact on Pitcairn history and culture, such as that of H.M. screw sloop *Pelican*, on October 18, 1886: "John I. Tay, a former seaman, and layman of the Seventh-day Adventist faith, arrives.... Given permission by the Pitcairners to reside and present the teachings of the Seventh-day Adventists, he stays five weeks before leaving on

The clean, contemporary cover design of Herbert Ford's *Pitcairn — Port of Call* was created by Brian Nash of Brian Nash Design in St. Helena, California. It features a square-rigged ship in partial silhouette and a small view of Pitcairn Island. Reprinted by permission of Herbert Ford.

the *General Evans*. At the request of the Islanders, Tay promises to return with an ordained minister of the Adventist faith to baptize those wishing to become members of the church."

The entry for December 23, 1934, notes the arrival of Dr. Harry L. Shapiro, an anthropologist at the American Museum of Natural History, on *Zaca*, a two-masted schooner sailing from Mangareva to Easter Island. Dr. Shapiro spent 10 days on the island, producing, as

Ford writes "The most comprehensive survey ever made of the physical and cultural anthropology of Pitcairn."

Dr. Shapiro's pioneering field work was the foundation for *The Heritage of the* Bounty: *The Story of Pitcairn through Six Generations*, published in 1936 and revised in 1962, as well as several other works about Pitcairn Island's people. His popular, yet scholarly, work introduced an entire generation to the history and residents of Pitcairn Island.

Pitcairn — Port of Call is an indispensable reference for students of Pitcairn history, and *Bounty*/Pitcairn enthusiasts also should consult Ford's other titles, including *Pitcairn*; *The Miscellany of Pitcairn's Island*; *Island of Tears: John I. Tay*; and his numerous articles in journals, magazines and newspapers.

Guide to Pitcairn: Published by the Government of The Islands of Pitcairn, Henderson, Ducie and Oeno, 1999. First published in 1963. Revised and reprinted, 1970, 1976, 1982 1990, 1999.

Guide to Pitcairn made its debut as a small booklet, and has grown with each succeeding issue to become one of the most useful, compact and attractive references on the Pitcairn Island. This official guide to the island is prepared for publication by the Pitcairn Islands Administration, based in Auckland, New Zealand. In the Preface, M.J. Williams, CVO, OBD, Governor of Pitcairn, Henderson, Ducie and Oeno Islands, explains the rationale for publishing *Guide to Pitcairn* and keeping it up to date: "To this day Pitcairn's inhabitants are descendants of the *Bounty* mutineers. There continues to be worldwide interest in them and their way of life. The *Guide to Pitcairn*, first published in 1963 and now into its sixth revision, is intended to answer some of the many questions that are most frequently asked about Pitcairn, including its history and current conditions on the Island."

Divided into four sections, the *Guide to Pitcairn* begins with a brief, fact-filled history of key events in Pitcairn history, including background on the mutiny, John Adams and his successors, emigration to Norfolk Island and changes in the islanders' religion and government. Other sections feature more difficult to find facts and information, such as "Pitcairn Island's Contribution to World War II," "Island Transport" and "The Other Islands." The "other islands" are Oeno, Ducie and Henderson, where the Pitcairners harvest miro wood for their carvings, sales of which make up an important part of their income.

The *Guide to Pitcairn* is filled with beautiful color and black and white photographs of the island and its residents, and covers just about every aspect of life on the island today, from its geography and climate to education, health and community recreation. Its four appendices cite population statistics, beginning with the births and deaths recorded in 1864, as well as details of Pitcairn's finances, office holders and a brief bibliography entitled "Pitcairn Island Reading List."

The 68-page *Guide to Pitcairn* is not intended to be a tool for more detailed research about the subject, but it is, along with the monthly newsletter *Pitcairn Miscellany*, the best source of information about contemporary life on the Island.

TREVOR LUMMIS: *Pitcairn Island: Life and Death in Eden*. Brookfield: Ashgate Publishing Co., 1997. First British edition published by Victor Gollancz, London, 1999. Revised, paperback edition published as *Life and Death in Eden: Pitcairn Island and the* Bounty *Mutineers* by Phoenix, London, 2000.

In *Pitcairn Island: Life and Death in Eden*, Trevor Lummis presents a fresh look at the Island's history, from the arrival of the *Bounty* in 1790 to 1859, when many of the islanders who had resettled on Norfolk Island returned to Pitcairn. *Life and Death in Eden: Pitcairn Island and the* Bounty *Mutineers*, a revised paperback edition published in 2000, adds a brief Epilogue highlighting Pitcairn history during the 19th and 20th centuries.

Both editions provide vital background information for readers unfamiliar with the events that led to the mutineers' secret settlement on Pitcairn Island. Lummis considers the various theories about why the mutiny occurred, rejecting Richard Hough's suggestion that a homosexual relationship existed between William Bligh and Fletcher Christian: "Such a relationship could hardly have been kept invisible on a small ship, where everyone lived cheek by jowl and where even Bligh's cabin was a busy companionway," he writes. Acknowledging that Bligh and Christian once enjoyed a friendship, he concludes that, "The reason why the relationship went so sour is inexplicable."

Lummis approaches Pitcairn's history from a somewhat different perspective than David Silverman in Pitcairn Island and Ian M. Ball in *Pitcairn: Children of Mutiny*. He states that "The role of the women in shaping events on the island and their input into the unique identity of the community, so often ignored, is fully considered. Their support for the men as rival groups — Tahitians or Europeans — or their concern for individuals largely decided which men lived or died." In 1989, Dr. Sven Wahlroos, in *Mutiny and Romance in the South Seas: A Companion to the Bounty Adventure*, also made this point: "The fact that most of the credit belonged to the Tahitian mothers escapes *Bounty* authors to this day." Lummis book is one of the first authors to fully address this topic.

He examines all of the sources of early Pitcairn history — John Adams' conflicting accounts, the journal of Edward Young, and especially the oral history of "Jenny," who told her version after returning to Tahiti in 1817 — and constructs what he believes to be the most convincing sequence of events. (For "Jenny's" oral history, see: Dillon, Captain Peter. "Pitcairn's Island — The *Bounty*'s Crew." *United Service Journal* Part II (November 1829): 589–593.)

Lummis agrees with Madge Darby and others that Edward Young masterminded a conspiracy to murder the Tahitians, as well as some of the white men. He also implicates two of the other mutineers: "It is more than possible that Adams and Mills (John Mills) were involved in the plot with Young from the beginning."

The Polynesian women began to assert themselves after the murders. They kept the skulls of the five murdered white men (a Tahitian custom), spurring a conflict with Young, who insisted that the skulls be buried. The women adamantly refused, an act that Lummis believes had significant repercussions: "This was quite an assertion, for not only were they disobeying the orders of a European male who had been accorded high status back in their own island, but were also denying the authority of a 'chief' among them ... in sharp contradiction to the great authority accorded to chiefs in their own culture."

Growing increasingly restive, the women attempted to return to Tahiti in a makeshift boat. When this failed, they hatched a plot to kill the white men, generating what Lummis calls "A gender war, albeit one deepened by racial lines and influenced by the brief but eventful history they had shared." A truce and period of relative calm followed, which was shattered when William McKoy perfected a still for brewing spirits. The ensuing period of alcohol-fueled violence finally ended after McKoy's death (possibly by suicide) and Adams and Young's decision to "execute" Matthew Quintal, whose violent behavior was endangering everyone. Following Quintal's death, Young and Adams began to hold prayer services,

Opposite: Four symbols of Pitcairn Island's early history are pictured on the cover of the paperback edition of *Life and Death in Eden* by Trevor Lummis: H.M.S. *Bounty*, a Polynesian woman, a pistol and an island flower. Illustration by Andy Bridge. Reprinted by permission of Orion Publishing Group Ltd.

teaching the children to read the Bible and write, hoping that their descendants would establish a peaceful community on Pitcairn. When Young died from asthma in 1800, Adams was the only adult male left on Pitcairn, and he became the patriarch, assuming moral authority over the population. Regardless of Adams' position as community leader, the women began to play a more dominant role in many aspects of day to day life, such as communal cooking and eating apart from the men, old domestic habits from their lives on Tahiti.

Lummis believes that we will never really grasp how the European and Tahitian cultures blended so successfully to form a pious new society, just as we will never learn the total truth about the murders: "The communal form of working by the Polynesian women contrasts sharply with the individualism of the European men. But it leaves something of a mystery as to how the two systems worked together but, once again, there is not sufficient detailed evidence to resolve it."

CAROLINE ALEXANDER: *The* Bounty: *The True Story of the Mutiny on the* Bounty. New York: Viking Press, 2003. First British edition published by HarperCollins, London, 2003.

The publication of Caroline Alexander's *The* Bounty: *The True Story of the Mutiny on the* Bounty, attracted a generous amount of attention from the media, once again demonstrating the public's perennial fascination with the *Bounty* Saga. An illustrated article appeared on the front page of the *New York Times* Book Review section and, several weeks later, *The* Bounty appeared on the *Times'* non-fiction best-seller list. The *New York Times* selected it as one of the "Best Books of 2003," and Alexander discussed *The* Bounty on a 15-city news and 20-city radio satellite tour, as well as on C-Span's *History* on *Book TV.*

In the popular mind, William Bligh's name has been synonymous with tyranny and brutality for more than 200 years. Alexander, the author of Endurance: *Shackleton's Legendary Antarctic Expedition*, sets out in *The* Bounty to argue the case for Bligh before a wide audience. Verlyn Klinkenborg's *New York Times* review goes to the heart of the matter: "What got into Fletcher Christian? Already he had sailed twice with Captain Bligh, a gifted seaman, not a tyrannical flogger. In '*The* Bounty,' Caroline Alexander tells how Bligh became the villain of the *Bounty*'s story instead of the hero."

The Bounty is far more than a vindication of Bligh; this 512-page volume is arguably the most comprehensive study of the *Bounty* Saga to date. Alexander also wanted to bring the little-known tale of *Pandora* to the attention of a larger reading public. In fact, she devotes considerably more space to *Pandora*'s voyage than to the mutiny itself.

Popular films have made Bligh, Fletcher Christian and the *Bounty* mutiny common knowledge, but Captain Edward Edwards and *Pandora* are far from being household names. Although *Pandora* made a brief appearance in the 1935 *Mutiny on the* Bounty, this segment of the film was filled with historical inaccuracies, the most blatant showing Bligh as commander of *Pandora* and Edwards as his lieutenant. Subsequent film treatments completely ignored *Pandora*'s voyage.

Few, if any, popular magazine articles about *Pandora* have appeared since the publication of Luis Marden's "In *Bounty*'s Wake: Finding the Wreck of H.M.S. *Pandora*," in the October 1985 issue of *National Geographic Magazine.* In its August 4, 2003 issue, *The New Yorker* magazine — under its "Annals of the Sea" banner — treated readers to an advance look at *The* Bounty, which would not appear in bookstores until later that year.

The article, "Wreck of the *Pandora*: The Fate of the Men Sent to Hunt Down the *Bounty* Mutineers," is a lengthy excerpt from *The* Bounty, with evocative illustrations by Mark Ulriksen. Readers must have been surprised to discover that there is so much more to *Bounty*'s story

William Bligh, the Bounty's ill-fated commander.   *Mutineer (and later Captain) Peter Heywood.*

These portraits of "William Bligh, the *Bounty*'s ill-fated commander," and "Mutineer (and later Captain) Peter Heywood" illustrated "Wreck of the *Pandora*: The Fate of the Men Sent to Hunt Down the *Bounty* Mutineers," which appeared in the August 4, 2003, issue of *The New Yorker*. The sinking of *Pandora* is pictured behind Heywood. Illustrations by permission of Mark Ulriksen.

than the mutiny itself. In addition to *Pandora*, Alexander discusses the mutineers' attempt to settle at Tubuai, Bligh's second breadfruit voyage on H.M.S. *Providence* and the outcome of the court-martial.

In *The* Bounty, Alexander presents a perceptive account of what Christian may have been thinking in the days preceding the mutiny. She emphasizes Fletcher's fear of corporal punishment and links that to a meeting with his brother, Charles, before the *Bounty* sailed:

> Central to Christian's state of mind appears to have been the extraordinary idea that Bligh might either break or flog him.... It is not impossible that he made such a threat in one of his passions. But if so, one would expect an event of such blazing significance to be referred to by Morrison or Fryer; or Heywood in his letters; or in testimony in the court-martial; or in later rumored accounts. No such allegation was ever made.

She quotes a primary account reporting that Christian, in tears, confided in Ship's Carpenter William Purcell who, as a warrant officer, could not be flogged for disagreeing with a commanding officer. Christian had clearly reached the point where he could no longer refrain from confronting Bligh, and Alexander stresses that his fear of punishment and the shame of being demoted prevented him from doing so. Christian said to Purcell, who confronted Bligh at Adventure Bay, "You have something to protect you, and can speak again; but if I should speak to him as you do, he would probably break me, turn me before the mast, and perhaps flog me; and if he did, it would be the death of us both, for I am sure I should take him in my arms, and jump overboard with him."

Charles Christian's involvement in the *Middlesex* mutiny surely was on Fletcher Christian's mind, as suggested by Glynn Christian, who discovered Charles' unpublished memoir of that event, and by Alexander, who states: "Sixteen months earlier, at the riverside inn with his Brother Charles ... Fletcher Christian had gained a breathtaking insight into how powerless a man could be made, officer or seaman, in the hands of a tyrannical captain, as his brother related all that had happened on the *Middlesex*."

In his memoir, Charles Christian reported the words of one of the men involved in the mutiny against Captain John Rogers of *Middlesex*: "His (Captain Roger's) passions were raised against me, to a more violent degree than formerly. Let him speak the truth, and he cannot assign a reasonable cause ... sent for me, beat me, ordered me to be flogged to death." Alexander comments, "So had Fletcher learned one of the men in the *Middlesex* mutiny had protested his treatment. From his impassioned brother, who had leaped into the fray, Fletcher had also learned there was honor in resistance." She also believes that Christian's disheveled appearance on the morning of the mutiny suggests that he had been drinking, a factor that may have tipped the balance from anger to outright rebellion.

In her defense of Bligh, Alexander presents what may be the most extensive account to date on the Christian and Heywood families' efforts to blacken his reputation, damage that persists to this day. Bligh's absence from England before the court-martial was convened — he was commanding *Providence* on a second breadfruit voyage — made this easier to achieve. When he returned from this successful mission, Bligh was shocked to learn that he had become persona non grata: "Bligh's reception was the result of considerable, at times concerted, outside effort. While the Heywood family connections and interest-making had done damage within Admiralty and naval circles, the most public and audacious attack on Bligh was to come from, of all quarters, Fletcher Christian's family." Alexander's extensive research reveals how the two families sought to mitigate their association with the crime of mutiny by suggesting that Bligh was largely to blame.

Unlike many books about the *Bounty* Saga, *The* Bounty does not end with the court-martial and execution of three mutineers. It ties up many of the saga's loose ends, including the later careers of John Fryer, Robert Tinkler and Heywood, who rose from pardoned mutineer to a life devoted to the Royal Navy, where he served more than 27 years at sea: "(When) young Heywood had been summoned before the assembled company of the *Hector* to receive His Majesty's pardon, he had pledged his 'future Life' would be faithfully devoted to his sovereign's service. This pledge he held good. A humble awareness that he had been reprieved — when others had not — combined with his strong religious feeling seemed to have forged of his life a kind of penance."

Generally, reviewers and readers applauded The *Bounty*, particularly Alexander's defense of Bligh. The *USA Today* review was headlined, "You had Capt. Bligh all wrong, Mr. Christian." The *Boston Globe* reviewer, referring to motion picture portrayals of Bligh, stated, "The picture of Bligh as a sadist is baloney. The 35-year-old navy lieutenant was unusually considerate of his men. He was loath to punish and did so sparingly, even when provoked by balky and insolent officers. Despite his temper and sharp tongue, there's no record of cruelty, and none was alleged by the court-martialed mutineers."

The Bounty, which also appeared in a trade paperback edition, has enjoyed a larger audience than many excellent volumes — such as those by Owen Rutter, George Mackaness and Rolf Du Rietz — that were published in small quantities or limited editions, and addressed primarily to a scholarly audience. These groundbreaking works by Du Rietz, Mackaness and Rutter, which also presented a fairer view of Bligh, led the way for a book like *The* Bounty. Its publication may mark a crucial turning point in the effort to explode the myths about Bligh initiated in the 1790s, propagated in the 19th century and confirmed in the popular mind by the 1935 and 1962 films.

Additional Works

Books

Allen, Kenneth. S. *That Bounty Bastard: The True Story of Captain William Bligh.* London: Robert Hale and Co., 1976.
    A fully illustrated biography of Bligh that strives to rehabilitate William Bligh's reputation as a villain.
Allward, Maurice. *Pitcairn Island: Refuge of the Bounty Mutineers.* Stroud: Tempus Publishing, 2000.
    Maurice Allward's photographic survey is filled with more than 100 photos and illustrations of Pitcairn Island and its people through the years.
Anthony, Irvin, Ed. *The Saga of the Bounty: Its Strange History as Related by the Participants Themselves.* New York: Putnam, 1935.
    This popular volume, reprinted several times (and as a paperback tie-in with the 1962 film *Mutiny on the Bounty*) must be approached with caution. It collects extracts from a wide range of authentic documents, including *The Journal of John Fryer* and *The Journal of James Morrison*, but includes one of the fraudulent *Letters from Mr. Fletcher Christian*. The editor's note to this section (Chapter XII), states, "May I remind the reader that Fletcher Christian aimed to tell his story here, yet hide the location of the wrecked *Bounty*, so that his companions might live securely on Pitcairn Island."
(Barrow, Sir John.) *The Mutiny and Piratical Seizure of H.M.S. Bounty.* London: Folio Society, 1976.
_____. *The Mutiny and Piratical Seizure of H.M.S. Bounty.* London: Oxford University Press, 1914.
_____. *The Mutiny of the Bounty.* Boston: David R. Godine, 1980.
_____. *Mutiny! The Real History of the* H.M.S. Bounty. New York: Cooper Square Press, 2003.
    See Chapter 2 for details of these editions of Sir John Barrow's *The Eventful History of the Mutiny and Piratical Seizure of H.M.S. Bounty.*
_____. *The Mutiny of the 'Bounty.'* Illustrated by Nigel Lambourne. London and Glasgow: Blackie and Son, 1961.
    See Chapter 5 for details.
Beaglehole, J. C. *Captain Cook and William Bligh: The Dr. W. E. Collins Lecture Delivered at the University on 3 August 1967.* Wellington: Victoria University of Wellington, 1967.
    This lecture by the preeminent biographer of Captain James Cook ponders how Bligh and Cook, who had so many traits in common, could have ended up with such different reputations. Both were great explorers, courageous navigators, short-tempered officers and "exceedingly humane men, careful of the lives of those who served under them." Why is Cook's memory revered, while most people associate Bligh with tyranny?
F. W. Beechey, R.N. *Narrative of a Voyage to the Pacific and Beerings Strait, to Co-operate with the Polar Expeditions: Performed in His Majesty's Ship Blossom, Under the Command of Captain F. W. Beechey, R.N. F.R.S. &c. In the Years 1825, 26, 27, 28.* New York: Da Capo Press, 1968.
    A two-volume, complete facsimile edition of F.W. Beechey's famous voyage. See Chapter 2 for a full discussion of this important work.
Bligh, William. *An Account of the Mutinous Seizure of the Bounty.* Guildford: Genesis Publications, 1987
See Chapter 1 for details.
_____. *The Log of H.M.S. Bounty, 1787–89.* Guildford: Genesis Publications, 1975.
    See Chapter 1 for details.
_____. *The Log of H.M.S. Providence 1791–1793.* Surrey: Genesis Publications, 1976.

        See Chapter 1 for details.
_____. *Narrative of the Mutiny on Board His Majesty's Ship the Bounty.* Philadelphia: Franklin Court, 1977.
        See Chapter 1 for details.
_____. *A Narrative of the Mutiny on Board His Majesty's Ship* Bounty. Sydney: The Library Shop, 1991.
        See Chapter 1 for details.
_____. *A Narrative of the Mutiny on Board His Majesty's Ship* Bounty ... *Minutes of the Court-Martial ... Bligh's Answer to Certain Assertions ... Edward Christian's Short Reply.* Melbourne: Georgian House 1952, for The Australiana Society. Limited to 1,000 copies.
        See Chapter 1 for details.
_____. *A Voyage To The South Sea.* Honolulu: Rare Books, n.d.
_____. *A Voyage To The South Sea.* Richmond: Hutchinson of Australia, 1979. Facsimile edition.
_____. *A Voyage to the South Sea.* Edited by Robert Bowman. Gloucester: Alan Sutton Publishing, 1981.
        See Chapter 1 for details of these three titles.

Bligh, William and Edward Christian. *The Bounty Mutiny.* Introduction by R. D. Madison. New York: Penguin Books, 2001.
        See Chapter 1 for details.

Bowker, R. M., and William Bligh. *Mutiny!! Aboard H. M. Armed Transport* 'Bounty,' *in 1789.* Old Bosham, Sussex, England: Bowker and Bertram, 1978.
        See Chapter 1 for details.

Brodie, Walter. *Pitcairn's Island and the Islanders in 1850.* New York: AMS Press, 1980. Facsimile edition.
        See Chapter 2 for details.

Brunton, Paul, ed. *Awake, Bold Bligh! William Bligh's Letters Describing the Mutiny on HMS Bounty.* Honolulu: University of Hawaii Press, 1989.
        Three of Bligh's personal letters to family and friends, written after his arrival in Timor, are reproduced here in facsimile for the first time, with a full introduction and notes.

Clarke, Peter. *Hell and Paradise: The Norfolk-Bounty-Pitcairn Saga.* New York: Viking Penguin, 1986. Also published in an edition limited to 275 copies, signed by the author and descendants of *Bounty* mutineers.
        As a resident of Norfolk Island, where many descendants of *Bounty* mutineers live to this day, Peter Clarke brings a special perspective to this beautifully illustrated volume — one of the most attractive published on the subject to date. Although many people are well acquainted with the *Bounty* mutiny and Pitcairn Island, the story of Norfolk Island is far less familiar. Norfolk has a notorious history of once being, as stated on the dust jacket, "The world's most abominable penal colony." Clarke's well written volume provides a broad account of Norfolk Island's history and its relationship to the *Bounty*/Pitcairn Saga.
        Also see Clarke's article "Norfolk Island" in *National Geographic Traveler.*

Delano, Amasa. *Delano's Voyages of Commerce and Discovery. Amasa Delano in China, the Pacific Islands, Australia, and South America, 1789–1807.* Stockbridge, Massachusetts: Berkshire House Publishers, 1994.
        See Chapter 2 for details.

Dening, Greg. *Mr. Bligh's Bad Language: Passion, Power And Theatre on the Bounty.* Cambridge: Cambridge University Press, 1992.
        Mr. Bligh's Bad Language is one of the more original books written on the *Bounty* Saga in recent years. Greg Dening interprets the mutiny in its historical and cultural context, explaining how the events became a "mythology" that is still being written and filmed. Not everyone will agree with his conclusions, but this is a fresh, fascinating volume.

Fryer, John. *The Voyage of the Bounty Launch: John Fryer's Narrative.* Guildford: Genesis Publications, 1979.
        See Chapter 1 for details.

Gesner, Peter. *Pandora: An Archaeological Perspective.* South Brisbane: Queensland Museum, 1991. Revised edition published in 2000.
        Bounty Saga enthusiasts across the globe were thrilled when, in 1977, the wreck of *Pandora* was discovered off the eastern coast of Australia. A continuing series of excavations by the Queensland Museum has yielded a great many artifacts, including the ship's stove, Captain Edward

Edwards' dinner service, and Surgeon George Hamilton's pocket watch and medical equipment. *Pandora: An Archaeological Perspective* is a well-photographed summary of discoveries up to 2000. Also see Luis Marden's "Finding the Wreck of H.M.S. *Pandora*."

Hall, James Norman. *The Tale of a Shipwreck: Adventures in the Wake of the Bounty.* Boston: Houghton Mifflin Co., 1934. Illustrations by W. Alister Macdonald.

_____. *Shipwreck: An Account of a Voyage in the Track of the* Bounty *from Tahiti to Pitcairn Island in 1933.* London: Chapman and Hall, 1935.

The Tale of a Shipwreck first appeared as *From Med to Mum*, a five-part serial in *Atlantic Monthly*, from March to July, 1934. It describes Hall's first visit to Pitcairn Island on the schooner *Pro Patria*, which nearly ended in disaster. On the return voyage, he and a crew of 17 were shipwrecked on an uninhabited coral island.

As the dust jacket copy states, "There followed a reproduction in miniature of Captain Bligh's experience described in 'Men Against the Sea.'" Although they did not experience the rigors and suffering faced by Bligh and his men, Hall's tale of his voyage in a small vessel is stirring. *The Tale of a Shipwreck* also includes a vivid account of his stay on Pitcairn Island.

Kennedy, Gavin. *Bligh.* London: Gerald Duckworth and Co., 1978.

_____. *Captain Bligh: the Man and his Mutinies.* London: Gerald Duckworth and Co., 1989.

These two volumes are the most comprehensive, up-to-date biographies of William Bligh written since George Mackaness's *Life of Vice-Admiral William Bligh*. Gavin Kennedy builds on Mackaness's achievements by considering important recent scholarship, and documents that have come to light since the 1930s — especially the letters of John and Francis Godolphin Bond. (*See* Chapter 2 for a discussion of these documents.) Kennedy's books are balanced, comprehensive and very readable.

McKay, John. *The Armed Transport Bounty.* Annapolis: Naval Institute Press, 1989. Anatomy of the Ship Series.

_____. *The Armed Transport Bounty.* London: Conway Maritime Press, 2002. Revised edition.

_____, and Ron Coleman. *The 24-Gun Frigate Pandora 1779.* Cedarburg: Phoenix Publications, 1992.

These titles provide an incredible array of details about the construction of these two famous vessels. They are of special appeal to readers interested in shipbuilding and modeling. They are fully illustrated with line drawings and diagrams, and descriptions of masts, rigging, fittings, sails, armament and every other conceivable part of the *Bounty* and *Pandora*.

Michener, James A., and A. Grove Day. *Rascals in Paradise.* New York: Random House, 1957.

Bounty enthusiasts will find two chapters of interest in this highly readable discussion of Pacific adventurers: "Bligh, Man of Mutinies," and "Louis Becke, Adventurer and Writer."

H.S. Montgomerie. *William Bligh of the "Bounty" in Fact and in Fable.* London: Williams and Norgate, 1937.

H.S. Montgomerie's *William Bligh of the "Bounty" in Fact and in Fable*, written at a time when Bligh's character was being completely reevaluated, is one of the more comprehensive and "pro-Bligh" biographies. His account of Bligh's later naval career and his appointment as governor-general of Australia is especially thorough. The book includes an extensive set of useful appendices, chronological outline, and two foldouts: a map of the open boat voyage and a photograph of Bligh's Royal Naval commission as Admiral of the Blue.

Mutiny on the Bounty, 1789–1989. London: Manorial Research PLC, 1989.

See Chapter 5 for details.

Mutiny on the Bounty: The Story of Captain William Bligh, Seaman, Navigator, Surveyor and of the Bounty Mutineers. Sydney: Mitchell Library, 1991.

Mutiny on the Bounty: The Story of Captain William Bligh, Seaman, Navigator, Surveyor and of the Bounty Mutineers. Sydney: Rolf Harris Productions Pty Ltd in association with State Library of New South Wales Press, 1998.

See Chapter 5 for details.

Oliver, Douglas. *Return To Tahiti: Bligh's Second Breadfruit Voyage.* Honolulu: University of Hawaii Press, 1988.

Captain Bligh's Second Voyage to the South Sea by Ida Lee is a scarce collector's item, but Douglas Oliver's *Return To Tahiti: Bligh's Second Breadfruit Voyage* features the full text of the journal Bligh kept for three months in Tahiti, as well as selections from his fellow officers' journals. It also reproduces a number of George Tobin's watercolors, many of them in full color for the first time.

The dust jacket of Douglas Oliver's *Return to Tahiti: Bligh's Second Breadfruit Voyage*, features a watercolor of *Providence* and *Assistant* in Matavai Bay by George Tobin, who served as third lieutenant on the voyage. ©1988 by Melbourne University Press. Reprinted by permission of Melbourne University Press.

Rawson, Geoffrey. *Bligh of the 'Bounty.'* London: Philip Alan and Co., 1930.

_____. *Bligh of the 'Bounty.'* New York: George R. Gorman, n.d. Nautilus Library edition.

    The first full-length biography of William Bligh appeared just one year before the publication of George Mackaness's *Life of Vice-Admiral William Bligh*, which quickly superseded it. Rawson takes a generally impartial view of the Bligh vs. Christian controversy.

Ross, A. S. C. *The Pitcairnese Language.* New York: Oxford University Press, 1964.

    The descendants of *Bounty* mutineers living on Pitcairn and Norfolk Islands eventually developed unique spoken languages (slightly different from each other) that blend English and Tahitian. *The Pitcairnese Language* is a serious linguistic study of both "Pitcairnese" and "Norfolkese."

Rutter, Owen. *Turbulent Journey: A Life of William Bligh, Vice-Admiral of the Blue.* London: Ivor Nicholson and Watson, 1936.

    Owen Rutter is one of the primary figures in the 1930s "renaissance" of *Bounty* scholarship, so it is not surprising that he wrote one of the better, more balanced biographies of William Bligh, *Turbulent Journey*. Rutter maintains an admirable degree of objectiveness, always willing to recognize Bligh's vices and virtues: "So far from having the gift of winning popularity, his tactlessness and passionate temper were the bane of his career. But he had both physical and moral courage, and he was a fine seaman with an intense devotion to what he conceived to be his duty. Even those outbursts of passion, of which some writers have made so much, sprang from his professional zeal."

_____, ed. *The Court-Martial of the "Bounty" Mutineers.* Edinburgh and London: William Hodge and Company, 1931. Introduction and notes by Owen Rutter. Notable British Trials series. Reprinted in 1989 as part of the "Notable Trials Library," with an introduction by Alan M. Dershowitz.

    This essential volume includes the evidence for the defense from the *Bounty* court-martial, as well as Owen Rutter's extensive introduction, which covers the voyage, mutiny, open boat voyage and fate of the mutineers. (Stephen Barney's *Minutes of the Proceedings of the Court-Martial* includes only evidence for the prosecution.) Reading the actual language used during the court-martial is a riveting experience. Charles Nordhoff and James Norman Hall recognized that this language is inherently compelling, adapting some of it in *Mutiny on the Bounty*.

Schreiber, Roy E. *The Fortunate Adversities of William Bligh.* New York: Peter Lang, 1991.

_____. *The Fortunate Adversities of William Bligh.* Lincoln, Nebraska: iUniverse.com, Inc., 2000. Reprint.

    The *Bounty* mutiny occupies a fairly small portion of Roy E. Schreiber's biography of Bligh, but his account is lucid, summarizing the many theories and stressing the multiple factors that must have come into play. Like Sven Wahlroos in *Mutiny and Romance in the South Seas*, he emphasizes that Christian's honor as a gentleman was at stake when Bligh accused him of stealing coconuts: "To charge publicly the heir of Deemsters of the Isle of Man with being such a low-life was beyond endurance." Schreiber also suggests that the painful symptoms of venereal disease may have been a minor factor that affected Christian's general mood.

    The Fortunate Adversities of William Bligh also provides a succinct account of the campaign to ruin Bligh's reputation. Unfortunately, this book does not have an index.

Shapiro, Harry L. *The Heritage of the Bounty: the Story of Pitcairn through Six Generations.* New York: Simon and Schuster, 1936.

_____. *Heritage of the Bounty.* Garden City: Doubleday and Co., Inc., 1962. Revised with a new postscript.

_____. *The Pitcairn Islanders* (Formerly *The Heritage of the Bounty*) New York: Simon and Schuster, 1968. Revised with a new postscript.

    The Heritage of the Bounty is one of the seminal works on Pitcairn Island. Harry L. Shapiro approaches the subject primarily from anthropological and historical perspectives. His knowledge was first hand, having performed research on Pitcairn itself and throughout the South Pacific. Well-illustrated with photographs, it also has some useful appendices.

Articles

Alexander, Caroline. "Wreck of the *Pandora*: The Fate of the Men Sent to Hunt Down the *Bounty* Mutineers." *The New Yorker*, August 4, 2003, 44–59.

A preview of Alexander's *The* Bounty*: The True Story of the Mutiny on the* Bounty, this article is enjoyable reading as an independent work, with its own unique merits.

Amis, Peter. "The 'Bounty' Timekeeper." *Horological Journal* 99, no.1191 (December 1957): 760–70.

    The *Bounty* chronometer has a fascinating story that Peter Amis presents in this article. Amis also was charged with restoring the chronometer, and his article appeals to *Bounty* Saga enthusiasts, as well as horologists and those interested in the history of navigation. *Bounty*'s chronometer, also known as "K2," was modeled on John Harrison's fourth timekeeper. Harrison won a prize of £20,000 for creating the first timekeeper that could measure longitude to a highly accurate standard. His story is told in Dava Sobel's *Longitude: The True Story of a Lone Genius Who Solved the Greatest Scientific Problem of His Time.*

Bonner Smith, D. "Some Remarks about the Mutiny of the Bounty." *Mariner's Mirror* 22, no. 2 (April 1936): 200–237.

    D. Bonner Smith's extensive article discusses Sir John Barrow's *Eventful History of the Mutiny and Piratical Seizure of H.M.S. Bounty* and the "authorities" that Barrow consulted. It throws a great deal of light on Barrow's book, revealing inaccuracies, as well as hidden agendas — some of them responses to the publication of F.W. Beechey's *Narrative of a Voyage to the Pacific and Beerings Strait* in 1831. (See Chapter 2.)

Bonner Smith draws on *The Journal of James Morrison*, which had just been published by the Golden Cockerel Press, and includes a facsimile of *Bounty*'s crew complement, transcribed from the ship's Muster Book and Pay Book.

    For *Bounty* Saga enthusiasts, the April 1936 issue of *The Mariner's Mirror* is a rich source of information. In addition to "Some Remarks about the Mutiny of the Bounty," there are articles by Geoffrey Callender, Owen Rutter and C. Knight, accompanied by several portraits of Bligh and foldout, schematic drawings of the *Bounty* and her launch.

_____. "More Light on Bligh and the Bounty." *Mariner's Mirror* 23, no. 2 (April 1937): 210–228.

    This article appeared at a vital period in *Bounty* scholarship. D. Bonner Smith called 1936, "Bligh Year." New biographies of Bligh were appearing, as well as Lawrence Irving's *Bligh and the "Bounty,"* Owen Rutter's *The Court Martial of the "Bounty" Mutineers* and the Golden Cockerel Press' *Log of the Bounty*. Bonner Smith contributes to this list of important publications by presenting, with commentary, Edward Christian's *Appendix* to Stephen Barney's *Minutes of the Proceedings of the Court-Martial*— a particularly rare item that was not easily available in 1936.

Christian, Glynn. "Pitcairn's Revolutionary Women." *CANVAS* (*New Zealand Herald*'s Saturday magazine), October 2, 2004, pp. 14–16.

    Glynn Christian discusses how the Polynesian women who settled on Pitcairn Island with the mutineers shaped a society where, by 1838, a law was written guaranteeing "the right of all women to vote and that education for both boys and girls be both free and compulsory.... They had created a new ethnic group with unique ethics, language and culture and, now, unheard of rights. It was not the mutineers, but these Tahitian women who had the last laugh on the British."

Conrad, Barnaby. "What Happened to Mr. Christian of H.M.S. *Bounty*?" *Smithsonian*, (February 1988): 203–204.

    Conrad's beautifully illustrated feature article provides a basic overview of *Bounty*/Pitcairn history.

Darby, Madge. "Bligh's Disciple: Matthew Flinders' Journals of HMS *Providence* (1791–3)." *The Mariner's Mirror* 86, no. 4 (November 2000): 401–411.

    William Bligh's behavior during the second breadfruit voyage on *Providence* sheds a great deal of light on his personality and leadership. In this article, Madge Darby explores Matthew Flinders' account of the *Providence* voyage, as recorded in his journal. Flinders, who became one of Australia's great explorers, served as an officer on *Providence*.

_____. "The Crown and Sceptre Inn, Greenwich." *UK Log* no. 25 (January 2003): 28–30.

    Madge Darby neatly summarizes how Edward Christian conducted interviews at the Crown and Sceptre Inn following the court-martial, and provides useful information on the later whereabouts of Michael Byrne, Joseph Coleman and Lawrence Lebogue.

_____. "The Glorious First of June: An Account of the Battle by Peter Heywood." *Mariner's Mirror* 64, no. 4 (November 1978): 361–366.

    This article provides a glimpse into the successful naval career of Peter Heywood through a long letter that he wrote to his friend Isaac Littledale on June 13, 1794, describing this great sea battle between England and France. In addition to providing a detailed account of the fight, Heywood alludes to his near-drowning on *Pandora* when he describes the men who were wounded, and "who had been so unfortunate to receive Wounds in Action that rendered them unable to extricate themselves from the Jaws of a Death I know from Experience (as you know my dear Isaac I once all but felt it) to be of all others the most dreadful." Heywood's letter did not come to light until 1977.

Denman, Arthur. "Capt. Bligh and the Mutiny of the Bounty." *Notes and Queries,* 9th Series 12 (December 1903): 501–502.

This article prints, for the first time, extracts from several letters written by Thomas Ledward, who took over as Surgeon on H.M.S. *Bounty* following the death of Thomas Huggan in Tahiti.

Du Rietz, Rolf. "The Voyage of H.M.S. Pandora, 1790–1792: Some Remarks Upon Geoffrey Rawson's Book on the Subject." *Ethnos* 28 (1963): 210–218.

Rolf Du Rietz takes Geoffrey Rawson to task for ignoring a number of important publications when he wrote *Pandora's Last Voyage*. Although the book was published in 1963, it makes no reference to scholarship after the year 1938. Du Rietz is generally critical of the book, although he does admit that *Pandora's Last Voyage* is "vividly written."

Ford, Herbert. "The Mutiny's Cause: A New Analysis." *Pitcairn Log* 25 (October — December 1998): 8–10.

This intriguing article points out that on April 27, 1798, the day before the mutiny, William Bligh did not appear on deck before 12 noon — a highly unusual occurrence that John Fryer and James Morrison recorded in their respective journals. It was customary for a Royal Navy commander to appear at dawn and give his standing orders. Interestingly, Bligh never referred to his own absence. Later that day, he accused the crew and officers of stealing his coconuts, an incident that triggered the mutiny at 4 A.M. the following day.

Herbert Ford asks, "Why would a stern disciplinarian like Bligh fail to be on deck for the dawn lookout procedure, and not appear until midday? And why was he so radically out of sorts when he did appear, ranting as he did about the coconuts?" Ford documents the response of some naval officers to these questions. They opined that Bligh, "Had a staggering hang-over, and when he did at last appear on deck he had an almighty bad temper, and he took it out on his subordinates." Ironically, Christian may have been in a similar physical state the next morning, just before the mutiny.

Heydt, Bruce. "Mutiny!" *British Heritage* 10 (June/July 1989): 60–65.

Bruce Heydt's article, which alludes to the speculation that Bligh and Christian may have had a homosexual relationship, provoked a flurry of letters denouncing the theory in the following issue of *British Heritage*. The hypothesis was first developed in Madge Darby's *Who Caused the Mutiny on the Bounty* and expanded by Richard Hough in *Captain Bligh and Mr. Christian*. It remains controversial.

Johnson, Irving, and Electa Johnson. "The *Yankee's* Wander-world." *National Geographic Magazine,* January 1949, 1–50.

_____. "Westward Bound in the Yankee." *National Geographic Magazine,* January 1942, 1–44.

These articles describing the voyages of brigantine *Yankee*, filled with wonderful photographs, are of considerable interest to enthusiasts of 20th century Pitcairn Island, Tahiti and the South Seas in general. Also see Luis Marden's "Saga of a Ship, the *Yankee*," and the accounts published in book form.

Lacy, Gavin de. "Plagiarism on the Bounty." *The Mariner's Mirror* 83, no. 1 (February 1997): 671–673.

When *The Journal of James Morrison* was published in 1935, thanks to Owen Rutter and the Golden Cockerel Press, *Bounty* scholars immediately began to make use of this important primary material. Because the Morrison's observations often conflict with Bligh's own accounts of the *Bounty* voyage and mutiny, the *Journal*'s authenticity, date and place of composition continue to be points of controversy.

Gavin de Lacy's article contributes new information to consider: the possibility that some of Morrison's content may have been heavily influenced by his reading of John Hawkesworth's *An Account of the Voyages Undertaken by the Order of His present Majesty for Making Discoveries in the Southern Hemisphere*, early editions of *Encyclopaedia Britannica* and other contemporary sources of information on the South Pacific.

The Morrison controversy has been going on for some time. The discussion has played out in H.S. Montgomerie's biography of Bligh, *William Bligh of the "Bounty" in Fact and in Fable,* his

The Morrison Myth: Pendant to William Bligh of the Bounty in Fact and in Fable and in two articles by Montgomerie and Ida Leeson, both entitled "The Morrison Myth" and published in *The Mariner's Mirror.*

Lyman, John. "*Pitcairn*, Missionary Packet." *American Neptune* 11, no. 3 (July 1951): 203–208.

After briefly discussing the South Sea travels of the Seventh-day Adventist Church, John Lymam provides numerous technical details about the construction of *Pitcairn*, the Church's missionary schooner. This famous vessel made six missionary voyages, each one with a stop at Pitcairn Island. Most Pitcairners have been members of the Seventh-day Adventist Church since 1890.

Additional information about *Pitcairn* and its missionary voyages is available in Alta Hilliard Christensen's *Heirs of Exile: the Story of Pitcairn Island, Paradise of the Pacific*, Sadie Engen's *John Tay, Messenger to Pitcairn* and the periodicals *Review and Herald, Pacific Union Recorder, Missionary Magazine,* and *San Francisco Morning Call.*

Marden, Luis. "I Found the Bones of the *Bounty*." *National Geographic Magazine,* December 1957, 725–789.

_____. "Finding the Wreck of H.M.S. *Pandora*." *National Geographic Magazine,* October 1985, 422–551.

_____. "The Friendly Isles of Tonga." *National Geographic Magazine*, March 1968, 345–367.

_____. "The Islands Called Fiji." *National Geographic Magazine,* October 1958, 526–561.

_____. "A New *Bounty* Sails to Tahiti." *National Geographic Magazine,* April 1962, 435–459.

_____. "Saga of a Ship, the *Yankee*." *National Geographic Magazine,* February 1966, 263–269.

_____. "Tahiti, "Finest Island in the World." *National Geographic Magazine*, July 1962, 1–48.

Luis Marden, who passed away in 2003, was one of *National Geographic Magazine*'s finest writer/photographers. He had a passionate interest in the *Bounty* Saga, and his *National Geographic* articles, published over a span of several decades, are outstanding examples of "on location" research and photography.

All of Marden's articles are required reading for *Bounty* enthusiasts, but "I Found the Bones of the *Bounty*," is especially noteworthy. It's a beautifully photographed narrative of the *Bounty* / Pitcairn story, as well as a record of Marden's successful expedition to find the remains of the *Bounty*. It also is an unforgettable pictorial record of life on Pitcairn Island in the 1950s.

Other *National Geographic Magazine* articles of interest are Ed Howard's "Pitcairn and Norfolk: The Saga of Bounty's Children," and T. C. Roughley's "Bounty Descendants Live on Remote Norfolk Island."

Maude, H. E. "The Edwards Papers." *Journal of Pacific History* 1 (1966): 184–185.

_____. "In Search of a Home: From the Mutiny to Pitcairn Island (1789–1790)." *Journal of the Polynesian Society* 67, no. 2 (June 1958): 106–116.

In "The Edwards Papers," H. E. Maude recounts the discovery of the log that Captain Edward Edwards kept during the *Pandora* voyage. It includes extracts from the journals of Peter Heywood and George Stewart, whose original journals were lost when *Pandora* sank off the Great Barrier Reef. This new information, supplemented by James Morrison's *Journal* and the accounts of Teehuteatuaonoa ("Jenny"), allowed Maude to reconstruct the wanderings of the *Bounty* after the mutiny. He provides a detailed account of their adventures on Tubai and Tahiti, and makes a convincing case that they discovered Rarotonga before settling on Pitcairn Island.

_____. "The Voyage of Pandora's Tender." *The Mariner's Mirror* 50, no. 3 (August 1964): 217–235.

One of the many intriguing tales that comprise the *Bounty* Saga concerns *Resolution*, the schooner constructed by James Morrison and several of the mutineers on Tahiti. She was rechristened *Matavy* after Captain Edward Edwards appropriated the vessel and refitted it as a tender for *Pandora*. *Matavy* disappeared off the Samoan Islands during Edwards' search for Fletcher Christian. Four months later, after the wreck of *Pandora*, Edwards discovered that it had made landfall in the Dutch East Indies. He presented the sturdy vessel to the Governor of Timor as thanks for taking such good care of *Pandora*'s crew after their grueling open-boat voyage.

H.E. Maude's article presents an account of *Matavy*'s four-month voyage written by Midshipman David T. Renouard. The actual ship's log has never come to light, but Renouard's narrative is, as Maude writes, "A very human narrative of adventure at sea, worth reading for its own sake." Following the publication of "The Voyage of Pandora's Tender," several articles discussing the adventures and fate of *Matavy* appeared in *The Mariner's Mirror*, by Andrew C.F. David, Alan Reid and

G.A. Rogers. They are required reading for those intrigued by this facet of the *Bounty* Saga.

Oster, Gerald, and Semalree Oster. "The Great Breadfruit Scheme." *Natural History* 94 (March 1985): 34–41.

    Food and drink, including tea, coffee and spices, have played major roles throughout history. The discovery of breadfruit eventually led to the voyages of the *Bounty* and *Providence*. The authors of this article include information on breadfruit's nutritional value and how it is prepared by the Polynesians.

Rutter, Owen. "The Vindication of Captain Bligh." *Quarterly Review* 261, no. 518 (October 1933): 279–291.

    In this lengthy review of G. C. Henderson's *The Discoverers of the Fiji Islands*, Owen Rutter takes the opportunity to emphasize the more positive aspects of Bligh's character, although he does concede, "Bligh was a truculent, irascible, overbearing fellow."

Wahlroos, Sven. "HMS *Bounty*: The Bloodless Mutiny." *Pacific Islands Monthly* 59 (April/May 1989): 54.

    In this essay, published on the 200th anniversary of the *Bounty* mutiny, Dr. Wahlroos discusses key events that occurred prior to the mutiny, such as Bligh calling Christian a "cowardly rascal" at the island of Nomuka and, of course, the infamous "coconut" incident. Dr. Wahlroos stresses, as he does in the revised edition of *Mutiny and Romance in the South Seas*, the importance of honor in the late 18th century: "A gentleman simply did not call another a coward: in England, the insult could well have resulted in a duel."

_____. "What Caused the Mutiny on the Bounty? Separating Fact From Speculation." *British Heritage* 24 (January 2003): 19–25.

    In a follow-up to his article in *Pacific Islands Monthly*, Sven Wahlroos makes a convincing case that "Neither Bligh nor Christian caused the mutiny. It was their interaction, combined with several other lesser but contributing factors, which caused the mutiny." These factors include the value placed on the *taio* friendship experienced by the crew on Tahiti, the possibility that Fletcher Christian suffered from borderline personality disorder, and, perhaps above all, Christian's sense of honor, severely wounded by Bligh's behavior.

Zerega, Nyree J. C. "The Breadfruit Trail." *Natural History* 112 (December 2003/January 2004): 46–51.

    Explores the origins of breadfruit, its propagation, and how it is associated with population migrations throughout the Pacific.

Supplemental Bibliography

Books

Allen, Kenneth S. *Sea Captains and Their Ships*. London: Odhams Books, 1965.

Allen, P. S. *Stewart's Handbook of the Pacific Islands* (Annual). Sydney: McCarron, Stewart and Co., 1908–1923.

Armstrong, Warren. *Mutiny Afloat: A Dramatized Record of Some Famous Sea Mutinies*. London: Frederick Muller, 1956.

Askew, John. *Guide to Cockermouth*. Cockermouth: Isaac Evening, 1872. Reprinted in 2000 by The Printing House, Cockermouth.

Aston, Paul. *True Sea Stories*. London: Constable and Robinson, 1997.

Aymar, Gordon C. *A Treasury of Sea Stories*. Illustrations by Rockwell Kent. New York: A.S. Barnes, 1948.

Baarslag, Karl. *Islands of Adventure*. New York: Farrar and Rinehart, 1940.

Badger, Geoffrey. *The Explorers of the Pacific*. Kenthurst: Kangaroo Press, 1988.

Barclay, Ian. *The Bounty Bible*. Hildenborough: Bishopsgate Press, 1993.

Barrett, Charles. *The Island World: An Anthology of the Pacific*. London: Oxford University Press, 1944.

_____, ed. *The Pacific: Ocean of Islands*. Melbourne: N. H. Seward, n.d. (1950).

(Barrow, Sir John). *The Eventful History of the Mutiny of the Bounty. A Description of Pitcairn's Island and Its Inhabitants. With an Authentic Account of the Mutiny of the Ship Bounty, and of the Subsequent Fortunes of the Mutineers*. New York: Harper and Brothers, 1936.

_____. *A Description of Pitcairn Island and its Inhabitants: With an Authentic Account of the Mutiny of the Ship Bounty.* New York: Haskell House Publishers, 1972.
Beach, Susan Hicks. (Susan Christian). *The Yesterdays Behind The Door: A Family Biography.* Liverpool: Liverpool University Press, 1956.
Beaglehole, J. C. *The Exploration of the Pacific.* London: Adam and Charles Black, 1934.
_____. *The Life of Captain James Cook.* London: Adam and Charles Black, 1974.
Beeching, Jack. *An Open Path: Christian Missionaries, 1515–1914.* London: Hutchinson and Co., 1979.
Benton, Tim, and Tom Spencer. *The Pitcairn Islands: Biogeography, Ecology and Prehistory.* London: Academic Press, 1995.
Bligh, J. H. *Vice Admiral William Bligh FRS: A Biography.* Rochester: John Bligh, 2001.
Bligh, William. *Mutiny on the H.M.S. Bounty.* Retold by Kenton K. Smith. Ashland: Landoll, Inc., n.d. (1995).
_____. *The Mutiny on Board H.M.S. Bounty.* West Haven: Academic Industries, 1984.
_____. *The Mutiny on Board H.M.S. Bounty.* Adapted by Deborah Kestel. New York: Baronet Books, n.d. (1992).
_____. *The Mutiny on Board H. M. Bounty.* Introduction by N. R. Teitel. New York: Airmont Publishing Co., 1965. Airmont Classic edition.
_____. *The Mutiny on Board H.M.S. Bounty.* Afterword by Milton Rugoff. New York: New American Library of World Literature, 1961. Signet Classic edition.
_____. *The Mutiny on Board H.M.S. Bounty.* Santa Barbara, California: The Narrative Press, 2003.
_____. *The Mutiny on Board H.M.S. Bounty 1789.* London and Melbourne: Pageminster Press/Argot Press, 1981.
_____. *A Narrative of the Mutiny on Board His Majesty's Ship* Bounty. Ann Arbor: University Microfilms International, 1985. Authorized facsimile printed by microfilm/xerography on acid-free paper.
_____. *Mutiny on the "Bounty."* Vercelli, Italy: White Star Publishers, 2006.
Bonham, W., and F. C. and Sons. "William Bligh and the Bounty Mutineers: the Property of Angela and Stephen Walters." London: W. and F.C. Bonham & Sons, Ltd., 1996. Auction catalog.
Bowley, Robert. *In Search of Truth: A New Version of the Episodes Leading Up to, During and Following the Mutiny on The Bounty.* Peterborough: Rebel Publishing, 1995.
Brady, Cyrus Townsend. *Sea Stories.* Boston: Hall and Locke Co., 1902.
Bullocke, J. G. *Sailors' Rebellion: A Century of Naval Mutinies.* London: Eyre and Spottiswoode, 1938.
Calderon, George. *Tahiti.* New York: Harcourt, Brace and Co., 1922.
Cameron, Hector C. *Sir Joseph Banks.* London: Batchworth Press, 1952.
Cameron, Ian. *Lost Paradise: The Exploration of the Pacific.* Topsfield: Salem House Publishers, 1987.
Campbell, A. B. *Yarns of the Seven Seas.* London: Sir Isaac Pitmans and Sons, 1940.
Carlsson, Susanne Chauvel. *Pitcairn: Island at the Edge of Time.* Rockhampton: Central Queensland University Press, 2000.
Carter, R. M. *The Geology of Pitcairn Island, South Pacific Ocean.* Honolulu: Bishop Museum Press, 1967.
Casey, Robert J. *Easter Island: Home of the Scornful Gods.* Indianapolis: Bobbs-Merril, 1931.
Chambers, Leanne, and Merval Hoare, eds. *Thomas Stewart's Journal: Norfolk Island 1855: Waiting for the Pitcairn Islanders.* North Geelong: Pearce Printing and Publishing, 1992.
Chandler, J. E. (Jess Eric). *Beloved, Respected and Lamented: A Story of the Mutiny of the Bounty.* Marlborough: J. E. Chandler, 1973.
Chatterton, E. Keble. *Seamen All.* Boston: Little, Brown and Co., 1924.
Christensen, Alta Hilliard. *Heirs of Exile: the Story of Pitcairn Island, Paradise of the Pacific.* Washington, D.C.: Review and Herald Publishing Association, 1955.
Christian, Glynn. "Tubai: Fort George Revisited." *The UK Log* no. 33 (January 2007): 16–17.
Christian-Bailey, B. E. *The Pitcairn Tradition on Norfolk Island: A Lecture.* Norfolk Island, n.d. (1969)
Claver, Scott. *Under the Lash: A History of Corporal Punishment in the British Armed Forces.* London: Torchstream Books, 1954.
Clement, Russell T. *Mutiny on the Bounty. An Exhibition Commemorating the Two-Hundredth Anniversary of the Mutiny.* Provo: Friends of the Brigham Young University Library, 1989.

Clune, Frank. *Journey to Pitcairn.* Sydney: Angus and Robertson, 1966.
_____. *The Norfolk Island Story.* Sydney: Angus and Robertson, 1967.
Conrad, Winston Stuart. *Fabled Isles of the South Seas, with Insights by Literary Greats.* Introduction by James Michener. San Francisco: Wild Coconuts Publishing Co., 1997.
Conway, Christiane. *Letters from the Isle of Man, The Bounty Correspondence of Nessy and Peter Heywood.* Onchan (Isle of Man): 2005.
Cook, Judith. *"To Brave Every Danger:" The Epic Life of Mary Bryant of Fowey.* London: Macmillan, 1993.
Coombe, Florence. *School Days in Norfolk Island.* London: Society for Promoting Christian Knowledge, 1909.
Cooper, Gordon. *Isles of Romance and Mystery.* London: Lutterworth Press, 1949.
Copplestone, B. *The Boat Voyage of Bounty Bligh.* Oxford: Blackwell, 1925.
Couper, J. M. *The Book of Bligh.* Carlton: Melbourne University Press, 1969.
Cox, Philip, and Wesley Stacey. *Building Norfolk Island.* Sydney: Thomas Nelson, 1971.
Currey, C. H. *The Transportation, Escape and Pardoning of Mary Bryant (neé Broad).* Sydney: Angus and Robertson, 1963.
Currey, John, ed. *Australian Sea Stories.* North Melbourne: Cassell Australia, 1972. Illustrated by Don Angus.
Danielsson, Bengt. *Love in the South Seas.* London: George Allen and Unwin, 1956.
Darby, Madge. *Captain Bligh in Wapping.* N.p.: History of Wapping Trust, 1990.
_____. "Lieutenants' Passing Certificates: Peter Heywood." *The Mariner's Mirror* 87, no. 2 (May 2001): 227.
_____. Lieutenants' Passing Certificates: William Bligh and Peter Heywood." *The Mariner's Mirror* 86, no. 2 (May 2000): 197–199.
_____. *William Peckover of Wapping: Gunner of the* Bounty. N.p.: History of Wapping Trust, 1989.
David, Andrew C. F. *The Surveyors of the Bounty: a Preliminary Study of the Hydrographic Surveys of William Bligh, Thomas Hayward and Peter Heywood and the Charts Published From Them.* Taunton: Hydrographic Department, 1982.
_____. "The Surveys of William Bligh." *The Mariner's Mirror* 63, no. 1. (February 1977): 69–70.
_____, ed. *The Voyage of H.M.S. Herald to Australia and the South-west Pacific 1852–1861 Under the Command of Captain Henry Mangles Denham.* Carlton: Melbourne University Press, 1995.
Davidson, Louis B., and Eddie Doherty. *Strange Crimes at Sea.* New York: Thomas Y. Crowell, 1954.
_____. *Strange Crimes at Sea.* New York: Grosset and Dunlap, 1966. Reprint.
Davies, K., and K. A. Davies. *Old Norfolk Town: The Past in Pictures.* Norfolk Island: K. and K. A. Davies, n.d. (1980).
Day, A. Grove. *Adventurers of the Pacific.* New York: Meridith Press, 1969.
_____. *The Lure of Tahiti.* Honolulu: Pacific Trade Group, 1988.
_____. *Rogues of the South Seas.* Honolulu: Mutual Publishing LLC, 1986.
Day, A. Grove, and Carl Stroven, Eds. *True Tales of the South Seas.* New York: Souvenir Press, 1966.
Dening, Greg. *The Bounty: An Ethnographic History.* Parkville: University of Melbourne, 1988.
Divine, David. *Six Great Sailors: Howard of Effingham, Blake, Morgan, Bligh, Keyes, Ramsey.* London: Hamish Hamilton, 1955.
Dodge, Ernest S. *Beyond the Capes: Pacific Explorations from Captain Cook to the* Challenger. Boston: Little, Brown and Co., 1971.
Dugan, James. *The Great Mutiny.* New York: G. P. Putnam's Sons, 1965.
Duke, Mary-Lorraine. *Tale of Two Islands.* Norfolk Island: Tern Publications, n.d. (1991).
Dunphy, Jocelyn. "Insurrection and Repression: Bligh's 1790 Narrative of the Mutiny on Board H.M.S. Ship Bounty," in *Reading, Writing, Revolution: Proceedings of the Essex Conference on the Sociology of Literature, July 1981,* ed. Francis Barker et al., 281–301. Colchester: University of Essex, 1982.
DuRietz, Rolf E. *The Bias of Bligh.* Uppsala: Dahlia Books, 2003.
_____. *Fresh Light on John Fryer of the "Bounty." Banksia 2.* Uppsala: Dahlia Books, 1981. Limited edition of 250 copies.
_____. *Peter Heywood's Tahitian Vocabulary and the Narrative by James Morrison: Some Notes on their Origin and History. Banksia 3.* Uppsala: Dahlia Books, 1986. Limited edition of 250 copies.
_____. *Thoughts on the Present State of Bligh Scholarship. Banksia 1.* Uppsala: Dahlia Books, 1979. Limited edition of 250 copies.

Dyall, Valentine. *A Flood of Mutiny.* London: Hutchinson of London, 1957.
Edgecombe, Jean. *Norfolk Island—South Pacific: Island of History and Many Delights.* Thornleigh: J. M. Edgecombe, 1991.
Edmond, Rod. *Representing the South Pacific: Colonial Discourse from Cook to Gauguin.* Cambridge, U.K.; New York: Cambridge University Press, 1997.
Edwards, Kenneth F., and Adrian Small. *A Voyage to New South Wales: The Journal of the Master of H. M. A. V. Bounty, 1987–1988.* Melbourne: Australia Post, 1988.
Edwards, Philip. *The Story of the Voyage.* Cambridge: Cambridge University Press, 2004.
Edwards, Roselyn. *Mutineer: The Story of Pitcairn Island.* Nashville: Southern Publishing Association, 1975.
Elizabeth Bligh. Hampshire: William Bligh Trust, 1989.
Engen, Sadie. *John Tay, Messenger to Pitcairn.* Mountain View: Pacific Press Publishing Association, 1981. Illustrations by Robert Hunt.
Ernst, Pauline Fargher. *Book Relics from H.M.S. Bounty; Comprised of Two Monographs: History of Two Bibles from H.M.S. Bounty and History Behind 'Relics of the Book Kind' from H.M.S. Bounty.* Mountain View: Ernst Associates in Graphics, 1993.
Evatt, Herbert Vere. *Rum Rebellion: A Study of the Overthrow of Governor Bligh by John Macarthur and the New South Wales Corps.* Sydney: Angus and Robertson, 1938.
"Exploration and Travel, including the Bligh Relics." London: Christie's International UK, 2002. Auction catalog.
Famous Islands and Memorable Voyages. Boston: D. Lothrop and Co., n.d.
Ferdon, Edwin N. Jr. *One Man's Log.* London: George Allen and Unwin, 1966.
_____. *Early Tahiti: As the Explorers Saw It 1767–1797.* Tucson: University of Arizona Press, 1981.
Ferrell, Vance. *Beyond Pitcairn.* Altamont: Pilgrims' Books, 1984.
Ferris, Norman. *The Story of Pitcairn Island.* Washington, D.C.: Review and Herald Publishing Association, 1957.
Fitzgerald, Ross, and Mark Hearn. *Bligh, Macarthur and the Rum Rebellion.* Kenthurst: Kangaroo Press, 1988.
Fogle, Ben. *The Teatime Islands.* London: Michael Joseph, 2003.
Ford, Herbert. *Island of Tears: John I. Tay and the Story of Pitcairn.* Boise: Pacific Press Publishing Association, 1990.
_____. *The Miscellany of Pitcairn's Island.* Mountain View: Pacific Press Publishing Association, 1980.
_____. *Pitcairn.* La Verne: El Camino Press, 1972.
French, Joseph Lewis, ed. *Great Sea Stories.* New York: Tudor Publishing Co., 1944.
Frost, Alan. *Sir Joseph Banks and the Transfer of plants to and from the South Pacific, 1786–1798.* Melbourne: Colony Press, 1993.
Fullerton, W. Y. *The Romance of Pitcairn Island.* London: Carey Press, 1923.
Furnas, J. C. *Anatomy of Paradise.* New York: W. Sloane Associates, 1948.
Gambier, J. W. *Links In My Life on Land and Sea.* New York: E. P. Dutton and Co., 1906.
Gazzard, Albert S. *The Bounty and After: a Short History of the Descendants of the Mutineers of the "Bounty."* Norfolk Island: Albert S. Gazzard, 1983.
Gessler, Clifford. *The Leaning Wind.* New York: Appleton-Century Co., 1943.
Giblin, R. W. *The Early History of Tasmania.* London: Methuen and Co., 1928.
Gordon, Jeremy. *A Portrait of Fletcher Christian and Pitcairn Island Landscapes.* Workington: Jeremy Gordon, 1994.
Gothesson, Lars-Ake. *Plants of the Pitcairn Islands: Including Local Names and Uses.* Sydney: Centre for South Pacific Studies, University of New South Wales, 1997.
Gough, Barry M., ed. *To the Pacific and Arctic with Beechey: The Journal of Lieutenant George Peard of H.M.S. 'Blossom,' 1825–28.* Cambridge: Published for the Hakluyt Society at the University Press, 1973.
Grant, James Shaw. *Morrison of the Bounty: A Scotsman: Famous but Unknown.* Stornoway: Acair, 1997.
Green, Terence M. *Children of the Rainbow.* Toronto: McClelland and Stewart, 1992.
A Guide to Pitcairn. Suva: 1963. Revised and reprinted, 1970, 1976, 1982, 1990, 1999.
Gunson, Niel, ed. *The Changing Pacific: Essays in Honour of H. E. Maude.* Oxford: Oxford University Press, 1978.
Guttridge, Leonard F. *Mutiny: A History of Naval Insurrection.* Annapolis: Naval Institute Press, 1992.

Hamilton, A.G. *The Restless Wind*. Edinburgh and London: William Blackwood and Sons, 1961.
Hamilton, Bruce J. *The Bligh Museum of Pacific Exploration, Adventure Bay*. Adventure Bay: Tasmania the Museum, 1956.
Hancock, W. K. *Politics in Pitcairn, and Other Essays*. London: Macmillan and Co., 1947.
Hawkey, Arthur. *Bligh's Other Mutiny*. London: Angus and Robertson, 1975.
Hayes, Walter. *The Captain from Nantucket and the Mutiny on the Bounty: A recollection of Mayhew Folger, Mariner, who discovered the Last Mutineer and his Family on Pitcairn's Island: together with Letters and Documents Never Previously Published*. Ann Arbor: William L. Clements Library, 1996. Limited to 1500 copies, 500 enclosed in a slipcase and signed by the author.
Hearn, Bob. *Shipwrecked on Pitcairn: The Diary of Bob Hearn, September to November 1989*. Peacehaven: Bob Hearn, 2001.
Heinemann, J., and G. Heinemann, eds. *H.M.S. Bounty: A Selection of Texts*. N.p.: Pantheon, 1995.
Henderson, George C. *The Discoverers of the Fiji Islands: Tasman, Cook, Bligh, Wilson, Bellinghausen*. London: John Murray, 1933.
Hiller, R.S. *The Norfolk Island Book*. Norfolk Island: Anson Publications, 1984.
Hoare, Merval. *Norfolk Island: An Outline of Its History*. St. Lucia: University of Queensland Press, 1969.
_____. *Norfolk Island: An Outline of Its History. 1774–1977*. St. Lucia: University of Queensland Press, 1978.
_____. *The Winds of Change: Norfolk Island, 1950–1982*. Christchurch: Whitcoulls, 1983.
Hobbs, Raymond. *George Hunn Hobbs, 1799–1884: Chaplain on Pitcairn and Norfolk Island*. Norfolk Island: Pitcairn Descendants Society, 1984.
Hoehling, A. A. *Epics of the Sea*. Chicago: Contemporary Books, 1977.
Hook, Milton. *"Dame of the Deep: The Six Voyages of the Pitcairn."* N.p.: South Pacific Division Department of Education, n.d. (1990). No. 7 of the Seventh-day Adventist Heritage Series.
Hook, Taffy. *The Pitcairn Radio Station and its Postal History*. La Canada: Bounty Sagas, n.d.
Hough, Richard. *The Last Voyage of Captain James Cook*. New York: William Morrow, 1979.
_____. *The Murder of Captain Cook*. London: Macmillan, 1979.
Horwitz, Tony. *Blue Latitudes: Boldly Going Where Captain Cook has Gone Before*. New York: Henry Holt and Co., 2002.
Hughes, E. A., ed. *Bligh of the Bounty: Being The Narrative of the Mutiny of the Bounty and The Voyage in the Open Boat*. London: J. M. Dent and Sons, 1928.
Humble, Richard. *Captain Bligh*. London: Arthur Barker, 1976.
Huntress, Keith. *A Checklist of Narratives of Shipwrecks and Disasters at Sea to 1860, with Summaries, Notes and Comments*. Ames, Iowa: Iowa State University Press, 1979.
Hurd, Edith Thatcher. *The Course of the Wild Wave: to her Wreck Upon Oeno, of her Boat to Pitcairn, and of the John Adams to the Marquesas*. London: Oxford University Press, 1942.
Hymns of Pitcairn and Norfolk Islands. Published on occasion of the eighty-fifth anniversary of the establishment of the Seventh-day Adventist Church on Norfolk Island. N.p., n.d.
"Important Natural History Books, Travel and Atlases, including Bligh's Manuscript Account of his Voyage in the Bounty's Launch after the Mutiny." London: Christies, November 24, 1976. Auction catalog.
Introducing the British Pacific Islands. London: Her Majesty's Stationery Office, 1951.
"Island of Peace." *Living Age* 209 (May 23, 1896): 511–512.
Jackson, G. Gibbard. *Ships, Seas and Sailors*. London: Heath Cranton, 1933.
James, Naomi. *Courage at Sea*. London: Stanley Paul, 1987.
Johnson, Irving, and Electa Johnson. *Sailing to See: Picture Cruise in the Schooner* Yankee. New York: W. W. Norton and Co., 1939.
_____. *Westward Bound in the Schooner* Yankee. New York: W. W. Norton and Co., 1936.
_____. *Yankee's People and Places*. New York: W. W. Norton and Co., 1955.
_____. *The* Yankee's *Wander World*. New York: W. W. Norton and Co., 1949.
Joy, William. *The Exiles*. Sydney: Golden Press, 1983.
Kahlström, C. *I Sailed on the Pitcairn and other Stories*. Nashville: Southern Publishing Association, 1957.
Kennedy, Gavin. *The Death of Captain Cook*. London: Duckworth, 1978.
Kennedy, Ludovic, ed. *A Book of Sea Journeys*. London: Collins, 1981.

_____. *A Book of Sea Journeys.* New York: Rawson, Wade Publishers, 1981.

Kent, Graeme. *Co. of Heaven: Early Missionaries in the South Seas.* Wellington: A. H. and A. W. Reed, 1972.

Knowles, Josiah N. *The Crusoes of Pitcairn Island. Being an Account of the Wreck of the "Wild Wave" of Boston on Oeno Island in the Pacific, and the Subsequent Adventures of her Master and Crew on Pitcairn's Island as Related in the Diary of Captain Josiah Nickerson Knowles of Brewster.* Privately printed for Henry Sears Hoyt and J. King Hoyt, Jr., 1938. Limited to 100 copies.

_____. *Crusoes of Pitcairn Island: the Shipwreck Diary of Josiah N. Knowles, Master of the California Clipper Wild Wave.* Edited by Richard S. Dillon. Los Angeles: Glen Dawson, 1957. No. 38 of the Early California Travels Series. Limited to 250 copies.

Lamb, Jonathan, Vanessa Smith and Nicholas Thomas, Eds. *Exploration & Exchange: A South Seas Anthology.* Chicago: University of Chicago Press, 2000.

Lareau, Paul J. *The H.M.S. Bounty Genealogies.* St. Paul: Paul J. Lareau, 1992.

Laws of Pitcairn, Henderson, Ducie and Oeno Islands, 1971. N.p.: Government of the Islands of Pitcairn, Henderson, Ducie and Oeno Islands, 1971. Revised edition.

Langdon, Robert. "New Light on the 'Bounty' Mutiny: Lost 'Pandora' Logbook Turns Up in U.K. after 170 Years." *Pacific Islands Monthly* 36 (April 1965): 33–35.

_____. *Tahiti, Island of Love.* London: Cassell and Co., 1959.

Lee, Georgia. *Te Moana Nui: Exploring Lost Isles of the South Pacific.* Los Osos: Easter Island Foundation, 2001.

Lloyd, Christopher. *Mr. Barrow of the Admiralty.* London: Collins, 1970.

Loukakis, Angelo, and Gunther Deichmann. *Norfolk, an Island and its People.* Adelaide: Rigby Publishers, 1984.

MacDonald, A. C. *Discovery of Pitcairn Island—Mutiny of the Bounty—Life of the Mutineers on Pitcairn and their Removal to Norfolk Island.* Sydney: W. E. Smith, 1912.

Mackay, David. *In The Wake of Cook: Exploration, Science and Empire, 1780–1801.* New York: St. Martin's Press, 1985.

Marks, Percy. *Norfolk Island and the Bounty Mutiny.* Sydney: Harris and Son, 1935. Limited edition of 200 copies for private circulation.

Marrett, Barbara John Neal. *Mahine Tiare: Pacific Passages.* Friday Harbor: Pacific International Publishing, 1993.

Marrington, P. *In the Sweet Bye and Bye: Reminiscences of a Norfolk Islander.* Wellington: A. H. and A. W. Reed, 1981.

Marshall, David. *Breadfruit Buccaneers and the Bounty Bible.* Grantham: Stanborough Press, n.d. (1989). Foreword by Glynn Christian.

Marshall, James, and Carrie Marshall, compilers. *Pacific Voyages: Selections from* Scots Magazine, *1771–1808.* Portland: Binfords and Mort, 1960.

Maude, H. E. *In Search of a Home: From the Mutiny to Pitcairn Island (1789–1790).* Washington, D.C.: Smithsonian Institution, 1960.

_____. *Of Islands and Men: Studies in Pacific History.* London: Oxford University Press, 1968.

McGoogan, Ken. *Ancient Mariner.* New York: Carroll & Graf, 2004.

McGuffie, T. H. *Stories of Famous Mutinies.* London: Arthur Barker, 1966.

McKinney, Sam. *Bligh, the Whole Story of the Mutiny Aboard H.M.S. Bounty.* Victoria: Horsdal and Schubart Publishers, 1999.

Mercer, Brian. *An Island Education: A History of the Norfolk Island Public School (1856–1987).* Norfolk Island: Norfolk Island P and C Association, 1987.

Merrett, John. *Famous Voyages in Small Boats.* New York: Criterion, 1957.

Merrill, John. *"Old Glory" Driver.* New York: Vantage Press, 1956.

Mitchell, Carleton. *Beyond Horizons: Sea Adventure in the Age of Discovery.* London: William Kimber, 1953.

Mjelde, Michael Jay. *Glory of the Seas.* Middletown: Wesleyan University Press, 1970.

Montgomerie, H. S. *The Morrison Myth: Pendant to William Bligh of the Bounty in Fact and in Fable.* London and Woking: Unwin Brothers Ltd., 1938. Privately printed.

Montgomery, Helen Barrett. *Christus Redemptor: An Outline Study of the Island World of the Pacific.* New York: Macmillan Co., 1906.

Moore, A. W. *Manx Worthies or Biographies of Notable Manx Men and Women.* Douglas: S. K. Broadbent and Co., 1901.

_____. *Manx Worthies or Biographies of Notable Manx Men and Women.* Douglas: Manx Museum and National Trust, 1971. Facsimile edition.

_____. *Nessy Heywood.* Douglas: Brown and Sons, 1913.

Moorehead, Alan. *The Fatal Impact.* London: Hamish Hamilton, 1966.

Morris, Roger. *Pacific Sail: Four Centuries of Western Ships in the Pacific.* Southampton: Ashford, 1987.

Morton, Harry A. *The Wind Commands: Sailors and Sailing Ships in the Pacific.* Middletown: Wesleyan University Press, 1975.

Murchie, Jr., Guy. *The Mutiny of the Bounty and Other Sea Stories.* Chicago: Spencer Press, 1937.

_____. *The Mutiny of the Bounty and Other Sea Stories.* New York: Book League of America, Inc., 1939. Reprint.

Murray, Spencer. *The Five Neighbors of Pitcairn Island, Oeno, Henderson, Temoe, Ducie, Mangareva, with an Overview of Pitcairn Geology.* La Canada: Spencer Murray, 1993.

The Mutiny of the 'Bounty' with History of the Survivors on Pitcairn Island and Elsewhere. Hobart: J. Walch and Sons, 1936.

Mutiny on the Bounty: The Story of Captain William Bligh, Seaman, Navigator, Surveyor and of the Bounty Mutineers. New South Wales: Rolf Harris Productions, 1998.

Nackington, M. *With Bligh of the Bounty or From Tofoa to Timor.* London: Sheldon Press, n.d. (1932).

Neill, J. S. *Ten Years in Tonga.* London: Hutchinson and Co., 1955.

Nicholson, Joyce. *Man Against Mutiny: The Story of Vice-Admiral William Bligh.* London: Lutterworth Press, 1961.

Nicolson, Robert B. *The Pitcairners.* Sydney: Angus and Robertson, 1965.

Nixon, Dalkin R. *Colonial Era Cemetery of Norfolk Island.* Sydney: Pacific Publications, 1974.

Nobbs, Raymond. *George Hunn Nobbs 1799–1884: Chaplain on Pitcairn and Norfolk Island.* Norfolk Island: Pitcairn Descendants Society, 1984.

_____, ed. *Norfolk Island and its First Settlement, 1788–1814.* Sydney, 1988.

O'Brien, Frederick. *Atolls of The Sun.* New York: Century Co., 1923.

_____. *Mystic Isles of the South Seas.* New York: Century Co., 1921.

_____. *White Shadows in the South Seas.* New York: Century Co., 1919.

Palmer, Beryl Nobbs. *A Dictionary of Norfolk Words and Usages plus English-Norfolk Appendix.* Norfolk Island: B. N. Palmer, 1992.

Paluka, Frank. *The Three Voyages of Captain Cook.* Pittsburgh: Beta Phi Mu, 1974.

Parker, Everett L., ed. *The Pitcairn Anthology: A Quarter Century of* The Pitcairn Log. N.p.: Pitcairn Islands Study Group, 1998.

_____. *From Palm Trees to Antarctic Ice, The Byrd Expedition at Pitcairn Island, 1939.* Greenville, ME: Moosehead Publications, n.d.

Pearn, John, and Peggy Carter, eds. *Islands of Incarceration: Convict and Quarantine Islands of the Australian Coast.* Brisbane: Royal Children's Hospital, 1995.

Pears, Randolph. *Young Sea Dogs.* London: Putnam, 1960.

Petty, Jr., Thurman C. *The Wreck of the Wild Wave: The Untold Saga of Captain Knowles and Pitcairn Island.* Boise: Pacific Press Publishing Association, 1991.

_____, and Martha Petty. *Stories from Pitcairn Island.* N.p.: Pettyprint Original, 1989.

Pilling, H. G. *Report on A Visit To Pitcairn Island, 1929.* London: His Majesty's Stationery Office, 1930.

Pitcairn Hymns and Norfolk Favourites. Norfolk Island: Church of England, n.d.

Ramsden, Eric. *Strange Stories from the South Seas.* Wellington: A. H. and A. W. Reed, 1944.

_____. *The Strange Case of Mary Bryant.* London: Robert Hale, 1938.

_____. *The Strange Case of Mary Bryant.* New York: E.P. Dutton, 1939.

Reeman, Douglas. *Adventures on the High Seas: True Sea Stories from Captain Bligh to the Nautilus.* New York: Walker and Co., 1971.

Richards, Harold Marshall Sylvester, Jr. *Mutineers on Pitcairn Island.* Nashville: Southern Publishing Assoc., 1980.

Rientis, Rex, and Thea Rientis. *The Three Voyages of Captain Cook.* London: Paul Hamlyn, 1968.

Ritchie, John. *A Charge of Mutiny: The Court Martial of Lieutenant Colonel George Johnston for Deposing Governor William Bligh in the Rebellion of 26 January 1808.* Canberra: National Library of Australia, 1988.

Rodwell, Sir. C. "Report on a Visit to Pitcairn Island." *Colonial Reports* no. 93 (1921).

Rowe, Newton A. *Voyage to the Amorous Islands: The Discovery of Tahiti.* London: Andre Deutsch, 1955.

Schubert, E. *The Pitcairn Island Story.* London: Longmans Green and Co., 1961.
Scott, Ernest. *The Life of Captain Matthew Flinders, R. N.* Sydney: Angus and Robertson, 1914.
_____. *The Life of Matthew Flinders.* Sydney: Angus and Robertson/HarperCollins, 2001. Reissue.
Search, Pamela, ed. *Great True Tales of Human Endurance: 22 of the World's Greatest Stories of Courage from Ancient to Present Times.* London: Arco Publications, 1957.
Shapiro, Harry L. *Descendents of the Mutineers of the Bounty.* Honolulu: Bernice P. Bishop Museum, 1929.
_____. *Descendants of the Mutineers of the Bounty.* Millwood: Kraus Reprint, 1974. Reprint.
Sharp, Andrew. *The Discovery of the Pacific Islands.* Westport: Greenwood Press, 1960.
Smith, Vanessa. "Pitcairn's 'Guilty Stock': The Island as Breeding Ground." *Islands in History and Representation.* Eds. Rod Edmond and Vanessa Smith. London and New York: Routledge, 2003, 116–132.
Snow, Edward Rowe. *Amazing Sea Stories Never Before Told.* New York: Dodd, Mead and Co., 1954.
Snow, Philip, and Stefanie Waine. *The People From the Horizon: An Illustrated History of the Europeans Among the South Sea Islanders.* Oxford: Phaidon Press, 1979.
Southworth, Dr. Rufus. *A Doctor's Letters from Pitcairn, 1937.* Wenham, Mass.: privately printed, 2003. Limited to 500 copies.
Spence, S. A. *Captain Wm. Bligh, R. N., (1754–1817) and Where to Find Him: Being a Catalogue of works wherein reference is contained to this remarkable seaman.* London: S. A. Spence, 1970. Limited to 75 Copies.
Spreadbury, I.D. *Famous Men and Women of Cornish Birth.* Cornwall: Kingston Publications, 1972.
States, John A. *Extracts From the Journal of John A. States of Stonington, Conn. on a Whaling Voyage, 1844–1846: A Visit to Pitcairn's Island.* Mystic: The Marine Historical Association, Inc., 1931.
Stories of the Sea in Former Days: Narratives of Wreck and Rescue. London: Gresham Publishing Co., n.d. (1923).
Stroven, Carl, and A. Grove Day, eds. *The Spell of the Pacific, an Anthology of its Literature.* New York: Macmillan Co., 1949. Introduction by James A. Michener.
Toohey, John. *Captain Bligh's Portable Nightmare: From the Bounty to Safety — 4,162 miles across the Pacific in a Rowing Boat.* Sydney: Duffy and Snellgrove, 1998.
_____. *Captain Bligh's Portable Nightmare: From the* Bounty *to Safety — 4,162 miles across the Pacific in a Rowing Boat.* London: Fourth Estate, 1999.
_____. *Captain Bligh's Portable Nightmare: From the* Bounty *to Safety — 4,162 miles across the Pacific in a Rowing Boat.* New York: HarperCollins, 2000.
Treadgold, M. L. *Bounteous Bestowal: the Economic History of Norfolk Island.* Canberra: Australian National University, 1988.
Varman, Robert V. J. *The Bounty and Tahitian Genealogies of the Pitcairn Island Descendants of Norfolk Island.* Berkeley Vale: Robert V. J. Varman, n.d. (1992).
Vaughan, Crawford. *The Last of Captain Bligh.* London: Staples Press, 1950.
Veitch, Anthony Scott. *Spindrift: The Mary Bryant Story, a Colonial Saga.* Sydney: Angus and Robertson, 1980.
Villiers, Alan. *Pioneers of the Seven Seas.* London: Routledge and Kegan Paul, 1956.
Wallis, Helen, ed. *Carteret's Voyage Round the World 1766–1769.* Cambridge: Hakluyt Society at the University Press, 1965.
Walters, Stephen, ed. *William Bligh, Extraordinary Seaman, a Look at his Life and Times.* London: Pitcairn Press, 1982. Catalogue of an exhibition held by the Earl and Countess of Devon.
Watson, Thomas J. *Pacific Passage.* Mystic, CT: Mystic Seaport Museum, 1993.
Welsby, Thomas. *Discoverers of the Brisbane River.* Brisbane: H. J. Diddams, 1913.
Whipple, A. B. C. *Yankee Whalers in the South Seas.* Rutland, Vt.: C. E. Tuttle Co., 1973.
Winchester, Simon. *The Sun Never Sets: Travels to the Remaining Outposts of the British Empire.* New York: Prentice Hall Press, 1985.
Woodman, Richard. *A Brief History of Mutiny.* London: Constable and Robinson, 2005.
Wyatt, H. G. *The Tale of the Bounty.* London: Oxford University Press, 1972.
Young, Sir George. *Young of Formosa.* Reading: Poynder and Son, n.d. (1928).
Young, Irwin. *The Bligh Saga.* Sydney: School Projects, 1966.

Articles

Adams, Alan. "The Adams Family: In the Wake of the Bounty." *UK Log* no. 22 (July 2001): 16–18.
Adams, M., and M. R. Adams. "News from Pitcairn." *Australasian Record* no. 19 (July 12, 1915): 5–6.
Adams, M. R. "A Long Isolation Broken." *Australasian Record* no. 21 (June 4, 1917): 2.
Adams, Miriam. "By Faith Alone," Parts 1–6. *Australasian Record* 60 (April 30, 1956): 2; (May 7, 1956): 2–3; (May 14, 1956): 2–3; (May 21, 1956): 2; (May 28, 1956): 2; (June 4, 1956): 2.
_____. "Letter From Pitcairn Island." *Review and Herald* 91 (1914): 24–25.
Alexander, Caroline. "Foolscap and Favored Sons." *New York Times,* July 23, 2004, A23.
Alexander, Cyril. "Norfolk Island and 'Morinda.'" *Nautical Magazine,* August 1969, 93–96.
Allward, Maurice. "John Adams' Prayer: A Piece of History is Preserved for England." *UK Log* no. 23 (January 2002): 17–20
_____. "The New Pitcairn Longboat." *UK Log* no. 10 (July 1995): 10–11.
_____. "Riddle of the Bounty Anchors." *UK Log* no. 21 (January 2001): 12–15.
_____. "Visit to History." *UK Log* no. 20 (July 2000): 25–27.
"Ambassadors for Pitcairn." *Australasian Record* 67 (April 29, 1963): 5.
Anderson, Carl D. "Cabin Boy on the Pitcairn." *The Youth's Instructor* 84 (May 12, 1936): 5–13.
Anderson, N. D. "A Story of Pitcairn." *The Youth's Instructor* 73 (January 20, 1925): 4.
Atkins, A. S. "Pitcairners in a Shipwreck." *Australasian Record* 38 (February 26, 1934): 3–4.
"Background of Bounty Bible." *Pitcairn Log* 13 (June-August 1986): 21.
"Background to Norfolk Island." *Pacific Islands Monthly* 45 (November 1974): 72.
Badagliacca, Ralph. "Pitcairn's History Linked to Ships." *Pitcairn Log* 18 (December – February 1991): 14–18.
Baker, John F. "Behind the Book: 'Pitcairn: Children of Mutiny.'" *Publisher's Weekly,* May 28, 1973, 31.
Ball, Ian M. "A Mutineer's Blood Ebbs in the South Seas." *Daily Telegraph,* September 7, 1973.
_____. "The World's Oldest Commune." *Nutrition Today* 8 (September – October 1973): 13–16.
Ballis, P. Harry. "Religion on Pitcairn Island: The first Hundred Years, 1790–1890." *Adventist Heritage* 9, no. 2 (Fall 1984): 40–56.
"Baptism on Pitcairn." *Australasian Record* 33 (October 28, 1929): 8.
Barlow, Joanna. "Keeping Pitcairn in Touch With the World." *Geographical Magazine* 56, no. 3 (March 1984): 140–147.
Baronian, Barrie, and Debbie Baronian. "In God's Hands." *Record* (South Pacific Division) 103 (May 9, 1998): 9.
_____. "God at Work on Pitcairn." *Record* (South Pacific Division) 102 (August 16, 1997): 8.
_____. "God at Work on Pitcairn." *Pacific Record* 4 no. 1 (1998): 4.
Bath, Arthur J. "Missionaries to Pitcairn." *Australasian Record* 89 (May 19, 1984): 7.
Bauer, David H. "Eric Hare Gives South Pacific Materials to Heritage Room." *Review and Herald* 150 (November 8, 1973): 22.
Baynham, Henry. "Lieutenants' Passing Certificates." *The Mariner's Mirror* 87, no. 4 (November 2001): 488.
Bechervaise, E. "The Mutiny of the Bounty: Lieut. Bligh's Voyage in the Ship's Boat to Timor." *Victorian Geographical Journal* 28 (1910–11): 78–87.
Bedingfield, Roger. "Lt. John Hallett." *UK Log* no. 27 (January 2004): 31–32
Behrens, Rae. "By Faith Alone." Parts 1–4. *The Youth's Instructor* 104 (May 8, 1956): 3–4; (May 15, 1956): 5–6; (May 22, 1956): 9–10; (May 29, 1956): 15–16.
Bellarosa, James M. "Odyssey for Survival: The Wreck of the 'Wild Wave.'" *American History Illustrated* 17 (March 1982): 24–29
Bentley, Patricia. "Questions on William Bligh Emerge." *Pitcairn Log* 17 (December 1989 – February 1990): 7–14
Benton, Ida E. "Pitcairners, Descendants of Kings." *Australasian Record* 67 (July 22, 1963): 16.
Bergherm, Wm. H. "Two Pitcairn Islanders Visit California." *Review and Herald* 139 (January 4, 1962): 20.
Berthold, Peter H. "A View of Pitcairn in 1858." *Pitcairn Log* 15 (June – August 1988): 13–14.
Billingsley, Laura. "Setting Sail on the 'Bounty' and Honours for Two of Britain's Greatest Sons." *British Heritage* 10 (June – July 1989): 72.

Birkett, Dea. "Fletcher Christian's Children." *New York Times Magazine*, December 8, 1991, 66–78.
_____. "Island of Lost Girls." *New York Times*, October 29, 2004, A25.
Bladen, F. M. "The Deposition of Governor Bligh." *Australian Historical Society, Journal and Proceedings* 1 (June 1908): 192–200.
_____. "Settlement of the Pitcairn Islanders on Norfolk Island." *Australian Historical Society, Journal and Proceedings* 2, part 1 (1906): 1–12.
Bligh, Maurice. "Regurgitating Some Old Myths." *UK Log* no. 24 (July 2002): 36–39.
"Bligh Meets Christian." *Lake Union Herald* 64 (January 11, 1972): 18.
"Bligh Meets Christian Again." *Australasian Record* 76 (March 13, 1972): 3.
"Bligh of the 'Bounty': A John Smart Portrait that has come to Light." *Illustrated London News*, March 13, 1937, p. 141.
"Bligh's Baptism Enigma Deepens." *Pitcairn Log* 17 (March — May 1990): 8.
Blunden, H. M. "How the Pitcairn Islanders Pay Tithe." *Pacific Union Recorder* 29 (May 15, 1930): 8.
Bolton, Charles Knowles. "John Adams of Pitcairn's Island." *American Neptune* 1, no. 3. (July 1941): 297–300.
Bolton, W. W. "An Impudent Fraud: How 'Lord' Hill Governed Pitcairn Is." *Pacific Islands Monthly* 7 (December 1936): 37–38.
_____. "A Link with the Bounty." *Pacific Islands Monthly* 15 (April 1945): 25–28.
Borthwick, John. "In the Wake of the Bounty." *Australian Geographic* no. 20 (Oct — Dec 1990): 58–73.
"The 'Bounty' Bible." *Bulletin of the Connecticut Historical Society* 19, no. 2 (April 1954): 63–64.
"*Bounty* Men's Graves." *Pacific Islands Monthly* 9 (December 1938): 6.
"*Bounty* Relic: Recovered from Sea Bottom." *Pacific Islands Monthly* 4 (December 1933): 4.
"*Bounty* Relics: Taken from Pitcairn Island." *Pacific Islands Monthly* 8 (April 1937): 6.
"Bounty's Last Relics." *Life*, Feb. 10, 1958, 38–41.
Bowen, T. E. "Shipwrecked Pitcairn Islanders Rescued." *Review and Herald* 97 (August 19, 1920): 24.
Bowley, R. E. "Letters: More on Tablets." *Pitcairn Log* 23 (April — June 1996): 20–21.
Bowley, Robert. "Letters: Lawless Pitcairn?" *Pitcairn Log* 25 (January — March 1998): 20.
_____. "More about Continuing Bligh Controversy." *Pitcairn Log* 26, no. 3 (September 1999): 6–9.
Branster, G. "News Notes From Central Pacific Union Mission: Pitcairn." *Australasian Record* 58 (June 14, 1954): 4–5.
_____. "A Visit to Pitcairn." *Australasian Record* 56 (November 10, 1952): 6–7.
Brash, Thomas. "Pitcairn — Pacific Sentinel." Parts 1–2. *Australasian Record* 51 (June 30, 1947): 4; *Review and Herald* 124 (May 1, 1947): 16.
Britten, Verna R. "A Pitcairner at Avondale." *Australasian Record* 40 (July 13, 1936): 4.
Bryant, Reverend J. "Pitcairn Island: A Lonely Isle and a Curious People." *Scottish Geographical Magazine*, February 1914, 83–87.
Buckland, J. V. "Captain Bligh of the Bounty." *Contemporary Review* 215, no. 1243 (August 1969): 80–83.
Buckle, Winifred F. "Southampton Saints and Pitcairn Islanders." *British Advent Messenger* 81 (June 25, 1976): 9.
Bull, Malcolm J. "Governor Presents New Flag." *Australasian Record* 89 (December 22, 1984): 8.
_____. "One Hundred and Twenty Years After." *Australasian Record* 90 (February 23, 1985): 8.
_____. "Triumphs, Tragedies and Transportation: A Quarter-Century on Pitcairn Island, 1890–1924." *Adventist Heritage* 16, no. 1 (Spring 1993): 56–69.
_____. "Wellington Holds Pitcairn Centennial Service." *South Pacific Record* 92 (January 17, 1987): 9.
Bunkin, Mitchell F. "Getting the Mail to Pitcairn." *Pitcairn Log* 22 (September — November 1994): 10–15.
_____. "My Voyage to Pitcairn." *Pitcairn Log* 21 (June — August 1994): 5–11.
_____. "A Pitcairn Mystery Partially Solved." *Pitcairn Log* 23 (April — June 1996): 8–11.
Bush, Bruce. "Pitcairn Assignments." *Pitcairn Log* 7 (March 1980): 10–12.
Butz, Edwin S. "Missionary Adventures of 1894." *Australasian Record* 46 (December 7, 1942): 4–5.
_____. "Pitcairn Island Camp Meeting." *Australasian Record* 34 (January 13, 1930): 3.
_____. "Present When the 'Pitcairn' Was Dedicated." *Australasian Record* 39 (July 29, 1935): 7.
_____, and Florence M. Butz. "Leaves From Our Diary." *Australasian Record* 33 (April 29, 1929): 2–3.
Cady, B. J. "The Eastern Polynesian Mission." *Review and Herald* 86 (April 1, 1909): 12–13.

_____. "Pitcairn Island." *Union Conference Record* (Australasian) 11 (August 5, 1907): 4.

_____. "A Visit to Pitcairn Island," parts 1–2. *Union Conference Record* (Australasian) 11 (August 26, 1907): 3–4; (September 2, 1907): 2–3.

Caine, P. W. "New Light on the 'Bounty' Mutiny." *Manx Quarterly* 6 (1921): 177–183.

Caldwell, Gayle. "Breadfruit: Captain Bligh's Bounty." *Islands* (December 1988): 33–36.

Callender, Geoffrey. "The Portraiture of Bligh." *The Mariner's Mirror* 22, no. 2 (April 1936): 172–178.

Campbell, Janet. "Eighteenth Century Wooden Clubs from HMS Pandora: A Preliminary Analysis." *The Bulletin of the Australian Institute for Maritime Archaeology* 21, nos. 1–2 (1997): 1–8.

Campbell, R. J. "*Bounty* Mutineer Commemorated in the Antarctic." *The Mariner's Mirror* 73, no. 4 (November 1987): 350.

Cape, Peter. "To Serve on Pitcairn." *Australasian Record* 73 (April 21, 1969): 1.

Carriker, Clyde. "An American on Pitcairn." Parts 1–2. *Pitcairn Log* 7 (September 1979): 4–6; (December 1979): 6–7.

_____. "Rosalind A. Young's Story." *Pitcairn Log* 5 (December 1977): 4–6.

Carver, James E. "Pacific's Biblical Buccaneers." *Nautical Magazine* 189 (February 1963): 77–80.

Castleton, Phillip. "William Bligh: Man in a Longboat." *GEO: Australia's Geographical Magazine* 12, no. 4 (Dec. 1990–Feb. 1991): 26–37.

Cates, Beryl. "Motor Power Has Made Life Easier on Pitcairn." *Pacific Islands Monthly* 36 (June 1965): 29–30.

Chandler, J. E. "Bounty's Muster Roll." *Pitcairn Log* 7 (September 1979): 8–11.

_____. "Death By Hanging." *Pitcairn Log* 6 (September 1978): 4–6.

Choice, Harriet. "Pitcairn Island: From Bligh's Bounty to Long, Lonely Decline." *Van Nuys* (California) *Daily News,* December 22, 1985, 1–3.

Christensen, Alta Hilliard. "Prized Possession." *The Youth's Instructor* 101 (May 5, 1953): 7–19.

Christian, A. Munro. "H.M.S. Bounty Society, International." *Pitcairn Log* 17 (September–November 1989): 14.

Christian, Ada M. "Boatmen's Nightlong Fight Against Storm Off Pitcairn Is." *Pacific Islands Monthly* 14 (June 1943): 26–27.

_____. "Early Ships at Pitcairn Island." *Pacific Islands Monthly* 11 (October 1940): 30.

_____. "Joy on Pitcairn Island." *Australasian Record* 39 (December 16, 1935): 7.

_____. "Landing Supplies in Dangerous Waters." *Review and Herald* 120 (May 20, 1943): 17–19.

_____. "A Letter From Pitcairn Island." *Review and Herald* 119 (November 26, 1942): 1.

_____. "Life on Pitcairn Island." *Review and Herald* 111 (August 2, 1934): 21.

_____. "New Administrative Group: Three Islands Joined With Pitcairn." *Pacific Islands Monthly* 14 (January 1943): 11.

_____. "Pitcairn Holidays." *The Youth's Instructor* 94 (October 29, 1946): 8.

_____. "Pitcairn Island—no. 1: A Community Saved From Heathenism." *Review and Herald* 112 (June 20, 1935): 15–16.

_____. "Pitcairn Island—no. 2: How the Sabbath Truth Came to Pitcairn." *Review and Herald* 112 (June 27, 1935): 14–15.

_____. "An Unsuccessful Voyage to Henderson Island From Pitcairn." *Review and Herald* 113 (October 1, 1936): 13–14.

Christian, Arthur Munro. "Christian Responds to Grave Issue." *Pitcairn Log* 19 (June–August 1992): 12–14.

_____. "In Defense of Fletcher Christian." *Pitcairn Log* 17 (June–August 1990): 18–19.

_____. "Information Surfaces on Rosalind Young." *Pitcairn Log* 18 (September–November 1990): 17.

Christian, Betty. "A Letter From Betty Christian." *Pitcairn Log* 19 (March–May 1992): 14–16.

Christian, Edwin. "An Answer to Prayer: Related on Pitcairn Island." *Australasian Record* 35 (September 7, 1931): 8.

Christian, Elsie. "Mutiny and Conversion." *The Youth's Instructor* 85 (June 29, 1937): 5–10.

Christian, Evelyn, and Elwyn Christian. "A Recent Letter From Pitcairn." *Review and Herald* 134 (November 21, 1957): 32.

Christian, Evelyn R. "Heyerdahl Expedition Visits Pitcairn." *Australasian Record* 60 (July 2, 1956): 8.

_____. "News From Lonely Pitcairn." *Australasian Record* 54 (November 6, 1950): 4.

_____. "News From Pitcairn." *Australasian Record* 53 (June 27, 1949): 4–5.

_____. "The President Visits Pitcairn Island." *Australasian Record* 56 (December 1, 1952): 6.
Christian, F. M. "Pitcairn Island Camp-Meeting." *Australasian Record* 32 (January 30, 1928): 4.
Christian, Irma D. "Pitcairn Pathfinder Club." *Australasian Record* 69 (May 24, 1965): 3–4.
Christian, Tom. "Dear Fellow Pitcairners at Home and Abroad." *Pitcairn Log* 2 (March 1975): 12–14.
Christian, Warren Clive. "A New 'Kaiulani' Visits Pitcairn." *Sea History* no. 50 (Summer 1989): 35.
Clark, Roy Palmer. "Accident at Pitcairn." *Australasian Record* 41 (September 27, 1937): 3–4.
_____. "Almost a Disaster on Pitcairn Island." *Australasian Record* 51 (July 21, 1947): 5–8.
_____. "Arrival at Pitcairn." *Australasian Record* 42 (August 8, 1938): 3–4.
_____. "Busy Days on Pitcairn Island." *Australasian Record* 40 (July 20, 1936): 3.
_____. "Busy Days on Pitcairn Island." *Australasian Record* 41 (June 28, 1937): 4.
_____. "Camp Meeting on Pitcairn." *Australasian Record* 39 (February 11, 1935): 2–3.
_____. "Camp Meeting on Pitcairn." *Review and Herald* 112 (April 11, 1935): 24.
_____. "The Community Bell, Pitcairn Island." *Australasian Record* 40 (November 30, 1936): 3–4.
_____. "Description of Pitcairn." *Australasian Record* 38 (May 28, 1934): 3–4.
_____. "Does God Answer Prayer? An Experience on Pitcairn." *Australasian Record* 40 (January 27, 1936): 4–5.
_____. "From Pitcairn Island." *Australasian Record* 32 (March 19, 1928): 5.
_____. "Great Grandson of a Mutineer." *Australasian Record* 39 (September 30, 1935): 8.
_____. "How *Bounty*'s Rudder Was Found." *Pacific Islands Monthly* 5 (April 1934): 5.
_____. "The Most Joyous Sound on Pitcairn." *Australasian Record* 38 (February 26, 1934): 3.
_____. "A Perilous Voyage." *Australasian Record* 40 (July 13, 1936): 2–3.
_____. "Pitcairn Co-operates." *Australasian Record* 37 (May 1, 1933): 8.
_____. "Pitcairn Island." *Australasian Record* 36 (June 6, 1932): 5–6.
_____. "Pitcairn Island: A Thought Journey." *Australasian Record* 38 (July 23, 1934): 3–4.
_____. "Pitcairn Island Camp Meeting." *Australasian Record* 38 (January 15, 1934): 8.
_____. "Pitcairn Rejoices." *Australasian Record* 42 (April 18, 1938): 2–3.
_____. "Pitcairn's Week of Prayer." *Australasian Record* 38 (July 16, 1934): 8.
_____. "Providence on Pitcairn." *The Youth's Instructor* 95 (September 30, 1947): 9–10, 20.
_____. "School on Pitcairn." *Atlantic Monthly* 159, no. 4 (April 1937): 482–484.
_____. "Schoolmaster of Pitcairn." *Atlantic Monthly* 157, no. 5 (May 1936): 576–579.
_____. "A Thrilling Day on Pitcairn Island." *The Youth's Instructor* 81 (December 12, 1933): 3–4.
_____. "A Unique Voyage." Parts 1–3. *Australasian Record* 40 (February 3, 1936): 4–5; (February 10, 1936): 3–4; (February 17, 1936): 4–5.
_____. "Voices From Pitcairn Heard by Millions." *Australasian Record* 42 (June 13, 1938): 3.
Clarke, Peter. "Norfolk Island." *National Geographic Traveler* 16 (September 1999): 106.
"Clewline." "Bligh and the 'Bounty'!" *Nautical Magazine* 136 (September 1936): 246–249.
Cobbin, Rex E. "Providential Protection on Pitcairn." *Australasian Record* 63 (November 2, 1959): 5.
Cobbin, Win E. "Sunshine and Shadow on Pitcairn." *Australasian Record* 65 (March 13, 1961): 2–3.
Collins, B. M. "Unsung Hero of Pitcairn Island." *Christian Science Monitor*, September 2, 1950, 15.
Conrad, Barnaby. "Legacy of the Bounty." *Signature* 22 (August 1987): 46–49, 88B, 92.
Conard, Claude. "The Passing of the Pitcairn." *The Youth's Instructor* 85 (May 18, 1937): 3–4, 10.
Currey, C. H. "An Outline of the Story of Norfolk Island and Pitcairn's Island, 1788–1857." *Royal Australian Historical Society Journal and Proceedings* 44 part 8 (1958).
("D. B"). "The Mutiny of the 'Bounty.'" *The Nation* 71 (August 2, 1900): 90–92.
Dalrymple, Gordon F. "Faith for Today Films Are Sent to Pitcairn Island." *Pacific Union Recorder* 70 (January 11, 1971): 1.
Danielsson, Marie-Therese and Bengt Danielsson. "Bligh's Cave: 196 Years On." *Pacific Islands Monthly* 56 (June 1985): 25–26.
Darby, Madge. "*Bounty* Mutineer Commemorated in the Antarctic." *The Mariner's Mirror* 73, no. 2 (May 1987): 213.
_____. "Lieutenant Francis Godolphin Bond and the Bligh Family." *The Mariner's Mirror* 85, no. 2 (May 1999): 203–205.
_____. "Losses in the Pandora." *UK Log* no. 22 (July 2001): 10–12.
David, Andrew C. F. "Bligh's Notes on Cook's Last Voyage." *The Mariner's Mirror* 67, no. 1 (February 1981): 102.

_____. "Broughton's Schooner and the Bounty Mutineers." *The Mariner's Mirror* 63, no. 3 (August 1977): 207–213.

_____. "Peter Heywood and Northwest Australia." *The Great Circle: Journal of the Australian Association for Maritime History* 1, no. 1 (1979).

Davies, May. "Millionaires and a Doctor on Pitcairn." *Australasian Record* 65 (December 11, 1961): 4–5, 8.

"A Day on Pitcairn Island During a Voyage from Australia to San Francisco." *American Neptune* 37, no. 1 (January 1977): 66–69.

Dean, Ivy. "The Loneliest Islanders: Visit to Pitcairn." *London Daily Mail,* September 13, 1921. Reproduced in *Review and Herald* 98 (October 20, 1921): 13.

DeBleser, Steven. "The Bounty, Her Crew and Their Discoveries." *UK Log* 22 (July 2001): 24–27.

_____. "The 'Bounty,' Her Crew and Their Discoveries." *Pitcairn Log* 28 (July – September 2001): 5–9.

Delaney, Arthur A. "Admiral Byrd's Pitcairn Interlude — Part One." Parts 1–2. *Pitcairn Log* 4 (June 1977): 4–6; *Pitcairn Log* 5 (September 1977): 4–7.

DeMontmorency, J.E.G. "Pitcairn Island." *Contemporary Review* 135 (May 1929): 671–673.

Denman, A., editor. "Capt. Bligh and the Mutiny of the Bounty." *Notes and Queries*, 9th Series 12 (1903): 501–502.

Diamond, Jared. "Paradises Lost." *Discover* 18, no. 11 (November 1997): 68–78.

_____. "Pitcairn Before the 'Bounty.'" *Nature* 369 (23 June 1994): 608–609.

Dick, Ernest D. "Pitcairn Island." *Review and Herald* 117 (February 8, 1940): 24.

Dillon, Richard. "CQ-PITC Radio Station Important to Pitcairn Islanders." *Radio News* 25 (May 1941): 6–7.

Dillon, Richard H. "Breadfruit Bligh: Bligh Papers in the Banks Collection." *American Neptune* 13, no. 3 (July 1953): 253–270.

_____. "Two Drawings by Bligh of *Bounty*." *American Neptune* 11, no. 2 (April 1951): 146–147.

Donnan, Tad. "The Longboats of Pitcairn Island." *Wooden Boat* 13 (November 12, 1976): 22–25.

Dorling, H. T. "The Mutiny of the *Bounty* by 'Taffrail.'" *Chamber's Journal* 18 (October 20, 1928).

Doyle, J. "Christmas on Pitcairn." *Pitcairn Log* 5 (December 1977): 13–14.

Dunbabin, Thomas. "Voyage of *Jenny* of Bristol." *American Neptune* 13, no. 3 (July 1953): 212–213.

Dunn, L. L. "Isolation Island." *The Youth's Instructor* 94 (March 19, 1946): 12–13, 16.

Du Rietz, Rolf. "Three Letters from James Burney to Sir Joseph Banks." *Ethnos* 27 (1962): 115–125.

_____. "The Voyage of H.M.S. Pandora, 1790–1792: Some Remarks Upon Geoffrey Rawson's Book on the Subject." Lund: Hakan Ohlsson, 1965. Reprint.

Ebbink, R. H. "German Liner Visits Pitcairn." *Adventist Review* 161 (May 17, 1984): 23.

Edmonds, M. "Pitcairn's Island." *Saturday Review,* February 23, 1935, 252.

Edwardy, Fredrik W. "Captain Jones, Missionary Mariner, Part 6: From Papeete to Pitcairn." *The Youth's Instructor* 97 (January 18, 1949): 7–22.

Eliott, L. S. "Romance of Pitcairn Island." *The Trident* 1, no. 3 (July 1939): 150–151.

Ellis, M. H. "The Mutiny on the Bounty — Bligh Whitewashed Again." *The Bulletin* (Sydney), February 16, 1963.

Elsberry, Richard B. "The Bounty Bibles." *Yankee,* August 1990, 122–123.

Emory, Kenneth P. "Stone Implements of Pitcairn Island." *Journal of the Polynesian Society* 37, no. 2 (June 1928): 125–135.

Ernst, Pauline F. "The 'Bounty' Bible and Pitcairn Bible." *Pitcairn Log* 15 (March – May 1988): 7–8.

Erskine, Nigel. "Pitcairn After the 'Bounty.'" *Maritime Life and Traditions* no. 21 (Winter 2003): 58–69.

_____. "Reclaiming the Bounty." *Archaeology* 52, no. 3 (May/June 1999): 42–43.

Eustis, Nelson. "New Issues Backgrounder: Captain Folger Discovers the 'Bounty' Mutineers." *Pitcairn Log* 11 (December – February 1984): 13–14.

Evans, Adelaide Bee. "Early Seed Sowing in the South Pacific Islands." *The Youth's Instructor* 64 (March 21, 1916): 3–5.

_____. "Later Work in the South Pacific Islands Mission Field." *The Youth's Instructor* 64 (April 4, 1916): 6–10.

_____. "Report from Pitcairn." *The Youth's Instructor* 65 (July 10, 1917): 9–10.

Ferdon, Edwin N., Jr. "Pitcairn Island, 1956." *Geographical Review* 48 (January 1958): 69–85.
Ferguson, Wallace R. "Christmas on Pitcairn." *Australasian Record* 82 (March 7, 1977): 10.
_____. "Islanders Give Medical Aid." *Adventist Review* 155 (April 20, 1978): 26.
_____. "Life Sketch of Mrs. Evelyn Christian." *Australasian Record* 82 (July 25, 1977): 11.
_____. "Pitcairn Plays Good Samaritan of the High Seas." *Pitcairn Log* 5 (June 1978): 10–11.
Ferren, J. R. "Pitcairn Island Soon to Be on Regular Line of Commerce." *The Youth's Instructor* 68 (June 8, 1920): 5–6.
Ferris, Norman A. "A Loyal Church on Pitcairn Island." *Review and Herald* 131 (July 22, 1954): 20.
_____. "A Loyal Church on Pitcairn Island." *Australasian Record* 58 (October 4, 1954): 10.
_____. "The Pitcairn Island Story." *These Times* 64 (October 1955): 16–17.
_____. "The Story of Pitcairn Island." Parts 1–12. *Review and Herald* 134 (August 1, 1957): 16–17, 31; pt. 2, "Injustice Leads to Mutiny." (August 15, 1957): 16–17; pt. 3, "The Mutineers Find a Home." (August 22, 1957): 16–17; pt. 4, "Reform Follows Strife and Tragedy." (August 29, 1957): 16–17, 24; pt. 5, "The Mystery of the Bounty is Solved." (September 5, 1957): 16–26; pt. 6, "Pitcairn's Family Grows." (September 12, 1957): 16–26; pt. 7, "Through Droughts and Turmoil." (September 19, 1957): 16–26; pt. 8, "Moses Young and Others Return." (September 26, 1957): 7–24; pt. 9, "The Dawn of a New Day for Pitcairn." (October 3, 1957): 16–26; pt. 10, "The Journeys of the Mission Ship Pitcairn." (October 10, 1957): 16–17; pt. 11, "Pitcairn After the Turn of the Century." (October 24, 1957): 7–25; pt. 12, "Pitcairn Today." (October 31, 1957): 3–5.
_____. "Tiny Pitcairn a Bulwark Against Evolution." *Australasian Record* 60 (February 20, 1956): 7–8.
Ferris, Walter G. "The Light of the Advent Message Shines Brightly on Pitcairn Island." *Review and Herald* 141 (August 27, 1964): 17–19.
_____. "Spiritual Blessings on Pitcairn." *Australasian Record* 68 (December 7, 1964): 6.
Ferris, W. G. "Letter From Pitcairn." *Pacific Islands Monthly* 40 (May 1969): 15–16.
Ferris, W. G., and Myrtle Ferris. "Happy on Pitcairn Island." *Australasian Record* 67 (July 8, 1963): 12.
"First Airmail for Pitcairn." *Australasian Record* 88 (July 30, 1983): 10.
"First for Pitcairn." *Record* (South Pacific Division) 102 (August 9, 1997): 7.
"First Government Teacher for Pitcairn: Pre-fab. Schoolhouse Goes As Well." *Pacific Islands Monthly* 19 (April 1948): 38.
Fisher, Emma. "William Bligh's Pocket Notebook." *The Mariner's Mirror* 64, no. 1 (February 1978): 2.
"A Fishing Experience off Pitcairn Is." *Pacific Islands Monthly* 25 (February 1954): 147.
Fitch, D. D. "Baptism on Pitcairn Island." *Review and Herald* 129 (December 4, 1952): 18–19.
_____. "Disaster on Pitcairn Island." *Review and Herald* 116 (August 3, 1939): 20.
_____. "How the Sabbath Came to Pitcairn Island." *Review and Herald* 128 (June 28, 1951): 17–18.
_____. "Ingathering Papers to Pitcairn Island." *Review and Herald* 123 (May 2, 1946): 19.
_____. "News From Pitcairn Island." *Review and Herald* 123 (October 3, 1946): 16.
_____. "News From Pitcairn Island." *Review and Herald* 129 (November 6, 1952): 36.
_____. "News From Pitcairn Island." *Review and Herald* 131 (May 6, 1954): 31.
_____. "No Taxes!" *The Youth's Instructor* 101 (March 10, 1953): 6.
_____. "Pitcairn Island." *Review and Herald* 113 (March 19, 1936): 9.
_____. "Pitcairn Island." *Review and Herald* 116 (April 6, 1939): 19–20.
_____. "Pitcairn Island." *Review and Herald* 120 (March 4, 1943): 19.
_____. "Pitcairn Island: Burned Wreck of the Ship 'Bounty' Recovered From the Ocean." *Review and Herald* 111 (January 11, 1934): 20.
_____. "Pitcairn Island Up to Date." *Review and Herald* 122 (May 3, 1945): 12–13.
_____. "Sail O — O!" *Review and Herald* 123 (February 28, 1946): 16.
_____. "Wireless on Pitcairn." *The Youth's Instructor* 102 (August 24, 1954): 16–23.
"Fletcher Christian in Bermuda." *Review and Herald* 139 (July 12, 1962): 14.
Forbes, Harry A. "The Strange Story of Pitcairn Island." *Missionary Review of the World* 62, no. 11 (November 1939): 487–491.
Ford, Graham, and Dennis Christian. "Pitcairn's Postal Service." *UK Log* 24 (July 2002): 33.
Ford, Herbert. "Change of Schedule for Ship Visiting Pitcairn." *Pacific Union Recorder* 69 (October 30, 1969): 1.
_____. "Christian Mission Ship Visits Adventist Colony." *Adventist Review* 168 (November 7, 1991): 29–30.

_____. "The Dream Finally Came True." *Pitcairn Log* 19 (December – February 1992): 5–7.
_____. "Early Pitcairn Mail Records." *Pitcairn Log* 22 (July – September 1995): 8–9.
_____. "Governors, Pitcairn Islanders Join in Bible Reading." *Review and Herald* 147 (January 8, 1970): 22.
_____. "Islanders Face Modern Problems." *Review and Herald* 150 (July 12, 1973): 17.
_____. "Letters: Wee Drop of Kickapoo Joy Juice?" *Pitcairn Log* 22 (December – February 1995): 14.
_____. "A Look Back at Pitcairn Island." *South Pacific Record* 92 (January 17, 1987): 8–9.
_____. "Mutiny on the Bounty: The Rest of the Story." *Signs of the Times* 128 (January 2001): 24–26.
_____. "Notable Figures of Pitcairn." *Pitcairn Log* 29 (July – September 2002): 17–18.
_____. "Paving the 'Hill of Difficulty.'" *Pacific Union Recorder* 93 (October 18, 1993): 8–9.
_____. "Pitcairn: Isle of Romance and Tragedy." *Pitcairn Log* 29 (July – September 2002): 8–10.
_____. "Pitcairn Now Has E-mail Access." *Pitcairn Log* 29 (July – September 2002): 11–13.
_____. "Pitcairn Study Center is Begun at PUC." *Review and Herald* 154 (June 16, 1977): 22.
_____. "Recovering the Bounty Anchor." *UK Log* no. 28 (July 2004): 6.
_____. "The Schooner 'Pitcairn': Launching Marked Start of South Sea Mission Work." *Pacific Union Recorder* 78 (October 16, 1978): 1, 8.
_____. "The 'United States' Will Wait for Pitcairn." *Australasian Record* 73 (November 24, 1969): 1.
_____. "World War II Came Early to Pitcairn Island." *Pitcairn Log* 16 (September – November 1988): 5–7.
Fowlie, Dave. "William Bligh: One of History's Most Enigmatic Figures." *Pitcairn Log* 17 (September – November 1989): 5–9.
_____. "Plymouth Versus St. Tudy: The Birthplace of Bligh." *Pitcairn Log* 20 (June – August 1993): 18–19.
_____. "Response to Christian's Grave Site Question." *Pitcairn Log* 19 (June – August 1992): 7–9.
Fox, U. "Bounty's Launch." *Sailing, Seamanship and Yacht Construction* 2 (1935): 137–139.
Foxwell, F. W. "Pitcairn Mailboats." *Pitcairn Log* 3 (June 1976): 12–14.
_____. "Pitcairn Rock." *Pitcairn Log* 2 (December 1974): 10–11.
Foxwell, Joan, and Frank Foxwell. "Our Cruise to Pitcairn Island." *UK Log* no. 21 (January 2001): 8–9.
"From Mutineers' Hideout to Pacific Paradise: Romantic Story of Pitcairn Island As Told by Parkin Christian to Donald A. Webster." *Signs of the Times* 86 (January 1959): 12–13.
Fulton, James Edwin. "Report of the Australasian Division: Pitcairn." *Review and Herald* 103 (June 11, 1926): 22.
_____. "Pitcairn Island: The Reason for a Transformation of Rascality." *Watchman Magazine* 36 (November 1927): 22–28.
Game, Alan. "In the Wake of the Bounty." *UK Log* 5 (July 1995): 17–20.
_____. "Tablets From the 'Bounty'?" *Pitcairn Log* 23 (January – March 1996): 10.
Garrard, Edward J. "Pitcairn International." *Australasian Record* 71 (June 19, 1967): 13.
Gates, E. H. "Development, Openings, and Needs of the Work in Polynesia: Pitcairn Island." *Union Conference Record* 3 (June 1, 1900): 12.
_____. "Pitcairn Island." *Australasian Union Conference Record* 4 (February 11, 1901): 5.
_____. "Pitcairn Island." *Review and Herald* 101 (April 3, 1924): 24.
Gesner, Peter. "Situation Report: HMS *Pandora*." *Bulletin for the Australian Institute of Maritime Archaeology* vol. 14, no. 2 (1990): 47.
Gilmour, Robert. "Fletcher Christian's Mysterious Last Days." *Isle of Man Family History Society Journal*, 8, no. 2 (April 1986): 55–56.
Goldhurst, William. "Martinet or Martyr: Captain Bligh." *Horizon* 5, no. 7. (September, 1963): 42–48.
"Good News from Pitcairn Island." *Australasian Record* 21 (July 30, 1917): 4.
Good, T. C. "The *Pandora* and the *Bounty*." *Journal for AutoCAD Users* 3, no. 2 (1986).
Gould, Rupert T. "Bligh's Notes on Cook's Last Voyage." *The Mariner's Mirror* 14, no. 4 (October 1928): 371–385.
Graham, Edith M. "Pitcairn Island." *Review and Herald* 94 (May 17, 1917): 13.
Gravelle, Kim. "Bligh's Cave Revisited." *Pacific Islands Monthly* 59 (September 1985): 45.
Green, R. C. "Pitcairn Island Fishhooks in Stone." *Journal of the Polynesian Society* 68, no. 1 (March, 1959): 155–138.

Greene, Marc T. "Lonely Isle." *Asia and the Americas* 45 (December 1945): 588–591.
_____. "Pitcairn's Island is Losing its 'Mutineers.'" *American Mercury* 79 (August 1954): 33–36.
_____. "Pitcairn Island." *Spectator* 174 (March 25, 1945): 471.
_____. "Pitcairn Island: Port of Call." *Christian Science Monitor* (June 16, 1945): 16–17.
_____. "Pitcairn's Future." *Spectator* 182 (January 21, 1949): 74.
_____. "Pitcairn Island Population Decreasing." *Nautical Magazine* 173 (February 1955): 85–86.
Gregg, Lizzie M. "A Good Word From Pitcairn Island." *The Youth's Instructor* 68 (June 29, 1920): 5.
_____. "News From Pitcairn Island." *The Youth's Instructor* 65 (January 23, 1917): 4–5.
Greive, Constance N. "Pitcairn Mission Activities Win Royal Approval." *Review and Herald* 132 (March 17, 1955): 1.
Grenier, Richard. "What Really Happened on the 'Bounty.'" *Commentary* 78 (August 1984): 56–62.
Hamilton, David. "The 'Yankee' Visits Pitcairn." *Review and Herald* 139 (January 25, 1962): 20.
Hancock, W. K. "Politics on Pitcairn." *Nineteenth Century and After* 109 (May 1931): 575–587.
Hannay, David. "Some Naval Mutinies." *Blackwood's Magazine* 187 (April 1910): 497–501.
Harder, Fred M. "Pitcairn: Ship and Symbol." *Adventist Heritage* 6, no. 1 (Summer, 1979): 3–15.
Hare, Robert. "How the Pitcairn Islanders Pay Tithe." *Review and Herald* 107 (July 3, 1930): 28.
_____. "Home Life on Pitcairn Island." *Australasian Record* 28 (June 2, 1924): 2.
_____. "Leaving for Pitcairn." *Australasian Record* 28 (May 12, 1924): 2.
_____. "Pitcairn Island Camp Meeting." *Australasian Record* 28 (December 8, 1924): 8.
_____. "Pitcairn Island in History." *Australasian Record* 28 (September 15, 1924): 5.
_____. "Sabbath on Pitcairn Island." *Australasian Record* 28 (June 9, 1924): 8.
_____. "Sabbath on Pitcairn Island." *Pacific Union Recorder* 24 (November 6, 1924): 6, 7.
_____. "Sketches of Pitcairn Life." *Australasian Record* 28 (August 11, 1924): 8.
_____. "The Topography of Pitcairn." *Australasian Record* 28 (June 23, 1924): 3.
_____. "The Week of Prayer on Pitcairn." *Australasian Record* 28 (July 21, 1924): 8.
_____. "The Island of the Golden Age." *The Youth's Instructor* 72 (December 2, 1924): 3–4.
Harré, John. "A Model for the Analysis of Island Emigration." *Journal of the Polynesian Society* 77, no. 2 (June 1968): 177–186.
Harvey, Claire. "The Pitcairn Paradise, or an Island of Depravity?" *New York Times,* October 29, 2004, A4.
Hathaway, Bradford A. "Visit of a Whaling Ship to Pitcairn." *Pitcairn Log* 3 (March 1976): 4–7.
Hattersley-Smith, G. "Bounty Mutineer Commemorated in the Antarctic." *The Mariner's Mirror* 73, no. 1 (February 1987): 70.
"Havoc at Pitcairn." *Pacific Islands Monthly* 17 (May 1946): 28.
Hawkes, Lester N. "Bergensfjord: 'Thank you, Pitcairn, for a Lovely Day.'" *Australasian Record* 62 (March 24, 1958): 1–2.
_____. "Landing by Tidal Wave." *The Youth's Instructor* 105 (November 5, 1957): 3–4.
_____. "Pitcairn Boats: On the Crest of a Tidal Wave." *Australasian Record* 61 (April 29, 1957): 16.
Helm, Christine. "About Thomas Denman Ledward." *UK Log* 27 (January 2004): 29–30.
Henderson, Graeme, David Lyon and Ian MacLeod. "H.M.S. Pandora: Lost and Found." *Archaeology* 36 (January/February 1983): 28–35.
Hilliard, E. "A Visit to Pitcairn Island." *Australasian Record* 38 (August 6, 1934): 3.
Himelfarb, Elizabeth J. "Underwater Bounty." *Archaeology's Dig* 1, no. 4. (October/November 1999): 28–32.
"The Homesickness of Polynesians: Pitcairners Who Went Home." *Pacific Islands Monthly* 9 (April 1938): 58.
Hooker, Brian. "Down with Bligh — Hurrah for Tahiti: A Fresh Look at the Mysterious Voyage of the Bounty." *Mercator's World* 6, no. 5. (September/October 2001): 38–43.
Hornadge, Bill. "Early Pitcairn Letters." *Pitcairn Log* 11 (June – August 1984): 4–8.
_____. "The Pitcairn Military Force During W. W. II." *Pitcairn Log* 8 (June 1981): 4–6.
_____. "Women Authors of Pitcairn Island." *Pitcairn Log* 17 (June – August 1990): 6–8.
Houghton, John. "Pitcairn Island: Utopia of the Pacific Ocean." *English Review* 60 (March 1935): 338–343.
Houston, Neil B. "The Mutiny On the Bounty: An Historical and Literary Bibliography." *Bulletin of Bibliography and Magazine Notes* 26, no. 2 (April – June 1969): 37–41.
"How the Descendants of the 'Bounty' Live Today." *Australasian Record* 40 (April 13, 1936): 2–3.

Howard, Ed. "Pitcairn and Norfolk: The Saga of Bounty's Children." *National Geographic Magazine*, October 1983, 510–541.

Howard, Richard A. "Captain Bligh and the Breadfruit." *Scientific American* 188 (March 1953): 88–94.

Howay, F. W. "Some Lengthy Open-boat Voyages in the Pacific Ocean." *American Neptune* 4, no. 1 (January 1944): 53–57.

Howse, E. W. "The Isle of Mystery." *Australasian Record* 56 (September 1, 1952): 3–4.

Huffey, Eric. "In the Wake of Fletcher Christian." *Pitcairn Log* 23 (July – September 1996): 9, 11–13.

"In Brief: Atlantic Union." *Review and Herald* 135 (July 24, 1958): 26.

"In the Wake of the Bounty — 200 Years Later." *Lauritzen News*, no. 124 (September 1989): 24–26.

"In the Wake of the Britannia." *Pacific Islands Monthly* 42 (May 1971): 36.

Inder, Stuart. "Norfolk Island." *Australian Geographic*, no. 20. (Oct – Dec 1990).

"The Internet and E-mail Set Up on Pitcairn." *UK Log* no. 24 (July 2002): 20–22.

"Intimate Glimpses of Pitcairn Life." *Australasian Record* 68 (April 6, 1964): 5–6.

"An Island In the Sun." *Gangway*. Number 37 (Summer 1984): 20–23.

"Islanders Row Out to See Duchess." *Australasian Record* 51 (March 17, 1947): 8.

"Isolated Pitcairn." *Australasian Record* 27 (December 17, 1923): 8.

"It Started 150 Years Ago." *Australasian Record* 39 (April 1, 1935): 3.

Jackson, G. G. "Pitcairn's Strange Story." *Review of Reviews* (London) 84 (December 1933): 51–54.

Janzen, Brenda. "Pitcairn Pioneer." *Guide* 47 (November 27, 1999): 2–7.

"Jawbone Found on the 'Bounty.'" *Pitcairn Log* 22 (December – February 1995): 10.

Jones, G. F. "Finding Pitcairn Island." *Review and Herald* 116 (March 23, 1939): 18.

_____. "Pitcairn Island." *Review and Herald* 80 (May 12, 1903): 15.

_____. "Reminiscences of Pitcairn." *Review and Herald* 121 (December 14, 1944): 18.

_____. "A Trip on the Cutter 'Pitcairn.'" *Review and Herald* 79 (November 18, 1902): 17.

Juberg, Morten. "'Bounty Returns to Pitcairn.'" *Lake Union Herald* 55 (October 8, 1963): 1–3.

_____. "'Bounty Returns to Pitcairn.'" *Australasian Record* 68 (February 24, 1964): 3.

_____. "Thirty – Year Dream Realized With Stay on Pitcairn Island." *Gleaner* 82 (March 2, 1987): 4–5.

Judge, Gwen M. "Adieu, Pitcairn." *Australasian Record* 43 (April 17, 1939): 4.

_____. "At Home on Pitcairn." *Australasian Record* 42 (December 5, 1938): 8.

_____. "Pitcairn Island as It Is Today." *Missionary Review of the World* 62, no. 11 (November 1939): 491–492.

Kallgard, Anders. "Pitcairn Language Fascinating Study." *Pitcairn Log* 13 (January – March 1986): 17–21.

Karr, Eldyn. "Pitcairn Islanders Less Isolated." *Voice of Prophecy News* 43 (December 1985): 7.

_____. "Pitcairn to Be Less Isolated." *Adventist Review* 162 (August 22, 1985): 18.

Kennane, Janet. "People of Pitcairn." *Oceans* 16, no. 5. (September – October 1983): 42–51.

Kennedy, Gavin. "Bligh and the *Defiance* Mutiny." *Mariner's Mirror* 65, no. 1. (February 1979): 65–68.

Kern, M. E. "A Long Silence Broken." *The Youth's Instructor* 65 (September 25, 1917): 6–7.

King, Henry. "Extract from the Journal of Captain Henry King of the *Elizabeth*." *Edinburgh Philosophical Journal* 3, no. 6, article 22 (1820): 380–388.

Kinnane, Janet. "People of Pitcairn." *Oceans* 16 (September – October 1983): 42–51.

Kinross, John S. "The Bligh Family." *The Mariner's Mirror* 85, no. 4. (November 1999): 484–485.

Kirch, Patrick V. "Polynesia's Mystery Islands." *Archaeology* 41 (May/June 1988): 26–31, 64.

Kisling, Vernon N. "Education Officer." *Pitcairn Log* 7 (March 1980): 14–15.

_____. "Pitcairn Island's Fauna and Flora Issues." *Pitcairn Log* 9 (December 1981): 4–9.

Kisling, Vernon N., Jr. "Pitcairn Wildlife." *Pitcairn Log* 4 (December 1976): 16–18.

Kitching, Cy. "Out of the Past." *Pitcairn Log* 16 (June – August 1989): 13–15.

_____. "Out of the Past." *Pitcairn Log* 17 (March – May 1990): 13, 19–21.

Klein, Hilary Dole. "Bounty Booty." *Islands*, July/August 1999, 22–24.

Knight, C. "H.M. Armed Vessel Bounty." *The Mariner's Mirror* 22, no. 2 (April 1936): 183–199.

"Lamp for Pitcairn." *Pacific Islands Monthly* 44 (February 1973): 131.

"'Land Reform' Is Pitcairn's Cry." *Pacific Islands Monthly* 50 (July 1979): 18–19.

Langdon, Robert. "Ancient Cornish Inn is Link with the *Bounty*." *Pacific Islands Monthly* 31 (April 1961): 75–76.

_____. "'Dusky Damsels': Pitcairn Island's Neglected Matriarchs of the Bounty Saga." *Journal of Pacific History* 35, no. 1 (2000): 29–47.
_____. "The Lost Tahitian Vocabulary of Peter Heywood." PAMBU no. 3 (October 1968): 6–10.
_____. "'Lost' Manuscript May Tell ... Have These Men a Place in Fiji History?" *Pacific Islands Monthly* 32, no. 1 (August 1961): 29–33.
_____. "Tahiti as the Early Explorers Saw It." *Pacific Islands Monthly* 53 (March 1982): 43–44.
_____. "Tahiti: Island of Love and Politics." *Pacific Islands Monthly* 39 (June 1968): 81–95.
Lareau, Paul. "Few Genetic Problems on Pitcairn." *UK Log* no. 28 (July 2004): 12.
_____. "The H.M.S. Bounty Genealogies—A Project." *Pitcairn Log* 16 (June—August 1989): 7.
_____. "Matt Quintal, Bounty Seaman and Pitcairn Settler." *Pitcairn Log* 21 (December—February 1994): 14–15.
_____. "Pitcairn Internet Update." *Pitcairn Log* 24 (October—December 1996): 8.
_____. "Pitcairn Island Home Page on the Internet." *Pitcairn Log* 23 (October—December 1995): 19.
_____. "Richard Skinner, the 'Bounty' Barber." *Pitcairn Log* 22 (July—September 1995): 15.
_____. "Summer on the 'Bounty.'" *Pitcairn Log* 22 (April—June 1995): 11.
_____. "William Brown, 'Bounty' Gardener and Pitcairn Settler." *Pitcairn Log* 22 (September—November 1994): 8–9.
_____. "William Purcell: 'Bounty' Carpenter." *Pitcairn Log* 21 (September—November 1993): 14–15.
"Last Resting-place of Captain Bligh's Bounty: This Year's Find off Pitcairn." *Illustrated London News*, December 21, 1957, 1093.
"The Launching of the Pitcairn 'Messenger.'" *Review and Herald* 94 (May 24, 1917): 17–18.
"A 'Lawless' Pitcairn Island?" *Pitcairn Log* 25 (October—December 1997): 9, 15.
Lay, Peter. "The Rangitoto's Call at Pitcairn, Boxing Day 1951." *UK Log* no. 24 (July 2002): 40–41.
Leach, Sharon. "Historical Diaries From Pitcairn." *Australasian Record* 79 (October 14, 1974): 10–11.
_____. "Pitcairn Collection Given to Heritage Room Details Early SDA Mission Work." *Focus* 10 (August—September 1974): 29–30.
_____. "Pitcairn Diaries Tell of Early Mission Life." *Lake Union Herald* 66 (December 24, 1974): 8–9.
Leeson, Ida. "The Morrison Myth." *The Mariner's Mirror* 25, no. 4 (October 1939): 433–438.
_____. *The Morrison Myth*. London: Messrs. Williams and Norgate, 1938.
LeFevre, Louis. "Pitcairn Island: A Study in the Evolution of Rascality." *Forum* 77 (June 1927): 903–911.
Leventhall, Alan. "The Discovery of John Fryer's Grave." *UK Log* no. 27 (January 2004): 13–14.
_____. "The Several Deaths of John Hallet." *UK Log* no. 26 (July 2003): 31–32.
Lewis, J. R. "Happy Sequel to 'The Mutiny on the Bounty.'" *Bible and Our Times* 80 (March 1964): 14–15, 29.
"Life on Pitcairn Island." *Australasian Record* 41 (October 4, 1937): 2–3.
"Life's Not So Tame on Pitcairn." *Pacific Islands Monthly* 45 (March 1974): 19.
Lincoln, A. "Beechey on Pitcairn." *Pacific Discovery* 35, no. 3 (May/June 1982): 1–10.
"A Little Bounty for Pitcairn." *Geographical Magazine* 56 (March 1984): 113.
Lloyd, Christopher. "Mr. Barrow of the Bounty." *Folio*, spring 1976, 16–23.
"Lonely Pitcairn Gets Electricity." *Australasian Record* 59 (October 10, 1955): 3–4.
Lord, Clive. "Notes on Captain Bligh's Visits to Tasmania." *Papers and Proceedings of the Royal Society of Tasmania* (1922): 11.
Lord, Eliza H., Daniel M. Lord, Herbert G. Lord and Harriet Lord Bradford. "The Pitcairn Bible." *Bulletin of the New York Public Library* 28 (June 1924): 543–552. Reprinted July 1924 in *Bulletin of the New York Public Library*.
_____. "The Pitcairn Bible." Reset and reprinted, with revisions, from the *Bulletin of the New York Public Library* (October 1934): 3–14.
_____. "The Pitcairn Bible: Further Notes." *Bulletin of the New York Public Library* 28 (September 1924): 682–683.
Loughborough, J. N. "Fishers of Men." *Pacific Union Recorder* 16 (September 28, 1916): 2–3.
MacDonald, A. C. "Discovery of Pitcairn Island—Mutiny of the 'Bounty'—Life of the Mutineers on Pitcairn and their Removal to Norfolk Island." *Report of the Thirteenth Meeting of the Australasian Association for the Advancement of Science, Held at Sydney, 1911* (1912): 382–384.
MacDonald, Alexander. "Pitcairn Today: An Isle of Peace." *Walkabout* 5 (December 1, 1938): 13–18.

Mackaness, George. "Extracts from a Log-book of H.M.S. *Providence* kept by Lieut. Francis Godolphin Bond." *Journal and Proceedings of the Royal Australian Historical Society* 46 (1960): 24–66.

———. "Fresh Light on Bligh: Some Correspondence of Captain William Bligh, RN, with John and Francis Godolphin Bond, 1776–1811." *Journal and Proceedings of the Royal Australian Historical Society* 35 (1949): 26–57.

MacKay, David. "Banks, Bligh and Breadfruit." *New Zealand Journal of History* 8 (1974): 61–77.

MacPherson, R. C. "A Link with the Bounty." *Pacific Islands Monthly* 15 (November 1944): 38–39.

MacTaggart, A. E. "A Pitcairn Island Experience." *Nautical Magazine* 135 (April 1936): 339–341.

Maddox, Kempson, MD. "Touching at Pitcairn." *Sydney University Medical Journal* 29, part 1 (August 1935): 26–30.

Maloney, Raymond James. "Mutiny On the Bounty: Questions And Answers." *Nautical World* 2 (October 1998): 37–40.

———. "Where Did the Mutiny on the Bounty Occur?" *American Neptune* 56, no. 4 (Fall 1996): 383–387.

Marshall, David. "Aye, Aye, Mr. Christian!" *Family Life* 8, no. 1 (1987): 4–7.

"Matthew Quintal: 'The Outstanding 'Heavy' in the Pitcairn Cast.'" *UK Log* no. 24 (July 2002): 5.

Maude, H. E. "The Development of the Pitcairner Settlement on Norfolk Island, 1856–1959." *Australian Geographer* 8 (September 1961): 103–115.

———. "Tahitian Interlude: The Migration of the Pitcairn Islanders to the Motherland in 1831." *Journal of the Polynesian Society* 68 (June 1959): 115–140.

Maxton, Donald A. "Hunting for the Grave of Peter Heywood." *UK Log* no. 33 (January 2007): 24–26.

McCandlish, James. "You Can't Drink Beer in Paradise." *National Enquirer*, December 11, 1990, 12.

McCarthy, Cormac. "The Bounty Story." *Yale Review* 54 (March 1965): 368–374.

McComish, J. D. "The McCoys of Pitcairn." *Pacific Islands Monthly* 13 (August 1942): 30–31.

McCoy, E. M. "Excerpts From a Letter From Pitcairn Island." *Review and Herald* 100 (August 2, 1923): 16–17.

———. "Letter From Pitcairn." *Australasian Record* 26 (March 27, 1922): 3.

———. "A Letter From Pitcairn." *Australasian Record* 26 (April 17, 1922): 8.

———. "Letter From Pitcairn." *Australasian Record* 28 (January 7, 1924): 3.

———. "Pitcairn Island." *Review and Herald* 99 (April 6, 1922): 24.

———. "Pitcairn Island." *Review and Herald* 99 (July 6, 1922): 19.

———. "Pitcairn Island: Miracle in Ethnology." *Independent* 57 (September 29, 1904): 712–719.

———. "Pitcairn Island: A Yearly Diary." *Review and Herald* 103 (December 23, 1926): 17–18.

———. "Tithing on Pitcairn Island." *Pacific Union Recorder* 21 (June 29, 1922): 2.

McCoy, F. H. "Pitcairn: New Angles on the Old Story of the *Bounty*." *Pacific Islands Monthly* 13 (July 1942): 13.

McCoy, J. R. "Letter From Pitcairn." *Missionary Magazine* 12 (May 1900): 225–227.

———. "Mangareva, Gambier Islands." *Missionary Magazine* 13 (April 1901): 172–173.

———. "Pitcairn Island." *Missionary Magazine* 13 (April 1901): 178–179.

———. "Pitcairn Island." *Missionary Magazine* 14 (May 1902): 233–234.

———. "Pitcairn Island." *Review and Herald* 81 (June 23, 1904): 15.

———. "A Thrilling Experience." *Union Conference Record* 4 (May 1, 1901): 5.

McDonald, William N. III. "Bounty Mutineer: James Morrison of Lewis." *Highlander* 26, no. 1 (Jan.–Feb. 1988): 52–53.

———. "James Morrison of Lewis: Saga of a Bounty Mutineer." *Pitcairn Log* 20 (December–February 1993): 6–8.

McIlraith, Shaun. "No Money and No Liquor: The Story of a Lonely Community." *People*, June 27, 1956, 36–39.

McKee, Alexander. "New Clues to the Bounty Mystery." *True, the Man's Magazine*, December 1962, 123–136.

McLoughlin, Donald. "An Account of the Development of the System of Government and Laws on Pitcairn Island in the Twentieth Century." Reprinted from *Transactions and Proceedings of the Fiji Society of Science and Industry* 11 (1966–1967): 63–87. Suva, Fiji: Fiji Society of Science and Industry, n.d.

"Mechanisation Brings New Life to Pitcairn." *Pacific Islands Monthly* 37 (August 1966): 75–76.

"Medical Survey of Pitcairn Island." *Pacific Islands Monthly* 21 (September 1950): 73.
"Member Profile: Spencer Murray." *Pitcairn Log* 19 (December — February 1992): 15.
Miller, Bryan. "Returning to Pitcairn." *Pitcairn Log* 10 (September 1982): 10–11.
Miller, David F. "News From Pitcairn." *Pitcairn Log* 17 (June — August 1990): 12–13.
_____. "News Update From Pitcairn." *Pitcairn Log* 17 (September — November 1989): 10–11.
_____. "Pitcairn Island — A Ham's Paradise." *Pitcairn Log* 20 (March — May 1993): 7–9.
Minogue, Tim. "Policing Paradise." *World Press Review* 44 (September 1997): 42.
Montgomerie, H. S. "The Morrison Myth." *The Mariner's Mirror* 27, no. 1 (January 1941): 69–76.
Moon, Allen. "The 'Pitcairn.'" *Missionary Magazine*, 11 (February 1899): 88–89.
"More News From Pitcairn." *Review and Herald* 91 (July 30, 1914): 11.
"More Early Letters." *Pitcairn Log* 9 (June 1982): 4–5.
Morgan, Jill. "Mister Christian's Island." *Saturday Review*, March 17, 1979, 42–43.
"Motor Cycling Comes to Pitcairn." *Pacific Islands Monthly* 37 (May 1966): 45.
"Movements of the 'Pitcairn.'" *Review and Herald* 69 (March 8, 1892): 148.
Moverley, J. "A Non-Adventist's Tribute." *Australasian Record* 53 (September 12, 1949): 4.
"Mr. Buffett Returns." *Pacific Islands Monthly* 44 (November 1973): 33, 35.
Murray, John. "H.M.S. Pandora: On the Trail of the Bounty." *Sea Frontiers* 35, no. 6 (Nov.— Dec. 1989): 328–335.
Murray, Spencer. "The 1831 Move to Tahiti." *Pitcairn Log* 27 (April — June 2000): 9–10, 14.
_____. "Believe It ... Or Not." *Pitcairn Log* 23 (January — March 1996): 14–15.
_____. "Bligh's Launch." *Pitcairn Log* 20 (June — August 1993): 5–8.
_____. "The 'Bounty' Pursuer." *Pitcairn Log* 21 (December — February 1994): 9–11.
_____. "Bounty's Forgotten Crewmen." *Pitcairn Log* 17 (March — May 1990): 16–17.
_____. "The Breadfruit Caper." *Pitcairn Log* 19 (September — November 1991): 11–13.
_____. "By the Dawn's Early Light." *Pitcairn Log* 25 (October — December 1997): 6–7.
_____. "The Carteret Error." *Pitcairn Log* 17 (March — May 1990): 6–8.
_____. "The Christian/Adams Question." *Pitcairn Log* 19 (March — May 1992): 5 — 7.
_____. "Close Calls." *Pitcairn Log* 21 (September — November 1993): 5–9.
_____. "The Day the 'Bounty' Roared." *Pitcairn Log* 18 (March — May 1991): 5–6.
_____. "Eclipsing the 'Bounty.'" *Pitcairn Log* 23 (October — December 1995): 5–6.
_____. "Jenny Says..." *Pitcairn Log* 21 (December — February 1994): 5–9.
_____. "The John Adams Markers" *Pitcairn Log* 20 (March — May 1993): 10–12.
_____. "Letters: Those 'Bounty' Tablets." *Pitcairn Log* 23 (April — June 1996): 20.
_____. "Oh, Say Can You See..." *Pitcairn Log* 22 (September — November 1994): 5–7.
_____. "Pitcairn and the 'Geographic.'" *Pitcairn Log* 24 (January — March 1997): 12–13, 18.
_____. "The Pitcairn Bible Enigma." *Pitcairn Log* 17 (June — August 1990): 16–17.
_____. *Pitcairn Island: The First 200 Years.* La Canada, CA: Bounty Sagas, 1992. Foreword by Sven Wahlroos.
_____. "Pitcairn Papers Are Perhaps Unique." *Pitcairn Log* 19 (June — August 1992): 5–6.
_____. "Pitcairn's Coinage." *Pitcairn Log* 17 (June — August 1990): 9–11.
_____. "The Pitcairners' 1831 Move to Tahiti." *Pitcairn Log* 24 (April — June 1997): 6–8.
_____. "A Question of Secession." *Pitcairn Log* 22 (December — February 1995): 7–9.
_____. "Sails and Other Tales." *Pitcairn Log* 21 (September — November 1993): 11–12.
_____. "Say What?" *Pitcairn Log* 23 (January — March 1996): 6–9.
_____. "Toys for (Tahitian) Tots?" *Pitcairn Log* 20 (March — May 1993): 5–6.
_____. "The Wheels of Pitcairn." *Pitcairn Log* 22 (December — February 1995): 12–14.
"Mutiny on the Bounty Sequel." *Adventist Review* 160, no. 37 (1983): 20.
"Mutiny on the Pitcairn." *Pitcairn Log* 10 (June 1983): 17.
"Names of Students Enrolled: Pitcairn Island: Miss Nessie Young." *Australasian Union Conference Record* 3 (March 1, 1900): 8.
Neal, John, and Barbara Marrett. "Mahina Tiare: Adventures on Pitcairn Island." *Bay and Delta Yachtsman* 23, no. 4 (April 1988): 52–56.
_____. "Voyage of *Mahina Tiare.*" *Bay and Delta Yachtsman* 23, no. 3 (March 1988): 42–43.
Neill, J. S., and D. Cook. "Pitcairn Island: Abstract." *Geographical Journal* 93 (April 1939): 373–374.
Nelson, P. G. "Captain Werge of the Pitcairn." *Review and Herald* 126 (October 6, 1949): 1.
Newman, Barry. "Bounty Descendants Mutiny Again." *Pitcairn Log* 8 (September 1980): 10–11.

Newman, J. H. "Great Days for Pitcairn." *Australasian Record* 81 (August 16, 1976): 13.
"New Map Pinpoints Adamstown Buildings." *Pitcairn Log* 16 (September – November 1988): 13.
"News from the Missionary Ship." *Review and Herald* 68 (February 24, 1891): 118.
"News From Pitcairn." *Harper's Weekly* 55 (May 1911): 21.
"News From Pitcairn." *Outlook* (December 9, 1893): 1093.
Nichol, F. D. "Pitcairn Island." *Review and Herald* 134 (August 1, 1957): 7.
Nichol, Helen. "A Hurricane Provided One of His Moments: Another Was a Volcano.'" *Australasian Record* 77 (February 19, 1973): 6–7.
Nightingale, Lorna. "Police Officer Reports from Pitcairn." *Messenger* 103, nos. 15, 16, 17 (July 1998): 7.
"No Biological Ill Effects of Inbreeding of Islanders." *Science News Letter* (April 24, 1937): 268.
"Norfolk Islanders at Sea: Descendants of the Bounty." *Sea Breezes* 8 (June 1926): 351–352.
"Nurse Queen of a Sinless Isle." *Literary Digest* 53 (Aug 12, 1916): 372.
Odell, Garner Scott. "Third Time's A Charm." *Pitcairn Log* 30 (October – December 2003): 11–12.
"An Official Report on Pitcairn." *Australasian Record* 46 (June 22, 1942): 8.
Olesen, Bill. "The Big Bounty." *Compass Rose* 9 (Winter 1990): 3.
"'On a Clear Day You can See Pitcairn Island from About Forty-seven miles Away'...." *Australasian Record* 89 (July 7, 1984): 16.
Pack, A. J. "Bligh's Identification List of Mutineers." *The Mariner's Mirror* 69, no. 4 (Nov. 1983): 459–460.
Paddock, Charles L. "Pirates of the South Seas." *Watchman Magazine* 40 (August 1931): 20–24.
"Pandora." *UK Log* 24 (July 2002): 23–25.
"'Pandora' Yields Up Secrets." *Pacific Islands Monthly* 55 (February 1984): 51.
Parker, Everett L. "Early Island Culture Diverse." *Pitcairn Log* 13 (March – May 1986): 8–10.
Peet, C. C. "Lonely Pitcairn." *Yachting Magazine*, December 1975, 44–45.
Peeters, Richard. "Ham Radio Operators Abound on Tiny Pitcairn Island." *Pitcairn Log* 24 (October – December 1996): 5–18.
Petersen-Roil, Almuth. "Was John Adams Really Fletcher Christian?" *Pitcairn Log* 19 (December – February 1992): 16–17.
Petty, Thurman C., Jr. "Peril at Pitcairn Island." *Mid-America Adventist Outlook* 7 (September 1986): 6–7.
_____. "Peace From a Storm." *Australasian Record* 88 (December 17, 1983): 9.
Photoplay Magazine, September 2, 1916.
"Pitcairn." *Australasian Record* 24 (January 26, 1920): 8.
"Pitcairn." *Blackwood's Magazine* 286 (July 1959): 1–12.
"Pitcairn, Bligh, 'Bounty' Items At Auction." *Pitcairn Log* 23 (July – September 1996): 14–15.
"Pitcairn Celebrates Bicentenary of Settlement." *Record* (South Pacific Division) 94 (December 16, 1989): 10–12.
"Pitcairn on the Air." *Mentor* 17, no. 1 (February 1929): 66.
"Pitcairn: From Man Power to Horse Power." *Australasian Record* 69 (May 3, 1965): 8.
"Pitcairn Island: Death of Fletcher Christian's Great Grandson." *Pacific Islands Monthly* 9 (June 1938): 19.
"Pitcairn Island Letter of 1849 Discovered." *Pitcairn Log* 5 (March 1978): 10–14.
"Pitcairn Island Letter of 1849 Discovered." *Pitcairn Log* 20 (December – February 1993): 9–13.
"Pitcairn Island Life." *Australasian Record* 38 (September 24, 1934): 3.
"Pitcairn's Plight." *Time* (November 20, 1939): 28.
"Pitcairners on Norfolk." *Pacific Islands Monthly* 8 (June 1937): 75.
Platner, C. Elwyn. "'Canvasback' Rechristening Recalls 'Pitcairn' Launch During Adventist Mission Centennial." *Pacific Union Recorder* 90 (December 17, 1990): 8–9.
Plummer, L. Flora. "More About the 'Pitcairn.'" *The Youth's Instructor* 59 (August 8, 1911): 10.
_____. "The Ship 'Pitcairn.'" *The Youth's Instructor* 59 (June 6, 1911): 11–12.
Pocknall, David. "Vintage Views of Pitcairn." *UK Log* no. 22 (July 2001): 19–23.
Pollard, Chris. "The Padstow Mutineer." *UK Log* no. 24 (July 2002): 6–8.
Powell, Dulcie. "The Voyage of the Plant Nursery, H.M.S. Providence, 1791–1793." *Bulletin of the Institute of Jamaica*, Science Series 15, no. 2 (1973).

Ramsden, Eric. "The Pitcairners Return to Tahiti." *Pacific Islands Monthly* 7 (August 1936): 41–42.
Reid, Alan. "Broughton's Schooner." *The Mariner's Mirror* 64, no. 3 (August 1978): 241–244.
"Relief: Byrd's North Star Brings Aid." *Time* (January 1, 1940): 18–19.
Richards, Harold Marshall Sylvester, Jr. "Pages of Power." *Signs of the Times* 101 (February 1974): 15–17.
Robertson, David. "Pitcairn Island: 'I'll Have You Swinging at a Yardarm Before Two Years Have Passed, Mr. Christian!'" *GEO*, March-May 1985, 102–113.
Robinson, A. H. W. "Captain William Bligh R.N., Hydrographic Surveyor." *Empire Survey Review* 9, no. 85 (1952): 301–306.
Robson, L.L. "Bligh — Hero or Villain?" *Australia's Heritage* 1, no. 6. Sydney: Paul Hamlyn, 1970.
Rogers, G. A. "Sojourn of the *Pandora's* Tender at Ono-I-Lau, Fiji." *The Mariner's Mirror* 69, no. 4 (Nov. 1983): 452–455.
Rolett, Barry Vladimir. "Voyaging and Interaction in Ancient East Polynesia." *Asian Perspectives* 41, no. 2 (Fall 2002): 182–194.
Rønne, Arn Falk. "Pitcairn's New Mutineers?" *Geographical Magazine*, January, 1966, 669–678.
Roughley, T. C. "Bounty Descendants Live on Remote Norfolk Island." *National Geographic Magazine*, October 1960, 559–584.
Royle, Stephen A. "Health and Health Care in Pitcairn Island in 1841: The Report of Surgeon William Gunn of HMS Curacoa." *Journal of Pacific History* 35, no. 2 (2000): 213–218.
Rudd, Arthur M. "Correction on *Pacific Queen*." *American Neptune* 16, no. 2 (April 1956): 137–138.
Rutter, Owen. "Bligh's Log." *The Mariner's Mirror* 22, no. 2 (April 1936): 179–182.
Salwey, C. M. "Pitcairn Island of the South Pacific Ocean." *Asiatic Review* (new series) 26 (January 1930): 59–64.
Samuel, Edward. "Life on Pitcairn Island." Parts 1–3. *Man Junior,* March 1940, 121–126; April 1940, 121–126; May 1940, 93–96.
Sansom, C. E. "The 'Bounty' Story — Is This the End?" *Nautical Magazine* 191 (March 1964): 137–139.
Scott, Brian W. "The True Identity of John Adams." *The Mariner's Mirror* 68, no. 1 (February 1982): 31–39.
Shaffer, Richard. A. "Pitcairn Island Through Native Eyes." *Travel*, January 1948, 11.
Shapiro, Deborah. "Legacy of the Bounty." *Sail* 21 (January 1990): 120–125.
Shapiro, Harriet. "Trouble in Christian's Paradise." *People Weekly*, April 17, 1989, 42–49.
Shapiro, Harry L. "Pitcairniana: A Commentary on the Mutiny of the *Bounty* and its Sequel on Pitcairn Island." *Natural History* 41 (January 1938): 34–80.
_____. "The Romance of the Norfolk Islanders: Modern Descendants of Mutineers Furnish Material for Research." *Scientific American* 135 (September 1926): 182–184.
_____. "Robinson Crusoe's Children: Life and Heredity of the Descendants of the First Settlers on Pitcairn and Norfolk Islands." *Natural History* 28 (May 1928): 290–301.
_____. "The Heritage of H.M.S. Bounty." *UNESCO Courier* 22 (August — September 1969): 20–21.
Shermer, Michael. "A Bounty of Science." *Scientific American*, May 9, 2005.
Simons, R. T. "Pitcairn Island/Report by Mr. R.T Symons." *Colonial Reports*. London: H.M.S.O., 1905.
Simmons, Laurence. "Jean Baudrillard and Captain Bligh's Breadfruit." In *Baudrillard West of the Dateline*. Edited by Victoria Grace, et al. Palmerston North: Dunmore, 2003: 57–79.
Slocum, V. "Voyage of the Bounty's Launch." *Yachting* 40 (July 1926): 37–40, 82–84.
Smith, Helen Frances. "An Island Saga." *The Youth's Instructor* 90 (September 22, 1942): 3–4, 13.
Smith, W. D. "Busy Days on Pitcairn." *Australasian Record* 38 (March 5, 1934): 3–4.
_____. "Cheering News From Pitcairn." *Australasian Record* 38 (April 16, 1934): 2–3.
_____. "An Interesting Discovery at Pitcairn Island." *Australasian Record* 38 (January 8, 1934): 3.
_____. "Journeying to Pitcairn." *Australasian Record* 37 (July 24, 1933): 4.
_____. "Letter From Pitcairn Island." *Australasian Record* 38 (July 2, 1934): 2–3.
_____. "The Most Isolated Island Engages in the Appeal." *Australasian Record* 38 (April 30, 1934): 2–3.
_____. "Pitcairn Island." *Australasian Record* 37 (October 23, 1933): 8.
_____. "Remarkable Dreams on Pitcairn Island." *Australasian Record* 38 (March 19, 1934): 8.
Smith, William. "Pitcairn Saga Continued in Penang." *Review and Herald* 140 (January 3, 1963): 23
Snow, Edward Rowe. "Letters From Rosa Young." *Pitcairn Log* 8 (June 1981): 9–10.

Spain, Ernest C. "Visit of the Four Masted Topsail Schooner 'William Taylor' to Pitcairn Island Sunday, November 25, 1923." *Pitcairn Log* 2 (June 1975): 13–15.

Spalding, Arthur W. "The Building of the Ship." *The Youth's Instructor* 100 (September 2, 1952): 7–9.

_____. "Men and Events of Our Early Days: In the South Seas." *Review and Herald* 129 (May 29, 1952): 11.

Speirs, George M. "Bethia or Bounty." *Pitcairn Log* 6 (March 1979): 12–13.

_____. "From Down Under." *Pitcairn Log* 10 (September 1982): 13.

Spicer, W. A. "Boat Building on Pitcairn." *The Youth's Instructor* 69 (February 22, 1921): 3–4.

_____. "How John I. Tay Came to Pitcairn." *Review and Herald* 108 (July 16, 1931): 7.

_____. "The Islands Were Waiting." *Review and Herald* 119 (June 25, 1942): 9.

_____. "The Light on Pitcairn." *Review and Herald* 119 (April 2, 1942): 1.

_____. "Providences of Pitcairn Island." *Review and Herald* 96 (May 15, 1919): 9.

_____. "Report From Pitcairn Island." *Review and Herald* 102 (February 12, 1925): 24.

Stacey, Brenton. "Allegations of Sex Abuse Saddening, Say Adventist Church Leaders." *Record* (South Pacific Division) 107 (August 10, 2002): 4.

Stackpole, Edouard. "Nantucket and Pitcairn: An Islander Unravels an Island Mystery Half a World Away." *Sea History*, no. 42 (Winter 1986–87): 16–17.

Steed, Ernest H. J. "H.M.S. Bounty's Anchor Raised at Pitcairn Island." *Australasian Record* 61 (April 1, 1957): 4–5.

_____. "Link with 'Bounty' Mutiny Discovered." *Australasian Record* 62 (June 30, 1958): 1.

Steley, Dennis. "Letters of a Leader." *Australasian Record* 90 (November 16, 1985): 12.

Stewart, A. G. "In the Wake of the Pitcairn." *Review and Herald* 126 (March 17, 1949): 1, 19–20.

_____. "Life Sketch of Pastor Robert Hare." *Australasian Record* 57 (September 21, 1953): 14–15.

_____. "Our South Sea Islands Mission 70th Anniversary." *Australasian Record* 64 (August 1, 1960): 1–2.

_____. "Our South Sea Islands Missions." *Australasian Record* 64 (August 22, 1960): 2–3.

_____. "Our South Sea Islands Missions." *Australasian Record* 64 (August 29, 1960): 2–3.

_____. "The Pitcairn Island Story." *These Times* 70 (February 1961): 24–27.

Stewart, G. G. "The First Voyage of the 'Messenger.'" *Australasian Record* 21 (April 23, 1917): 8.

Stewart, M. M. "Queenslanders Thrill to the Saga of Pitcairn." *Review and Herald* 142 (October 7, 1965): 18–19.

Sundelius, Björn. "The Bligh Notebook." *The Mariner's Mirror* 73, no. 4 (November 1987): 420.

Taylor, Ron W. "In the Wake of the 'Pitcairn.'" *Australasian Record* 67 (August 12, 1963): 2–3.

_____. "Pitcairn History Unearthed." *South Pacific Record* 92 (March 14, 1987): 11.

_____. "Pitcairn Island's Double Centennial." *Adventist Review* 167 (March 15, 1990): 16–17.

_____. "Thomas Hall, the 'Bounty' Cook." *Pitcairn Log* 22 (December – February 1995): 10.

"Termites Eat Out Homes on Pitcairn Island." *Science News Letter*, July 16, 1955, 44.

Thomas, Jeff. "Cook's *Bounty* Men." Part one. *UK Log* no. 25 (January 2003): 9–11.

_____. "Cook's *Bounty* Men." Part two. *UK Log* no. 26 (July 2003): 6–8.

_____. "The Voyage of the *Swallow* (1766–1769), and the Discovery of Pitcairn Island." *UK Log* no. 24 (July 2002): 9–13.

Thorsen, Douglas M. "A Pitcairn Visit." *Pitcairn Log* 12 (March – May 1985): 5–8.

_____. "A Pitcairn Visit," Part II. *Pitcairn Log* 12 (June – August 1985): 12–13.

Tomeraasen, David. "Letter From Pitcairn," (Concluded). *Pitcairn Log* 18 (June – August 1991): 11–13.

_____. "Letter From Pitcairn in 1930s Shows Insight." *Pitcairn Log* 18 (March – May 1991): 11–13.

_____. "Unique Trip to Pitcairn." *Pitcairn Log* 13 (September – December 1985): 7–8.

Toombs, Jennifer M. "The Story of the Bounty Ring." *UK Log* no. 21 (January 2001): 10–11.

_____. "Through 19th Century Eyes." *Pitcairn Log* 12 (June – August 1985): 7–8.

_____. "My Visit to the Pitcairn Islands – Part One." Parts 1–3. *Pitcairn Log* 4 (March 1977): 4–6; (June 1977): 8–11; *Pitcairn Log* 5 (September 1977): 8–11.

Totenhofer, Evelyn R. "Shipwreck at Pitcairn." *Australasian Record* 48 (October 2, 1944): 4–5.

_____. "To Pitcairn via Rarotonga." *Australasian Record* 48 (August 7, 1944): 3.

Townend, M. G. "Pitcairn Island: Islanders Cooperate for Community Growth." *Review and Herald* 146 (November 6, 1969): 39.

Trim, John B. "A Layman's Dream." *Adventist Review* 167 (November 29, 1990): 18–19.
Tubbs, Jack. "American Influence on the History of Pitcairn Island." *Pitcairn Log* 9 (March 1982): 4–9.
Tupper, H. "Many Happy Returns from the South Pacific. *Reader's Digest*, May 1958, 56–60.
Vandeman, George. "The Bounty Bible." *Channels* 17 (Fall 1991): 10–11.
Walston, Shirley. "People of the World's Tiniest Country Have Big Hearts." *On Line* (Fall 1991): 3.
_____. "Pitcairn — Born in Violence, Redeemed Through Jesus." *On Line* (Fall 1991): 3.
_____. "Pitcairn: The End ... and the Beginning." *Charisma and Christian Life* 17 (December 1991): 48–71.
Walters, Stephen. "The Literature of Bligh." *Sea Breezes* 50, no. 370 (October 1976): 608–611.
Ward, David. "Pitcairn Population Sees Serious Decrease." *Pitcairn Log* 24 (April – June 1997): 9.
Ward, F. Percival. "Baptisms on Pitcairn." *Australasian Record* 54 (March 27, 1950): 3.
_____. "'The Disaster,' Pitcairn Island." *Australasian Record* 42 (June 26, 1939): 3.
_____. "The Bounty Bible Is Welcomed Home." *Review and Herald* 127 (April 27, 1950): 1–11.
Ibid., pt. 2, *Australasian Record* 54 (May 1, 1950): 5–6.
Ward, Myrtle L. "From Lonely Pitcairn: A Visit From the 'Yankee.'" *Australasian Record* 44 (March 25, 1940): 3.
_____. "Jottings From Pitcairn Island." *Australasian Record* 54 (March 6, 1950): 5.
_____. "Many Ships Call at Pitcairn." *Australasian Record* 52 (May 17, 1948): 3–8.
_____. "Pitcairn Island Women Pioneers." *Australasian Record* 64 (November 7, 1960): 5.
Warren, Royal. "A History of Nursing on Pitcairn." *Pitcairn Log* 21 (March – May 1994): 16–17.
Waugh, Frances N. "Pitcairn Island." *Union Conference Record* (Australasian) 12 (January 13, 1908): 5–6.
Wawrzyniak, William J. "My Quest for Beechey's 'Narrative of a Voyage to the Pacific and Beering's Strait.'" *Pitcairn Log* 17 (December – February 1990): 15.
Webster, Donald A., and Parkin Christian. "From Mutineers' Hideout to Pacific Paradise." *Signs of the Times* 86 (January 1959): 12–13.
Webster, L.A.J. "Path finding on Pitcairn Island." *Australasian Record* 77 (January 1, 1973): 10.
_____. "Why Go Again to Pitcairn Island?" *Australasian Record* 75 (October 4, 1971): 6.
Weigle, John. "Surviving Mutineers Turn to God: Tragedy Stalked Bounty Crew on Pitcairn." *Vista* (May 18, 1980): 30.
Were, Eric W. "Heritage of the 'Bounty.'" *Signs of the Times* (Australia) 79 (July 1964): 16–19.
_____. "They Live Cheerfully With Danger." *Australasian Record* 67 (September 23, 1963): 1–2.
_____. "Pitcairn Today: Ten Weeks with the Sons of the Bounty Mutineers." *Signs of the Times* 91 (August 1964): 10–13.
White, E. E. "Our Faithful Pitcairn Believers." *Review and Herald* 126 (November 10, 1949): 17.
Wilder, Gerrit P. "The Breadfruit of Tahiti." Honolulu: *Bernice P. Bishop Museum Bulletin no. 50* (1928).
Williams, F. Winston. "Chasing the Ghosts of Pitcairn's Past." *Cruising World* (February 1998): 32–39.
Winchester, Simon. "Pitcairn, The Loneliest Island in the World." *Islands,* March – April 1994, 126–137.
"Won: A Constitution." *Time* (August 17, 1943): 32.
Woodward, H. G. "Captain Bligh's Bible: The Book That Converted an Island." *Signs of the Times* 77 (July 18, 1950): 7–14.
"Wreck of the Bounty and the Way of the Geographic. *Newsweek* (December 9, 1957): 62.
Yarham, E. R. "Pacific Eden of Biblical Mutineers." *Nautical Magazine* 217 (February 1977): 100–104.
Yazell, Harry. "Fishing an Important Part of Pitcairn Life." *Pitcairn Log* 13 (June – August 1986): 19–20.
_____. "Importance of the Bounty Bible." *Pitcairn Log* 13 (June – August 1986): 16.
Young, Andrew. "The Beginnings of Pitcairn's Wireless." *Pitcairn Log* 11 (September – November 1983): 8–9.

4

Fiction, Poetry, and Plays

The multifaceted story of H.M.S. *Bounty* is proof positive that history can be more fascinating than fiction. Nevertheless, novelists, short story writers, poets and authors of children's literature have been mining this large body of material — with mixed results — for nearly 200 years, beginning in 1811, with Mary Russell Mitford's narrative poem *Christina, the Maid of the South Seas.*

Mitford wrote *Christina* at the beginning of her literary career, while Lord Byron published a long poem, *The Island, or Christian and His Comrades*, in 1823, near the end of his life. Readers who agree with the theories of C.S. Wilkinson (*The Wake of the* Bounty) would add Samuel Taylor Coleridge's "The Rime of the Ancyent Marinere" to the relatively brief list of *Bounty* poems. Wilkinson suggests that this famous poem had its genesis in a phrase that Coleridge jotted down in his notebook: "Adventures of Christian the Mutineer." Other 19th-century *Bounty*-related poetry includes William Cullen Bryant's lyric poem, "A Song of Pitcairn's Island," Abraham Oulton's "The Mutiny of the Bounty," and John McGilchrist's long dramatic poem, *The Mutineers.*

Jack Adams, the Mutineer, a popular three-volume novel by Captain Frederic Chamier that was reprinted several times, marks the beginning of prose fiction inspired by the *Bounty* Saga, although novelists ignored the material until the publication of Louis Becke and Walter Jeffery's *The Mutineer: A Romance of Pitcairn Island* in 1898.

In the nascent world of literature written specifically for children, story collections such as *Peter Parley's Tales About the Sea, and the Islands in the Pacific Ocean, Round the World and Other Stories* and Maria Hack's *Winter Evenings, or Tales of Travellers* appealed to many young readers, as did R.M. Ballantyne's novel *The Lonely Island*. Unfortunately, the authors' moralizing tone severely dates them, and they are rarely read today.

In the late 19th century, fiction of greater sophistication based on events in the *Bounty* Saga began to appear, including Mark Twain's short story "The Great Revolution in Pitcairn" (published in *The Stolen White Elephant, Etc.*), *The Mutineer: A Romance of Pitcairn Island* and "The Seed of McCoy," one of Jack London's finest short stories from *South Sea Tales.* Twain's and London's stories, based on true incidents, are excellent examples of how historical material can be creatively shaped into compelling fiction.

Bounty Saga fiction reached a pinnacle of success with Charles Nordhoff and James Norman Hall's *Bounty Trilogy* novels: *Mutiny on the Bounty*, *Men Against the Sea* and *Pitcairn's Island*. All three titles are excellent examples of historical fiction, although their status has been somewhat eclipsed in recent years by Patrick O'Brian's superb Aubrey/Maturin novels — one of which, *Desolation Island*— features a brief appearance by Peter Heywood. Still, the *Bounty Trilogy* novels are likely to remain classics of their genre for many years to come.

Recent authors of novels for children and young adults have found that the people and places of the *Bounty* Saga are a good source of suitable material. The roster includes I. G. Edmonds' The *Bounty*'s Boy, James Barbary's *The Boy Mutineer* and Ethel Harper's *Paths of the Sea*. The most recent example is *Mutiny's Daughter* by Ann Rinaldi, which appeared in 2003.

A list of mainstream adult fiction about H.M.S. *Bounty* published between 1950 and 2006 would include Erle Wilson's *Adams of the Bounty*, Stanley Miller's *Mr. Christian! The Journal of Fletcher Christian*, John Maxwell's *H.M.S. Bounty*, William Kinsolving's *Mr. Christian: the Further Adventures of Fletcher Christian*, Bill Collett's *The Last Mutiny: The Further Adventures of Captain Bligh*, Fiona Mountain's *Isabella, The Haunting Love Story of Fletcher Christian and Isabella Curwen*, Dan L. Thrapp's *Mutiny's Curse* and Val McDermid's *The Grave Tattoo*. These novels vary in quality, but each one is worth examining to see how the authors employ *Bounty* Saga material to reach their artistic goals. They often present a more balanced view of Bligh than Nordhoff and Hall's, and most of them focus on Fletcher Christian, suggesting that he survived the bloodshed on Pitcairn Island and eventually returned to England.

Given its high drama, it is surprising that the *Bounty* Saga has not inspired more playwrights. When *The Mutineer* was published in 1898, Louis Becke wrote to his co-author, Walter J. Jefferey, "I hope to see *The Mutineer* dramatized, by the best dramatist in England." This never came to pass. Stanley Miller's *Acquit or Hang!*, an unpublished ITV Network "Play of the Week" based on the court-martial, was broadcast in England on June 1, 1964. It also was produced as a radio play. In August 1987, *The Longboat* by John L. Chodes opened at New York City's Off Broadway Harold Clurman Theatre, where it ran for six weeks. The musical *Mutiny!* enjoyed a successful run on the London stage from 1985 to 1986. (*Mutiny!* is discussed in Chapter 6.)

Bounty enthusiasts surely would welcome serious drama based on events in the saga. Some of Herman Melville's most complex works of fiction — including *Moby-Dick* and *Billy Budd*, both of them set against a nautical backdrop — have been successfully produced as plays. It stands to reason that the many facets of the *Bounty* Saga will inspire some future playwright.

Major Works

MARY RUSSELL MITFORD: *Christina, the Maid of the South Seas; A Poem*. London: Printed by A. J. Valpy, Took's Court, Chancery Lane, for F. C. and J. Rivington, St. Paul's Cathedral; Sold also by J. Hatchard, Piccadilly, 1811.

Poet and essayist Mary Russell Mitford wrote one of the first works of creative literature based on the *Bounty* Saga. Inspired by the discovery of the Pitcairn Island community in 1808 by Captain Mayhew Folger of *Topaz*, she composed *Christina, the Maid of the South Seas*, a long narrative poem about Fletcher Christian's daughter — whose true name was Mary Ann. Known as "The Fair Maid of the South Seas" in her youth, Mary Ann Christian was born soon after, or, according to some accounts, on the very day that her father was murdered by a South Seas native. In the "Advertisement" or preface to *Christina*, Mitford discloses that she was not only inspired, but also "irresistibly attracted," to the "gallant and amiable (Fletcher) Christian." At the same time, she was careful not "to extenuate his crime" in her poem.

Several notable people assisted Mitford with her work. Captain James Burney, who befriended William Bligh when they served on Captain Cook's third voyage — and who later edited Bligh's *A Voyage to the South Sea*— helped Mitford amass 150 pages of notes about the mutiny and geography of Pitcairn Island as an appendix to *Christina*. She acknowledges Burney's help in the "Advertisement," thanking him for the "friendly assistance which he has rendered her in arranging and revising her notes." Her father, Dr. George Mitford, arranged for its publication, and secured the services of the great Romantic poet Samuel Taylor Coleridge to read and amend the press proofs.

Coleridge performed a thorough job, and also contributed several lines of his own to the third canto of *Christina*. Interestingly, Mitford's mother was not pleased when he deleted some clumsy verse that interrupted the flow of the narrative. Mitford had a more judicious view of her poetic gifts, commenting, "Mr Coleridge has only taken out what could well be spared from my poem. I wish he had taken more for what remains is really detestable, always excepting his own beautiful lines."

A blend of fiction and fact, *Christina*'s central episode is the heroine's romantic entanglement with Hubert, a young Pitcairner betrothed to her, and Henry, a sailor whose ship has harbored at Pitcairn to gather supplies. The poem is set one year after the death of Christina's mother, Iddeah. Henry and his fellow shipmate Seymor admire the beautiful island maiden, and when Hubert reveals her name, "Christina Christian," Seymor instantly recalls the *Bounty* mutiny:

> "Christian!" As Hubert breath'd the name,
> Suspicion quick to Seymor came;
> For well he knew — who knows it not?
> Misguided Christian's ruthless plot.
> And he had read, with horror pale,
> The suffering Bligh's heart-thrilling tale.
> [first canto, XXVII, 394–399].

Henry falls in love with Christina and the two meet with Fitzallan, the island patriarch, whose character is clearly based on John Adams. Fitzallan describes the event that instigated the mutiny: Fletcher Christian had asked Bligh permission to bring Iddeah and their child Christina to England on the *Bounty*— fearing that when the vessel left Tahiti, Christina, as an unwanted baby, would be strangled by Tahiti's warrior priests, the Arreoys: "Slaves to their superstition wild, / "Th' Arreoys will destroy my child! / "With its first breath will seize their prize, / "Unfather'd, unreveng'd it dies!" (second canto, XXIV, 384–387).

Bligh's refusal enrages Christian, who enlists the aid of his shipmates to take the ship. Fitzallan says, "I swore: and Christian told me then, that three and twenty valiant men/Like oath had sworn: at his command/Was each brave heart, and trusty hand" (second canto, XXIV, 384–387). He also tells Henry and Seymor about the murders that occurred after the mutineers settled on Pitcairn Island: "Beneath the Otaheitean knife, /Each *Briton* yielded up his life; / In that one breath of love and dread,/All fell, and all but I were dead" (third canto, XXIX, 432–435). He also reveals that Fletcher Christian eventually fell into madness. Haunted by the "spectre" of Bligh, he jumped off a cliff to his death.

With a Pitcairner and an Englishman both vying for Christina's love, Mitford's poem

> CHRISTINA,
>
> THE
>
> MAID OF THE SOUTH SEAS;
>
> A Poem.
>
> BY
>
> MARY RUSSELL MITFORD.
>
> LONDON:
> PRINTED BY A. J. VALPY, TOOK'S COURT,
> CHANCERY LANE,
> FOR F. C. AND J. RIVINGTON, ST. PAUL'S CHURCHYARD;
> SOLD ALSO
> BY J. HATCHARD, PICCADILLY.
>
> 1811.

The title page of Mary Russell Mitford's *Christina, the Maid of the South Seas*, an all-but-forgotten narrative poem that was quite popular in its day. Today, it is extremely rare (courtesy the British Library).

could have ended in bloodshed and tragedy. Fitzallan insists that Christina must marry Hubert and pulls her away from Henry, who draws his sword. Christina manages to separate the men and Henry dejectedly returns to the ship.

When the marriage ceremony begins on the following day, Hubert fails to appear, and everyone fears that he has canoed out to the ship to kill Henry. But Hubert, realizing that Christina is in love with his rival, returns with Henry so that he and Christina can marry. Hubert's selfless act of generosity averts further violence from erupting on Pitcairn's already blood-soaked soil.

In the hands of a more gifted poet, *Christina*'s subject matter might have inspired a more stirring narrative. Russell's verse, on the whole, is pedestrian and *Christina* is not a very compelling piece of literature. Vera Watson, in her biography *Mary Russell Mitford*, acknowledges *Christina*'s literary weaknesses, yet finds in it the seeds of literary promise: "It is a remarkable production for a young woman, both for its execution, the skilful handling of so many characters and the versifying. But it still falls short of the highest standards of poetry."

Nevertheless, *Christina* was popular in its day and sold well, especially in the United States. Today, it is all but forgotten, and only a handful of literary and *Bounty* scholars bother to read the poem — if they can find a copy — for *Christina* is one of the scarcer volumes of *Bounty*-related literature. Mitford continued to compose poetry and verse dramas, such as

Rienzi and *Blanche of Castile,* but she achieved her greatest literary success with *Our Village,* a collection of essays about life in a Berkshire village that endures as a minor classic.

GEORGE NOEL GORDON (LORD BYRON): *The Island, or Christian and His Comrades.* By the Right Hon. Lord Byron. London, 1823 Printed for: John Hunt, 22, Old Bond Street.

The author of such literary masterpieces as *Don Juan, Childe Harold's Pilgrimage* and many brilliant lyric and satiric poems, George Noel Gordon — better known as Lord Byron — holds a high rank among the great English poets of the Romantic Age. Toward the end of his life, he versified the tale of H.M.S. *Bounty* as *The Island, or Christian and His Comrades.* Byron's narrative poems are filled with strong, forceful protagonists, and the image of Fletcher Christian must have been irresistible to him, although he sympathized more with William Bligh than the mutineers, characterizing them as the "rudest sea boys" and "outlaws."

Byron's sources for *The Island* were Bligh's *A Narrative of the Mutiny on Board His Majesty's Ship Bounty,* and *Mariner's Account of the Tonga Islands.* This blend of unrelated material yielded odd, unsatisfying results. In an introduction to *The Island* in *The Works of Lord Byron,* Ernest Hartley Coleridge writes, "The story of the mutiny of the *Bounty,* which is faithfully related in the first canto, is not, as the second title implies, a prelude to the 'Adventures of Christian and his Comrades,' but to a description of 'The Island,' an Ogygia (a mythical island in Homer's *Odyssey*) of the South Seas."

The fate of Christian and the other mutineers on Pitcairn Island was public knowledge well before Byron composed *The Island,* but evidently he did not have access to this information. Coleridge writes, "Whatever may have been his opportunities of ascertaining the facts of the case, it is certain ... that he did not know what became of Christian, and that whereas in the first canto he follows the text of Bligh's *Narrative,* in the three last cantos he draws upon his imagination, turning Tahiti into Toobouai and transporting Toobouai from one archipelago to another — from the Society to the Friendly Islands."

At a time when Bligh's reputation was being vilified, Byron portrays him as a "Gallant Chief" and "Bold Bligh." He chose not to versify the open boat voyage in *The Island,* writing, "But 'tis not mine to tell their tale of grief, /Their constant peril, and their scant relief; /Their days of danger, and their nights of pain; /Their manly courage even when deemed in vain" (first canto, IX, lines 9–11).

Byron leaves historical accuracy far behind when he transforms Toobouai — the island where Christian failed to establish a permanent settlement due to the natives' hostility — into a South Sea paradise. He then introduces the poem's true hero: not Bligh or Christian, but George Stewart, the midshipman from the Orkney Islands who drowned in the wreck of *Pandora*! Byron calls him "Torquil," quite a departure from "George," but this Scottish name of Norse origin is appropriate for a native of the Orkneys, which have a rich Scandinavian heritage.

Stewart's Tahitian bride, "Peggy," had borne him a daughter and died of a broken heart soon after *Pandora*'s departure. In *The Island* she becomes "Neuha," a fit companion for Torquil because they both are islanders: "Both children of the isles, though distant far; /Both born beneath a sea-presiding star" (second canto, XII, lines 3–4).

When a British vessel approaches Toobouai and a battle ensues, Christian is mortally wounded. A true Byronic hero, he is unrepentant to the end and falls off a cliff to his death, as he does in Mitford's *Christina.* Byron's graphic description of Christian's death reveals his ambivalent attitude toward the mutineer:

> Then, like a serpent, coiled
> His wounded, weary form, to where the steep

An illustration from an early edition of Byron's *The Island*, fourth canto, stanza VIII, lines 1–2: "And Neuha took her Torquil by the Hand, / And waved along the vault her kindled brand."

> Looked desperate as himself along the deep;
> Cast one glance back, and clenched his hand, and shook
> His last rage 'gainst the earth which he forsook;
> Then plunged: the rock below received like glass
> His body crushed into one gory mass,
> With scarce a shred to tell of human form,
> Or fragment for the sea-bird or the worm;
> A fair-haired scalp, besmeared with blood and weeds,
> Yet reeked, the remnant of himself and deeds;
> [fourth canto, XII, 56–66].

Byron, who clearly empathized with the true story of Stewart and Peggy, creates a happy ending for Torquil and Neuha in *The Island*. They survive the battle and return to Toobouai, where they are welcomed with a great feast:

> A hundred fires, far flickering from the height,
> Blazed o'er the general revel of the night,
> The feast in honour of the guest, returned
> To Peace and Pleasure, perilously earned;
> A night succeeded by such happy days
> As only the yet infant world displays
> [fourth canto, XV, 15–20].

The Island is an intriguing, entertaining poem, especially for readers familiar with the true story of H.M.S. *Bounty*, but it does not approach the quality of Byron's finest work. Samuel Taylor Coleridge maintained that very little of *The Island* was worthy of the great poet. Byron himself, in a letter to author Leigh Hunt dated January 25, 1823, acknowledged its weaknesses: "I am merely trying to write a poem a little above the usual run of periodical poesy, and I hope that it will at least be that."

Byron was close to the mark, and his great popularity ensured that *The Island* would find faithful readers. It was reprinted twice in the year of publication. Most readers and critics have ignored *The Island* since that time. We can only wonder what Byron might have achieved if he had crafted the story of H.M.S. *Bounty* at the peak of his poetic powers.

MARIA HACK: "Adventures of Captain Bligh" in *Adventures by Land and Sea*. Pages 113–185. Every Boy's Library. London: George Routledge and Sons, Broadway, Ludgate Hill. New York: 416 Broome Street. N.d. (1891).

Maria Hack published four volumes of *Winter Evenings, or Tales of Travellers*, books that became schoolroom classics, between 1818 and 1820. She firmly believed that children would learn lessons more effectively if they read stories about real events as opposed to nursery tales, "stories of giants and castles (that) do not accord with the taste of the present day." She used history as her source material, believing that young readers would prefer the truth to fantasy.

The fourth volume of *Winter Evenings*, reprinted as *Adventures by Land and Sea* in 1891, collects several tales of nautical adventure, including "Adventures of Captain Bligh." (The stories were titled "The Escape of Captain Bligh" and "Pitcairn's Island" in earlier printings.) Hack's sources for these adaptations are William Bligh's *A Voyage to the South Sea* and *The Quarterly Review* for July 1815.

Hack liked to use a "story time" framework in her tales: A "Mrs. B." tells the stories while her children, "Harry" and "Lucy," pepper her with questions. This format provided Hack the opportunity to provide basic instruction on a wide range of topics, from the botany and geography of the South Seas to the use of nautical instruments. As she discusses the equipment that Bligh used to navigate *Bounty*'s launch, Harry asks:

"I know the use of a compass very well; but what was the quadrant for?"

"It is by means of a quadrant that sailors can tell the height of the sun at noon: and that, you know, is a very important thing."

"Oh, yes, I remember!" said Harry, "When they know that, they can find out the latitude. Ah, I understand it now! The quadrant was to show them the place they really were in; and the compass, which way they ought to sail."

The *Bounty* story also provided plenty of opportunities for Hack to infuse her content with moral lessons. For example, Lucy asks about the meaning of suffering as she ponders the plight of Bligh and his men in the open boat:

"Mamma, do you believe that if people suffer with fortitude, they can really bear more than if they are impatient or cowardly?"

"I have not the least doubt of it. If you have, my dear Lucy, I advise you the next time any painful or vexatious accident happens to you, to make the experiment for yourself."

Although this heavily didactic style of writing for children has gone out of fashion, books like *Adventures by Land and Sea* are still worth examining for their historical and cultural interest: they provide a clear window into 19th century reading habits, education and teaching.

PETER PARLEY (PSEUDONYM FOR SAMUEL GRISWOLD GOODRICH): "Pitcairn's Island," Chapter XXII, *Tales About the Sea, and the Islands in the Pacific Ocean.* By Peter Parley, Author of Tales about Natural History, Etc. Embellished with Engravings. London: Printed for Thomas Tegg, No. 73, Cheapside; Tegg and Co. Dublin; R. Griffin and Co. Glasgow; and J. and S.A. Tegg, Sydney and Hobart Town. 1841. Fourth Edition. "The Bounty," Chapter CXCVL, *Peter Parley's Universal History on the Basis of Geography.* New York: Ivison, Blakeman & Co., n.d. (1886).

"Peter Parley" was the pseudonym of Samuel Griswold Goodrich, an American author, editor and publisher who produced more than 150 illustrated books, among the first American works of literature written specifically for children. Like Hack, he was determined to purge children's literature of nursery tales, and his subjects included ancient and modern history, biography, geography, science and natural history.

Goodrich hired a number of writers, most of them hacks, to compose the Peter Parley tales, although he did a good deal of editing. They were composed in a friendly, chatty style that is rather tiresome to our ears today, although it appealed to children in the 19th century. The following excerpt about Pitcairn Island from Chapter 22 of *Tales About the Sea, and the Islands in the Pacific Ocean* is a good example of the Peter Parley style:

"I will now tell you a story that I think you will find interesting. To the west of Easter Island you will see a little place on the map, called Pitcairn's Island. This is six miles long, and is a fertile and beautiful spot. Well! In the year 1789, the sailors on board the British ship *Bounty*, while sailing in the Pacific, mutinied against their officers. They took possession of the ship, put the officers on board the launch, a kind of large boat, and left them to their fate. These officers fortunately reached the island of Timor, north of New Holland."

It is difficult to identify the anonymous authors of the Peter Parley books, with one significant exception. From letters he wrote in 1836, we know that Nathaniel Hawthorne, who would gain fame as the author of *The Scarlet Letter* and *The House of the Seven Gables*, was hired by Goodrich to write *Peter Parley's Universal History on the Basis of Geography*. Some scholars maintain that the writing actually was done by Hawthorne's sister, Elizabeth Manning Hawthorne, or was a joint effort. *Peter Parley's Universal History* includes an account of the *Bounty* mutiny that is clear, succinct, and still quite readable. The following description of Pitcairn Islanders rowing out from Bounty Bay to greet H.M.S. *Tagus* may have come from Nathaniel Hawthorne's pen:

An engraving from *Tales About the Sea, and the Islands in the Pacific Ocean* depicts John Adams, the last of the *Bounty* mutineers, meeting the officers and crew of *Briton* and *Tagus* (courtesy Pitcairn Islands Study Center).

As Sir Thomas Staines looked from the deck of his vessel to the shore, he was amazed to perceive that the island was cultivated, and that there were small houses on it... While Sir Thomas Staines and his sailors were wondering at these circumstances, a small boat put off from the shore. The waves rolled very high, but the boat skimmed like a sea-bird over the tops of them, and soon came alongside of the vessel.

Peter Parley's Universal History and other Peter Parley titles were so popular that numerous publishers began to issue unauthorized editions, including *Tales About the Sea, and the Islands in the Pacific Ocean*, from English publisher Thomas Tegg. The American edition, published in Philadelphia by Thomas, Cowperthwait & Co., is titled *Peter Parley's Tales About the Islands in the Pacific Ocean*.

This frequently reprinted volume, which features stories about the *Bounty*, Pitcairn Island, whaling, Captain Cook, Hawaii, Pacific missionaries and many other subjects, was a treasure trove of history for young readers eager to learn more about the world.

ANONYMOUS: "The Ship and the Island" in *Round the World and Other Stories*. London: Groombridge and Sons, 1871. Unpaginated.

The historically based tales for children in *Round the World and Other Stories* are written in a didactic, "story time" format, very much in the vein of Maria Hack and Peter Parley. Here, the storyteller is "Grandfather," and when his grandchildren ask him to relate an "adventure on the sea," he tells the tale of H.M.S. *Bounty*, providing appropriate lessons along the way.

The anonymous author of "The Ship and the Island" clearly admires and respects the South Pacific islanders. An accompanying illustration shows the mutineers landing at Toobouai, where, Grandfather says, the mutineers hoped to indulge in a life of ease and pleasure: "But when they came near to Toobouai, and made ready their boats to go on shore, the natives rushed down to the seaside armed with clubs, spears, and stones, to prevent their landing. So brave and resolute were they in keeping off the strangers that the ship's cannon were fired at them, and the men in the boats discharged their muskets against the troop of naked islanders, who were only defending their own property."

Christian and the mutineers gain a foothold on Toobouai because the islanders' weapons are no match for the firepower of an English armed vessel: "Their spears and clubs were no defence against cannon balls and bullets; and they were forced to give way. It too often happens that strength and power prevail over weakness and justice."

Of course, the islanders did prevail in the end. Faced with constant attacks, the mutineers constructed "Fort George," but soon realized that settling on Toobouai would only lead to a state of endless conflict. Christian's actual attempt to create a safe haven on Toobouai has rarely been addressed in fiction or in film — probably because popular culture tends to portray Christian as a virtuous rebel and leader, and this particular episode in the *Bounty* Saga reveals his weaknesses.

The primary concern of the author of "The Ship and the Island" is teaching children to treat all human beings with fairness, dignity and respect. He drives this lesson home as he tells the story of Pitcairn Island: "The island was divided into nine equal portions, one to each Englishman, but none was given to the native Tahitians. The black men, as they were called, were made to clear and till the land, and assist in all the heavy labour, and before long their masters treated them little better than slaves. The Tahitians generally are a mild-tempered race, and they would not have complained of this treatment but for the cruelty and injustice to which they were gradually subjected."

The anonymous author of "The Ship and the Island" stands out as a writer intent on teaching children respect for the entire human race, certainly not a widespread concept in 1871.

R. M. BALLANTYNE: *The Lonely Island, or the Refuge of the Mutineers*. New York: Thomas Nelson & Sons, n.d. (1880).

Robert Michael Ballantyne, a prolific author of fiction for young readers, enjoyed popularity and success during his lifetime and is remembered chiefly for *The Coral Island* (1858), an exciting tale of three young boys shipwrecked on a South Seas island. He wrote *The Lonely Island*, which was inspired by the history of Pitcairn Island, 22 years after *The Coral Island* was published. In his preface, Ballantyne characterizes his tale as "essentially a 'true story,' the merest spider-web of fiction having been employed to bind it together."

Ballantyne holds a significant position in the history of children's literature for his pioneering practice of placing characters in a genuine historical setting — a technique that gives his best stories an air of authenticity. The true story of the *Bounty* is one of the most compelling of all stories, but its vibrant subject matter does not guarantee a good historical tale. Like most writers for children in his day, Ballantyne's tone in *The Lonely Island* is preachy and didactic, focusing primarily on the moral and religious implications of the mutiny. He writes, "Its object is to show the remarkable manner in which it has pleased God, in connection with this event, to bring light out of darkness, good out of evil, by means of the Bible."

Fletcher Christian and the *Bounty* mutineers face fierce resistance from natives as they attempt to land at Toobouai, in an illustration from "The Ship and the Island," collected in *Round the World and Other Stories* (courtesy Pitcairn Islands Study Center).

A scene in *The Lonely Island* that clearly illustrates Ballantyne's religious tone is a discussion between Fletcher Christian and John Adams in Christian's Cave on Pitcairn Island. Christian, who has repented his actions during the mutiny, is praying and reading the *Bounty*'s Bible as Adams enters the cave. He says to Adams:

> "Repentance is not enough. Why, man, do you think if I went to England just now, and said ever so earnestly or so truly, 'I repent,' that I'd escape swinging at the yard-arm?"
>
> "Well, I can't say you would," replied the sailor, somewhat puzzled; "but then man's ways ain't the same as God's ways; are they sir?"
>
> "That's true, Adams; but justice is always the same, whether with God or man. Besides, if repentance alone would do, where is the need of a Saviour?"
>
> Adams' puzzled look increased, and finally settled on the horizon. The matter had evidently never occurred to him before in that light. After a short silence he turned again to Christian.
>
> "Well, sir, to be frank with you, I must say that I don't rightly understand it."
>
> "But I do," said Christian, again laying his hand on the Bible, "At least I think I do. God has forgiven me for Jesus Christ's sake, and His Spirit has made me repent and accept the forgiveness, and now I feel that there is work, serious work, for me to do. I have just been praying that God would help me to do it."

Ballantyne's evangelical tone was common among Victorian-era children's books. John Rowe Townsend comments in *Written for Children: An Outline of English-language Children's Literature* (1983), "Today hardly any children's writer would venture to put the Christian religion in the forefront of his picture, any more than he would the old imperialism.... Ballantyne was not an over-pious writer by temperament; he was just professing what it was obvious and proper that a decent British Christian should profess in his day and age."

The Lonely Island is heavily didactic and does not rank high among Ballantyne's works. He was at his best when writing from firsthand knowledge and experience, as he did in *The Young Fur Traders*, based on his experiences working in the Hudson Bay Territories.

ANDREW LANG, EDITOR: "A Wonderful Voyage" and "The Pitcairn Islanders" in *The Red True Story Book*. With Numerous Illustrations by Henry J. Ford. London: Longmans, Green and Co., 1895. Pages 226–246.

Andrew Lang is fondly remembered for his series of "color" fairy tale collections, including *The Blue Fairy Book, The Green Fairy Book* and many others, most of them illustrated by Henry J. Ford. Lang also adapted and edited several volumes of historical tales for children, publishing them in *The Blue True Story Book*, and *The Red True Story Book*—which collects two *Bounty*-related tales, "A Wonderful Voyage" and "The Pitcairn Islanders."

According to Lang's introduction, a "Miss May Kendall" and/or a "Mrs. Bovill" wrote these tales. They avoid the moralizing tone used in *Peter Parley's Tales About the Sea,* Hack's *Winter Evenings* and Ballantyne's *The Lonely Island*, making them more palatable to the modern reader. In "A Wonderful Voyage," an account of the mutiny and Bligh's open boat voyage, the authors acknowledge Bligh's navigational skills, but display the typical prejudice against him that persisted well throughout the 20th century: "This is a story of a man who, when in command of his ships and when everything went prosperously with him, was so overbearing and cruel that some of his men, in desperation at the treatment they received, mutinied against him. But the story shows another side of his character in adversity which it is impossible not to admire."

"The Pitcairn Islanders" tells the visit of H.M.S. *Briton* and H.M.S. *Tagus*, commanded by, respectively, Sir Thomas Staines and Captain Philip Pipon, to the mutineers' refuge in 1814. They are greeted by the sons of Christian and Edward Young, who board the ship and bring the captains ashore to meet John Adams and hear the story of what happened to the

Fletcher Christian and John Adams discuss repentance in this illustration from R.M. Ballantyne's *The Lonely Island* (courtesy Pitcairn Islands Study Center).

Sir Thomas Staines and Captain Philip Pipon meet with Thursday October Christian and George Young in this illustration from Andrew Lang's *The Red True Story Book*. Young is admiring a dog — the first one he has ever seen.

mutineers on Pitcairn Island. The author appropriately spares young readers the more gruesome details of Pitcairn's bloody history. It is refreshing that "The Pitcairn Islanders" acknowledges the contradictory accounts of Pitcairn's early history, including the fate of Fletcher Christian: "(Christian) Shut himself off from the others, and with only the sound of the roaring breakers as they beat on the shore below to disturb his solitude, the madman dwelt alone with his terrible history of the past. One story is that in a fit of maniacal insanity he flung himself over the rocks into the sea. Another that he was shot by one of the mutineers whilst digging in a plantation."

Although these two tales from *The Red True Story Book* are readable today, their style is not very inspired. If Lang had commissioned his friend H. Rider Haggard — author of *She* and *King Solomon's Mines*, and a contributor to both *The Red True Story Book* and *The Blue*

True Story Book— to tell the tale of H.M.S. *Bounty* and Pitcairn Island, he might have published a masterpiece.

Louis Becke and Walter Jeffery: *The Mutineer: A Romance of Pitcairn Island*. By Louis Becke and Walter Jeffery. London: T. Fisher Unwin, Paternoster Square, 1898. Sydney: Angus & Robertson, 1898. Colonial issue.

The Mutineer is rarely read today, but Louis Becke and Walter Jeffery deserve recognition for writing one of the first historical novels about the *Bounty* mutiny, even if their work does not approach the scope or quality of the more famous writing team of Charles Nordhoff and James Norman Hall. Fans of *The Bounty Trilogy* should be thankful that Nordhoff and Hall were completely unaware of *The Mutineer*'s existence when they were performing background research for *Mutiny on the Bounty*, *Men Against the Sea* and *Pitcairn's Island*. Otherwise, they might have chosen to abandon the project.

A major stumbling block for modern readers of *The Mutineer* is the authors' stilted prose. Glynn Christian calls the book "turgid with high passion and purple prose in the best manner of the Victorian novel." A formal, biblical-style language is used to distinguish Tahitian dialogue from the English spoken by the mutineers. It suits neither the characters nor the historical period, and plain English would have served much better. A good example is Mahina's statement to Fletcher Christian in the opening chapter: "My white lover," she murmured, "would that I could tell thee in thine own tongue how I love thee. But the language of Peretane is hard to the lips of us of Tahiti; yet, in a little time, when thou hast learned mine, thou wilt know all the great love that is in my heart for thee, and then thou shalt tell me all that is in thine for me."

Nevertheless, *The Mutineer* is worth reading, if only for its version of Christian's death, which Becke claimed was based on an authentic report related to him by the Pitcairn Islanders. As Glynn Christian notes in *Fragile Paradise; The Discovery of Fletcher Christian, Bounty Mutineer*, "*The Mutineer* said that Christian survived the gunshot wounds and recovered in his cave. When he was well enough, he attempted to put to sea in *Bounty*'s boat to join a sailing ship sighted off Pitcairn. Adams tried to prevent him to protect the secrecy of the community and in the struggle, shot and killed Christian."

Glynn Christian quotes a letter affirming Becke's belief that Fletcher Christian really did meet his end as written in *The Mutineer*: "It is, I believe, strictly true. Anyway, I prefer to believe the native account of the *Bounty* story to the vague surmises of the many authors who have written on the subject."

Becke and Jeffery present the death of Christian in a melodramatic fashion, but it is tantalizing to think that this may actually be what happened — especially since it accounts for John Adams' "inability" to show Christian's grave to the visitors who began arriving in Pitcairn in 1808: "Mahina ... wife ... come closer to me ... and you, Young and Smith, give me your hands. Promise me that no one but yourselves shall ever know where I lie. Let no other white man point to my grave and say, 'Fletcher Christian ... mutineer."

After visiting Pitcairn and making the arduous climb to Christian's Cave, Glynn Christian is convinced that a wounded Fletcher Christian could not have reached the cave and recovered. He believes that Becke either was misled by the Pitcairn Islanders or simply took plenty of poetic license while writing *The Mutineer*.

Jack London: "The Seed of McCoy" in *South Sea Tales*. New York: The Macmillan Co., 1911.

Jack London is best known for his novels and short stories set during Alaska's Klondike Gold Rush of 1897–98: *The Call of the Wild*, *White Fang*, "To Build a Fire" and many others. Readers are less familiar with the stories and novels based on his travels in *Snark*, a 45-foot yacht that he and his wife, Charmian, sailed through the South Pacific for two years. Eight stories inspired by their voyage are collected in *South Sea Tales*, including the frequently anthologized "The Seed of McCoy," first published in the periodical *Century*, in April 1909.

London based his quickly paced tale on the true story of *Pyrennes*, a steel bark out of Glasgow commanded by Captain Robert Bryce. Captain Bryce arrived at Pitcairn Island with a fire in his ship's hold, on December 1, 1900, hoping to beach the vessel there. After learning that Pitcairn had no beach or safe anchorage, he accepted the help of James Russell McCoy, a third-generation Pitcairn Islander and great-grandson of William McCoy, one of the most violent *Bounty* mutineers.

When the fictional McCoy boards *Pyrenees*, he realizes that the ship's cargo of wheat is burning below deck. The first mate, who thinks they can safely beach the vessel at Pitcairn Island and save the ship's metal hull, is outraged at McCoy's gentle, yet firm, explanation that Pitcairn has no suitable beach or anchorage. In stark contrast to the crew's fear and anxiety, he approaches their dangerous plight with clarity and steadfastness, agreeing to help pilot the ship to a safe harbor in Mangareva. Nevertheless, McCoy's actions continue to anger and puzzle the captain (renamed "Captain Davenport") and crew. He insists on first returning to Pitcairn to speak to the entire population, delaying their departure. McCoy's response to the captain's anger not only justifies his actions, but reveals the depth of his generosity:

> "In the name of reason and common-sense," the captain burst forth, "what do you want to assemble the people for? Don't you realize that my ship is burning beneath me?"
> McCoy was as placid as a summer sea, and the other's anger produced not the slightest ripple upon it.
> "But I must get permission to go with you. It is our custom," was the imperturbable reply.
> "Also, I am the governor, and I must make arrangements for the conduct of the island during my absence."

McCoy then explains that, since few ships stop at Pitcairn, he may be away from his home for as long as a year.

During its hazardous journey, *Pyrenees* is beset by gales, treacherous currents and dangerous shoals, bringing the crew, who prefer to abandon ship, to the brink of mutiny. Ironically, McCoy, descendant of a violent mutineer, peacefully quells the uprising. His expertise and experience finally bring the ship and crew to a safe harbor.

London portrays McCoy as nearly Christ-like in his ability to foster peace, describing his voice as "dovelike," suggesting not only the dove as a symbol of peace, but perhaps the Holy Ghost. Captain Davenport is amazed that such a man could be descended from someone like William McCoy: "This old man was merely the seed of McCoy, of McCoy of the *Bounty*, the mutineer fleeing from the hemp that waited him in England, the McCoy who was a power for evil in the early days of blood and lust and violent death on Pitcairn Island. Captain Davenport was not religious, yet in that moment he felt a mad impulse to cast himself at the other's feet — and to say he knew not what."

In *White Logic: Jack London's Short Stories*, James I. McClintock writes, "'The Seed of McCoy' is an affirmation that good can come of evil, that democracy can grow from an original tyranny and anarchy, and that tenderness, compassion and intelligence can guide men to safety."

London never visited Pitcairn Island, and he did not disclose how he met James Russell McCoy. He does refer to McCoy in a letter dated July 1, 1909, where he wrote, "I knew this McCoy of Pitcairn, and it is just the way he would have acted. In fact, he was a most charming personality." Jack and Charmian London did catch a glimpse of Pitcairn Island on their return voyage to California. In *The Log of the Snark*, published several years after her husband's death, Charmian London writes, "One last link of our South Sea chain we picked up one morning at sunrise, when a squall-curtain lifted and parted over Pitcairn Island, high and sheer, green and gold and unreal in the rainbow shimmer."

CHARLES NORDHOFF AND JAMES NORMAN HALL: *Mutiny on the Bounty*. Boston: Little, Brown and Company, 1932.

Charles Nordhoff and James Norman Hall, individually and as a team, wrote a large number of fictional and non-fiction works set in the South Pacific, including *The Pearl Lagoon*, *The Tale of a Shipwreck*, *Faery Lands of the South Seas* and *Botany Bay*. They are remembered primarily for three compelling, well-written historical novels closely based on events in the *Bounty* Saga: *Mutiny on the Bounty*, *Men Against the Sea* and *Pitcairn's Island*. Still in print, they usually are published together in a single volume as *The Bounty Trilogy*. In April 1989, *Mutiny on the Bounty* was reissued to mark the mutiny's 200th anniversary.

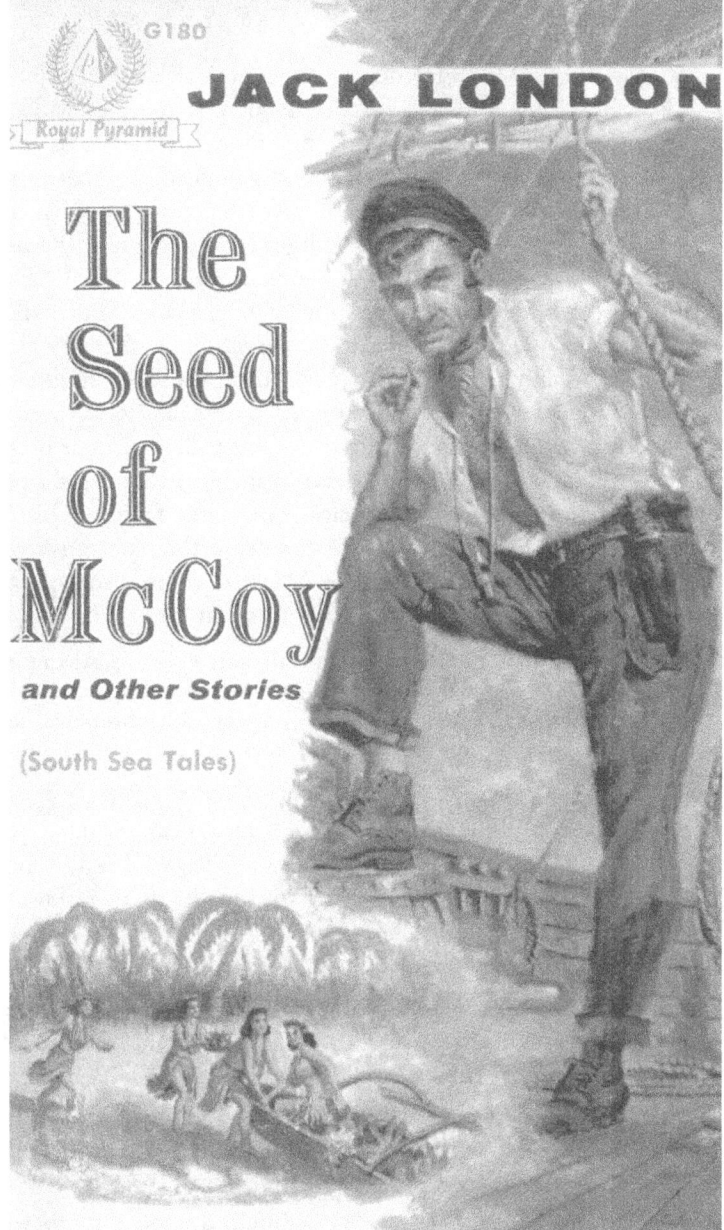

This paperback edition of Jack London's *South Sea Tales*, retitled *The Seed of McCoy and Other Stories*, published by Pyramid Books in 1956, reflects London's popular appeal as a rugged, "tough guy" writer.

The genesis of the *Bounty Trilogy* novels is recounted in Hall's autobiography, *My Island Home* (1952), and in Paul L. Briand, Jr.'s *In Search of Paradise; The Nordhoff-Hall Story* (1966). Hall had purchased the Oxford Classics edition of Barrow's *Eventful History of the Mutiny and Piratical Seizure of H.M.S. Bounty* at a Paris bookstore in 1916. More than a decade later, Hall was searching for a subject about which he could co-write with Nordhoff, and finding his copy of Barrow sparked the idea.

Although it is not documented in *My Island Home* or *In Search of Paradise*, Hall and Nordhoff must also have recalled a conversation they had several years earlier with one N.C. Reynolds, a mechanic who they met in Tahiti. Reynolds later became an acquaintance of Dr. Rufus Southworth, a physician who practiced on Pitcairn Island for several months in 1937. A collection of letters by Dr. Southworth privately published in 2003 —*A Doctor's Letters from Pitcairn, 1937*—casts additional light on the origin of the *Bounty Trilogy*. In 1937, Dr. Southworth wrote to his family, "It seems that he (Reynolds) knows both Nordhoff and Hall, in fact saw a great deal of them in his younger days. Shortly before he left Papeete, he told both the writers the story of the Bounty as he had gathered it from some Pitcairners who had left the island and had come to Tahiti. Reynolds suggested that the history of the Bounty would make a good story. When four years ago he read *Mutiny on the Bounty*, he found that the tale was substantially as he had told it." Regardless of their origin, *Bounty* scholar Rolf Du Rietz calls these works, "By far the best and most influential novels ever written on the subject," even though they were "Hopelessly outdated from the historian's point of view."

Nordhoff and Hall closely modeled their narrative of the mutiny on William Bligh's account in *A Voyage to the South Sea*. A comparison of the two texts illuminates how the authors infused Bligh's relatively prosaic account with color and immediacy.

> I continued my endeavours to turn the tide of affairs, when Christian changed the cutlass which he had in his hand for a bayonet that was brought to him, and holding me with a strong grip by the cord that tied my hands, he with many oaths threatened to kill me immediately if I would not be quiet; the villains round me had their pieces cocked and their bayonets fixed [*A Voyage to the South Sea*].
>
> Captain Bligh, naked except for his shirt, and with his hands tied behind his back, was standing by the mizzenmast. Christian stood before him, holding in one hand the end of the line by which Bligh was bound and in the other a bayonet, and around them were several of the able seamen, fully armed ... Christian placed the point of his bayonet at Bligh's throat with a look in his eye there was no mistaking" [*Mutiny on the Bounty*].

Unfortunately, Nordhoff and Hall did not have access to George Mackaness's *Life of Vice-Admiral William Bligh* and other scholarly works that present a more accurate portrait of Bligh's character than earlier literature on the subject. Barrow's *Eventful History of the Mutiny and Piratical Seizure of H.M.S.* Bounty and Lady Belcher's *The Mutineers of the Bounty and their Descendants in Pitcairn and Norfolk Islands* were two primary sources, and the generally "anti–Bligh" tone of those books provided justification for Nordhoff and Hall to characterize Bligh as a ruthless sadist who enjoys flogging his crew:

> "Bligh watched the punishment with folded arms. 'I'll show the man who's captain of this ship,' I heard him remark placidly to Christian. 'By God, I will!' The thirteenth blow broke the iron of Mills' self-control. He was writhing on the grating, his tongue bitten halfway through and the blood pouring from his lips. 'Oh!' he shouted thickly, 'Oh, my God! Oh!'
> 'Mr. Morrison,' called Bligh, sternly and suddenly. 'See that you lay on with a will.'"

Such scenes clearly inspired Charles Laughton's performance as Bligh in the 1936 MGM film

Opposite: **Henry C. Pitz executed the dust jackets for the first editions of Charles Nordhoff and James Norman Hall's *Mutiny on the Bounty* and *Pitcairn's Island*. His depiction of the mutineers casting the launch adrift is inaccurate, as the sea was quite calm on the morning of the mutiny. Reprinted by permission of Little, Brown and Company.**

based on the novel. Both offer exciting entertainment, but reinforce a simplistic, inaccurate image of Bligh as a tyrannical commander.

Nordhoff and Hall take the opposite tack with ship's surgeon Thomas Huggan, transforming him into "Old Bacchus," a convivial, good-natured drunkard. Huggan was a chronic alcoholic, and his carelessness contributed to the death of able-bodied seaman James Valentine, who died from an infection on the voyage to Tahiti. (Nordhoff and Hall did not include Valentine in the novel.) "Old Bacchus" dies from eating poisonous fish on Tahiti, but the real Huggan drank himself to death and was buried on Tahiti. Bligh records in his log on December 10, 1788, "This unfortunate Man died owing to drunkenness and indolence."

The authors' most significant departure from the historical record was replacing Midshipman Peter Heywood with the fictitious "Roger Byam," whose experiences are modeled closely—with several important exceptions—on Heywood's. Byam serves as the narrator of *Mutiny on the Bounty*, and is retired from the Royal Navy when the novel opens.

Byam tells a gripping tale that is by turn dramatic, lyrical and suspenseful. This stirring blend draws the reader into every facet of the story, climaxing in the court-martial, when Byam is condemned to death. He is later acquitted, in the nick of time, by the unexpected reappearance of Robert Tinkler, the only member of *Bounty*'s crew who can prove Byam's innocence and save him from the yardarm. This turn of events is completely fictitious—Peter Heywood was condemned, but immediately recommended to the King's mercy. But Nordhoff and Hall's alteration of reality in the episode heightens the drama, adding excitement and suspense.

In the "Epilogue," Roger Byam summarizes his subsequent career in the Royal Navy, including his promotion to Captain. He recalls that in 1809, he received orders to sail to the South Seas, which he had longed to revisit for many years. Arriving in Tahiti, Byam learns that Tehani, his Tahitian wife, died soon after *Pandora*'s departure, and that Tehani, their daughter, is a grown woman with a child. He is so moved by these revelations that he asks to be introduced to his daughter and granddaughter as, simply, "The English captain." The novel closes with these haunting lines as Byam sails away from Tahiti for the last time: "The moon was bright overhead when I reëmbarked in the pinnace to return to my ship. A chill night breeze came whispering down from the depths of the valley, and suddenly the place was full of ghosts,—shadows of men alive and dead,—my own among them."

The early printings of *Mutiny on the Bounty* close with another fictional episode. When Byam leaves Tahiti, he discovers the mutineers' refuge on Pitcairn Island. This device provides Nordhoff and Hall the opportunity to account for what happened to Christian and his followers. Byam is greeted by the sons of Christian and Edward Young and spends the night on shore. Alexander Smith (John Adams) tells Byam the story of Pitcairn's bloody years and how the survivors eventually created an idyllic, peaceful island community.

The novel ends when Christian's daughter, Mary, guides Byam to her father's cave refuge, where he meditates on the fate of his friend Fletcher Christian: "I could see him gazing out over the vast panorama of empty ocean that stretched away to horizons lonely as any in the world; listening to the faint cries of the sea fowl and the melancholy booming of the surf in the caverns at the bases of the cliffs."

This alternate ending was deleted after Nordhoff and Hall published *Pitcairn's Island* in 1934. The later novel is more accurate, ending with the arrival of Captain Mayhew Folger of *Topaz* in 1808.

CHARLES NORDHOFF AND JAMES NORMAN HALL: *Men Against the Sea*. Boston: Little, Brown and Company, 1934.

To narrate *Men Against the Sea*, Nordhoff and Hall chose Thomas Ledward, a survivor of the incredible, 3,600-mile open-boat voyage from Tofoa to Timor and *Bounty*'s acting surgeon, "whose medical knowledge and whose experience in reading men's sufferings would qualify him as a sensitive and reliable observer."

Ledward writes his account in Coupang, as he recovers from a serious leg ulcer that prevents his immediate return to England. He begins the tale on the day Master's Mate William Elphinstone is buried, the third of *Bounty*'s crew to die from malarial fever following the ordeal of the voyage, which left the survivors susceptible to the region's notoriously unhealthy climate. Quartermaster Peter Linkletter and Cook Thomas Hall also died. Bligh nearly succumbed to the disease, and was plagued by debilitating relapses long after leaving Coupang.

By choosing Ledward to tell the story, Nordhoff and Hall clearly chose to treat Bligh more objectively than they did in *Mutiny on the Bounty*. If they had selected one of Bligh's antagonists, such as John Fryer or William Purcell, *Men Against the Sea* would have been a much different novel.

After setting the stage with a brief account of the mutiny, Ledward tells one of the truly great epics of the sea. Nordhoff and Hall recreate this most famous of open boat voyages by weaving Ledward's narrative with authentic source material, including Bligh's own log and his *A Voyage to the South Sea*. Readers familiar with Bligh's accounts will note that the authors use this material judiciously to flesh out the action and add color. For example, here is Bligh's description of the impending attack of natives at Tofoa, followed by the same scene as written in *Men Against the Sea*:

A Voyage to the South Sea: "The onset was now preparing. Every one, as I have described before, kept knocking stones together.... All but two or three things were in the boat, when I took Nageete (an islander) by the hand and we walked down the beach, every one in a silent kind of horror.

Men Against the Sea: "Bligh had already instructed us in what order we should proceed to the beach. Cole, also armed with a cutlass, took his station with the Captain on the other side of Nageete; and the rest of us fell in behind, with Purcell and Norton bringing up the rear.

"Forward, lads!" said Bligh. "Let these bastards see how Englishmen behave in a tight place!"

"We then proceeded toward the beach, everyone in a kind of silent horror."

Nordhoff and Hall skillfully employ such techniques throughout the novel. *Men Against the Sea* is solidly based on fact, which makes their storytelling all the more compelling as Ledward recounts the horrors of near-starvation; incessant storms that batter the crew; the threat of the launch foundering on the open sea; the welcome respites on Restoration Island; and the excitement of the men when they finally sight Timor.

Readers who finish *Mutiny on the Bounty* convinced that Bligh was a cruel tyrant cannot leave *Men Against the Sea* without acknowledging at least a modicum of respect and admiration for the brave, brilliant navigator who saved the lives of his remaining crew under nightmarish conditions. Ledward himself clearly admires his captain, concluding his narration with Bligh's departure for England: "He was gone — the finest seaman under whom I have ever had the good fortune to sail. From the bottom of my heart I wished him God Speed."

Readers who do additional research on the aftermath of the open boat voyage will discover that Thomas Ledward's fate is something of a mystery. In *Bounty*'s muster book, opposite the name "Thomas Ledward," the following note is written: "17th Nov., 1789. Embarked

MEN AGAINST THE SEA

CHARLES NORDHOFF
JAMES NORMAN HALL
Authors of "MUTINY on the BOUNTY"

on board the Rotterdam Welfare. Q. What became of him?" Ledward probably died at sea on the *Rotterdam Welfare*, which sank on the passage from Coupang to Cape Town. However, records also reveal that a surgeon named Ledward served on the British vessel *Discover* from 1791 to 1795. There is no way to determine if he was Thomas Ledward of H.M.S. *Bounty*.

Men Against the Sea had the special distinction of being printed in a free, paperback "Armed Services Edition" during World War II. Thousands of sailors, soldiers and pilots must have enjoyed this quickly paced novel of survival under incredibly dangerous and difficult conditions.

CHARLES NORDHOFF AND JAMES NORMAN HALL: *Pitcairn's Island*. Boston: Little, Brown and Company, 1934.

The subject matter of the more leisurely paced *Pitcairn's Island* presented a far greater challenge to Nordhoff and Hall than either *Mutiny on the Bounty* or *Men Against the Sea*. While writing the first two novels, the authors had at their disposal a virtual library of resources, provided by their publisher, about the mutiny and open-boat voyage.

The only material relating to the history of Pitcairn Island from 1790 to 1808 are the conflicting accounts provided by Alexander Smith (John Adams); Arthur Quintal, the son of Matthew Quintal, as recorded by Walter Brodie, author of *Pitcairn's Island and the Islanders in 1850*; and Eliza Mills, the daughter of John Mills, published many years later in *Mutiny of the Bounty and Story of Pitcairn Island* by Rosalind Amelia Young. The Authors' Note states that "Each of these accounts is remarkable for its differences from the others, if for nothing else, and all contain discrepancies and improbabilities of human behaviour which can scarcely be in accordance with the facts. The authors, therefore, after a careful study of every existing account, have adopted a chronology and selected a sequence of events which seem to them to render more plausible the play of cause and effect."

Nordhoff and Hall also faced the challenge of describing the sheer amount of blood spilled in early Pitcairn history: 16 deaths in 10 years, 15 of them violent. They did not flinch from the facts, but they also did not want to repel their readers: "Certain details which would add nothing to the narrative and are too revolting for the printed page have been omitted." Because these bloody events were hidden from the rest of the world, narrating this tale of murder and redemption demanded more creativity from the authors than the first two *Bounty Trilogy* novels.

A pall hangs over the beginning of *Pitcairn's Island*. Although the mutineers have discovered what appears to be a perfect, even idyllic, refuge, providing everything they need to start new lives, Nordhoff and Hall prepare the reader for the tragedies that will follow. As Fletcher Christian and Maimiti explore the island, she senses that other people have lived there. Christian finds this difficult to believe, asking her,

"Why have they gone, then?"
"Who knows?" she replied. "Perhaps it is not a happy place."
"Not happy?" "An island so rich and beautiful?"
"The people may have brought some old unhappiness with them. It is not often the land that is to blame; it is those who come."

The mutineers, of course, have brought with them both the taint of mutiny and the knowledge that they probably are responsible for the death of Bligh and his loyalists. Only John Adams was to learn, in 1808, that they survived the open boat voyage.

Opposite: C. Alister Macdonald's dust jacket illustration for *Men Against the Sea* pictures the overloaded launch on one of the many days of torrential rain during the voyage. Reprinted by permission of Little, Brown and Company.

Nordhoff and Hall perform a masterful job of third and first person narration in *Pitcairn's Island*. They raise the level of suspense at a crucial point — when Smith is shot and Christian lies mortally wounded — by jumping ahead to the arrival of Captain Mayhew Folger on the American ship *Topaz* in 1808. Smith tells the rest of the tale to Captain Folger at a period of time when, as Nordhoff and Hall note, the Pitcairn colony "presented a veritable picture of the Golden Age."

The final pages of *Pitcairn's Island* serve as a kind of benediction — assuring the reader that at least one good thing did grow from the mutiny, which Adams admits was a "cruel, lawless deed." After baring his soul to Mr. Webber, mate of *Topaz*, about the bloody history of the mutineers and natives, including his own role in the violence and redemption, he says, simply, "I doubt if ye could find anywhere a family of human beings that lives together with more kindness and good will. We're at peace, in our lives and in our hearts."

The novel closes on a haunting note that suggests both the isolation of Pitcairn Island from the rest of the world and the warmth of the community that took root there. Smith watches *Topaz* depart from the island:

> The sun had set and the last light faded swiftly from the sky. In the east the first stars appeared. The ship was now but a mere speck almost on the verge of the horizon. Motionless, his chin in his hands, elbows on his knees, the old seamen gazed after her till she was lost to view in the gathering darkness. At length he rose and turned away, slowly descending the steep northern slope of the crag to the path which led to the settlement.

I. G. EDMONDS: *The Bounty's Boy*. New York: The Bobbs-Merrill Company, Inc., 1962.

Robert Tinkler, who played such a crucial, albeit fictional, role in Nordhoff and Hall's *Mutiny on the Bounty*, takes center stage as the protagonist of *The Bounty's Boy*, a historical novel for children. I.G. Edmonds had a specific goal in writing *The Bounty's Boy*: to rehabilitate William Bligh by presenting him in a more realistic light, not as the sadistic bully portrayed by Charles Laughton in MGM's film adaptation of *Mutiny on the Bounty*. Edmonds wanted young readers to discover that the popular notion of Bligh generated by most fiction and film is far from the truth: He writes, "When older people think of Bligh, they think of Laughton's Bligh, the monster of the sea. The real Bligh has been lost." Edmonds strikes this note early in the book, in an exchange between Tinkler and Christian (who has just been upbraided by Bligh): "Mr. Fryer says that Captain Bligh is not as bad as he makes out," Tinkler said, wanting to make Mr. Christian feel better. "It's just his way to shout all the time."

Although he succeeded in accentuating Bligh's positive qualities, Edmonds took a considerable number of liberties with the truth when characterizing some of the other crewmembers. His depiction of Fletcher Christian as a weakling — called "Fletch" by the mutineers — is at odds with contemporary reports. In *The Bounty's Boy*, the crew barely tolerates Christian's weakness, following him only because he knows how to navigate the *Bounty* back to Tahiti after the mutiny. They even understand why Christian was frequently the target of Bligh's tirades: "The men also knew that much of Bligh's constant anger at his lieutenant had been an attempt to make a good sailor of a man too lax and easygoing to be a proper seaman."

Tinkler is transformed into a 12-year-old in *The Bounty's Boy*, making it easier for young readers to identify with the main character — even though the real Robert Tinkler was 17 years of age when he joined H.M.S. *Bounty*, and already a capable seaman. Surprisingly,

Opposite: Henry C. Pitz's colorful dust jacket for the first edition of *Pitcairn's Island* portrays a violent confrontation between one of the Tahitian women and a mutineer. Reprinted by permission of Little, Brown and Company.

Edmonds makes Alexander Smith the most despicable character in the novel. Believing that Tinkler is a "Jonah" who endangers the ship, Smith is determined to kill the youngster. Strangely, it is Matthew Quintal, one of the most ruthless and violent members of *Bounty*'s crew, who befriends and protects Tinkler from Smith in *The Bounty's Boy*.

Unaccountably, Edmonds uses Fryer, one of Bligh's most implacable foes, as a mouthpiece to point out his positive qualities. He explains to Tinkler, who has been castigated by Bligh, "You are lucky to have been able to study seamanship under a master like Bligh. Even more important, you have been lucky to study leadership from one of the greatest examples I have ever seen."

Edmonds took steps to rehabilitate Bligh's reputation in *The Bounty's Boy*, but his young readers must have finished the book with equally misguided impressions of Christian, Fryer, Smith and Quintal.

JAMES BARBARY: *The Boy Mutineer.* Illustrated by Charlotte Mensforth. London: Max Parrish, 1966.

The story of midshipman Peter Heywood is one of the more gripping tales associated with the *Bounty* mutiny, and James Barbary's *The Boy Mutineer* is an exciting fictional account of his adventures for young readers. It is based more firmly on historical fact than I. G. Edmonds' *The Bounty's Boy*, although Edmonds' conception of Bligh is probably closer to the truth than Barbary's "mean and petty tyrant."

As the book begins, Heywood has a nightmare in which Bligh appears as a grotesque monster: "He saw Captain Bligh's face, whiskery, fat, choleric, irritable, come closer and closer until he appeared nothing but one huge red moist mouth ... the Captain's mouth opened cavernously wide, to show yellow teeth like broken tree stumps, and a tongue as broad as a red flannel blanket." When Heywood awakes from this dream, he learns that Christian has taken the ship. The story, which proceeds at a lively pace, is told through convincing dialogue and skillfully drawn characters, especially Fletcher Christian, James Morrison, George Stewart and Captain Edward Edwards of *Pandora*. During the mutiny, Barbary succinctly captures the mood of Heywood, who is genuinely puzzled about what he should do: "Peter could see that even George Stewart—nearly the same age as Christian himself, and a sailor of much experience—was standing there looking dazed, as if all these abrupt occurrences were beyond him. What exactly, as a midshipman, are you supposed to do at a moment like this? Peter asked himself. Not even George Stewart seemed to know."

Unwittingly, Heywood performs some actions that will put him at grave risk during the court-martial: he helps lower the launch into the water and rests his hand on a cutlass.

The Boy Mutineer's seven brief, action-packed chapters encompass a multitude of events: Christian's attempt to settle on Tubuai; Heywood's eighteen-month interlude in Tahiti; Morrison constructing the schooner *Resolution*; the nightmarish imprisonment in "Pandora's Box," the sinking of *Pandora* and open-boat voyage to Batavia; and Heywood's return to England, followed by his court-martial. Barbary even explains how Morrison saved his journal during the wreck of *Pandora* and how it proved useful during the trial. After Heywood receives his pardon and visits his home, he decides, much like Roger Byam in *Mutiny on the Bounty*, "That the sea was really his home, his chosen career." Lord Hood offers him a midshipman's berth on his flagship, H.M.S. *Victory*.

Barbary thoughtfully adds a short "Historical Note" that discusses Heywood's later career (including his "sighting" of Christian in Plymouth), Morrison's and Fryer's journals, the publications of Bligh and Sir John Barrow, the discovery of the Pitcairn settlement and John Adams' contradictory accounts of Christian's fate.

The Boy Mutineer closes on a tantalizing note that surely has encouraged many young readers to comb the library for more books about the *Bounty*: "Did Fletcher Christian — after instructing Smith to report him dead — somehow find a way of leaving his desert island and returning secretly to England? We can never be sure."

GEORGE MACKAY BROWN: "Lieutenant Bligh and Two Midshipmen," in *Winter Tales*. London: John Murray, 1995.

Poet, short story writer and novelist George Mackay Brown was born, and spent most of his life, in the Orkney Islands off the northern coast of Scotland. His beautifully crafted verse and prose are imbued with the Orkneys' rich seafaring history and traditions, and one of his stories concerns William Bligh and George Stewart.

Winter Tales, one of Brown's last short story collections, includes "Lieutenant Bligh and Two Midshipmen," a haunting tale about a visit Bligh made to the Orkneys in 1780. He arrived at the close of *Resolution*'s third voyage, during which Bligh served as sailing master under Captain James Cook. Making landfall at Stromness, Bligh was entertained by the prominent Stewart family. At their house, he met 14 year-old George Stewart, who would join H.M.S. *Bounty* as an acting midshipman in 1787, and drown four years later in the wreck of *Pandora*. He remains one of the more enigmatic members of *Bounty*'s crew, as Bligh considered him to be one of the mutineers, while others held different opinions.

Bligh briefly mentioned the event and his opinion of George Stewart in *A Voyage to the South Sea*: "Stewart was a young man of creditable parents, in the Orkneys; at which place, on the return of *Resolution* from the South Seas, in 1780, we received so many civilities, that, on that account only, I should gladly have taken him with me: but, independent of this recommendation, he was a seaman, and had always borne a good character."

In "Lieutenant Bligh and Two Midshipmen," Brown paints as authentic a portrait of Bligh's personality as we are likely to get. He captures many of Bligh's well-known habits — his fussiness, aversion to excessive drinking, and the good-natured affection he felt for his crew — when they followed the rules. Rowena and Brian Murray, in their critical study, *Interrogation of Silence: The Writings of George Mackay Brown*, point out that Brown's language, "bring[s] out the gruffly caring nature of a man who shrinks from the display of feeling at the same time as being a shrewd observer of others' emotions."

The *Booklist* reviewer termed this particular story "*Sui generis*, outstandingly so; read it to learn what historical fiction ought to sound like — an aural slice of its era, not modern speech dressed, as it were, in period drag." Patrick O'Brian frequently achieves similar results, and his novel *Desolation Island* is of special interest to *Bounty* Saga enthusiasts for the powerful, albeit brief, appearance of Peter Heywood. O'Brian gives Heywood the opportunity to express his opinion of Captain Edwards of *Pandora* in the appropriately salty language of a British post captain: "Edwards! There's a man I don't mind telling you my opinion of. He was a blackguard, and no seaman, neither; and I hope he rots in hell ... the infernal bugger ran his ship on to a reef at the entrance of the Endeavour Straits.... The scoundrel. If it were not uncharitable, I should drink to his damnation for ever and a day."

During his dinner with the Stewart family, Bligh sums up his philosophy of leadership: "Let but all do their prescribed work adequately and with a good heart, and life on shipboard would move as if to music." He is disgusted by the tipsy behavior of his host as well as the excessive drinking of *Resolution*'s Lieutenant James Brisco, who spends most of the evening flirting with Stewart's daughter.

The next day, the fastidious Bligh demands that Brisco deliver a letter of apology to the Stewarts, a letter that also includes an invitation for George Stewart to join the crew of the

Charles Shearer's wraparound dust jacket illustration for George Mackay Brown's *Winter Tales* evokes the maritime history of the Orkney Islands and the storytelling traditions of its people, symbolized by a ship and an oil lamp. Brown's story, "Lieutenant Bligh and Two Midshipmen" appears in this volume. Reprinted by permission of John Murray (Publishers).

Bounty. Bligh had observed Stewart closely during his visit and formed a favorable opinion of him:

> George Stewart was a well-favoured young man. There was no doubt about that. His modesty when his name had been under discussion recommended him to Bligh, and also his temperance with regard to drink. A young man's eyes conveyed much to Bligh. There was a steadiness of purpose in young Stewart's and a sense of outwardness and questing; but this only manifested itself now and then, when his eyes glanced momentarily to the window, going beyond the silhouettes of the sailor and the merchant, to the great ship, the harbour, and the islands of Scapa Flow.

Brown takes some chronological liberties in the story, as Bligh would not obtain his command of the *Bounty* for several more years after his meeting George Stewart.

In 1869, a few years before Lady Belcher published *The Mutineers of the Bounty and their Descendants in Pitcairn and Norfolk Islands*, she received a letter referring to Bligh's visit from George Stewart's sister, "Mrs. Barry," then 92 years of age. She wrote, "Bligh may possibly have understood that George was inclined to go to sea, and may have said that if he could be of any use in furthering his views he would do so; but whether or not the *Bounty* was the first ship George sailed in I do not know, but, poor fellow, it was his last."

Bligh branded Stewart, who remained on board the *Bounty* after the mutiny, as one of the guilty parties, although there is no solid evidence that he took an active part in the rebellion. The night before the mutiny, Fletcher Christian told Stewart of his suicidal plan to leave the ship by raft. Stewart's ambiguous response — "The men are ripe for anything!" — has been variously interpreted as an effort to dissuade Christian from his plan and an incitement to mutiny.

Since Stewart drowned in the wreck of *Pandora*, we can only speculate if he would have been acquitted, condemned or pardoned at the court-martial of the *Bounty* mutineers. His story is particularly poignant, as he left behind in Tahiti "Peggy," his native wife, who died shortly after *Pandora* sailed. Missionaries later took their orphaned daughter, also named Peggy, to California, where she died in 1871. Lord Byron made Stewart (renaming him "Torquil"), a major character in *The Island, or Christian and His Comrades*, but Brown's tale of Bligh and Stewart has a genuine air of authenticity, and is more likely to endure than Byron's largely forgotten poem.

Additional Works

Books

Bennett, Jack. *The Lieutenant: An Epic Tale of Courage and Endurance on the High Seas.* London: Angus and Robertson, 1977.

    The action in Jack Bennett's highly readable novel is confined to the voyage of *Bounty*'s launch, as is Nordhoff and Hall's *Men Against the Sea*. Bennett's characterization of Bligh is especially effective.

Briand, Jr., Paul L. *In Search of Paradise; The Nordhoff-Hall Story.* New York: Duell, Sloan and Pearce, 1966.

_____. *In Search of Paradise; The Nordhoff-Hall Story.* Honolulu: Mutual Publishing Co., 1986. Paperback "Centennial Edition."

    This joint biography of Charles Nordhoff and James Norman Hall documents the creation of *The Bounty Trilogy* and other novels co-written by the famous team. It also discusses the novels and stories written individually by each author, including Hall's *The Tale of a Shipwreck: Adventures in the Wake of the Bounty*. Paul L. Briand, Jr. includes a useful bibliography of books and magazine articles written by Nordhoff and Hall.

Bullen, Frank T. *A Bounty Boy: Being Some Adventures of a Christian Barbarian on an Unpremeditated Trip Round the World.* London: Holden and Hardingham, Adelphi, 1912.

    Frank T. Bullen is remembered primarily for his vivid whaling novel, *The Cruise of the Cachalot*. His primary objective in *A Bounty Boy*, a highly religious work, is to "sketch a community for whom I have the highest admiration, the descendants of the mutineers of the Bounty." The community is Norfolk Island, where many of the Pitcairners settled in the 19th century.

Chamier, Frederick. *Jack Adams, the Mutineer.* Three volumes. London: Henry Colburn, 1838. Later editions entitled *Jack Adams; or, the Mutiny of the Bounty*.

    Royal Navy Captain Frederick Chamier was a pioneer of naval fiction, along with Frederick Marryat and James Fenimore Cooper. Regardless, few readers today have the patience to make it through three long volumes of *Jack Adams, the Mutineer*. Chamier unfolds the tale in a very leisurely way, infusing events with a moralistic, didactic tone that has gone out of fashion. *Jack Adams, the Mutineer* does have historic value as the first novelistic treatment of the *Bounty* Saga, one of the few predecessors of Nordhoff and Hall's *Bounty Trilogy* novels.

Collett, Bill. *The Last Mutiny: The Further Adventures of Captain Bligh.* New York: W. W. Norton and Co., 1993.

    An aging Bligh approaches death in this powerfully atmospheric novel, reliving his naval career through a sequence of memories and dreams.

Day, A. Grove. *Louis Becke.* New York: Twayne Publishers, Inc., 1966.

    A perceptive discussion of Louis Becke and Walter Jeffery's *The Mutineer*, an important *Bounty* Saga novel, is included in this full-length critical study.

_____. *Mad about Islands: Novelists of a Vanished Pacific.* Honolulu: Mutual Publishing Co., 1987.

This entertaining volume features essays on several writers who have written *Bounty*- or Pitcairn Island-related novels and stories: Louis Becke, Jack London, Charles Nordhoff, James Norman Hall and Mark Twain.

Day, A. Grove and Carl Stroven, eds. *Best South Sea Stories.* New York: Appleton-Century, 1964.

An excellent selection of short fiction set in the South Seas, including Jack London's "The Seed of McCoy" and James A. Michener's "Mutiny."

Kinsolving, William. *Mr. Christian: the Further Adventures of Fletcher Christian.* New York: Simon and Schuster, 1996.

Mr. Christian: the Further Adventures of Fletcher Christian opens in 1810, in the London asylum Bedlam, where a filthy stranger has been confined after a suicide attempt. It turns out to be Fletcher Christian, who requests pen and paper to write his story.

Christian begins the tale on the day he was shot on Pitcairn Island. As he tills his garden, he is consumed by guilt, planning to jump from the cliffs into the sea: "I considered in explicit detail how a seed might grow in the rich red soil of Pitcairn. Yet every time I opened the earth with my wooden spade, I saw blood there, glistening." Moments later, he is wounded by one of the Polynesians, but soon recovers and makes his escape. William Kinsolving's tale of Christian's fictional adventures is thrilling and deeply moving — arguably the best *Bounty* novel since Nordhoff and Hall's *Mutiny on the Bounty.*

Maxwell, John (pseudonym for Brian Freemantle). *HMS Bounty.* London: Jonathan Cape, 1977.

Freemantle, Brian. *Hell's Paradise.* London: Severn House Publishers, 2001. Reprint of *HMS Bounty* (with new title).

In *HMS Bounty*, Christian not only survives the bloodshed on Pitcairn Island and returns to England, but also, with his brother Edward, confronts William Bligh during his tenure as Governor-General of new South Wales!

Richard Hough's *Captain Bligh and Mr. Christian,* published five years earlier, clearly influenced Miller's novel. Although the language is not explicit, it slowly becomes quite clear that the characters had a homosexual relationship that ended by the time the *Bounty* left Tahiti.

McClintock, James I. *White Logic: Jack London's Short Stories.* Grand Rapids: Wolf House Books, 1975.

James I. McClintock's perceptive study of London's short fiction includes commentary on "The Seed of McCoy."

Metcalfe, Rowan. *Transit of Venus.* Wellington, N.Z.: Huia Publishers, 2004. Reprinted in trade paperback format by Pandanus Books.

Rowan Metcalfe, a direct descendant of Fletcher Christian, characterizes her novel as "A meditation on my ancestors." It tells the story of the *Bounty* and Pitcairn Island through the eyes of Mauatua, who later becomes Christian's consort. The novel begins in 1869, with the arrival of James Cook on *Endeavour.*

Miller, Stanley. *Mr. Christian! The Journal of Fletcher Christian, Former Lieutenant of His Majesty's Armed Vessel Bounty.* New York: John Day Co., 1973.

So many "autobiographies" of Fletcher Christian have been appearing that they constitute a subgenre of *Bounty* historical fiction. The first example was Owen Rutter's *Cain's Birthday,* in which Christian's descendant discovers his journal. In Stanley Miller's *Mr. Christian! The Journal of Fletcher Christian, Former Lieutenant of His Majesty's Armed Vessel Bounty*, Christian survives the bloodshed on Pitcairn Island, writing his story from the safety of what he calls "Look-Out Hill ... my leafy bower hidden close under the highest crag of my island fortress." He narrates how he was picked up by an American ship, wandered the world from Boston to England, and then finally returned to Pitcairn.

Mountain, Fiona. *Isabella: The Haunting Love Story of Fletcher Christian and Isabella Curwen.* London: Orion Books Ltd., 1999.

This gothic novel of romance and suspense is based on the premise that Fletcher Christian returned to England.

Opposite: The Curwen family's unusual house on Belle Island in Lake Windermere is featured on the cover of Fiona Mountain's *Isabella*, a novel based on the premise that Christian returned to England. The privately owned house still stands today. Reprinted by permission of Orion Publishing Group Ltd.

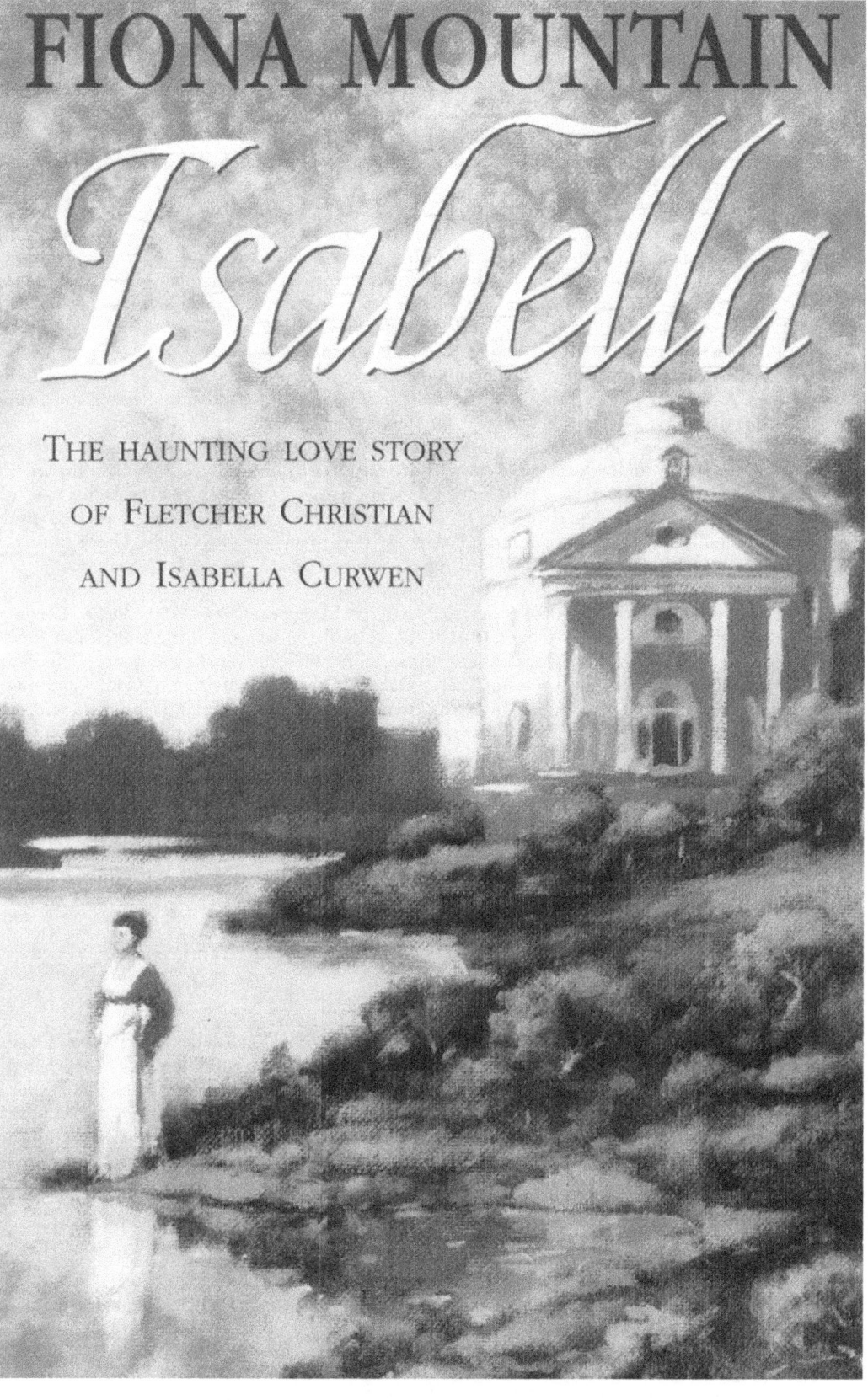

FIONA MOUNTAIN

Isabella

THE HAUNTING LOVE STORY
OF FLETCHER CHRISTIAN
AND ISABELLA CURWEN

Quayle, Eric. *Ballantyne the Brave: A Victorian Writer and his Family.* London: Rupert Hart-Davis, 1967.

    Eric Quayle's biographical study provides personal background on R.M. Ballantyne, author of *The Lonely Island.*

Roulston, Robert. *James Norman Hall.* Boston: Twayne Publishers, 1978.

    Nordhoff and Hall's *Bounty Trilogy* novels are discussed in this book-length, scholarly overview of James Norman Hall's work.

Rutter, Owen. *Cain's Birthday.* London: Hutchinson and Co, Ltd., 1930.

    The protagonist of *Cain's Birthday,* by *Bounty* scholar Owen Rutter, is Ursula Christian, a fictional descendant of Fletcher Christian who discovers her ancestor's journal. It tells the tale of the *Bounty* from Christian's point of view, anticipating works such as Stanley Miller's *Mr. Christian! The Journal of Fletcher Christian, Former Lieutenant of His Majesty's Armed Vessel Bounty* and William Kinsolving's *Mr. Christian: the Further Adventures of Fletcher Christian.*

    Rutter wrote several novels during his career, but his literary talents clearly lay in the field of historical scholarship, and most of his fiction is forgotten.

Snow, Philip. "A Single Unlucky Imposter." *Best Stories of the South Seas.* London: Faber and Faber, 1967.

    One of the lesser-known chapters in the *Bounty* Saga is the "reign" of Joshua Hill, an unscrupulous American who took advantage of the Pitcairn Islanders from 1832 to 1838, claiming British authority to rule the island. As Philip Snow states in this succinct account of the events that followed, Hill realized that "The chances of his authority and his authenticity being contested would seem more unlikely on Pitcairn a hundred years ago than anywhere that he could have chosen in the world." Mark Twain based "The Great Revolution in Pitcairn" on the same material.

Thrapp, Dan. *Mutiny's Curse.* Tulsa: RiverOak Publishing, 2002.

    Dan Thrapp creatively employs fictional material from *Letters from Mr. Fletcher Christian* and places the post-mutiny Fletcher Christian in the midst of war and intrigue in South America. This novel has a strong religious undertone, beginning with the very first sentence: "His name was Christian, though his faith was not." RiverOak Publishing is a division of Cook Communications Ministries, which specializes in Sunday school curriculum material. It follows a long tradition of using the history of the *Bounty* and Pitcairn Island for religious inspiration and instruction.

Twain, Mark. "The Great Revolution in Pitcairn." *The Stolen White Elephant, Etc.* Boston: James R. Osgood and Co., 1882.

    Twain takes an ironic look at Joshua Hill's dictatorial reign on Pitcairn Island, and how he imposed his own brand of tyranny on the Pitcairn Islanders in this fictional account. It was reprinted in *The Complete Humorous Sketches and Tales of Mark Twain* by Da Capo Press in 1996.

Van der Voort, P. J. *The Pen and the Quarter-Deck: A Study of the Life and Works of Captain Frederick Chamier, R.N.* Leiden: Leiden University Press, 1972.

    This first full-length critical study of Frederick Chamier includes a chapter discussing *Jack Adams, the Mutineer.*

Wilson, Erle. *Adams of the Bounty.* Sydney: Angus & Robertson, 1958.

_____. *Adams of the Bounty.* New York: Criterion Books, 1958.

    Unlike the many novels where Fletcher Christian is the primary character, Erle Wilson's *Adams of the Bounty* is told from John Adams' perspective. Although it was published at a time when the name "William Bligh" was a synonym for tyranny and brutality, Wilson claims, "The author is convinced that the popular legend ... which has branded Bligh as a bullying, inhuman monster, is very far from the truth." Wilson has a flair for effective dialogue and characterization, and *Adams of the Bounty* deserves more attention than it has received.

Poems

Beard, William. *Valiant Martinet: or the Adventures on Land and Sea of Captain William Bligh.* Foreword by George Mackaness. Sydney: William Beard, (1956). Limited to 125 copies.

    Bligh biographer George Mackaness contributed a foreword to this scarce narrative poem about Bligh.

Bryant, William Cullen. "A Song of Pitcairn's Island." *Poems by William Cullen Bryant.* New York: E. Bliss, 1832.

A Tahitian woman narrates this brief, sentimental lyric poem some 20 years after her arrival on Pitcairn Island, which she calls "This sweet lone isle amid the sea."

Byron, George Gordon. "The Death of Christian and the Mutineers." *Mirror of Literature, Amusement, and Instruction* 6, no. 32 (June 28 1823): 136–141.

An episode from Lord Byron's *The Island, or, Christian and His Comrades* was featured in this periodical, issued the same year as the poem's publication.

Coleridge, Ernest Hartley, ed. *The Works of Lord Byron. Poetry.* Vol. 5. London: John Murray, 1905. Second edition.

Ernest Hartley Coleridge provides a lengthy introduction to *The Island, or, Christian and his Comrades* in Volume 5 of this collected edition of Byron's works.

Coleridge, Samuel Taylor. "The Rime of the Ancyent Marinere, in Seven Parts." *Lyrical Ballads, with a Few Other Poems.* London: J. and A. Arch, 1798.

This famous poem is available in numerous editions and anthologies of English literature. Editions that incorporate annotations and critical commentary are the most useful for readers interested in ferreting out allusions to Fletcher Christian.

Heywood, Peter, and Raymond F. DaBall. *A Dream, Which Happened to Peter Heywood, Febry 6th, 1790, while he was at Taheite, an Exile from His Friends and Country Owing to the Fatal Mutiny on Board His Majesty's Ship Bounty in Which He Was Forced to Remain against His Inclination and Not Suffer'd to Accompany the Captain in the Boat.* N.p.: Bond Wheelwright Co., 1977. Limited to 1,200 copies.

A Dream, which Peter Heywood composed in 1790 during his long sojourn on Tahiti, was available only in the Heywood family papers until this limited edition appeared, printed in black and red calligraphic script. It is illuminating to read *A Dream* alongside passages in Edward Tagart's *A Memoir of the Late Captain Peter Heywood, R.N.* that describe Heywood's lifelong affection for Tahiti, its people and culture.

Children's Books

Anderson, David, and Margarette Lincoln. *The Mutiny on the Bounty.* London: Macdonald Children's Books, 1989.

See Chapter 5 for details.

Armstrong, Richard. *The Mutineers.* London: J. M. Dent, 1968.

A gang of teenage delinquents "emulates" Fletcher Christian by hijacking an ocean liner in this imaginative young adult novel.

Bingley, Thomas. "Uncle Thomas Tells About the Mutiny of the Bounty." *Tales of Shipwrecks and Other Disasters at Sea.* Chapter IV. Boston: Weeks, Jordan and Company, 1839.

Typical of much 19th century children's literature about the *Bounty*, the story as told by "Uncle Thomas" to his nephews is heavily paraphrased from Barrow's *The Eventful History of the Mutiny and Piratical Seizure of H.M.S. Bounty.*

Goodrich, Frank B. *Ocean's Story: or, Triumphs of Thirty Centuries.* Philadelphia: Hubbard Brothers, 1873. Chapter XLVII.

This collection of sea stories includes a nicely illustrated account of the *Bounty* mutiny and Pitcairn Island.

Hale, Edward Everett. "Pitcairn's Island." *Stories of the Sea, Told by Sailors.* Boston: Roberts Brothers, 1880.

Edward Everett Hale is best remembered for his story, "The Man Without a Country." Very few people are familiar with his collections of historically based stories for young readers: *Stories of War, Told by Soldiers* and *Stories of the Sea, Told by Sailors.* Hale's purpose in publishing these volumes was to "lead the way from story-books to history, by showing to the young reader how to pass from one to the other, and giving them a taste of the original narratives."

"Pitcairn's Island" tells one of the island's most famous and exciting true stories: "Wreck of the Wild Wave: The Crusoes of Pitcairn Island: The Shipwreck Diary of Capt. Josiah N. Knowles." In 1858, Captain Knowles of the California clipper ship *Wild Wave* was shipwrecked on the Oeno Atoll, 76 miles from Pitcairn Island. He and the crew reached Pitcairn in the ship's boat, but were surprised to find it uninhabited: the Pitcairners had emigrated to Norfolk Island. Luckily, there still was plenty of fruit, as well as livestock to sustain them while they awaited rescue.

Readers interested in this tale should consult Josiah N. Knowles' The *Crusoes of Pitcairn Island*, Edith Thatcher Hurd's *The Course of the Wild Wave*, James M. Bellarosa's "Odyssey for Survival: The Wreck of the 'Wild Wave,'" and Thurman C. Petty, Jr.'s, *The Wreck of the Wild Wave: The Untold Saga of Captain Knowles and Pitcairn Island*.

Harper, Ethel. *Paths of the Sea*. Douglas, Isle of Man: Shearwater Press, 1977.

Rich in atmosphere, most of Ether Harper's illustrated novel for young people is set on the Isle of Man, the ancestral home of Fletcher Christian and Peter Heywood.

Knox, Thomas W. "A Visit to Pitcairn's Island — The Mutineers of the 'Bounty.'" *The Young Nimrods Around the World: A Book for Boys. Hunting Adventures on Land and Sea, Part II*. New York: Harper and Brothers, 1882. Illustrated.

Chapter XV of this sequel to the popular *The Young Nimrods in North America*, entitled "A Visit to Pitcairn's Island — The Mutineers of the "Bounty," is told in the form of a dialogue between "Lieutenant Johnson," the "Doctor" and the youths on board as they sight Pitcairn Island.

Lincoln, Margarette. *Mutiny on the Bounty*. Illustrations by John Dillow. Loughborough: Ladybird Books, 1989.

See Chapter 5 for details.

Rinaldi, Ann. *Mutiny's Daughter*. New York: HarperCollins, 2005.

Fletcher Christian brings Mary, his 14-year-old daughter to England in this colorful, suspenseful novel for young adults.

Vicary, Tim. *Mutiny on the Bounty*. Oxford: Oxford University Press, 1994.

This graded children's reader, a volume in the "Oxford Bookworms" Library, features a cover photo of Mel Gibson as Fletcher Christian in *The Bounty*.

Von Horn, W. O. (Wilhelm Öertel). *The Lord Will Repay*. New York and Chicago: Ernst Kaufmann, n.d. (1914).

The Lord Will Repay surely is one of the most curious books inspired by the *Bounty* mutiny. Filled with wild inaccuracies, this children's story is a blend of fact, fiction and religious instruction. Telling an accurate story is secondary to Von Horn's primary objective of teaching young readers that "crime does not pay."

Weate, Philip, and Caroline Graham. *Captain William Bligh: An Illustrated History*. Sydney: Paul Hamlyn, 1972.

The many fine illustrations in this handsome biography of Bligh make it especially appropriate for young readers.

Stage Dramatizations

Chodes, John J. *The Longboat: A Play*. (Unpublished). First production: Harold Clurman Theatre, New York City, August 7, 1987. Sixty-eight page typescript.

Chodes' play, which features just four actors, is set during the voyage of *Bounty*'s launch, and suggests that differences in social class among *Bounty*'s crew triggered the mutiny.

Articles

Addison, Catherine. "Gender and Race in Byron's *The Island* and Mitford's *Christina*." *Antipodes* 18, no. 1 (June 2004): 72–76.

Catherine Addison discusses how Mitford's poem may have influenced Byron in the composition of *The Island, or Christian and His Comrades*, and how the two poets created quite different "utopias" in their work.

Houston, Neal B. "Fletcher Christian and the Rime of the Ancient Mariner." *Dalhousie Review* 45, no. 55 (Winter 1965–66): 431–446.

Neal B. Houston's scholarly interpretation of Coleridge's "The Rime of the Ancient Mariner" argues that Fletcher Christian's experiences lie at its very heart: "The Mariner's 'guilt and redemption' is the guilt and redemption Christian must have experienced, and it underlies the overt moral principle of the poem."

Leask, Nigel. "Resolving *The Corsair: Lara* and *The Island*." *Byron*. Edited by Jane Stabler. London: Addison Wesley Longman, 1998.

Nigel Leask's article in this general collection of essays about Byron characterizes *The*

A photograph from a performance of *The Longboat: A Play*, by John Chodes. This powerful drama, which takes place on *Bounty*'s launch, suggests that variations in social class aboard *Bounty* triggered the mutiny. The *New York City Tribune* reviewer wrote, "For Chodes, Bligh is both a hero and victim of his rise from the lowest rung of society." The cast consisted of Rob Donohoe as Ledward, Eddie Grossman as Tinkler, John Juback as Purcell and James Walch as Bligh (courtesy John Chodes).

    Island, or Christian and His Comrades as, "An anticolonial reworking of the theme of *Robinson Crusoe*."

Lowes, John Livingston. *The Road to Xanadu: A Study in the Ways of the Imagination*. Boston and New York: Houghton Mifflin Co., 1927.
    This legendary critical work discusses the genesis of Coleridge's great poems, including "The Rime of the Ancient Mariner."

Mariner, William. *An Account of the Natives of the Tonga Islands, in the South Pacific Ocean*. London: John Murray, 1817.
    Mariner's popular book was one of Lord Byron's sources for *The Island, or Christian and His Comrades*.

Menard, Wilmon. "The *Bounty* Mutiny Remembered." *Naval History* 5, no. 2 (Summer 1991): 24–30.
    This general article about the *Bounty* mutiny recounts a conversation that Wilmon Menard had with Charles Nordhoff at the Tahiti Yacht club in the late 1930s. Menard asked Nordhoff why he and James Norman Hall made Bligh such a villain in *Mutiny on the Bounty*, when history seemed to suggest otherwise. Nordhoff, who disagreed with Menard's higher opinion of Bligh, admitted, "Jimmy and I did perhaps treat him somewhat harshly, perhaps more than he deserved. However, we did need a full-fledged villain for story conflict in our novel."

Rutter, Owen. "The Travels of Fletcher Christian." *Blue Peter* 12, no. 123 (June 1932): 263–270.
    Bounty scholar Owen Rutter contributed an article about the fraudulent *Letters from Mr. Fletcher Christian* to this "Magazine of Sea Travel" for children. He liberally quotes from the letters, explaining how the first few obviously were derived from authentic sources, but that beginning with the fourth letter, "Fact ceases and fiction begins."

This article is useful for its excerpts from the rare *Letters from Mr. Fletcher Christian*, and for Rutter's excellent commentary. The illustrations include a reproduction of Bligh's dispatch to the Admiralty reporting the mutiny and his safe arrival at Timor.

Spence, Gordon. "Byron's Polynesian Fantasy." *Byron Journal* no. 24 (1996): 42–51.

Gordon Spence's critical discussion of Byron's *The Island, or Christian and His Comrades*, notes that Lord Byron did not like "fantasy," and had even criticized William Wordsworth for an inaccurate descriptions of Grecian landscapes. Yet, Byron takes extreme liberties with the true *Bounty* story in *The Island*, which Spence says we should regret: "With Bligh's and Mariner's books in front of him, he could have written a poem about Polynesia with some degree of authenticity."

Squire, John. "Was Fletcher Christian the Ancient Mariner?" *Illustrated London News*, May 9, 1953, 732.

In this enjoyable review and "appreciation" of *The Wake of the Bounty*, John Squire casts a doubtful eye on C.S. Wilkinson's theories about the return of Fletcher Christian to England, and how it may have inspired Samuel Taylor Coleridge's figure of the Ancient Mariner. Nevertheless, Squire appreciates the romance of these speculations, concluding, "A pity Sherlock Holmes can't get to work!"

Supplemental Bibliography

Books

Armstrong, Warren. *Mutiny Afloat: A Dramatized Record of Some Famous Sea Mutinies*. London: Frederick Muller, 1956.

Bruce, Charles. "The Mutiny of The Bounty." *The Book of Adventure and Peril: A Record of Heroism and Endurance on Sea and Land*. Edinburgh: Nimmo, Hay and Mitchell, 1876, 315–360.

Coleridge, Samuel Taylor. *The Rime of the Ancient Mariner and Other Poems*. New York: Dover Publications, 1992.

Gaunt, Mary. *Joan of the Pilchard*. London: Ernest Benn, 1930.

Hall, James Norman. *My Island Home: an Autobiography*. Boston: Little, Brown, 1952.

Hume, Robert. "'The Island' and the Evolution of Byron's 'Tales.'" *Romantic and Victorian: Studies in Memory of William H. Marshall*. Eds. W. Paul Elledge and Richard Hoffman. Rutherford, New Jersey: Fairleigh Dickinson University Press, 1971, 158–180.

Johnson, Robert Leland. *The American Heritage of James Norman Hall, the Woodshed Poet of Iowa and Co-author of Mutiny on the Bounty*. Philadelphia: Dorrance, n.d. [1969].

MacGilchrist, John. *The Mutineers: A Poem*. Edinburgh: Sutherland and Knox; London: Simpkin, Marshall and Co., 1859.

McDermind, Val. *The Grave Tattoo*. London: HarperCollins, 2006.

Merle, Robert. *The Island*. London: Michael Joseph, 1964. Translated from the French "L'Ile" by Humphrey Hare.

The Mutiny of the 'Bounty.' Whitcombe's Story Books, no. 527. Wellington: Whitcombe and Tombs, n.d.

Nash, Cyril. "'The Bounty Mutineers,' A Play written for Broadcasting by Cyril Nash, being an authentic presentation of the Voyage of the 'Bounty' and subsequent Court Martial based on Owen Rutter's book 'The True Story of the Bounty' (sic) and from contemporary records, which includes James Morrison's Journal, Bligh's Log and the Admiralty Records." Produced by Peter Creswell; Regional; 2nd September 1936, 8:30 to 9:40 pm.

Nordhoff, Charles. *Seeing The World: A Young Sailor's Own Story*. Edinburgh: W. P. Nimmo, n.d. (1880).

_____. *Faery Lands of the South Seas*. New York: Harper and Brothers, 1921.

_____. *Mutiny on the Bounty*. New York: Books, Inc., 1943. First paperback edition.

_____. *Men Against the Sea*. New York: Pocket Books, Inc., 1946. First paperback edition.

_____. *Pitcairn's Island*. New York: Pocket Books, Inc., 1947. First paperback edition.

O'Brian, Patrick. *Desolation Island*. New York: Stein and Day, 1978.

O'Brien, Patrick. *The Mutiny on the Bounty*. New York: Walker Books for Young Readers, 2007.

David Edgar as William Bligh curses Fletcher Christian and the mutineers in this scene from Richard Crane's *Mutiny on the Bounty—A Sea-Faring Show*, performed in 1972 at the University of Bradford, England: "You will see me again Mr. Christian! You will see me as you swing from the yards in Portsmouth Harbour!" His companions in the launch are, from left, Alan Bridger as John Fryer; Jackie Newbold, Liz Lester and Fiona Taylor as Midshipmen; and Arnie Kinbrum as "Bosun" (photograph by Roger Pearson). Reprinted by permission of Richard Crane.

Oulton, Abraham, Esq. "The Mutiny of the Bounty." *Poems by Abraham Oulton, Esq.* Dublin: 1839.
Rennie, Neil. *Far-fetched facts: the literature of travel and the idea of the South Seas.* Oxford: Clarendon Press; New York: Oxford University Press, 1995.
_____. *Far-fetched facts: the literature of travel and the idea of the South Seas.* Oxford: Clarendon Press, 1998. Clarendon paperback edition, with corrections.
Richardson, Robert. *Adventurous Boat Voyages.* London: Nelson & Sons, 1886.
Townsend, John Rowe. *The Islanders.* New York: J. B. Lippincott, 1981.
Watson, Vera. *Mary Russell Mitford.* London: Evans Brothers, n.d.
Wells, Carveth. *Adventure!* With a foreword by Lowell Thomas. New York: John Day, 1931.
Whiteing, Richard. *The Island, or, an Adventure of a Person of Quality.* Leipzig: Tauchnitz, 1888.
Wilkinson, Isaac. *The Poetical Works of Isaac Wilkinson.* Cockermouth: 1824.

Articles

Benchley, Peter. "Maison James Norman Hall." *New York Times Magazine,* May 2, 2004, 98.
Chodes, John. "Mutiny in Paradise." *Chronicles,* February 1988, 10–13.
Erskine, Nigel. "Reclaiming the Bounty." *Archaeology* 52, no. 3 (May–June 1999): 34–40.
Fleck, P. D. "Romance in Byron's 'The Island.'" *Byron: A Symposium.* Edited by John Jump. New York: Barnes and Noble, 1975, 163–183.
Glasgow, Jesse. "For What it's Worth: Patrick O'Brian on Capt. Bligh." *Pitcairn Log* 25 (October–December 1998): 6–7.
Hall, James Norman. "From Med to Mum: An Adventure of My Own." Parts 1–5, *Atlantic Monthly*

153 (March 1934): 257–268; pt. 2, "The Ghosts of Pitcairn." (April 1934): 404–414; pt. 3, "Wreck of the 'Pro Patria.'" (May 1934): 568–578; pt. 4, "Castaway." (June 1934): 708–718; pt. 5, "The Last Leg: From Med to Mum." *Atlantic Monthly* 154 (July 1934): 96–105.

Hare, Robert. "Pitcairn" (poem). *Australasian Record* 28 (August 18, 1924): 3.

_____. "Pitcairn" (poem). *The Youth's Instructor* 72 (December 2, 1924): 4.

Kennerley, Alston. "Frank Thomas Bullen, 1857–1915: Whaling and Nonfiction Maritime Writing." *American Neptune* 56, no. 4 (Fall 1996): 353–370.

Trodd, Anthea. "Collaborating in Open Boats: Dickens, Collins, Franklin, and Bligh." *Victorian Studies* Volume 42, Number 2 (Winter 1999/2000): 201–225.

Tubbs, Jack. "Research Paper on 'The Great Revolution in Pitcairn' by Mark Twain." *Pitcairn Log* 11 (September–November 1983): 4–6.

Warren, Nicholas W. "A Lexicographical Study of Bligh's *Narrative of the Mutiny on Board His Majesty's Ship Bounty*." *Bulletin of Fukuoka Women's Junior College*, no. 59 (February 2001).

Stage Dramatizations

Crane, Richard. *Mutiny on the Bounty—a Sea-faring Show*. Unpublished script. Performed at the University of Bradford, 1972.

Miller, Stanley. *Acquit or Hang!* ITV "Play of the Week." Broadcast January 6, 1964.

Radio Dramatizations

McAll, Kate. *The Real Captain Bligh*. BBC Radio 4.

Miller, Stanley. *Acquit or Hang!*

Mutiny on the Bounty. BBC Radio 4 Drama, 1996.

Directed by Adrian Bean.

Cast includes Roger Daltrey, Lionel Jefferies, Oliver Reed and Linus Roache.

"*Mutiny on the Bounty*." Independent Radio Drama Productions, 1989.

Welles, Orson. "Mutiny on the Bounty."

First broadcast January 13, 1939 on *Campbell Soup Playhouse*.

5

Illustrated Books

The episodes that constitute the *Bounty* Saga took place across the globe, against a wide variety of backdrops that artists have captured on canvas and paper. These settings include the decks of a square-rigged ship, vast expanses of the ocean in its ever-changing aspects, a court-martial on a British man-of-war, the turbulent waters of Pitcairn Island's Bounty Bay, and the lush island of Tahiti, with its mountains, waterfalls, azure sea and black sand beaches. Illustrations depicting these places and events appeared as early as 1790, with the publication of William Bligh's *A Narrative of the Mutiny on Board His Majesty's Ship* Bounty. The frontispiece of the first Dutch edition is a detailed engraving of *Bounty*'s launch that pictures Bligh at the rudder, several of the crew trimming the sails and others bailing water from the vessel.

Robert Dodd's famous 1790 painting of the mutineers forcing Bligh into the launch has been used as a dust jacket illustration for many books, including Alexander McKee's *The Truth about the Mutiny on the Bounty*, Bengt Danielsson's *What Happened on the Bounty*, Gavin Kennedy's *The Mutiny of the Bounty*, the American edition of Glynn Christian's *Fragile Paradise: The Discovery of Fletcher Christian, Bounty Mutineer*, and Bill Collett's novel, *The Last Mutiny: The Further Adventures of Captain Bligh*.

Midshipman Peter Heywood, one of the main participants in the *Bounty* Saga, made an eyewitness sketch of H.M.S. *Pandora* sinking that has been reproduced countless times since it first appeared in Sir John Barrow's *Eventful History of the Mutiny and Piratical Seizure of H.M.S.* Bounty. The publisher of Geoffrey Rawson's *Pandora's Last Voyage* created a striking dust jacket based on Heywood's sketch.

Bligh himself was a skilled artist, who focused much of his talent on painting the flora and fauna he encountered during his extensive travels. Even his rough sketches are worth examining, such as the ones he made in a small notebook during the open boat voyage under the most difficult conditions (reproduced in *The Bligh Notebook*). George Tobin, who served as a lieutenant on Bligh's *Providence* voyage, was an exceptional artist who painted many of the locales visited by the *Bounty* just a few years earlier, including Adventure Bay in Van Diemen's Land (Tasmania) and Tahiti's Matavai Bay. Many of his works are reproduced in Douglas Oliver's *Return To Tahiti: Bligh's Second Breadfruit Voyage*.

Early visitors to Pitcairn Island often created pictorial records of their experiences. Lieutenant John Shillibeer of H.M.S. *Briton*, admittedly an amateur, etched the first portrait of Thursday October Christian, son of the mutiny's ringleader. It was used as an illustration in Shillibeer's *Narrative of the Briton's Voyage to Pitcairn's Island*. Captain F.W. Beechey of H.M.S.

The unique frontispiece of the first Dutch edition of *A Narrative of the Mutiny on Board His Majesty's Ship the Bounty*, printed in Rotterdam, 1790, by Gerard Abraham Arrenberg. This is one of the earliest illustrations of Bligh and his crew in the open boat.

Blossom, another British seaman with an artistic flair, drew a much-reproduced portrait of John Adams when he visited Pitcairn Island in 1825. This, along with Beechey's drawings of longboats landing at Bounty Bay and of John Adams' residence, were first published in his *Narrative of a Voyage to the Pacific and Beerings Strait*. These have been reprinted in many other works.

Since the mid–20th century, illustrated books and articles about H.M.S. *Bounty* have been appearing with some regularity, with the quality of the artwork running the gamut from uninspired to exceptional. The latter would include the 12 illustrations that N.C. Wyeth created for the 1940 edition of *The Bounty Trilogy* by Charles Nordhoff and James Norman Hall. In the world of periodical art, Anton Otto Fischer and W.H.D. Koerner executed a number of illustrations to accompany the *Saturday Evening Post* serializations of, respectively, Nordhoff and Hall's *Men Against the Sea* and *Pitcairn's Island*. Roy Andersen painted several vibrant canvases for Luis Marden's "In *Bounty*'s Wake: Finding the Wreck of H.M.S. *Pandora*," published in *National Geographic Magazine* (1985).

Perhaps the most outstanding examples of *Bounty*-related illustrations to date are the wood engravings that accompany five volumes of important primary material published by the Golden Cockerel Press throughout the 1930s, starting with *The Voyage of the Bounty's Launch* and closing with *John Fryer of the Bounty*. The artists commissioned by the press for these works, which also are masterpieces of typography, were Robert Gibbings, Lynton Lamb, Peter Barker-Mill and Averil Mackenzie-Grieve.

Two other notable examples of fine illustration and bookmaking were issued by the Limited Editions Club: Nordhoff and Hall's *Mutiny on the Bounty*, illustrated by Fletcher Martin, and Bligh's *A Voyage to the South Sea*, featuring the work of Geoffrey C. Ingleton. Both are filled with well-executed watercolors and drawings. Laurence Irving's *Bligh & the Bounty*, illustrated with woodcuts, is another exceptional volume, as is A. Richard Mansir's *The Journal of* Bounty's *Launch*. Mansir's selection of texts from William Bligh's log is accompanied by his own drawings and watercolors.

Illustrated books and articles about H.M.S. *Bounty* continue to appear from specialty presses and prestigious magazines like *The New Yorker* and *The Atlantic Monthly*. Considering the consistently high level of interest in the people and events that make up the *Bounty* Saga, this trend seems likely to continue.

Major Works

WILLIAM BLIGH: John Fryer. *The Voyage of the Bounty's Launch as Related in William Bligh's Despatch to the Admiralty and the Journal of John Fryer*. With an Introduction by Owen Rutter and wood engravings by Robert Gibbings. [London]: Printed & made in Great Britain by the Golden Cockerel Press, 1934. Limited to 300 numbered copies.

The Voyage of the Bounty's Launch was the first volume to appear in a series of five "Bountiana" titles published by the Golden Cockerel Press, in uniform "sail cloth" bindings, from 1934 to 1939. Historian and novelist Owen Rutter, who became a partner of the Press in the early 1930s, shared an enthusiasm for the history of the South Seas and the *Bounty* Saga with Robert Gibbings, a noted wood engraver who acquired the press from its founder, Harold Midgely Taylor, in 1924.

The Golden Cockerel Press "Bountiana" volumes were expensive, fine press books issued in limited quantities for collectors, but they had a major impact on *Bounty* scholarship by making a number of important documents available to the public (albeit a small public) for the first time. All *Bounty* enthusiasts and scholars are thankful that the Golden Cockerel Press brought these manuscripts to the light of day.

Gibbings' wood-engraved frontispiece to *The Voyage of the Bounty's Launch* captures both the confusion and high emotion generated by the mutiny. Armed with a pistol, one mutineer shakes his fist at Bligh, who has been bound to a mast in his nightshirt; others brandish muskets and a cutlass; the boatswain hauls on a rope that will lower *Bounty*'s launch to the water; and, in the foreground, three crew members — two armed with muskets but not brandishing them — watch the scene. Perhaps they are debating whether to join Christian or risk their lives with Bligh in an open boat. Here is the scene as Bligh describes it in his "Despatch to the Admiralty," composed in Batavia just six months after the mutiny: "I was now haul'd upon Deck in my shirt without a rag else, and my hands tyed behind my back, held by Fletcher Christian and Charles Churchill with a Bayonet at my Breast, and two men, Alexr Smith and Thos Burkitt ... behind me, with loaded musquets cocked and Bayonets fixed. Under guard I was placed abaft the Mizzen Mast."

Bligh later used "Despatch to the Admiralty," along with his log, as a basis for *A Narrative of the Mutiny on Board His Majesty's Ship* Bounty, published in 1790. Before publication as part of *The Voyage of the Bounty's Launch*, it had appeared only once before, in *Historical Records of New South Wales* (1892).

The Voyage of the Bounty's Launch pairs the "Despatch" with a previously unpublished manuscript by John Fryer, Master of H.M.S. *Bounty*, that reveals his own unique view of the mutiny and open boat voyage. At first, Rutter worked with the transcript of an untraced original that contained a number of omissions and other editorial changes. Fortuitously, the original Fryer manuscript came up for auction at Sotheby's as Rutter proceeded with his work. W. F. Molloy, who purchased the manuscript for the Mitchell Library in Sydney, loaned it to Rutter for collation with the faulty transcript.

A facsimile of this transcript, now held by the National Maritime Museum, Greenwich, was published as *The Voyage of the Bounty Launch: John Fryer's Narrative*, in an illustrated, limited edition by Genesis Publications (1979).

By publishing the "Despatch" *and The Journal of John Fryer* together in a single volume, Rutter invites the reader to compare two very different accounts of the events. We learn that Fryer's antagonistic relationship with Bligh must have begun during the voyage to Tahiti, and continued until the two men made their separate ways back to England. Although Fryer was loyal to Bligh during the mutiny, his *Journal* makes plain their strained relations. Rutter states in the introduction, "Almost every page smoulders with a sulky resentment, and, as one reads on, it becomes plainer and plainer how Fryer hated Bligh."

Fryer insinuates that on the launch, Bligh secretly took more food than was allotted to him. He also questions Bligh's courage when the launch was being pursued by canoes in the Fiji Islands, and downplays Bligh's superb nautical skills: "I must till [sic] my Friends that there were others in the Boat that would have found their way to Timor as well as Captain Bligh and made every one with them more pleasant." His accusations are unfounded, and Rutter feels that Fryer comes off poorly in his *Journal*. Rutter states, "My feeling is — it may be shared or not — that the *Journal* is the work of a mean-souled man, a man of such surpassing pettiness that no niggling innuendo was too preposterous if it could serve to smirch the reputation of the detested Bligh. It does not contain a single direct accusation against Bligh's professional conduct supported by evidence."

Many *Bounty* scholars have discussed Fryer's personality and behavior and, like so many other topics associated with the mutiny, readers ultimately reach their own conclusions about *Bounty*'s Master. After giving evidence during the court-martial of the mutineers, Fryer went on to complete creditable service in the Royal Navy until his death in 1817, reaching the position of Master of the First Rate in 1798. Acknowledging Fryer's later successes, Rutter suggests that he, like many others, found it extremely difficult to tolerate Bligh's frequent outbursts of temper. For Christian, it became impossible.

A wood-engraved diptych by Robert Gibbings for *The Voyage of the Bounty's Launch* illustrates the attack at Tofoa and death of Quartermaster John Norton, the only member of Bligh's party lost during the open boat voyage. Gibbings, who purchased the Golden Cockerel Press in 1924, was one of the most influential figures during a renaissance of wood engraving that flourished in the early 20th century. *The Voyage of the Bounty's Launch* was the first volume in the Golden Cockerel Press's "Bountiana" series. Reprinted by permission of the Golden Cockerel Press.

JAMES MORRISON: *The Journal of James Morrison, Boatswain's Mate of the Bounty, Describing the Mutiny & Subsequent Misfortunes of the Mutineers, Together With an Account of the Island of Tahiti.* With an Introduction by Owen Rutter and Five Engravings by Robert Gibbings. London: The Golden Cockerel Press, 1935. Limited to 325 copies.

James Morrison's manuscript journal was first published in its entirety by the Golden

INTRODUCTION

UNTIL recently the whereabouts of the journal written by James Morrison, boatswain's mate of His Majesty's armed vessel *Bounty*, and here published for the first time, had remained a mystery for many years. I knew of the existence of the journal from Sir John Barrow's *Eventful History of the Mutiny of the 'Bounty'* and Lady Belcher's *Mutineers of the 'Bounty'*. Both these writers had handled the manuscript, vouched for its authenticity and quoted from it. Sir John Barrow examined it among the papers of Captain Peter Heywood, who as a midshipman had been tried by court-martial, together with Morrison and others of the *Bounty's* company, for complicity in the mutiny of which Fletcher Christian was the ringleader, and Heywood, like Morrison, had received the King's pardon after being found guilty and condemned to death. Sir John had access to the journal in 1830 and forty years later it was still among Captain Heywood's papers, for his stepdaughter, Lady Belcher, whose book was published in 1870, expressly stated that it was in her possession.

Lady Belcher was thus in a position to know the history of the manuscript. According to her (*op. cit.*, p. 152), Morrison had been in the habit of keeping notes 'of daily occurences from the period

Cockerel Press as *The Journal of James Morrison*, the second volume in its series of Bountiana. In his introduction, editor Owen Rutter discusses the history and provenance of this important, yet controversial, document by *Bounty*'s Boatswain's Mate.

A manuscript copy of the journal (Morrison's original holograph is lost), now at the Public Library of New South Wales, Mitchell Library, was among the private papers of Peter Heywood, who, along with Morrison, had been convicted of mutiny, sentenced to death and pardoned by King George III. The few people who had access to the manuscript before its publication in 1935 included Sir John Barrow, who used it as reference material in *Eventful History of the Mutiny and Piratical Seizure of H.M.S. Bounty*, and Heywood's stepdaughter, Lady Belcher, who quoted from it in *The Mutineers of the Bounty and their Descendants in Pitcairn and Norfolk Island*. William Bligh probably read an earlier version of the journal. Owen Rutter included Bligh's written response, titled "Remarks on Morrison's Journal." The latter work was included in *Bligh's Voyage in the Resource*, published by the Golden Cockerel Press in 1937.

The composition date of Morrison's original manuscript has been a subject of debate since the 19th century. Lady Belcher stated that Morrison managed to save his personal notebook — on which the journal was supposedly based — from the wreck of *Pandora*. Rutter points out how unlikely this would have been under the circumstances, and cites internal evidence in the manuscript that suggests a composition date after Morrison returned to England.

Rutter also speculates that "The meticulous detail, the niceness of observation and the accuracy of the dates in the journal make it improbable that the finished work could have been composed without the aid of notes taken on the spot. We must assume therefore that Morrison did preserve some form of diary and it is possible that Captain Edward Edwards, of the *Pandora*, impounded it when Morrison gave himself up at Tahiti, that it was saved from the wreck with the other ship's papers and returned to Morrison when he reached England."

We may never know if Morrison's diary survived or exactly when the manuscript was composed, but Rutter did establish that Lady Belcher gave a manuscript to the Rev. A. G. K. L'Estrange (author of *Lady Belcher and Her Friends*), who, in turn, presented it to the Public Library of New South Wales. By 1935, Rutter's scholarly reputation was well established, and the Mitchell Library granted him permission to edit and publish the journal.

The publication of *The Journal of James Morrison* provided *Bounty* scholars and enthusiasts an important primary text to compare with Bligh's published accounts. Morrison recorded a number of crucial events that occurred before, during and after the mutiny. One of the most significant of these incidents was Bligh's violent response, early in the voyage, to the crew's refusal to accept one pound of pumpkin in lieu of two pounds of bread. Morrison provides a glimpse of the salty, abusive language Bligh frequently used with his officers and crew: "Mr. Blighs being informd of it He Came up in a violent passion, and Calld all hands telling Mr. Samuel to Call the first Man of every Mess and let him see Who would dare to refuse it, or any thing else that He should order to be Served, saying 'you Dam'd Infernal scoundrels, I'll make you eat Grass or any thing you can catch before I have done with you.'"

Morrison's *Journal* fleshes out the story of H.M.S. *Bounty*. It includes the first account of Fletcher Christian's failed attempts to settle on the island of Tubuai and *Bounty*'s return to Tahiti; Christian's departure into the unknown; the mutineers' life on the Tahiti before the

Opposite: Robert Gibbings' wood engraving of H.M.S. *Bounty* invites readers to enter the world of *The Journal of James Morrison*, published by the Golden Cockerel Press. This fine press was well known for its skillful marriage of text and illustration, especially wood engravings. Reprinted by permission of the Golden Cockerel Press.

arrival of H.M.S. *Pandora*; and an account of her shipwreck off Australia's Great Barrier Reef. As Rutter states in the introduction, "The journal is the only original source of information as to the activities of the mutineers after they had cast Bligh adrift, and this part of the narrative has never previously been published in anything but a condensed form."

In one of the most interesting parts of the *Journal*, Morrison recounts how he and ten other members of *Bounty*'s crew began constructing a two-masted schooner in November 1789. Morrison intended to sail it to Batavia, and find a passage to England. As he describes the difficulties of taking on such an ambitious project, the reader can only gain respect for his skill and determination:

> Went in search of More timbers, & had tolerable Sucess. The business of searching for timber always took up a whole day, having Several Miles to go before any Could be found to answer our purpose, and when we found them we frequently had the misfortune to breake them by tumbling them down the precipices, which we could not avoid, it being impossible to Carry them along the Steep Clifts, and what we Cut in one day would keep McIntosh & Myself employd for three or four... Nor was the making of Plank less troublesome, having no Saws (except handsaws).

Morrison and his team were remarkably creative with the limited resources available for shipbuilding on Tahiti. They made pitch from breadfruit tree gum, rope from hibiscus bark and pegs from hardwood, which served as a substitute for scarce iron nails. Using simple hand tools and a homemade forge, Morrison, with some additional help from the Tahitians, constructed and launched the 35-foot, 18-ton *Resolution* in July of 1790. *Resolution* proved to be a remarkably seaworthy vessel, and when Captain Edwards arrived on *Pandora*, he confiscated it for use as a tender (rechristening it *Matavy*). As Edwards scoured the South Seas for the other *Bounty* mutineers, the schooner and its nine-man crew lost sight of *Pandora* during bad weather near the Samoan Islands. Four months later, after the sinking of *Pandora*, Edwards caught up with *Matavy* in the Dutch East Indies.

In addition to his flair for shipbuilding and leadership, Morrison had a keen eye for native social and cultural life, and Part Two of *The Journal* is a valuable, vividly written record of Tahiti in the late 18th century. The Golden Cockerel Press prospectus for the volume states, "The latter part of the book contains the first detailed description of Tahiti and of the islanders' customs, mode of life, erotic dances & human sacrifices, and is the outcome of the author's long residence among the Tahitians ... (Morrison) could write with a literary ability and dramatic power uncommon in a seaman of the day."

WILLIAM BLIGH: *Bligh and the Bounty. His Narrative of the Voyage to Otaheite with an Account of the Mutiny and of his Boat Journey to Timor.* With illustrations and a preface by Laurence Irving. N.P.: E. P. Dutton & Co., Inc., 1936.

This unabridged edition of William Bligh's *A Voyage to the South Seas* is notable for Laurence Irving's woodcuts, which are very much in the manner of noted American printmaker Rockwell Kent.

One particularly interesting print shows the rarely pictured Michael Byrne (or Byrn), playing a fiddle tune while crew members turn the capstan, weighing *Bounty*'s anchor. Byrne, rated as an able bodied seaman even though he was nearly blind, was engaged by Bligh for his musical talents. Bligh's determination to have a musician on board shows his concern for the crew's welfare: he believed that music and dancing would keep the crew both healthy and amused. As he wrote in a letter to Sir Joseph Banks prior to the voyage, "Some time for relaxation and mirth is absolutely necessary and I have considered it so much so that after 4 o'clock the evening is laid aside for their amusement and dancing. I had great difficulty before I left England to get a man to play the violin and I preferred at last to take one two-thirds blind than come without one."

A wood engraving by Robert Gibbings in *The Journal of James Morrison* depicts the construction of Morrison's schooner, *Resolution*. The history of this seaworthy vessel, which served as a tender to *Pandora* after the mutineers on Tahiti were captured, is a subject of great interest to *Bounty* researchers. Reprinted by permission of the Golden Cockerel Press.

Bligh took the exercise seriously. Toward the end of the voyage to Tahiti, some of the members of the crew complained about being forced to dance. Just one week before the *Bounty* arrived in Tahiti, the Gardener and Botanist's Assistant (who later joined the mutiny), refused to dance. Bligh reported the incident and punishment in his log for October 19, 1788: "John

Michael Byrne, the *Bounty*'s half-blind fiddler, plays a tune while the seamen weigh anchor in this Laurence Irving woodcut from *Bligh and the 'Bounty'* by William Bligh, preface, introduction and illustrations by Laurence Irving, copyright 1936, 1964 by Laurence Henry Forster Irving. Used by permission of Dutton, a division of Penguin Group (USA) Inc.

Mills & Wm Brown refusing to dance this evening, I ordered their Grog to be Stopt with a promise of further punishment on a Second Refusal."

In the list of mutineers compiled by Bligh, he described Byrne as "28 years, 5 feet 6 inches high. Fair complexion and is almost blind. Plays the fiddle. Has the mark of an issue in the back of his neck." Byrne's case is an interesting one. There is no evidence that he played a role in the mutiny — which probably would have been next to impossible, considering his weak vision — but he was tried at the court-martial, along with everyone else who remained with the ship. Byrne kept his defense short and to the point. Read by the Judge Advocate, it began:

> It has pleased the Almighty, amongst the Events of his unsearchable Providence, nearly to deprive me of Sight, which often puts it out of my Power to carry the Intentions of my Mind into Execution. I make no Doubt but it appears to this Honorable Court that on the 28th. of April, 1789, my Intention was, to quit His Majesty's Ship the "Bounty" with the Officers and Men who went away, and that the Sorrow I expressed at being detained was real and unfeigned.

Byrne was acquitted. His disability did not interfere with a strong instinct for survival, as he survived both the wreck of *Pandora* and the subsequent open-boat voyage to Timor.

One of Irving's more powerful illustrations in this edition of *A Voyage to the South Sea* depicts Bligh being violently shaken out of sleep by a group of mutineers brandishing bayonets. Irving captures the shocked expression that Bligh must have had on his face at that moment.

Bligh's *A Voyage to the South Seas* is readily available in a number of editions, but Laurence Irving's version stands as one of the most graphically distinctive productions to date.

This Laurence Irving woodcut from *Bligh and the 'Bounty'* captures the look of shock and surprise that must have been on Bligh's face on the morning of the mutiny. Used by permission of Dutton, a division of Penguin Group (USA) Inc.

CHARLES NORDHOFF AND JAMES NORMAN HALL: *The Bounty Trilogy*. Boston: Little, Brown and Company, 1936. Decorations by Henry C. Pitz. Boston: Little, Brown and Company, 1940. Wyeth Edition.

Charles Nordhoff and James Norman Hall's American publisher, Little, Brown and Company, published *Mutiny on the Bounty*, *Men Against the Sea* and *Pitcairn's Island* together in a single volume — *The Bounty Trilogy* — in 1936. Henry C. Pitz, who illustrated the dust jackets of the first and third books, created several small woodcuts to embellish the new work. These novels have been perennial favorites, so it is not surprising that *The Bounty Trilogy* went into a second printing during the month it was published. It also appeared in a "Tahiti Edition," with a different dust jacket, in 1938.

Recognizing that they had a potential classic on their hands, Little, Brown, and Company eventually commissioned N. C. Wyeth, one of America's greatest illustrators, to create a dust jacket and 12 full-color paintings for a new edition of *The Bounty Trilogy*, which they published in 1940. The "Wyeth Edition" has been reprinted countless times — in hardcover, paperback, and as a Book of the Month Club selection — although four of Wyeth's plates were deleted from most of the later printings.

Wyeth trained under the legendary artist Howard Pyle, originator of the "Brandywine School" of art. Pyle urged his students to infuse their compositions with action, urgency and drama. Wyeth later applied these techniques with great success, as demonstrated by his illustrations for Charles Scribner's Sons' "Classics" series, including Robert Louis Stevenson's *Treasure Island*, James Fenimore Cooper's *The Last of the Mohicans*, Jules Verne's *The Mysterious*

The BOUNTY TRILOGY

Comprising the three volumes
"Mutiny on the Bounty," "Men Against the Sea,"
and "Pitcairn's Island"

BY

CHARLES NORDHOFF

AND

JAMES NORMAN HALL

Decorations by Henry C. Pitz

BOSTON
LITTLE, BROWN, AND COMPANY
1936

The title page, with a woodcut by illustrator Henry C. Pitz, for the first edition of Nordhoff and Hall's *The Bounty Trilogy*, which predates the "Wyeth Edition" by four years. Pitz executed several small woodcuts for the volume. Reprinted by permission of Little, Brown and Company.

Island, and 13 other titles. In fact, some of the illustrations Wyeth executed for the Scribner's Classics and other publishers have gained more renown than the stories themselves.

Relatively little critical attention has been paid to Wyeth's illustrations for *The Bounty Trilogy*. Created late in his career, their reputation has been somewhat eclipsed by the power and popularity of his earlier work. Yet, Wyeth masterfully reflects the range of emotions found in each book, from the idyllic beauty of Tahiti to the dangers of the open sea and the stark violence of Christian's death on Pitcairn Island.

The Pitz and Wyeth editions of *The Bounty Trilogy* both included a new Preface by Nordhoff and Hall that discusses the writing of each volume. It also provides a useful list of source materials for readers interested in learning more about the *Bounty* Saga.

WILLIAM BLIGH: *The Log of the Bounty. Being Lieutenant William Bligh's Log of the Proceedings of his Majesty's armed vessel Bounty in a voyage to the South Seas, to take the Breadfruit from the Society Islands to the West Indies.* London: Golden Cockerel Press, 1937. Limited to 300 copies. 2 vols., 4to, 435pp & 2 woodblock engravings (&) 260 pp & 2 wood block engravings. Engravings on wood by Lynton Lamb. Three-color decorative cloth.

The publication of *The Log of the Bounty* by the Golden Cockerel Press made William Bligh's official log accessible to the general reading public for the first time. By providing an opportunity to read Bligh's day-to-day account of the voyage, the Press made a great contribution to the rehabilitation of Bligh's reputation.

As Owen Rutter notes in the prospectus for this handsome, two-volume production,

This wood engraving by Lynton Lamb depicts two of *Bounty*'s crew aloft during a storm. Lamb executed four wood engravings for the Golden Cockerel Press's two-volume edition of William Bligh's *The Log of the Bounty*—two vignettes for each title page spread. Reprinted by permission of the Golden Cockerel Press. Courtesy of Sterling Memorial Library, Yale University.

"Contemporary judgments on men and affairs are rarely sound. Records long hidden in official archives have caused posterity to reverse its verdict on many whom their fellows had condemned. So it may be with Bligh, commander of the *Bounty*, a man who deserved well of his country. Thousands who are familiar with his name as the villain of a melodrama of the sea know nothing of his legitimate claims to distinction."

Rutter was granted access to Bligh's original manuscript from the library of the Admiralty (it currently is held in the Public Record Office, London) and wrote a perceptive introduction. Rear-Admiral H. J. A. Edgell, O. B. E., Hydrographer of the Navy, was invited to provide comments about Bligh's navigational skills.

Although much of the information included in *The Log of the Bounty* had been available since 1790—in Bligh's *A Narrative of the Mutiny* and *A Voyage to the South Sea*—the official log provides a far richer account of the voyage. Rutter points out that parts of the log, especially the sections dealing with Bligh's attempt to round Cape Horn, are, "as vivid and as stirring as any in the literature of the sea."

Lynton Lamb's wood engraving of the launch as Bligh's loyalists row away from *Bounty* on the morning of the mutiny is far more accurate than many illustrations, which often depict the vessel in turbulent seas. The island of Tofoa appears in the distance. Reprinted by permission of the Golden Cockerel Press. Courtesy of Sterling Memorial Library, Yale University.

For example, the following extract from *The Log of the Bounty* for March 22, 1788 attests to the severity of the weather at the Horn and Bligh's concern for the crew's well-being: "The Gale encreased with much violence and continued so the whole Night with an exceeding high Sea... The Air is now become very Sharp, and some of my people begin to feel rheumatic pains, but as they are at three Watches and dry Births to sleep in without much fatigue, I hope that complaint will not hang much about them."

The log also includes a wealth of technical details and additional information on the Tahitians' way of life. Because a ship's log was not destined for verbatim publication, Bligh did not hesitate to describe, in vivid terms, Tahitian behavior that would have been considered unsuitable for the public. For example, on Friday, November 21, 1788, Bligh was invited to a Heiva, "An entertainment which I had not seen ... the Heiva began by the Men jumping and throwing their Legs and Arms into violent and odd motions, which the Women kept time with, and as they were conveniently cloathed for the Purpose, their persons were generally exposed to full view, frequently standing on one Leg and keeping the other up, giving themselves the most lascivious and wanton motions."

Like *The Journal of James Morrison*, *The Log of the Bounty* is filled with firsthand accounts that effectively draw the reader into the late 18th century world of the Royal Navy and South Pacific. *The Log of the Bounty* was quite expensive and limited to only 300 copies, and it remains a rare and expensive set today. In 1975, Genesis Publications released *The Log of HMS Bounty, 1787–89*, a deluxe facsimile limited to 500 copies. An inexpensive version entitled *Mutiny!! Aboard H. M. Armed Transport 'Bounty,' in 1789*, edited by R. M. Bowker, was published in 1978.

WILLIAM BLIGH: *Bligh's Voyage in the Resource. From Coupang to Batavia, Together with the Log of his Subsequent Passage to England in the Dutch Packet* Vlydt *and his Remarks on Morrison's Journal*. All Printed for the First Time from the Manuscripts in the Mitchell Library of New South Wales, with an Introduction and Notes by Owen Rutter, & Engravings on Wood by Peter Barker-Mill. (London): The Golden Cockerel Press, 1937. Limited to 350 copies.

Bligh's Voyage in the Resource collects three important *Bounty*-related documents in one handsome volume, illustrated with wood engravings by Peter Barker-Miller. The Golden Cockerel Press envisioned this title as "a natural sequel" to *The Log of the Bounty*. As in *The Journal of James Morrison*, Owen Rutter obtained permission from the Mitchell Library in Sydney, Australia, to publish these manuscripts for the first time. The *Resource* log is printed from an authenticated copy of Bligh's original, but the location of the original manuscript is unknown.

Bligh kept a log as he sailed from Coupang, where he purchased the schooner *Resource*, to Batavia, where he at last obtained passage back to England on the Dutch vessel *Vlydt*. Owen Rutter points out the historical significance of this log, which provides a detailed record of this brief, but eventful voyage.

In Bligh's *A Voyage to the South Sea* only a few pages are devoted to his activities after he left Timor. His friend Captain James Burney edited the book for publication, and either he or Bligh omitted the outbreak of insubordination that broke out among the ship's company while the *Resource* was at Sourabaya. In the log, however, Bligh gives the full details, and it is evident that but for his prompt action in placing the ringleaders under arrest and bringing them before the Dutch authorities, he might have been the victim of another mutiny.

The insubordinate "ringleaders" were Master John Fryer and Ship's Carpenter William Purcell, who had irritated Bligh so much that he refused to let them board the *Resource*. Instead, he forced them to follow in the native praus that accompanied the *Resource* as an escort against pirates. In the section of the *Resource* log titled "Particular transactions at Sourabaya," Bligh provides a fascinating, detailed account of the "Sourabaya incident," which included disobedience to his orders, insolence, complaints and drunkenness. Mr. Bonza, the Master Attendant at Sourabaya, reported to Bligh, "That they believed I had some Villains about me who I did not suspect, for that in their way to the Shore their Coxwain had told them My Officers & Men had spread a report that I should be hanged or blown from the Mouth of a Cannon as soon as I got home." The indignant Bligh had Purcell and Fryer arrested and demanded a formal hearing of the other men's complaints. Fryer apologized and was released, but Purcell refused, so Bligh had him court-martialed upon his return to England. Purcell was reprimanded for his behavior.

It seems astonishing that a group of men who had survived an ordeal as terrible as the open-boat voyage would continue to harbor such ill will toward each other. The incident at Sourabaya throws strong light on the personalities of these men and their volatile relationships. Rutter states, referring to Fryer, "The perils through which captain and master had come during those terrible six weeks in the open boat had done nothing to soften the animosity that had embittered both before the *Bounty* reached Tahiti."

BLIGH'S VOYAGE IN THE RESOURCE

FROM COUPANG TO BATAVIA, TOGETHER WITH THE LOG OF HIS SUBSEQUENT PASSAGE TO ENGLAND IN THE DUTCH PACKET *VLYDT* AND HIS REMARKS ON MORRISON'S JOURNAL. THE GOLDEN COCKEREL PRESS, 1937.

ALL PRINTED FOR THE FIRST TIME FROM THE MANUSCRIPTS IN THE MITCHELL LIBRARY OF NEW SOUTH WALES, WITH AN INTRODUCTION AND NOTES BY OWEN RUTTER, & ENGRAVINGS ON WOOD BY PETER BARKER-MILL.

Peter Barker-Mill's dramatic title page spread for *Bligh's Voyage in the Resource* shows the schooner *Resource* at anchor and at sea, with Bligh at the tiller. Reprinted by permission of the Golden Cockerel Press.

Bligh's brief "Remarks on Morrison's Journal," also held by the Mitchell Library and published here for the first time, is an important commentary on the *Journal of James Morrison*. Bligh energetically responded to each of Morrison's accusations, many of which pertain to Bligh's supposed stinginess with the food allowance. Bligh, who took great pride in how well he looked after his crew's health, wrote a vigorous response that reveals the extent of his indignity:

> [MORRISON]: Pease & oatmeal sparingly served & His Hogs would have starved, but for Bread & Indian Corn that was purchased for his Poultry &c &c.
>
> [BLIGH]: On investigation, these low charges could strongly mark the character of Morrison — they are convenient at a remote period. Captain Bligh declares every person had as much as was necessary; and what was never known in any Ship before, & perhaps in none but his own since, they had hot breakfasts every day of boiled wheat sweetnd with sugar, or Burgoo enriched with Portable Soup. So happily did every person with them feel themselves, that letters from the People & Warrant Officers from the Cape of Good Hope were particular in remarking how happy they were under Captain Bligh's Command.

Rutter says that "Making each of the fourteen charges a separate round he trounces Morrison until one can almost see him pursuing his adversary about the ring, landing blow after blow in a contest whose issue every reader may decide for himself on points."

Bligh is quite candid in the journal he kept on his passage to England on the Dutch packet *Vlydt*. Published here by the Golden Cockerel Press as the *Journal of Bligh's Voyage to England*, it is filled with pungent criticism of general shipboard conditions and on the way the ship is handled. Here is one of Bligh's remarks on the Dutch captain's seamanship:

> Days Out 3. "Under Single Reefs and no T.Gt. Sails. Any other Ship would be carrying every Steering Sail."
> Days Out 7. "I am certain that if I had the Command of this Vessel I could run 1 1/2 knot pr Hour More than this Man."

Bligh, who was more fastidious than many captains of his day, was particularly appalled at the lack of cleanliness aboard *Vlydt*: "The Men are stinking and dirty with long beards, and their Bedding a nuisance, as may be conceived when they have not washed Hammocks since they have been from Europe. The Capt. in his person and bedding equally dirty. Some of the people (have) not a second shift of Cloathes. Cookery so bad I cannot make a Meal: such nasty beasts."

The *Journal of Bligh's Voyage to England* paints a brief, vivid picture of 18th century shipboard conditions and also provides a window into Bligh's mind when he was not in command of a ship. Rutter's publication of this manuscript, the log of the *Resource* and the *Remarks on Morrison's Journal* in one volume, complemented by the wood engravings of Barker-Mill, marks an important milestone in *Bounty* scholarship as well as fine press production.

MARY ANN GAMBLE: *John Fryer of the Bounty. Notes on His Career Written by his Daughter Mary Ann.* With an Introduction and Commentary by Owen Rutter and Wood-Engravings by Averil Mackenzie-Grieve. [London]: Printed at the Golden Cockerel Press, 1939.

Limited to 300 copies, signed by the editor and the artist.

Owen Rutter expected Bligh's *Voyage in the Resource* to be the final volume in the Bountiana series published by the Golden Cockerel Press, but his plans changed when a correspondent sent him a letter providing additional information about John Fryer. Rutter states in his introduction, "It provided me with clues I had lacked six years previously [when he was working on *The Voyage of the Bounty's Launch*] and brought me out on Fryer's trail again." The result was a handsome volume that Rutter called a "postscript" to *The Voyage of the Bounty's Launch*.

John Fryer of the Bounty collects the fruits of Rutter's additional research, an intriguing group of manuscripts that includes the recollections of Fryer's eldest daughter, Mary Ann Gamble, and letters that her father wrote to the Navy Board prior to his retirement in 1812. Not surprisingly, we discover that Fryer's dislike of William Bligh shaped his daughter's opinion of the man: "I have heard him say many times he (Bligh) was as Tyrannical in his temper in the Boat as in the Ship, and that his chief thought was his own comfort if it was possible to have any in such a situation." Gamble attributes the mutiny to Bligh's superior attitude toward others, as well as to his "tyrannical conduct."

She summarizes Fryer's post–*Bounty* career in the Royal Navy, where he served creditably on a number of vessels, including a period of service when "He was five-years without seeing his family, in fact he never saw England." He also was involved in a number of shipboard actions. Gamble believed that the rigors of the open boat voyage eventually took a severe toll on her father's health. In a series of desperate letters to R. A. Nelson, Secretary of the Navy Board, Fryer pleaded that his physical and mental deterioration were making him unfit for duty: "I am sorry to inform you I am so very poorly, my mind is so much impaired, and my sight fails me so much at times, that the Ship is not safe under my charge."

Fryer retired on half pay at the age of sixty, and his health continued to deteriorate. Gam-

ble wrote that "The hardships he endured in the Boat laid the foundation for a premature old age; his subsequent Service, combined with a naturally anxious mind, reduced him to such a state of Nervous Debility that for the last two years and half of the five he lived at home he was confined to his bed helpless as an infant."

Fryer died in 1817, the year that Bligh passed away. Some *Bounty* scholars are critical of Fryer's character and competence as the ship's Master, charging that he frequently deserved Bligh's rebukes. Certainly, Fryer's insinuation that Bligh secretly took more than his fair share of food during the open boat voyage is completely unfounded. Yet Fryer performed his duties well under other commanders. Rutter's summation of Fryer's relationship with Bligh has the ring of truth: "Fine seaman and tough warrior that Bligh was, he had the unhappy faculty of bringing out the worst in a man and of inflaming the passions of those who served under him. He undoubtedly brought out the worst in Fryer."

CHARLES NORDHOFF AND JAMES NORMAN HALL: *Mutiny on the Bounty.* With a Preface by the Authors and an Appendix Containing the True Story of Peter Heywood. New York: The Limited Editions Club, 1947. Illustrated by Fletcher Martin. Limited to 1500 copies, signed by Fletcher Martin.

The vivid watercolors and evocative pen drawings of American artist Fletcher Martin are the major attractions in the Limited Editions Club's leatherbound edition of Nordhoff and Hall's *Mutiny on the Bounty*, limited to 1,500 copies for subscribers. Luckily for the larger reading public, the Heritage Press later reissued it in a less expensive, clothbound edition.

Martin, a self-taught painter, muralist and illustrator, working in the tradition of such artists as Thomas Hart Benton, Grant Wood and John Steuart Curry, is best known for his vigorous, action-filled canvases. His first color plate for this edition of *Mutiny on the Bounty* is a perfect accompaniment to the text, capturing the atmosphere of an 18th century vessel preparing to leave port. We see midshipman Roger Byam (the fictional narrator whose story is based on Peter Heywood's), boarding *Bounty* for the first time. Outfitted in a fine, new uniform that will be of little practical use on board, he is overwhelmed by the typical activities that occurred in and around a ship preparing to leave port on a long voyage: "All was new and strange to me on the morning when I presented myself to Lieutenant Bligh, the ship was crowded with women,— the sailors' 'wives,'— rum seemed to flow like water everywhere.... The crews of the bumboat men, the shrill scolding of the women, and the shouts and curses of the sailors made a pandemonium stunning to a landsman's ears."

Another memorable plate depicts a pivotal moment in *Mutiny on the Bounty* that occurs on the night before the mutiny. Fletcher Christian, despondent and near the breaking point, asks Byam to contact his family in England if, for some reason, he fails to reach home. Martin's painting captures the warm, moonlit evening that turns out to be the calm before the storm. Robert Tinkler is pictured "napping" on the deck while Christian and Byam converse.

Byam agrees to Christian's request, saying "You can count on me," and shaking hands with Christian just as Bligh approaches and overhears these words. In retrospect, Bligh convinces himself that this conversation must have concerned the mutiny and that Byam was one of the ringleaders. Fortunately for Byam, Tinkler heard the full conversation, which gives "You

Opposite: The wood engraved frontispiece of *John Fryer of the Bounty* by Averil Mackenzie-Grieve depicts the quay of Wells-next-the-Sea in Norfolk, the birthplace of *Bounty* Sailing Master John Fryer and his brother-in-law Robert Tinkler. Both survived the harrowing open boat journey with Bligh. Mackenzie-Grieve's dramatic wood engravings made *John Fryer of the Bounty* one of the Golden Cockerel Press' most attractive titles. Reprinted by permission of the Golden Cockerel Press.

"I joined the *Bounty* at Spithead." In his watercolor of Roger Byam boarding the *Bounty* for the first time, Fletcher Martin captures the noise and confusion that surrounded the departure of a ship in the late 18th century. Byam will soon discard his new midshipman's uniform for more comfortable clothing. Reprinted by permission of The Limited Editions Club.

"You can count on me," I said, shaking his hand

"'You can count on me,' I said, shaking his hand." Fletcher Martin's watercolor, commissioned by The Limited Editions Club for its edition of Charles Nordhoff and James Norman Hall's *Mutiny on the Bounty* captures the crucial moment where Roger Byam makes a solemn promise to Fletcher Christian. Robert Tinkler appears to be sleeping in the background, but hears every word that passes between Byam and Christian. Reprinted by permission of The Limited Editions Club.

can count on me," an entirely different meaning. His last-minute testimony, given to the court after Byam already has been found guilty and sentenced to death, leads to his full acquittal.

Heywood spent 18 months on Tahiti before the arrival of *Pandora*, but we do not have a complete account of his life there — his journal was lost during the sinking of *Pandora*. So, Nordhoff and Hall gave full rein to their imaginations in this part of the novel, creating a romantic interlude for Byam. One of Martin's loveliest watercolors illustrates a scene from Chapter 12, "Tehani," in which Byam takes a predawn walk along the beach toward Point Venus. In this idyllic setting, he observes a vessel landing at the beach: "Several of the crew came on land to build a fire of coconut husks and prepare food for the morning meal, and I saw two women helped ashore, who strolled away westward along the point and disappeared." Later, as Byam takes his morning swim in a river that empties into the sea, he meets Tehani, one of the two women. He has seen and admired her before, and the two begin a romance that quickly leads to marriage and the birth of a daughter, also named Tehani.

There is no evidence that Heywood fathered a daughter during his stay on Tahiti, as George Stewart did with his Tahitian wife, "Peggy," but the possibility exists. We know that Heywood was sexually active, as he was one of the many *Bounty* crewmembers who contracted venereal disease. Interestingly, the record suggests that Heywood did have an illegitimate daughter later in life. In 1810, he wrote a last will and testament expressing his desire to "make some provision for an Infant under my care." Payments were to be used for the care of "Mary Gray." However, unless new evidence comes to light, we probably will never know if Heywood became a father in Tahiti as well.

An appendix that provides extensive biographical information about Heywood is a welcome bonus in this edition of *Mutiny on the Bounty*. "The True Story of Peter Heywood" is a slightly abridged version of John Marshall's *Royal Navy Biography of Peter Heywood*, originally published in 1825. "The True Story of Peter Heywood" has undoubtedly encouraged readers of the novel to investigate other books and historical documents devoted to the *Bounty*. The Nordhoff and Hall novels are superb examples of historical fiction, but they also are — as stated in the newsletter for subscribers included with this volume —"A highly biased account of an enthralling happening."

WILLIAM BLIGH: *A Voyage To The South Seas.* Undertaken by command of His Majesty for the Purpose of Conveying the Bread-fruit Tree to the West Indies in His Majesty's Ship *Bounty* commanded by Lieutenant William Bligh including an account of the Mutiny on board the said ship and the subsequent voyage of part of the crew in the ship's boat from Tofoa, one of the Friendly Islands, to Timor, a Dutch Settlement in the East Indies. Introduced by Alan Villiers and illustrated with watercolours and drawings by Geoffrey C. Ingleton. New York: The Limited Editions Club, 1975. Limited to 1,500 copies signed by Geoffrey C. Ingleton and Douglas A. Dunstan (the designer).

This splendid edition of *A Voyage To The South Sea* gave Limited Editions Club subscribers an opportunity to read the story of H.M.S. *Bounty* from William Bligh's perspective. It features a vigorous introduction by author, adventurer and master mariner Alan Villiers, and watercolors and olive green line drawings by Geoffrey C. Ingleton, a noted Australian artist, illustrator and naval historian. Villiers was the perfect writer to introduce the reader to Bligh's book. The 1975–76 Limited Editions Club prospectus states, "Alan Villiers has a unique understanding of Bligh's cocky character and recognized accomplishments — and his introduction is written with tremendous gusto." Villiers, a seasoned mariner himself, expresses a great deal of respect and admiration for Bligh's skills as a navigator and seaman. He writes,

Two women who strolled away and disappeared

"Two women who strolled away and disappeared." Roger Byam glimpses his future Tahitian bride in Fletcher Martin's appropriately sensuous watercolor for The Limited Editions Club's edition of Charles Nordhoff and James Norman Hall's ***Mutiny on the Bounty.*** Reprinted by permission of The Limited Editions Club.

"He died in bed, after his often stormy life: and no man before or since showed greater courage against the natural and the man-made hazards of the sea. Bligh had his faults, like all men of character. But to me he has always been almost an inspiration."

Ingleton's choice of subjects for his illustrations in *A Voyage To The South Sea* is wide-ranging. In addition to depicting the mutiny, open boat voyage and other key events, he offers glimpses of the more prosaic activities that occurred during the voyage — gathering the breadfruit plants, anchoring the ship and cutting timber on shore to replace damaged or rotted wood. The *Bounty* anchored in Adventure Bay, Van Diemen's Land (now Tasmania), on August 21, 1788 and remained there for nearly two weeks to gather wood and water. It would be *Bounty*'s last landfall before arriving in Tahiti in late October.

After identifying the local trees that would provide the best lumber, Bligh, as reported in *A Voyage to the South Sea*, "Directed a saw-pit to be dug, and employed some of the people to saw trees into plank." One of Ingleton's drawings pictures a crew hard at work in the sawpit, using a whipsaw to convert a log into useful plank. This normally mundane task led to serious repercussions. In his journal, James Morrison wrote that in Adventure Bay, "Seeds of eternal discord between Lieut. Bligh & the Carpenter, and it will be no more than true to say, with all the Officers in general, were sown on this very day." Bligh argued with William Purcell about the way he was cutting wood and ordered him back to the ship. In *The* Bounty: *The True Story of the Mutiny on the* Bounty, Caroline Alexander suggests that Christian, who was in charge of the difficult task of getting the timber on board, also may have been criticized harshly by Bligh at this time.

CHAPTER FOUR

Passage towards Van Diemen's Land
Make the Island of St. Paul
Arrival in Adventure Bay - Natives seen
Sail from Van Diemen's Land

Geoffrey C. Ingleton depicts members of *Bounty*'s crew cutting wood in Adventure Bay, Van Diemen's Land (Tasmania), in The Limited Editions Club's lavish production of Bligh's *A Voyage to the South Sea*. Bligh anchored at Adventure Bay for wood and water on the voyage to Tahiti. According to Boatswain's Mate James Morrison, "Seeds of eternal discord between Lieut. Bligh & the Carpenter, and it will be no more than true to say, with all the Officers in general were sown" at Adventure Bay. Reprinted by permission of The Limited Editions Club.

Another drawing illustrates a medical examination on *Bounty* just before the ship's arrival at Tahiti, a scene that is illustrated here for the first time. Bligh's reports of this event in *A Voyage To The South Sea* was edited from his log entry for October 25, 1788: "As there was great probability that we should remain a considerable time at Otaheite, it could not be expected that the intercourse of my people with the natives should be of a very reserved nature. I therefore ordered that every person should be examined by the surgeon, and had the satisfaction to learn, from his report, that they were all perfectly free from any venereal complaint."

Bligh ordered the examination because he did not want to be held responsible for bringing additional cases of venereal disease to Tahiti, where it was already common. He had observed the uninhibited sexual habits of the Tahitians when he served under Captain James Cook as Sailing Master on *Resolution*. The fee for sexual intercourse usually was an iron nail. Ship's Surgeon Thomas Huggan might have been able to note acute signs of venereal disease when he examined *Bounty*'s crew, but there was no way for him to determine if any of the men were in a latent or asymptomatic stage of gonorrhea or syphilis. Eighteen of the ship's company, including Christian and Heywood, soon contracted venereal disease on Tahiti, and were treated in the accepted method of the time: large doses of toxic mercury.

Ingleton excels at capturing small details in his drawings. Another example is his illustration of Bligh and the crew of *Bounty*'s launch on a beach. One month after the mutiny, they went ashore on a small island lying within Australia's Great Barrier Reef, where they conducted an extensive search for food. To their great relief, they discovered fresh water, berries and enough oysters to make a stew. Ingleton's drawing faithfully captures the details of the scene as Bligh described it in *A Voyage to the South Sea*: We can see Bligh and the ship's car-

Ship's Surgeon Thomas Huggan examines *Bounty*'s crew for signs of venereal disease prior to the ship's arrival in Tahiti in Geoffrey C. Ingleton's illustration for The Limited Edition Club's *A Voyage to the South Sea*. Within weeks, a substantial number of the crew was infected, including Fletcher Christian and Peter Heywood. Reprinted by permission of The Limited Editions Club.

penter examining the boat's rudder, while some of the other men cook oyster stew in a copper pot, over an open fire:

> One of the gudgeons of the rudder had come out in the course of the night, and was lost. This, if it had happened at sea, might have been attended with the most serious consequences, as the management of the boat could not have been so nicely preserved as these very heavy seas required. It appears therefore a providential circumstance that it happened in a place of safety, and that it was in our power to remedy the defect, for by great good luck we found a large staple in the boat which answered the purpose.

Bligh comments that the stew, "might have been relished by people of far more delicate appetites." He named their landfall Restoration Island, "This day being the anniversary of the restoration of King Charles the Second, and the name not being inapplicable to our present situation (for we were restored to fresh life and strength)."

The combination of fine printing and evocative illustrations in this edition of *A Voyage To The South Sea* provide continual delight to the hand and eye.

FLETCHER CHRISTIAN: *The Letters of Fletcher Christian.* Introduction by Stephen Walters. Guildford: Genesis Publications Limited, 1984. Limited to 350 numbered copies, bound in half leather. Frontispiece by Keith West. Illustrations by Roy Williams.

This deluxe, illustrated edition of the spurious *Letters from Mr. Fletcher Christian* (first published in 1796), with the letters themselves printed in facsimile, attests to a continuing interest in the possibility that Christian did not die on Pitcairn Island. In addition to its evocative illustrations, this volume reproduces, in color, previously unpublished portraits of Fletcher Christian's parents.

William Bligh and Ship's Carpenter William Purcell examine the condition of the launch's rudder on the beach of Restoration Island, while other members of the party prepare a meal of stewed oysters. Reprinted by permission of The Limited Editions Club.

One of the more romantic aspects of the *Bounty* Saga is a theory—treated in depth by C. S. Wilkinson in *The Wake of the* Bounty—that Fletcher Christian somehow managed to return to England from Pitcairn Island. Speculation on this topic began as early as 1796, with the publication of *Letters from Mr. Fletcher Christian*. Although these seven letters have been proven to be fabrications by an unknown author, they were presented as "authentic" as recently as 1935, in Irvin Anthony's *The Saga of the* Bounty, printed side by side with material by William Bligh, James Morrison and John Fryer. First published more than ten years before the report that Christian had been killed on Pitcairn Island, *Letters from Mr. Fletcher Christian* evoked public curiosity and speculation about the mutineer's fate. In these fictitious letters, Christian describes his escape from Pitcairn Island and narrates a series of adventures in South America.

Several decades after the original publication of *Letters from Mr. Fletcher Christian*, an intriguing note in Sir John Barrow's *The Eventful History of the Mutiny and Piratical Seizure of H.M.S. Bounty* stimulated further discussion about Christian's return. Barrow recounts how, in 1808 or 1809, Captain Peter Heywood believed he saw Christian on Plymouth Dock. Other tantalizing hints can be found in the writings of Samuel Taylor Coleridge, William Wordsworth and Robert Southey. John Adams' conflicting accounts of the events that occurred on Pitcairn Island raised even more questions.

Did Christian return to visit, or live out his life, as a fugitive in his native Cumberland? If so, he may have hidden in the unusual house pictured by Roy Williams in *The Letters of Fletcher Christian*. This picturesque dwelling, which still stands on Belle Isle in Lake Windermere, was the home of Isabella Curwen, wealthy heiress to Workington Hall and wife of John Christian. John Christian was Fletcher Christian's first cousin and head of the Christian family, and Belle Isle was named after Isabella Curwen.

The romantic and dramatic aspects of Christian's return to England have been irresistible to novelists, including Owen Rutter (*Cain's Birthday*, 1930); Stanley Miller (*Mr. Christian! The Journal of Fletcher Christian*, 1973); Ethel Harper (*Paths of the Sea*, 1977); John Maxwell (*H.M.S. Bounty*, 1977); William Kinsolving (*Mr. Christian: the Further Adventures of Fletcher Christian*, 1996); Fiona Mountain (*Isabella, The Haunting Love Story of Fletcher Christian and Isabella Curwen*, 1999); Dan L. Thrapp (*Mutiny's Curse*, 2002); and Ann Rinaldi (*Mutiny's Daughter*, 2003).

This fascination with Christian seems likely to continue. Playwright Richard Crane, who wrote a spirited musical play called *Mutiny on the* Bounty—*A Sea-Faring Show* (1972) captured the whole controversy in a few amusing lines:

> The fate of Mr. Christian
> is a mystery, much debated;
> some scholars say on Pitcairn Isle
> he was assassinated;
> but some are certain he returned
> in secret, like a foreigner,
> met Coleridge, a meeting which
> inspired "The Ancient Mariner."

WILLIAM BLIGH: *The Journal of Bounty's Launch.* Annotated and illustrated by A. Richard Mansir. Los Angeles: Kittiwake Publications, 1989.

Painter and author A. Richard Mansir's selection of texts from William Bligh's log, titled *The Journal of Bounty's Launch*, is filled with well-executed watercolors and drawings that illus-

Roy Williams' dramatic illustration of the mutineers seizing Bligh in his cabin appeared in Genesis Publications' deluxe, limited edition of *The Letters of Fletcher Christian*. Reprinted by permission of Genesis Publications Limited.

trate the struggle and drama of the open-boat voyage — from the attack on the beach at Tofoa to the launch's arrival at Coupang. This inexpensive, attractive volume also includes technical illustrations of the launch and suggestions on how to craft a model of the vessel.

Mansir provides useful background information about *Bounty*'s voyage in his introduction, but many readers will disagree with his conclusion that the outbreak of venereal dis-

The Curwen family's round house on Belle Island, Lake Windermere, is pictured by Roy Williams in a deluxe, limited edition of *The Letters of Fletcher Christian*. Some scholars of the *Bounty* Saga believe that Christian took refuge here with relatives following his "escape" from Pitcairn Island. Reprinted by permission of Genesis Publications Limited.

ease among the crew in Tahiti—and Fletcher Christian's refusal, "To acknowledge Bligh's well-founded concern and demand that his officers help in stemming the epidemic"—were significant factors in the mutiny. However, his statement about Bligh's character rings very true: "The more he tried to enforce his authority, the more he exacerbated the friction and gradually dissipated his control of both ship and crew."

Mansir's dramatic cover illustration for *The Journal of Bounty's Launch* shows Bligh and his crew battling rough seas. His depiction of *Bounty*'s launch is quite accurate, clearly showing the modifications Bligh made to render the craft more seaworthy: "I got fitted a pair of shrouds to each mast and contrived a canvass Weather Cloth round the boat and made the quarters about 9 inches by Nailing on the Seats of the Stern Sheets."

Another atmospheric watercolor portrays the launch being pursued by native canoes as Bligh and his men sail through the Fiji Archipelago. Bligh reports in his log, "We now observed two large Sailing Canoes coming swiftly after us along shore, and being apprehensive of their intentions, we rowed with some anxiety being too sensible of our weak and Defenceless state."

In *A Voyage to the South Sea*, Bligh expanded his description of this event to include remarks about the stormy weather on that day, which is well depicted by Mansir: "All the afternoon we had light winds at NNE; the weather was very rainy, attended with thunder and lightning. Only one of the canoes gained upon us, which by three o'clock in the afternoon was not more than two miles off, when she gave over chase."

Bligh explains in the log why he avoided contact with the islanders sailing these canoes: "Whether these canoes had any hostile intention against us must remain a doubt. Perhaps we might have benefited by an intercourse with them, but in our defenceless situation to have made the experiment would have been risking too much." His handling of this situation has generated considerable speculation and discussion. In his own journal, Fryer implies that Bligh was excessively timid.

$15.95

The JOURNAL of
BOUNTY'S LAUNCH

BY LT. WILLIAM BLIGH, RN
ANNOTATED AND ILLUSTRATED BY A. RICHARD MANSIR

A SEA ADVENTURE

Bligh and his crew battling rough seas in *Bounty*'s launch on May 22, 1789, as depicted by A. Richard Mansir on the cover of *The Journal of Bounty's Launch*. Mansir portrays the launch quite accurately, right down to the hastily improvised, protective weather cloth. Bligh writes, in *A Voyage to the South Sea*, "In the afternoon I fitted a pair of shrouds for each mast, and contrived a canvas weather cloth round the boat, and raised the quarters about nine inches by nailing on the seats of the stern sheets, which proved of great benefit to us." Reprinted by permission of A. Richard Mansir.

May 7th, Chased by Canoes
"We now observed two large sailing canoes coming swiftly after us..."

H.M.S. *Bounty*'s launch, in its two-masted configuration, is pursued by natives through the Fiji archipelago on May 7, 1789, in A. Richard Mansir's *The Journal of Bounty's Launch*. Fearing attack by the Fijians, Bligh refused to land on any of these islands. Reprinted by permission of A. Richard Mansir.

John Bach, editor of *The Bligh Notebook*, comments that Sail maker Lawrence Lebogue, "Openly chastised his captain, for which he was reprimanded by Fryer. This is one of the several occasions on which Bligh, if Fryer's account is accepted, was not as cool and collected as his own account would have us believe." The reader must decide whether Fryer's accusation was warranted or not.

With its attractive blend of text, drawings, watercolors and schematics, *The Journal of Bounty's Launch* serves as a visual treat, even for readers already familiar with Bligh's narrative of the open boat voyage.

Additional Works

Books

Barrow, Sir John. *The Eventful History of the Mutiny and Piratical Seizure of H.M.S.* Bounty: *Its Causes and Consequences*. Illustrated by Six Etchings from Original Drawings by Lieut.-Colonel Batty. London: John Murray, Albermarle-Street; and Thomas Tegg, Cheapside (1832).

The six prints that illustrate the early editions of Sir John Barrow's famous volume are frequently reproduced in other works. Some of them were etched from drawings and sketches made by Lieutenant Smith of H.M.S. *Blossom* and Peter Heywood.

_____. *The Mutiny of the 'Bounty.'* Illustrated by Nigel Lambourne. London and Glasgow: Blackie and Son, 1961.

Publisher Blackie and Son selected *The Eventful History of the Mutiny and Piratical Seizure of H.M.S.* Bounty: *Its Causes and Consequences* as part of its "Chosen Books" series, designed "to provide exciting reading for children over ten and also to give them an encouraging introduction to adult literature." Sir John Barrow's book certainly fills the bill, and this edition has the added bonus of Nigel Lambourne's excellent drawings. His depiction of Bligh confronting the crew over the theft of his coconuts speaks volumes: it perfectly captures the furious, petulant expression that Bligh must have had on his face at that crucial moment.

Bligh, William. *Dangerous Voyage of Captain Bligh, in an Open Boat, Over 1200 Leagues of the Ocean in the Year 1789.* N.p.: T. Courtney, 1820.

This volume's crude woodcuts are among the earliest illustrations of events in the *Bounty* Saga. They depict *Bounty*'s launch in stormy seas, a breadfruit tree and a "kanguroo."

Cave, Roderick, and Sarah Manson. *A History of the Golden Cockerel Press, 1920–1960.* London and New Castle: The British Library and Oak Knoll Press, 2002.

This substantial reference work on the Golden Cockerel Press includes a full discussion of its "Bountiana" series of volumes and the artists who illustrated these beautiful books.

Fryer, John. *The Voyage of the Bounty Launch: John Fryer's Narrative.* Guildford: Genesis Publications, 1979. Introduction by Stephen Walters. Illustrated by Roy Williams.

See Chapter 1 for details.

Johnston, Sir Harry. "Bligh of the 'Bounty.'" *Pioneers in Australasia.* London: Gresham Publishing Co., n.d. (1900).

Alec Ball, whose artistic credits include a Sherlock Holmes story in *The Strand* magazine, provided an excellent color illustration to "Bligh of the 'Bounty'": "Captain Bligh and his men searching for oysters off the Great Barrier Reef."

Kane, Herb Kawainui. *Voyagers: Words and Images.* Bellevue: WhaleSong, 1991.

One of Herb Kane's colorful paintings, *Building Fort George*, is a superb, rarely pictured illustration of the fort (complete with moat), constructed by *Bounty* mutineers during their ill-fated attempt to settle on the island of Tubuai.

Marden, Luis. "Finding the Wreck of H.M.S. *Pandora*." *National Geographic Magazine*, October 1985, 422–551.

Roy Andersen, an artist more closely associated with American Western subject matter, created some striking illustrations for this article, including a depiction of *Pandora* at Tahiti.

McKinney, Sam. *Bligh: A True Account of Mutiny Aboard His Majesty's Ship Bounty.* Camden: International Marine Publishing Co., 1989. Drawings by Nathan Goldstein.

Nathan Goldstein's drawings are an added attraction to this appealing volume. Sam McKinney uses a wide range of primary sources for a thorough account of *Bounty*'s voyage and aftermath.

_____. *Mutiny on the Bounty.* Franklin Center, PA: Franklin Library, 1982. Illustrated by Ronald Keller.

Ronald Keller created a number of powerful illustrations for this leatherbound collector's edition of *Mutiny on the Bounty*. Originally available only to Franklin subscribers, it frequently turns up in the used book marketplace.

_____. *Mutiny on the Bounty. With a Preface by the Authors and an Appendix Containing the True Story of Peter Heywood.* Illustrated by Fletcher Martin. New York: Heritage Press, 1947.

This clothbound reprint of the Limited Editions Club *Mutiny on the Bounty* is less expensive and easier to find than the original, leatherbound production.

Opposite: "Captain Bligh and his men searching for oysters off the Great Barrier Reef." Alec Ball, whose artistic credits include a Sherlock Holmes story in *The Strand* magazine, provided this illustration for "Bligh of the 'Bounty,'" collected in Sir Harry Johnston's *Pioneers in Australasia*, published circa 1900. The men in the foreground pry oysters from the rocks while Bligh supervises. Several men carry shellfish to the rest of the party seated near the launch, which has one sail unfurled. A line of breakers marking the reef is visible in the background. Courtesy Pitcairn Islands Study Center.

Selborne, Joanna. *British Wood-Engraved Book Illustration, 1904–1940.* Oxford: Clarendon Press, 1998.

    Joanna Selborne's comprehensive study of the wood engraving "renaissance" that occurred in England during the early part of the 20th century discusses Robert Gibbings and other artists who illustrated the Golden Cockerel Press's "Bountiana" series.

Verne, Jules. *The Begum's Fortune. With an Account of The Mutineers of the "Bounty."* Translated by W. H. G. Kingston. London: Sampson Low, Marston, Searle and Rivington, 1880. Pages 241–272.

    In 1879, Jules Verne published a fantasy entitled *Les Cinq Cents Millions de la Bégum* (published in English as *The Begum's Fortune*). It was a short work and, one year later, was republished with "Les révoltés de la Bounty" ("The Mutineers of the Bounty") as filler, accompanied by five interesting illustrations. *Les révoltés de la Bounty* was translated into English by W. H. G. Kingston and published in *The Begum's Fortune*. Kingston reprinted it, with different illustrations, as "The Ship and the Island" in *The Burgomaster's Daughter*.

Whymper, F. *The Sea: Its Stirring Story of Adventure, Peril and Heroism.* London: Cassell & Co., n.d. (1877).

    Chapter XIV of this handsome volume features four large engravings depicting *Bounty*'s arrival at Tahiti, Bligh being seized by the mutineers, the launch being cast adrift and H.M.S. *Briton*'s visit to Pitcairn Island.

Articles

Alexander, Caroline. "Wreck of the Pandora: The Fate of the Men Sent to Hunt Down the Bounty Mutineers." *The New Yorker*, August 4, 2003, 44–59.

    Mark Ulriksen contributed several color illustrations to this article.

Nordhoff, Charles, and James Norman Hall. "Men Against the Sea." *Saturday Evening Post*, November 18, 25, December 2, 9, 1933.

    Noted marine artist Anton Otto Fischer, who also created cover art for *The Saturday Evening Post*, illustrated this serialization of the second book in *The Bounty Trilogy*. His illustrations are skillfully executed, but somewhat static for a book filled with so much action.

_____. "Pitcairn's Island." *Saturday Evening Post*, September 22, 29, October 6, 13, 20, 27, November 3, 1934.

    Although W.H.D. Koerner is remembered primarily for his illustrations with American Wild West themes—many of them published in *The Saturday Evening Post*—his illustrations for the final book in *The Bounty Trilogy* are atmospheric and quite compelling.

Supplemental Bibliography

Books

Allen, Douglas, and Allen Douglas, Jr. *N. C. Wyeth: The Collected Paintings, Illustrations and Murals.* New York: Bonanza Books, 1972.

Bibliography of the Golden Cockerel Press, 1921–1949. San Francisco: Alan Wofsy Fine Arts, 1975.

Bligh, William. *The Mutiny on Board H.M.S. Bounty.* Adapted by Deborah Kestel. Illustrated by Brendan Lynch. New York: Playmore, 1979.

_____. *The Mutiny on Board H.M.S. Bounty.* Belmont, California: Lake Education, 1994. Lake Illustrated Classic edition.

Opposite: "Tandis que les révoltés saluaient d'acclamations ironiques." ("As the mutineers gestured with sarcastic shouts.") In 1879, Jules Verne published a fantasy titled ***Les Cinq Cents Millions de la Bégum*** (published in English as *The Begum's Fortune*). It was a short work and, one year later, was expanded with "Les Révoltés de la Bounty" ("The Mutineers of the Bounty,") accompanied by five illustrations. The illustration opposite, by "Drée," pictures the mutineers taunting Bligh as he sails the launch away from *Bounty*. "Les Révoltés de la Bounty" was translated into English by W. H. G. Kingston and published with *The Begum's Fortune* in 1880. Courtesy the Beinecke Rare Book and Manuscript Library, Yale University.

Ebersole, Barbara. *Fletcher Martin*. Gainesville: University of Florida Press, 1954.
Edwards, Hugh. *The Trials and Triumphs of Captain William Bligh, RN*. Sydney: Paul Hamlyn, 1972. Illustrated by Arthur McNeil.
Houfe, Simon. *The Dictionary of British Book Illustrators and Caricaturists, 1800–1914*. Woodbridge, Suffolk: Antique Collectors' Club, 1981. Revised edition.
McCullagh, S. K. *Mutiny at Sea*. N.p.: J. Arnold Leeds, 1965. Illustrated by A. Harper.
Pearson, Julie. *Bounty: Beyond the Voyage*. Leatherhead: Trusson Publications, in association with the Self Publishing Association, 1989. Illustrated by T. E. M. Latham.
Reid, Frank. *The Romance of the Great Barrier Reef*. With illustrations by Geoffrey C. Ingleton. Sydney, London: Angus and Robertson, 1954.

6

Films, Magazines and Music

News of the *Bounty* mutiny and William Bligh's landmark voyage with the loyal members of his crew sparked the interest of people throughout England and Europe. The public remained attentive as subsequent events played out over the next several years. H.M.S. *Pandora*'s pursuit of the mutineers, its sinking off Australia's Great Barrier Reef and the arduous voyage of its survivors was an epic in its own right. The court-martial, sentences, pardons and executions were reported in newspapers and periodicals, and the case of young, well-connected Peter Heywood became a cause célèbre.

When Bligh departed on his second breadfruit voyage to Tahiti and the West Indies on H.M.S. *Providence*, he was known as "Breadfruit Bligh," a hero in the public eye. By the time he returned, behind the scenes machinations conducted by the Christian and Heywood families had successfully blackened Bligh's reputation, and the hero became known as "That Bounty Bastard." Regardless, Bligh went on to enjoy a successful, though stormy naval career, attaining the rank of Admiral of the Blue. Even so, his reputation has never fully recovered from the *Bounty* mutiny.

After the court-martial and punishment of the parties found guilty of mutiny, the entire *Bounty* affair was over as far as the Royal Navy was concerned. But for the public, an unresolved strand of the story remained: What became of Fletcher Christian and the other mutineers?

One enterprising charlatan made the most of this unanswered question by publishing, in 1796, *Letters from Mr. Fletcher Christian, containing a Narrative of the Transactions on board His Majesty's Ship Bounty, before and after the Mutiny, with his subsequent Voyages and Travels in South America*. This collection of seven letters, some of them first published in newspapers and periodicals, supposedly were from the pen of Christian himself. They eventually were proven to be fakes, but the book was popular and reprinted the following year, with illustrations.

The discovery of the mutineers' refuge on Pitcairn Island in the early years of the 19th century, and the conflicting accounts of Christian's fate, further stimulated the public's interest in H.M.S. *Bounty*. In 1831, the publication of Sir John Barrow's seminal *Eventful History of the Mutiny and Piratical Seizure of H.M.S. Bounty* crystallized, for the first time, all of the *Bounty*/*Pandora*/Pitcairn stories into a coherent whole, allowing readers to absorb the amazing breadth of the story. In particular, the story of John Adams' religious conversion and the transformation of tiny Pitcairn Island into a South Seas Eden caught the world's imagination, unleashing a steady flow of articles and stories in popular periodicals that continues to this day.

When popular cinema made its debut in the early 1900s, the *Bounty* Saga was a natural subject for portrayal on the silver screen. MGM's 1935 Academy Award winner *Mutiny on the Bounty* made the names "Bligh" and "Christian" familiar to everyone. Five film versions have been produced to date, each interesting in its own way, but none of them have attempted to dramatize every episode in the saga. Novelist and screenwriter George MacDonald Fraser writes, in *Hollywood History of the World*, "Hollywood has touched only part of it, and that perforce in condensed form; the full tale of the ship and its company is so complex and sensational — and still mysterious — that it would take several films to tell it properly. It is one of the factual dramas that outstrips fiction."

This is especially true of the tale of Pitcairn Island. Elsa Chauvel, who with her husband Charles Chauvel produced *In the Wake of The Bounty* in 1933, writes, "No adequate story of this phase of the Bounty's history had ever been fully recorded. What was the true history of Pitcairn, that forgotten isle at the Southern end of the Pacific which had served as a retreat for the mutineers?"

Someday, the entire *Bounty* Saga may finally reach the screen. The great director David Lean made an attempt to dramatize the full story in two separate films, but the project was stillborn. Director Peter Jackson has proven that an extremely long tale — the three books that comprise J.R.R. Tolkien's *The Lord of the Rings*— can be filmed successfully and profitably.

From April 28 to October 1, 1989, the National Maritime Museum in Greenwich, England, hosted an international exhibition to mark the mutiny's bicentenary. It gave the public an opportunity to take a fresh look at Bligh, Christian, and the other participants in this great human drama. Thousands of visitors thrilled to the display of *Bounty*-related artifacts and a variety of sophisticated audio-visual effects. A wide range of *Bounty*-associated items were sold, from tote bag souvenirs and children's books to *Mutiny on the Bounty, 1789–1989*— a superbly illustrated, 160-page guide to the exhibition that included articles written by renowned *Bounty* scholars. A version for children also was produced, titled *The Mutiny on the Bounty*.

Since the 1930s, a great deal of serious *Bounty* scholarship has been undertaken in an attempt to rehabilitate the public's negative opinion of Bligh, but most popular film and literature has, until recently, taken the opposite tack. The pendulum now is beginning to swing back. The fifth mutiny film, *The Bounty*, and the musical *Mutiny!* presented Bligh and Christian as real human beings, rather than the stereotypical villain and hero. The release of several well-made documentaries suggests that popular culture is finally assimilating the information that scholarship has been unearthing for 75 years. Those willing to take an objective view will discover that the true story of *Bounty* is far more compelling than any film or print interpretation.

Major Works

THOMAS JOHN DIBDIN: *The Pirates: or, The Calamaties of Capt. Bligh*. London, 1790.
When William Bligh returned to England in March 1790, he had a compelling tale to tell, one that immediately caught the public's attention. London's entertainment world also took note. Plays based on current topics, such as the *Siege of Quebec* and *The Triumph of Liberty, Or the Destruction of the Bastille* were quite popular. On May 6, 1790, barely two months

after Bligh's return, Thomas John Dibdin's hastily written "romantick operatick Ballet Spectacle," called *The Pirates: Or, The Calamaties of Capt. Bligh*, opened at the Royalty Theatre.

The first actors to play Bligh and Fletcher Christian were, respectively, Ralph Wewitzer and William Bourke. They were limited to performing in mime — "A Fact, Told in Action" as the advertisement describes — because the Royalty Theatre did not have a legitimate license. The absence of spoken dialogue in *The Pirates* proved to be a liability. In *Mr. Bligh's Bad Language*, Greg Dening notes that the audience was expected to "Construct a narrative out of some crib in the programme, such as the advertisement for *The Pirates*... The spectacle was the unthinking man's narrative, an animated cartoon."

The Pirates did not attract much of an audience, and it closed on June 30, 1790. *The Mutiny of the Bounty, or, the Traitor's Doom!*, an historical drama in three acts that incorporated several quotations from Bligh's *A Narrative of the Mutiny*, was performed in 1800.

Years later, news about Pitcairn Island from Captain Philip Pipon of H.M.S. *Briton* and Sir Thomas Staines of H.M.S. *Tagus* revived public interest in the *Bounty*, which led to additional stage adaptations. In April 1816, Thomas John Dibdin of the Theatre Royal presented *A New Romantick Operatick Ballet Spectacle (Founded on the Recent Discovery of a Numerous Colony, Formed by, and Descended from, the Mutineers of the Bounty Frigate,)* called *Pitcairn's Island*. In July 1823, Sadler's Wells Theatre presented a stage adaptation of Lord Byron's narrative poem about the mutiny, *The Island, or, Christian and his Comrades*.

Following these early stage productions, 19th century literature about the *Bounty* mutiny and Pitcairn Island appeared primarily in the form of books and articles in popular periodicals. The religious conversion and piety of the mutineers' descendants on Pitcairn Island was of particular interest to readers around the world. The *Bounty* story did not return to the stage until the late 20th century, when a handful of stimulating, entertaining works appeared. In 1972, playwright Richard Crane presented *Mutiny on the Bounty — a sea-faring show*, which he calls a "part pantomime, part rock musical, part seafaring extravaganza," at the University of Bradford in England.

Crane later produced a dramatic variation of the *Bounty* story that was acted by children in Brighton. This production attracted the attention of actor and singer David Essex, who collaborated with Crane on *Mutiny!*, a musical adaptation performed in London's West End from 1985 to 1986.

The Mutiny of the Bounty (1916)

Directed and produced by Raymond Longford. Screenplay by Raymond Longford and Lottie Lyell. Crick and Jones Production Company. Cast: Gwil Adams (Mrs. Bligh); Harry Beaumont (Mr. Samuels); Reginald Collins (Heywood); Ernesto Crosetto (Midshipman Hallett); George Cross (William Bligh); D.L. Dalziel (Sir Joseph Banks); Ada Guilford (Mrs. Heywood); Lottie Lyell (Nessy Heywood); Leah Miller (Baby); Wilton Powe (Fletcher Christian); John Storm (King George III); Meta Taupopoki (Otoo); Charles Villiers (Burkett).

No fewer than five film versions of the *Bounty* Saga have been produced to date, the first one during the early, silent days of cinema. Although there are unproven rumors of an even earlier version, Australian Raymond Longford wrote, directed and produced the first known motion picture treatment of the *Bounty* story. Unfortunately, the delicate celluloid film has deteriorated beyond repair. A handful of stills for only some of the scenes has survived. Reportedly, it originally included scenes of George III and Sir Joseph Banks.

The Mutiny of the Bounty, which premiered in 1916 at Hoyts Street Theatre in Sydney,

ROYALTY-THEATRE,
Well-Street, near Goodman's-Fields.

This present THURSDAY, May 6, 1790,
WILL BE PRESENTED
A NEW MUSICAL PIECE, called

TAR against PERFUME:
Or, The SAILOR PREFERRED.

Coxswain, Mr. MATHEWS. William, Mr. BIRKETT. Old Slop, Mr. REES.
And Monsieur Le Friz, (the Perfumer,) Mr. WEWITZER.
Susan, Miss WILLIAMS.

A NEW DANCE, composed by Mr. BOURKE, called

THE MERRY BLOCK-MAKERS.

By Monf. FERRERE, Mad. FOUZZI, Mad FERRERE. Mr. JEANI, Mr. BOURKE, &c.

A MUSICAL ENTERTAINMENT, called

A PILL FOR THE DOCTOR:
Or, The TRIPLE WEDDING.

Sailor, Mr. BIRKETT. Dr. Lotion, Mr. REES. Farmer, Mr. MATHEWS.
And Pestle, the Doctor's Man, Mr. WEWITZER.
Polly, Miss WILLIAMS Dorothy, Mrs. SAUNDERS.
Lydia, Miss E. WILLIAMS. And Goody, Mrs. BURNETT.
To conclude with a DANCE by the Characters.

A FAVOURITE SONG, by Miss DANIEL.

The Whole to conclude with (the 4th Time) A FACT, TOLD IN ACTION, called

The PIRATES:
OR, The Calamities of Capt. BLIGH.

Exhibiting a full Account of his Voyage, from his taking Leave at the Admiralty.
AND SHEWING,
The BOUNTY falling down the River THAMES.
The Captain's Reception at OTAHEITE, and exchanging the *British Manufactures*
for the BREAD-FRUIT TREES. With an OTAHEITEAN DANCE.
The Attachment of the OTAHEITEAN WOMEN to, and their Distress at parting from, the BRITISH SAILORS
An exact Representation of
The SEISURE of Capt. BLIGH, in the Cabin of the BOUNTY, by the Pirates.
With the affecting Scene of forcing the Captain and his faithful Followers into the Boat.
Their Distress at Sea, and Repulse by the Natives of One of the *Friendly Islands*.
Their miraculous Arrival at the *Cape of Good Hope*, and their friendly Reception by
the Governor.
DANCES and CEREMONIES of the HOTTENTOTS
On their Departure. And their happy Arrival in England.
Rehearsed under the immediate Instruction of a Person who was on-board the Bounty, Store-Ship.

*** The Doors to be opened at Half past Five and to begin at Half past Six o'Clock precisely.
BOXES, 3s. 6d.—PIT, 2s. 6d.—FIRST GALLERY, 1s. 6d.—UPPER GALLERY, 1s.
Nothing under full Price will be taken nor any Money returned:
Places for the Boxes may be taken at the Stage-Door from Ten till Three o'Clock every Day,
VIVANT REX & REGINA.

☞ BOOKS of the PILL for the DOCTOR to be had at the Theatre; and, to prevent Imposition,
the Proprietors have ordered that no more shall be taken for them than SIX-PENCE each.

was advertised as "The finest and most important motion picture ever produced in Australia... Book your seats now and avoid disappointment. Every man, women [sic] and child should see 'The Mutiny of the Bounty.'"

Longford's screenplay was well researched. He consulted the superb collection of historical records, which includes Bligh's log, at the Mitchell Library in Sydney. These primary materials are being preserved for future generations, and it is unfortunate that Longford's 74-minute film has not fared as well.

In some ways, Longford's *The Mutiny of the Bounty* is the most ambitious of the five *Bounty* films. Filmed in Rotorua, New Zealand and Norfolk Island, it includes scenes that no other filmmaker has attempted, such as William Bligh (accompanied by Sir Joseph Banks), receiving his commission for the breadfruit voyage from King George III; the reaction of Peter Heywood's family when they learn that he has been implicated in the mutiny, and their reunion after he receives the King's Pardon; the bloodshed on Pitcairn Island; and an older, wiser John Adams teaching the children of Pitcairn. Longford's vision of the Bligh/Christian relationship emphasizes the traditionally negative view of Bligh (played by George Cross), who is described in the screenplay as a commander with an "ungovernable temper" who "disgusts" Fletcher Christian (played by Wilton Power). In Longford's film, the famous "coconut incident" pushes Christian to the brink:

SCENE: Deck of *Bounty*
Bligh on coming on deck looks at nuts on deck flys [sic] into temper and calls Christian & other Officers to him and accuses them.
CHRISTIAN: Sir I hope you do not think me guilty of stealing.
BLIGH: Yes you d—-d hound I do, you are all thieves alike.
Bligh threatens and orders them away B (Bligh) in G (Great) Passion.

We can no longer judge the merits of this lost motion picture, but the few surviving reviews were enthusiastic. Frank Walter of the Australian Historical Society wrote to Longford, "The characters are all true to life, particularly the conception of the character of Captain Bligh, which was well sustained, and afforded an excellent idea of the kind of man he was.... All the scenes are well acted, and the pictures leave nothing to be desired." *Photoplay Magazine* for September 2, 1916, called it "Easily the best Australian historical photoplay produced here... The public opinion will be in favour of the picture produced by Mr. Longford."

Additional reviews, along with the screenplay submitted for copyright, stills, production credits, advertisements and other items may be found on line at www.screensound.gov.au.

In the Wake of The Bounty (1933)

Directed and Produced by Charles Chauvel. Script by Charles Chauvel. Expeditionary Films. Cast: Mayne Lynton (Captain Bligh); Errol Flynn (Fletcher Christian); Victor Gouriet (The Blind Fiddler); John Warwick (Young).

Millions of people throughout the world have seen the 1935, 1962 and 1984 film versions of the *Bounty* story, but few of them have heard of *In the Wake of The Bounty* by pioneer Australian filmmaker Charles Chauvel. Part historical drama and part travel documentary, it premiered at the Prince Edward Theatre in Sydney on March 15, 1933. Its distribution was limited to just a few movie houses in Australia and the film was never released in the United

Opposite: This broadside advertised a performance of *The Pirates: or, The Calamities of Capt. Bligh*, produced in London, 1790.

Advertisement for Raymond Longford's *The Mutiny of the Bounty*, the first movie about the mutiny. The actual film is lost, but a number of stills exist.

States. Metro-Goldwyn-Mayer, which was producing a far more expensive and opulent version of the *Bounty* Saga at the time, purchased the rights to Chauvel's movie. MGM even used some of Chauvel's footage to create two short advertising films—entitled *Pitcairn Island Today* and *Primitive Pitcairn*—to publicize its own *Mutiny on the* Bounty, released in 1935.

    In the Wake of The Bounty opens in 1810, at an English waterside tavern where the "locals"

The program cover for Charles Chauvel's *In the Wake of the Bounty* was written in pungent language, extolling the film's exotic Tahitian setting and its effect on *Bounty*'s crew: "Where dryads asked no vows and knew no shame — and thoughts of home, sweethearts and wives were buried under the demoralizing debris of scented nights and tropic madness!" The scenes of Tahitian dancing in the film were quite frank for 1933, and Chauvel had trouble with the censors.

ask blind fiddler Michael Byrne (played by Victor Gouriet) to tell the story of *Bounty*'s voyage. The subsequent historical segments, narrated by Byrne, are confined to a handful of brief scenes, including William Bligh's violent reaction to some "stolen" cheeses; his attempt to round Cape Horn; a flogging; *Bounty*'s arrival at Tahiti; and the mutiny itself, which Chauvel attributes to Bligh's unbearable temper, poor rations and the crew's desire to return to Tahiti.

Unfortunately, a poor script hampers the performances, and none of the characters are fully developed. Only five are actually named: Byrne, Christian, Bligh, Edward Young and Isabella, Christian's paramour. Mayne Lynton depicts Bligh as a snuff-taking tyrant who starves and flogs his crew. Errol Flynn's performance as Christian, in his first film performance, is stilted and dull. It was an unremarkable debut, but Flynn would soon achieve worldwide fame as a swashbuckling hero in such Hollywood classics as *Captain Blood*, *The Charge of the Light Brigade* and *The Adventures of Robin Hood*. With a better screenplay, he might have provided a more memorable interpretation of Christian. Interestingly, Flynn claimed to be a distant relative of Edward Young.

Although the historical segments (Chauvel refers to them as the "threads of a story") fail to dramatize the *Bounty* story in a compelling way, Chauvel's footage of Pitcairn Island in the early 1930s is impressive. The first visitors to document the island and its people on motion picture film, Charles and his wife, Elsa Chauvel provide a wonderful look at Pitcairn, making this footage the high point of *In the Wake of The Bounty*.

This film is an invaluable record of island life in the early 1930s, capturing the Pitcairners performing everyday chores and activities, as well as special occasions, like the wedding of Eva and Allan Christian. We see the Islanders rowing in and out of dangerous Bounty Bay, attending church services, exercising, cooking, swimming and creating curios for ships calling at the island. There are many dramatic shots of the island itself, including Adamstown, John Adams' grave, Christian's Cave and the hieroglyphic drawings of Pitcairn's past inhabitants.

Now widely available in VHS and DVD format, *In the Wake of The Bounty* is well worth viewing, despite its uninspired script, poor acting and generally primitive production values. Its repetitive, sometimes inappropriate soundtrack is particularly annoying. Nevertheless, *In the Wake of The Bounty* is redeemed by its lively, on-location footage.

Mutiny on the Bounty (1935)

Directed by Frank Lloyd. Screenplay by Talbot Jennings, Jules Furthman and Carey Wilson. Metro-Goldwyn-Mayer. Cast: Charles Laughton (Capt. William Bligh); Clark Gable (Lt. Fletcher Christian); Franchot Tone (Midshipman Roger Byam); Herbert Mundin (Smith); Eddie Quillan (Seaman Thomas Ellison); Dudley Digges (Dr. Bacchus); Donald Crisp (Seaman Thomas Burkitt); Henry Stephenson (Sir Joseph Banks); Francis Lister (Capt. Nelson); Spring Byington (Mrs. Byam); Movita Castenada (Tehanni); Mamo Clark (Maimiti); Byron Russell (Quintal); Percy Waram (Seaman Coleman); David Torrence (Lord Hood); John Harrington (Lt. Purcell); Douglas Walton (Midshipman Stewart); DeWitt Jennings (1st Lt. Fryer); Vernon Downing (Midshipman Hayward); Stanley Fields (Seaman William Muspratt); Wallis Clark (Bos'un Morrison); Pat Flaherty (Bos'uns Mate Churchill); Alec Craig (Seaman William McCoy); Charles Irwin (Seaman Matthew Thompson); Dick Winsol (Tinkler).

Metro-Goldwyn-Mayer's 1935 blockbuster *Mutiny on the Bounty* is undoubtedly the most famous film version of the *Bounty* Saga. MGM spared no expense, investing more than $2 million in the project over a two-year period. Two old schooners were refurbished to resemble the *Bounty* and *Pandora*, a replica of *Bounty*'s launch was constructed, and a 27-foot scale model of *Bounty* was built to film the wreck of the ship on Pitcairn Island.

MGM's investment paid off. *Mutiny on the Bounty* grossed nearly $4.5 million and was nominated for seven Academy Awards, winning an Academy Award for Best Picture. Arguably the most entertaining of the five *Bounty* movies, it is filled with inaccuracies that make it an unsatisfying experience for the more historically minded viewer.

Director Frank Lloyd owned the rights to film Nordhoff and Hall's *Bounty Trilogy* novels, and the team-written script was based on *Mutiny on the Bounty* and *Men Against the Sea*. However, the screenwriters took considerable liberties with the novels, which adhere far more closely to historical truth than the script. The more obvious examples include Fletcher Christian heading up a press gang to man the *Bounty* when the crew actually consisted of volunteers, and presenting 15-year-old Thomas Ellison as a married man with a child. The mutiny itself—in reality a bloodless event—is filmed as a knockdown, drag-out battle, with the crew using knives, clubs and bayonets.

The script also ignores the important interlude at Tubuai. After the mutiny, Christian sails *Bounty* directly back to Tahiti, where he and the rest of the crew live comfortably until H.M.S. *Pandora* arrives, escaping just hours before the ship enters the harbor. William Bligh, not Captain Edward Edwards, commands *Pandora*, and is responsible for the wreck of the vessel. Bligh also testifies at the court-martial, which would have been impossible, since he was commanding H.M.S. *Providence* at the time.

Regardless of these gross inaccuracies, there is no question that *Mutiny on the Bounty* succeeds as sheer cinematic entertainment. The cinematography and strong performances from Charles Laughton as Bligh, Clark Gable as Christian and Franchot Tone as Roger Byam—the fictional narrator invented by Nordhoff and Hall for the first volume of the *Bounty* Trilogy—make this film a memorable one. For the first time in Academy Award history, three actors from one film were nominated for Best Actor.

Unfortunately, *Mutiny on the Bounty* has accomplished more than any other book, magazine article or film to perpetuate the image of Bligh as a merciless tyrant. For many people, it is their first, and only, exposure to the story. Charles Laughton's unforgettable portrayal of Bligh as a sneering, sadistic commander who starves and mercilessly flogs his men firmly established the public perception of Bligh as an icon of cruelty and injustice. In one notorious scene, Bligh keelhauls a seaman who begs for water, resulting in his death. As Glynn Christian comments in his article, "Film-makers and *Bounty*," "The infamous keel-hauling scene could never have happened, as it had long been banned by the time *Bounty* sailed—indeed if Bligh were really as tough as this film made out, there might not have been a mutiny."

Many *Bounty* enthusiasts would agree with film scholar Ed Reardon, who suggests in his article "Captain Bligh in Film" that a masterful actor like Laughton could have presented a more balanced performance of Bligh if the script had allowed it:

> Given his range as an actor, why then did he invest Bligh with a demonic quality that has frozen this character in the American psyche as the personification of evil? Whatever possibilities existed for shading this quality and investing the character with even a modicum of humanity are absent. Why Laughton's interpretation is limited in this way has more to do with the other creative forces brought to bear on it and concerns among the filmmakers that irrevocably shaped the production in significant and far-reaching ways.

Ironically, *Mutiny on the Bounty* appeared at a time when the publication of such works as George Mackaness's *Life of Vice-Admiral Bligh* and the Golden Cockerel Press's "Bountiana" series were presenting a far more accurate view of not only Bligh but virtually all aspects

of the *Bounty* Saga. Nearly 50 years would pass until Hollywood caught up with scholarship and presented Bligh in a more reasonable, realistic light.

CHARLES NORDHOFF AND JAMES NORMAN HALL: *Mutiny on the Bounty. Classics Illustrated*, No. 100. *Men Against the Sea. Classics Illustrated*, No. 103. *Pitcairn's Island. Classics Illustrated*, No. 109. New York: Gilberton Company, Inc., 1952–1953. Reprinted by arrangement with Little, Brown & Company.

Created by Albert Kantner as *Classic Comics* in 1941, which he changed to *Classics Illustrated* six years later, these avidly collected comic books attracted millions of readers until the series ended in the early 1970s. *Classics Illustrated* abridged and illustrated 167 well-known novels and works of non-fiction — from Alexandre Dumas' *The Three Musketeers* (No. 1) to Goethe's *Faust* (No. 167). Titles were reprinted on a regular basis, sometimes with new cover artwork.

The *Classics Illustrated* pledge — "To bring you the world's finest literature in an authentic, absorbing, and colorful manner" — was printed on the inside front cover of the 100th issue, adapted from James Nordhoff and Charles Norman Hall's *Mutiny on the Bounty*.

Whether *Classics Illustrated* successfully reached its lofty goal is still disputed. Many critics complained that the content and characters were oversimplified or that school students would use them as cribs. The writing and artwork varied in quality, and comic books obviously were no substitute for the original work. But supporters noted that the friendly, familiar comic book format enticed children to approach serious literature and eventually "graduate" to the unabridged versions. In fact, the *Classics Illustrated* editors encouraged readers, at the close of each story, to tackle the "real thing": "Now that you've read the *Classics Illustrated* Edition, don't miss the added enjoyment of Reading the original, obtainable at your school or Public Library."

Nordhoff and Hall's *Mutiny on the Bounty*, *Men Against the Sea* and *Pitcairn's Island* made their appearance as *Classics Illustrated* from 1952 to 1953. *Mutiny on the Bounty*, illustrated by Morris Waldinger, was even packaged with a recording of the comic book text as part of the "Classics Story Teller" series. *Men Against the Sea* and *Pitcairn's Island* featured artwork by Rudy Palais, a versatile, well-known comic artist who also adapted works by Robert Louis Stevenson and James Fenimore Cooper for *Classics Illustrated*. *Mutiny on the Bounty* also appeared as no. 11 of *A Classic in Pictures*, a United Kingdom edition of *Classics Illustrated* that ran for only 12 issues.

With its straightforward narrative, *Men Against the Sea* must have been the easiest of the three novels to adapt to a comic book format. The editors also were fairly faithful to the content of *Mutiny on the Bounty*. *Pitcairn's Island*, filled with sexual jealousy, violence, alcoholism and racial discrimination, must have presented a significant challenge to the artist and editor, as it did to Nordhoff and Hall, who stated in their "Author's Note" to the original novel: "If at times, in the following narrative, blood flows overfreely, and horror seems to pile on horror, it is not because the authors would have it so: it was so, in Pitcairn history."

The Gilberton Company needed to ensure their comics' acceptability in the marketplace, and they managed to create a straightforward, tasteful adaptation of *Pitcairn's Island*. Understandably, they omitted some of the more gruesome events that occur in the novel, such as the "execution" by axe of Matthew Quintal.

Opposite: This advertisement for the 1935 film *Mutiny on the Bounty* shows some of the key characters: Clark Gable as handsome, rugged Fletcher Christian; Mamo Clark as his Tahitian love Maimiti; Franchot Tone as Roger Byam; and Charles Laughton as Captain Bligh.

Alexander Smith and Isaac Martin battle it out on the sheer cliffs of Pitcairn Island on the cover of the *Classics Illustrated* version of Charles Nordhoff and James Norman Hall's *Pitcairn's Island*.

While the *Classics Illustrated* versions obviously are no match for Nordhoff and Hall's great trilogy, these colorful comics must have motivated many young readers to explore the riches of their novels and the fascination of the entire *Bounty* Saga.

JACK PEARL: "Captain Bligh of the *Bounty.*" *Saga: The Magazine for Men*, January 1961.

Until actor Anthony Hopkins' portrayal of William Bligh as a harsh, but humane, character in *The Bounty* (1984), films typically presented him as a ruthless, sadistic naval officer who delighted in starving his crew, flogging and keelhauling them at every opportunity. Charles Laughton played this role to perfection in MGM's 1935 version of *Mutiny on the Bounty*.

One year before the release of MGM's 1962 production — when Trevor Howard picked up where Laughton left off—*Saga*, a pulp magazine, posed the following question on the cover of its January 1961 issue: "Was Captain Bligh the Bounty Villain?" This popular magazine's illustrated, "Triple-Length Feature" cover story by Jack Pearl, titled "Captain Bligh of the Bounty," presented a more accurate interpretation of Bligh than either of the MGM film versions.

The editor prefaces this blend of fact and fiction with a note that asks the reader to keep an open mind: "The very name 'Captain Bligh' has become a synonym for tyranny and brutality, while 'Mister Christian' has become something of a folk hero, a symbol of the nobility of man and his determination to live in freedom and dignity. It's a romantic idea, but is it true?"

In the story's first scene, Pearl dismisses the notion that Bligh was a notorious flogger. Following the punishment of Able Seaman Matthew Quintal, Bligh returns to his cabin, "His hands still clasped behind his back, his head bent in depression." Noting this behavior, Midshipman Thomas Hayward asks Christian:

"What's wrong with the captain?"

Master's Mate Fletcher Christian shrugged. "He had hoped to go the whole voyage without putting the lash to anybody."

Hayward's eyebrows lifted superciliously. "Why should he care about that? Has he got a weak stomach or something?"

"It's not that. With that back, Matt Quintal won't be any good to us for a couple of days. Captain Bligh just doesn't like to see any of his crew taking it easy in the hammock."

In this incident, as well as in his description of *Bounty*'s attempt to round Cape Horn, Pearl makes it clear that Bligh usually did a superb job taking care of his crew's health — even if his ultimate goal was the success of the voyage, not the men's personal comfort. By and large, Pearl sticks to the historical facts, but adds a provocative touch by suggesting that Midshipman Hayward encouraged Christian to take the ship. Hayward is an unsympathetic character in most versions of the story, but he is particularly odious here, deserting Christian after the mutiny and joining Bligh's party in the launch.

Unlike many popular versions of the *Bounty* story, "Was Captain Bligh the *Bounty* Villain?" clearly focuses on Bligh's dilemma: "He could excel as a leader only under the most severe circumstances: As impressive as Bligh's navigating skills were the qualities he displayed as a leader of men — qualities which he never had shown before the mutiny and which unhappily became dormant again at the completion of the journey to Timor. But during those 41 days in the open boat, Lieutenant Bligh, as if by divine inspiration, was magnificent."

Ironically, this inexpensive, ephemeral pulp magazine served up an entertaining story with a higher degree of historical accuracy than MGM's two multimillion dollar motion pictures.

"Although he was a hard taskmaster, Bligh hated to use the lash on his men." This drawing by Brendan Lynch from Jack Pearl's "Captain Bligh of the *Bounty*," which appeared in *Saga: The Magazine for Men* in January 1961, presents Bligh in a more realistic light than the motion picture that appeared the following year.

Mutiny on the Bounty (1962)

Directed by Lewis Milestone. Screenplay by Charles Lederer and others. Metro-Goldwyn-Mayer. Cast: Marlon Brando (Fletcher Christian); Trevor Howard (Capt. William Bligh); Richard Harris (John Mills); Hugh Griffith (Alexander Smith); Richard Haydn (William Brown); Percy Herbert (Matthew Quintal); Tarita (Maimiti); Chips Rafferty (Michael Byrne); Eddie Byrne (John Fryer); Tim Seely (Edward Young); Noel Purcell (William McCoy); Gordon Jackson (Edward Birkett); Duncan Lamont (John Williams); Ashley Cowan (Samuel Mack); Keith McConnell (James Morrison); Frank Silvera (Minarii); Ben Wright (Graves); Henry Daniell (Court Martial Judge); Torin Thatcher (Staines); Yvon Arai (Tahitian Native).

When Marlon Brando passed away in 2004, the *New York Times* obituary stated that Metro-Goldwyn-Mayer's 1962 remake of *Mutiny on the Bounty*, starring Brando as Fletcher Christian and Trevor Howard as William Bligh, was, "the most celebrated movie disaster of its day." Many moviegoers and critics believe that it also is the weakest film interpretation of the *Bounty* story to date. Its budget was ten times that of the 1935 version, yet the film was a box office flop. And, unlike its predecessor, it failed to capture a single Academy Award.

Mutiny on the Bounty opens promisingly, with gardener William Brown explaining the voyage's breadfruit mission to John Mills, John Adams and other members of the crew — accurately described as volunteers — as he boards the *Bounty* in Portsmouth.

Unfortunately, the film begins to go downhill when Christian arrives in a splendid coach, dressed in foppish, un-seamanlike clothing and accompanied by two French-speaking women. Brando speaks his lines in a peculiar, distracting accent that makes it difficult to regard his character seriously. He plays Christian as a wealthy dilettante who has joined the Royal Navy because, as he tells Bligh, "one must have something to do." Although he proves to be a competent seaman, he doesn't take the voyage seriously, calling *Bounty* "a river scow on a grocer's errand" and ridiculing Bligh at every opportunity.

For example, when Christian's companions insist on meeting Bligh, we learn that he cannot speak French. From this point on, the film focuses on the social class difference between Bligh and Christian, suggesting that this tension culminated in the mutiny. The introduction to the film's souvenir book states that the mutiny was "led by an Englishman of good birth named Fletcher Christian against an officer of modest background named William Bligh."

This well-worn theory was proposed in 1831 by Sir John Barrow in *The Eventful History of the Mutiny and Piratical Seizure of H.M.S.* Bounty: *Its Causes and Consequences*: "It was Bligh's misfortune not to have been educated in the cockpit of a man-of-war among young gentlemen, which is to the navy what a public school is to those who are to move in civil society.... (Bligh) was a man of coarse habits, and entertained very mistaken notions with regard to discipline.... His temper was irritable in the extreme."

Sir Cyprian A. G. Bridge echoes Barrow's thoughts in his introduction to the World's Classics edition of Barrow's work: "In fact he was not a gentleman either by bringing up or by nature. To speak plainly, he was a bully... In the matter of social position, (Christian, George Stewart and Peter Heywood), were all gentlemen by birth, and members of families of exceptionally good position." John Chodes, in his play *The Longboat*, took a similar approach: "It was the clash of the lower and aristocratic classes, not Bligh's cruelty, that brought on the mutiny."

Trevor Howard's performance as a seaman of "modest background" is solid and far more convincing than Brando's, although he was too old for the role. Like Laughton's Bligh, he is fairly one-dimensional, despising the crew, ruling them by fear, and ordering numerous floggings, as well as a keelhauling. When Bligh's "gentlemanly" officers remind him that keelhauling is illegal on an English ship, he insists on enforcing the punishment, and sharks devour the unfortunate seaman.

Bligh also recklessly attempts to round Cape Horn in an effort to impress the Admiralty by harvesting and delivering the breadfruit plants as quickly as possible. This action causes the death of Carpenter's Mate Charles Norman (in reality, one of the men acquitted at the court-martial), who is crushed by a barrel in the ship's hold during rough seas.

In this film, the mutiny is sparked by a completely fictional event. On the voyage to Jamaica, the breadfruit plants begin to die for lack of water and Bligh, who is more concerned about the plants than the crew, forces them to climb to the yardarm for a drink. When he refuses water to a man who has been drinking sea water, Christian takes the ship. The film does not dramatize Bligh's open boat voyage, but concentrates on the fate of the mutineers, which leads to a strange, unsatisfying conclusion that has no basis in fact.

Marlon Brando as Fletcher Christian and Trevor Howard as William Bligh are pictured on the title page of *Mutiny on the Bounty*, a souvenir book packaged with the soundtrack of the 1962 film.

Soon after arriving on Pitcairn Island, Christian tries to convince his fellow mutineers that the only way they will ever find peace is by returning to England to face a court-martial — which he believes will vindicate their actions. He gives them a night to consider his proposal, during which they thwart Christian by setting fire to the ship. Christian attempts to save the *Bounty*, but is fatally burned and dies in the arms of his consort, here named Maimiti.

Given the high caliber of the cast, including Richard Harris as John Mills, audiences and critics anticipated a far more satisfying film. Nevertheless, this "movie disaster" has a number of saving graces that make it worthwhile viewing. Filmed in Technicolor, it is filled with spectacular scenery of the South Seas. Brando was so impressed by the locale that he actually purchased the coral atoll of Tetiaroa as a retreat from Hollywood. The film also boasts a haunting soundtrack by Bronislau Kaper.

The Bounty (1984)

Directed by Roger Donaldson. Screenplay by Robert Bolt. Dino De Laurentiis Productions, Bounty Productions Ltd. Cast: Mel Gibson (Fletcher Christian); Anthony Hopkins (Lieutenant William Bligh); Laurence Olivier (Admiral Hood); Edward Fox (Captain Greetham); Daniel Day-Lewis (John Fryer); Bernard Hill (William Cole); Philip Davis (Edward Young); Liam Neeson (Charles Churchill); Wi Kuki Kaa (King Tynah); Tevaite Vernette (Mauatua); Philip Martin Brown (John Adams); Simon Chandler (David Nelson); Malcolm Terris (Dr. John Huggan); Simon Adams (Peter Heywood); John Sessions (John Smith); Andrew Wilde (William McKoy); Neil Morrissey (Matthew Quintal); Richard Graham (John Mills); Dexter Fletcher (Thomas Ellison); Pete Lee-Wilson (William Purcell); Jon Gadsby (John Norton); Brendan Conroy (Robert Lamb); Barry Dransfield (Michael Byrne); Steve Fletcher (James Valentine); Jack May (Prosecuting Captain); Mary Kauila (Queen Tynah); Sharon Bower (Mrs. Bligh); Tavana (King Tynah's Councillor).

Loosely based on Richard Hough's *Captain Bligh and Mr. Christian*, with an intelligent script by playwright and screenwriter Robert Bolt, *The Bounty* is the most historically accurate film adaptation of the story to date. Even the full-size replica of *Bounty* constructed for this film follows the dimensions of the original vessel more closely than the earlier reproductions. Filmed on location in England, Tahiti and New Zealand, it is colorful and visually attractive, although some prefer the cinematography of the 1962 version.

Hough's fresh, controversial approach to the mutiny inspired David Lean, the director of *Lawrence of Arabia, Doctor Zhivago* and other acclaimed screen epics, to create two films about the *Bounty* Saga. His working titles were *The Lawbreakers* and *The Long Arm*. The first film would cover the voyage to Tahiti, the mutiny and open boat voyage, while the second would treat the voyage of *Pandora*, the court-martial and the fate of the mutineers on Pitcairn Island. According to film historian Adrian Turner, Lean was "astonished by the complexity and richness of the story, as well as its striking divergence from the familiar MGM films of 1935 and 1962. The truth of the *Bounty* mutiny and its even more dramatic aftermath was far stranger than any fiction." Lean engaged Bolt, a past collaborator, to write the screenplays.

Bolt finished the scripts, writing much of them in Tahiti and Bora Bora, but Warner Brothers balked at the estimated production expenses and dropped the project. After several unsuccessful attempts to raise funds on his own for a one-film version, to be titled *Pandora's Box*, Lean reluctantly gave up. During this time, Bolt suffered a massive stroke. Producer Dino De Laurentiis, who had purchased Bolt's screenplays as well as the new replica of *Bounty*, hired Roger Donaldson as director. In 1984, *The Bounty* was finally released, as one film.

The events are presented through a series of flashbacks during Bligh's testimony before Lord Hood, at the obligatory court-martial all commanders faced for the loss of a ship. *The Bounty*'s early scenes focus on the friendship that Bligh and Christian once enjoyed. One episode pictures Christian visiting Bligh's house and playing with his children. When Bligh invites Christian to join his crew, Christian eagerly accepts, although it is clear that he is more interested in the chance to sample life on a South Sea island than in Bligh's mission to gather breadfruit.

When *Bounty* arrives in Tahiti and the crew begins relationships with the native women, discipline slips and trouble starts to brew. Christian, especially, is full of enthusiasm about native life and even endures the painful process of tattooing. Bligh remains chaste, but it is clear that the more he represses his sexuality, the more irascible he becomes, especially with Christian.

In *Captain Bligh and Mr. Christian*, Hough expanded on the hypothesis, suggested earlier by Madge Darby in *Who Caused the Mutiny on the Bounty?*, that repressed homosexuality generated a love/hate relationship between Bligh and Christian. Hough maintains that the two men actually did have a consensual, homosexual relationship on earlier voyages as well as during *Bounty*'s voyage to Tahiti, and that Christian broke it off when *Bounty* left the island. Rejected, Bligh begins to act out his rage by mercilessly criticizing Christian, culminating in the accusation that he stole some of his coconuts.

The Bounty does not present a literal interpretation of Hough's hypothesis, but it does suggest that repressed homosexual feelings may have led to the mutiny. Bligh is not only angry with Christian's "going native" and consequent lack of discipline, but clearly jealous of the fact that he is involved in a sexual relationship. The film has one strange inaccuracy. Bligh tells his crew that he wants to circumnavigate the globe and make another attempt at rounding Cape Horn, a statement that provides additional motivation for the men to mutiny.

While it may have failed at the box office, *The Bounty* has a number of strengths, notably in its presentation of Bligh and Christian, who are far more human and believable than in the earlier films. It gave moviegoers the opportunity to see Bligh as a brilliant navigator and flawed leader of men. Gibson does not portray Christian as a paragon of virtue and romantic hero the way Clark Gable did, but as a sensitive, hedonistic man who puts pleasure before his duty as an officer.

Unfortunately, *The Bounty*, like its predecessors, does not tell the complete story, leaving out the voyage of *Pandora*, the court-martial and the Pitcairn Island settlement. Glynn Christian writes, "Despite the millions of pounds, dollars, and other currencies spent, the story of *Bounty* still awaits factual transferral to large or small screen. This is a story where truth is far more spectacular than the fictions of scriptwriters."

DAVID ESSEX AND RICHARD CRANE: *Mutiny!* Music by David Essex. Book by Richard Crane. Lyrics by Richard Crane and David Essex. Freedman Panter Productions Ltd. in association with Theatre Productions LC, 1985. Cast: Frank Finlay (William Bligh); Neville Jason (John Fryer); David Essex (Fletcher Christian); David Oakley (William Elphinstone); Shaun Curry (William Cole); Hugh Craig (Thomas Ellison); Daire O'Dunlaing (Robert Tinkler); Jack Dolman (Edward Young); Paul Firth (Peter Heywood); William Snape (John Adams);

Opposite: Mel Gibson, Anthony Hopkins and the third, most accurate replica of *Bounty* are pictured on the cover of *The Bounty*, a paperback, movie tie-in edition of Richard Hough's *Captain Bligh and Mr. Christian: the Men and the Mutiny*. Copyright © 1979, 1984 by Hough Writing Ltd. Reprinted by permission of Penguin Group (USA) Inc.

Peter Rutherford (Thomas Burkitt); Stanley Fleet (Henry Hillbrandt); Patrick Clancy (William McCoy); Tony Carpenter (John Millward); Mark Adams (William Muspratt); Ken Drury (Matthew Quintal); Ray Mangion (Valentine); Simon Packham (Byrne — Blind Fiddler); Paul Hardy, Anthony Johncock or Tim Woodman (John Hallett); William Snape (President of Court Martial); Frank Olegario (King Hiti-Hiti); Nicola Blackman (Queen Hitimahana); Sinitta Renet (Miamiti).

In 1983, playwright/lyricist Richard Crane and pop singer turned actor David Essex — who gained theatrical fame for his performances in *Godspell* and *Evita*— joined forces to compose *Mutiny!*, a concept record album about H.M.S. *Bounty*. The two artists then created an ambitious stage musical based on the album, starring Essex as Fletcher Christian and Frank Finlay as William Bligh.

Mutiny! opened in July 1985, at London's Piccadilly Theatre. The critical response was mixed, but audiences loved the play, which was nominated for an Ivor Novell award as "Best Musical" by the British Academy of Composers and Songwriters. Three songs from the show became hit singles.

The production team went to extraordinary lengths to simulate the appearance of a ship at sea. Supported by hydraulic legs that moved up and down, *Bounty*'s "deck" mimicked the motion of a swaying vessel. This was especially effective during the storm scenes, but dangerous for the actors. In his autobiography, *A Charmed Life*, Essex writes, "Without any doubt it was the most complicated and dangerous set you could wish to work on. Quite simply, as the boat pitched and tossed as it rounded the imaginary Cape Horn, if you fell from the rigging you were dead."

Mutiny! is filled with appealing songs and scenes, including "Saucy Sal," a sea shanty, the Tahitian "War Dance," and "Breadfruit," chanted by the crew as they toil in Tahiti. In "Pumpkin," the crew complains about their food and Bligh's theft of the cheeses; Christian and Sinitta Renee as Miamiti celebrate their love in a duet, "Tahiti."

The musical's portrayal of Bligh and Christian as friends at the start of the voyage echoes the psychological dynamics of Anthony Hopkins and Mel Gibson in *The Bounty*. Their relationship is established early in *Mutiny!* through the duet, "Friends." The song's musical accompaniment and strong vocal performances create a haunting quality that resonated throughout the play — especially for members of the audience who knew the final outcome.

The *Mutiny!* souvenir brochure sold at the theatre also emphasized their friendship by printing a quote from Lawrence Lebogue, *Bounty*'s Sail maker: "I knew Captain Bligh was always a friend to Christian, when he sailed with him to the West Indies as well as afterwards. Captain Bligh was the best friend Christian ever had."

Finlay interpreted Bligh as a rigid perfectionist who took his duty so seriously that the failure to round Cape Horn leaves him in a morbid psychological state. As he sings "Failed Cape Horn," he imagines that Captain Cook is berating him for his failure, while the crew notes that Bligh sulks in his cabin for nine days. Glynn Christian, who consulted with the playwrights, criticized reviewers who complained about Finlay's performance, "For playing Bligh as mercurial with ever changing moods and no definable character. To me, it was by far the best and most accurate portrayal of Bligh and the impossibility of dealing with him, no matter how much you admired his undoubted skills."

Several motivations for mutiny arise during the play. Bligh's harsh discipline, intolerably cramped conditions on the homeward voyage and, above all, the crew's longing for the freedom of Tahiti, all of which make the *Bounty* a "hell." Richard Crane's note in the theatre program, reprinted from the concept album, puts the play in its historical context:

A colorful souvenir book was sold at performances of *Mutiny!* The cover shows David Essex as Fletcher Christian, Frank Finlay as William Bligh and Robert Dodd's famous illustration of the mutiny. Reprinted by permission of David Essex.

The *Bounty* Mutiny was a minor ripple in a deluge of rebellion that was sweeping the world... The French and American Revolutions had overturned more than a century of tranquillity... The *Bounty* would have sunk without trace in this watershed of history, were it not that the temper of the men, the tensions between the officers, and the eruption that followed, seemed to sum up, in fascinating detail, the end of one era and the beginning of another.

Following the mutiny, the crew strives for revolutionary dignity in the song "Fallen Angels Riding:" "We arose and cried for freedom, /freedom was our right, /We have sold our lives for freedom /and sailed into the night." Unfortunately, they soon descend into a hell of their own making on Pitcairn Island.

By playing Christian as an idealistic, world-weary fighter for freedom, Essex may have taken a cue from the life and work of Lord Byron — a role he acted in Romulus Linney's play *Childe Byron* in 1981. Byron himself died during Greece's war of independence against Turkey. Ultimately, Christian's actions cut him off not only from his country, but also from his remaining companions. He summarizes their fate on Pitcairn Island (taking some artistic license), and his closing lines suggest that he will soon take his own life:

> We ran the *Bounty* on the rocks. We stripped her to the hulk. We burned her alive. She laughed and roared and lit up the sky and cursed us as we killed each other. Adams and Young shot Mills

and Williams. McCoy fell to his death from a cliff. The women killed Quintal with an axe. Young died of a fever. Only Adams is left with the care of the women and children. They won't come to my cave. I live as I will. Free — within a chain of rock. Safe — on the edge of a sheer drop to the sea.

Mutiny! may not have reached the pinnacle of success, but it did provide an entertaining, thoughtful evening of musical theater for thousands of people. It ran for a respectable 526 performances over 16 months, attesting to both the enduring popularity of the story and quality of the production.

CHRISTOPHER BUCKLEY: "Scrutiny on the Bounty: Captain Bligh's Secret Logbook." *The Atlantic Monthly*, December 2003.

During 2003 and 2004, publications as disparate as *Publishers Weekly, Scientific American, The New Yorker, USA Today* and *People* featured articles that confirm the public's continuing fascination with the *Bounty* Saga, more than 200 years after the mutiny.

Soon after the release of Caroline Alexander's *The* Bounty: *The True Story of the Mutiny on the* Bounty, a whimsical article by humorist Christopher Buckley appeared in the December 2003 issue of *The Atlantic Monthly*. "Scrutiny on the Bounty: Captain Bligh's Secret Logbook" is a comic response to Alexander's mission to rehabilitate Bligh's reputation. Behind its wit and playfulness lies familiarity with Bligh and the *Bounty*. Buckley prefaced "Scrutiny on the *Bounty*" with a direct quote from the *USA Today* review of *The* Bounty, titled "You had Capt. Bligh all wrong, Mr. Christian":

> No monster on the high seas has equaled the infamous ship captain William Bligh. And no movie fan can forget the scene in which Charles Laughton, the definitive Bligh in the 1935 film, instructs his crew to keep flogging a man. That he's dead makes no difference to Bligh, lips curled with unfettered malignancy. "Everything you think you know about Bligh is utterly wrong," says best-selling writer Caroline Alexander.

The first "secret logbook entry" reveals that Bligh is deeply concerned about Christian's puzzling behavior:

> February 2, 1789. Position is 18°52 3 S. 129°27 45 W. Winds light W. by WSW. Seas 2–4 feet. Am much vexed on account of Mr. Christian. His mood-compass vacillated sharply between Hysterical Agitation and Sullen Lethargy. I had so wanted this Voyage to be special for him.

Another "entry" alludes to Bligh's love of hydrography as well as his tendency to be highly critical of others' efforts: "Calmed myself by re-drawing the Admiralty charts of the North and South Atlantick, which I found to be rife with Errors." Buckley also satirizes Bligh's interest in providing the crew a healthy diet by having their commander offer them "Dolphin and Sharke ceviche in a lyme-cilantroe Reduction with julienned mangoes and mashed wasabi taro. (My own Recipe.)" The more he coddles the crew, the more defiant Christian becomes, until Bligh asks to be set adrift, with some food, water and a few loyal crew members. By the time he reaches the Dutch East Indies, his temper has cooled:

> June 12. Batavia. By the time we reached Timor, I had exhausted my anger at him (Christian) and was resolved to say nothing against him in the event of an Inquest, having no wish to put at risk his future in H. M. Navy. He is a decent fellow at heart and will make a fine Officer of the Line, if only he would purge himself of these Demons that afflicte him. Do earnestly hope he delivered my Bread-fruit safely to West Indies. Must go and make a Poultice for my men.

In a review of Caroline Alexander's *The* Bounty, David Curtis Wright of the University of Calgary alluded to "Scrutiny on the Bounty," writing that "She is by no means the first writer to challenge the commonplace view of Bligh as the heartless and mindless disciplinarian ... but popular reaction to her book (including a recent piece in the *Atlantic Monthly*)

Bligh holds a dainty china teacup in this illustration by Tim Bower from "Scrutiny on the Bounty: Captain Bligh's Secret Logbook," published in *The Atlantic Monthly*, December 2003. The picture suggests that a genteel personality lay beneath Bligh's rough appearance. Actually, Bligh had delicate features and was startlingly pale (courtesy Tim Bower).

seems to indicate that many people think she is." The laughter evoked by articles like "Scrutiny on the Bounty" can only help set the record straight about William Bligh.

Additional Works

Books

Anderson, David, and Margarette Lincoln. *The Mutiny on the Bounty*. London: Macdonald Children's Books, 1989.

This illustrated companion to "Mutiny on the Bounty, 1789–1989," the National Maritime Museum's 1989 Bicentenary Exhibition, was written for older school children.

Chauvel, Charles. *In the Wake of "The Bounty"; to Tahiti and Pitcairn Islands.* Sydney: Endeavour Press, 1933.

This volume is an excellent companion to Charles Chauvel's film. In fact, reading his full account of the *Bounty*/Pitcairn adventure is more satisfying than watching the historical segments of the movie. The book includes a number of stills, behind the scenes photos, a description of the Chauvels' filming excursions and a personal record of their experiences on Tahiti and Pitcairn Island.

Like so many other visitors, the Chauvels found it difficult to leave Pitcairn: "We were embraced by each island man and woman able to accompany us to sea, and although we were homeward bound from our isolation, this parting will always have the fondest and saddest memories for us as we regretfully said good-bye to those wonderful people who had given their best to us."

Chauvel, Elsa. *My Life with Charles Chauvel.* Sydney: Shakespeare Head Press, 1973.

Elsa Chauvel devotes several chapters of her memoir to the time she spent with her husband on Pitcairn Island and Tahiti, filming *In the Wake of The Bounty*, along with their discovery of Errol Flynn. She includes a riveting account of their arrival on Pitcairn in stormy weather: "Walls of basalt loomed above us as a watery roller lifted our boat on to its crest, drenching us again with its salty mane and carrying us high and wide through the two serrated and forbidding rocks to the foot of the boat ramp of Bounty Bay."

Carlsson, Susanne Chauvel. *Charles and Elsa Chauvel, Movie Pioneers.* St. Lucia: University of Queensland Press, 1989.

Susanne Carlson includes a well-illustrated chapter on *In the Wake of The Bounty* in this delightful study of her parents' film career.

Hough, Richard. *The Bounty.* Harmondsworth: Penguin Books, 1984.

Movie stills enliven this paperback, movie tie-in edition of Hough's 1979 *Captain Bligh and Mr. Christian: the Men and the Mutiny.*

Lincoln, Margarette. *Mutiny on the Bounty.* Illustrations by John Dillow. Loughborough: Ladybird Books, 1989.

This nicely illustrated account of the *Bounty* Saga for young readers was produced in association with the National Maritime Museum to commemorate the Museum's 1989 Bicentenary Exhibition.

"London Exhibition Does Justice to Captain Bligh." *Pacific Islands Monthly* 59, no. 17 (June 1989): 39–41.

The anonymous author of this article calls the National Maritime Museum's 1989 Bicentenary Exhibition "extraordinary ... a display that traces in punctilious detail the most famous mutiny in history, capturing not just the record of events but their precise feel and texture." He was especially impressed by the tableaux that allowed visitors to vicariously experience the voyage of *Bounty*'s launch and the court-martial sentencing.

Mutiny on the Bounty. N.p.: Metro-Goldwyn-Mayer and Arcola Pictures Corp., 1962. "A Random House Book." Hardcover.

Mutiny on the Bounty. N.p. Softcover version, printed for the British market.

Both the American and British versions of this souvenir book for the 1962 film *Mutiny on the Bounty* are illustrated in color and black and white, with numerous stills from the film, historical background, production notes and profiles of the cast. The American edition was part of a boxed set with the film's soundtrack.

Mutiny on the Bounty: A Coloring Book Based on the Metro-Goldwyn-Mayer Motion Picture. Drawings by Sam Burlockoff. New York: Saalfield Publishing Co., 1963.

Following the release of the 1962 *Mutiny on the Bounty*, Saalfield Publishing created this coloring book for children, and even recycled the vibrant cover art for a Saalfield jigsaw puzzle!

Mutiny on the Bounty, 1789–1989. London: Manorial Research PLC, 1989.

This fully illustrated companion to "Mutiny on the Bounty, 1789–1989," the National Maritime Museum's Bicentenary exhibition, is indispensable for *Bounty* Saga enthusiasts. In addition to cataloging the 194 museum exhibits, it includes a number of commissioned essays by noted *Bounty* scholars, including Glynn Christian, Bengt Danielsson, Andrew David and Gavin Kennedy.

Mutiny on the Bounty: The Story of Captain William Bligh, Seaman, Navigator, Surveyor and of the Bounty Mutineers. Sydney: Mitchell Library: 1991.

In 1990, the State Library of New South Wales displayed 123 items from the National Maritime Museum's Bounty Bicentenary exhibition. This illustrated catalog also reprints four essays from *Mutiny on the Bounty, 1789–1989* and adds "Arresting Bligh," by Paul Brunton, editor of *Awake, Bold Bligh! William Bligh's Letters Describing the Mutiny on H.M.S. Bounty.*

Mutiny on the Bounty: The Story of Captain William Bligh, Seaman, Navigator, Surveyor and of the Bounty Mutineers. Sydney: Rolf Harris Productions Pty Ltd in association with State Library of New South Wales Press: 1998.

This revised edition was published as a companion to a television series about William Bligh. It features a new foreword by Rolf Harris, an additional article, "Torment in Tofua," by Bruce Harris and the latest information about the *Pandora* wreck, by Peter Gesner.

Sudbury, Neil, Ed. *Return of the Bounty: Flagship of the Fleet.* Mona Vale: Australian HiFi Publications, 1988.

Return of the Bounty is a photographic, commemorative record of Australia's bicentennial re-enactment of the 1787 "First Fleet" voyage to New South Wales. The *Bounty* replica constructed for the 1985 film served as flagship of the contemporary fleet.

Turner, Adrian. *Robert Bolt: Scenes from Two Lives.* London: Hutchinson, 1998.

Adrian Turner's chatty, entertaining volume includes a detailed discussion of the proposed David Lean/Robert Bolt *Bounty/Pandora* film projects.

Articles

Axon, Tim. "A Brief History of 'The Bounty' (1984)." *UK Log* (July 2000): 11–19.

_____. "'The Bounty' Re-experienced." *UK Log* no. 25 (January 2003): 5–8.

Tim Axon discusses the complex genesis of the 1984 film version of the mutiny in "A Brief History of 'The Bounty' (1984)," which includes thumbnail sketches of some of the movie sets. He comments that "*The Bounty* is a very good film indeed — not perhaps a great film, and certainly not the film that Lean would have produced, but (bearing in mind the many agonies that attended its birth) it is a surprisingly good film."

Axon provides valuable commentary on the wide screen video and DVD versions of *The Bounty* in "'The Bounty' Re-experienced." He closely examines the extra features, including the theatrical trailer, a 50-minute documentary on the making of the film, and an illustrated booklet by historical consultant Stephen Walters.

"Ballyhoo and Bali'hai: Hollywood's Love Affairs with the South Seas." *Islands,* October 1994, 155–182.

Islands' nicely illustrated survey of Hollywood movies made in the South Pacific includes Nordhoff and Hall's *The Hurricane*, and the 1935, 1962 and 1985 *Bounty* films.

Clowes, Peter. "The 'Bounty' Sails on and on." *Sea Breezes* 64, no. 533 (May 1990): 332–337.

The three replicas of H.M.S. *Bounty* constructed for the 1935, 1962 and 1984 film versions of the *Bounty* story, are discussed in this informative article.

Murray, Spencer. "The Fifth Bounty Film (or is it sixth?)." *Pitcairn Log* 23 (October — December 1995): 11–12.

In this brief discussion of the five *Bounty* films, Spencer Murray speculates that there may have been a sixth, predating the 1916 Raymond Longford production.

_____. "The 'Forgotten' *Bounty* Movie." *Pitcairn Log* 27 (March 2000): 11–12.

The Women of Pitcairn Island undoubtedly is the most obscure *Bounty*-related film. Few people have seen this completely fictional movie, but reportedly it is set in the late 18th century, when a band of pirates lands on Pitcairn Island to find stolen pearls and dally with the women.

_____. "Why Roger Byam?" *Pitcairn Log* 26 (September 1999): 10–11.

Spencer Murray explains how *Bounty* Midshipman Peter Heywood became the fictional "Roger Byam," created by Charles Nordhoff and James Norman Hall to narrate *Mutiny on the Bounty*. Roger Byam also was a character in the 1935 film adaptation of Nordhoff and Hall's novel.

Pew, Curtis E. "Mutiny on the Bounty (ex-Bethia)." *Journal of Maritime Law & Commerce* 31, no. 4 (October 2000): 609–614.

Curtis E. Pew discusses the 1935, 1962 and 1985 *Bounty* films in the general context of popular maritime movies. He observes that each film interpretations comes to quite a different conclusion about Fletcher Christian's motives for mutiny.

Journal of Maritime Law & Commerce is difficult to find outside a research library, but it may be consulted at http://www.jmlc.org/index.php.

Reardon, Ed. "Captain Bligh in Film." *Films about Polynesia: Scholarly Interpretations.* http://www.fiu.edu/~harveyb/filmsx2.html.

Ed Reardon discusses the three major film interpretations of William Bligh in this scholarly article. He also examines the films against the cultural and political contexts of their times.

"Secrets of the Movie Ships." *Popular Mechanics Magazine* (July 1936): 74–114a.

Popular Mechanics' illustrated article includes technical information about the *Bounty* replica created for the 1935 MGM film, *Mutiny on the Bounty.*

Solomon, Jon. "Celluloid Bountys." *Archaeology* 52 (May/June 1999): 41.

Jon Solomon covers the *Pandora* diving expeditions, and briefly discusses the five film versions of the *Bounty* Saga.

Stevens, Jack. "I Survived the Savage Mutiny on the Bounty." Art by Earl Norem. *Man's World*, February 1969, 16–89.

The publisher of this amusingly trashy article claims that it is based on the letters of Peter Heywood, "Pieced together by an expert on historical matters such as this and presented with as much vivid, true-to-life details as the letters provided." An illustration of two bare-breasted Tahitian women, inexplicably on board *Bounty* during the mutiny, suggests that the magazine was not concerned with historical accuracy. The article focuses on Peter Heywood's experiences: "He was only a teenager, but his voyage taught him more about women and vicious men than he would ever have learned at home."

Sturma, Michael. "Women, the *Bounty*, the Movies." *Journal of Popular Film and Television* 23, no. 2 (Summer 1995): 88–93.

Michael Sturma shows how the relationship of women and sex to the *Bounty* mutiny is treated in each of the three major *Bounty* films. He differentiates them into "Christian's Family Values" (1935), "Sexual Utopia Lost" (1962) and "Voyeurism and Moral Ambiguity" (1985).

Supplemental Bibliography

Books

Cunningham, Stuart. *Featuring Australia: The Cinema of Charles Chauvel.* Sydney: Allen and Unwin, 1991.
Dening, Greg. "Mutiny on the Bounty." *In Past Imperfect: History According to the Movies.* Ed. Ted Mico, et. al. New York: Henry Holt, 1995.
Essex, David. *A Charmed Life: The Autobiography of David Essex.* London: Orion, 2002.
Fraser, George MacDonald. *The Hollywood History of the World.* London: Michael Joseph, 1988.
Vera, Hernán, and Andrew M. Gordon. *Screen Saviors: Hollywood Fictions of Whiteness.* Oxford: Rowman and Littlefield, n.d. (2003).

Articles

Barry, Roger. "Mutiny on the Bounty." *Boys' Super Colour Annual.* London: Beaverbrook Newspapers, n.d. (1950).
"Bounty Sails Again." *Motor Boating*, April 1961, 37–39.
Cameron, Joseph. "H.M.S. Bounty Reappears." *Jetaway,* March – April 1982.
Holmes, C. "Bounty Sails Again." *Look and Listen,* December 1984.
"Mutiny on the Bounty." *Boys World* 1, no. 3 (February 9, 1963). Dunedin, New Zealand: Longacre Press.
"Mutiny on the Bounty." *Picturegoer*, September 19, 1936. With a 16-page supplement on the 1935 MGM film, *Mutiny on the Bounty.*
"New Zealand Firm to Build Bounty Replica." *Pacific Islands Monthly* 49 (August 1978): 31.

O'Reilly, Gray. "Mutiny on the Bounty: Performance Photographs." *Stage*, May 1936, 44–45.
Parker, John. "The Bounty." *Metro* 42 (1984): 186–188.
Pitcairn, A Souvenir Booklet. Oakland: Pacific Press Publishing Co., 1890.
"Pitcairn Film." *Adventist Review* 160 (January 20, 1983): 18.
"'Pitcairn Island Today' (1935) Preserved by the British Film Institute." *UK Log* 5 (July 1995): 25–26.
Sawyer, Beryl. "New *Bounty* Brings Film-Makers to Eager Tahiti." *Pacific Islands Monthly* 32 (January 1961): 27.
Smith, J. L. "Cinematographer and Pitcairn Island." *Review and Herald* 110 (January 12, 1933): 24.
_____. "Cinematographer and Pitcairn Island." *Australasian Record* 37 (March 6, 1933): 4.
Wahlroos, Sven. "Happy Birthday H.M.S. *Bounty*." *Pacific Islands Monthly* 58 (March 1988): 58.
Wheat, Gilbert. "Legacy of the Bounty." *Sports Illustrated*, November 20, 1961, 40–59.
"William Bligh: Portrait." *Time* (September 7, 1936): 57.

Films

The Women of Pitcairn Island, 1956. Regal Films, Inc. Original screenplay by Aubrey Wisberg. Directed by Jean Yarbrough. Distributed by 20th Century–Fox. Cast includes James Craig and Lynn Bari. See Murray, Spencer. "The 'Forgotten' *Bounty* Movie." *Pitcairn Log* 27 (March 2000): 11–12.

Audio Recordings

The Bounty. One World Music OWM-9503/4, 1984/1995. Music by Vangelis. Soundtrack from the Mel Gibson, Anthony Hopkins film, 1984.
Mutiny! Lyrics by Richard Crane and David Essex. Music by David Essex, book by Richard Crane. London: Mercury/Phonogram, MERH-30/UK, 1983. Studio Cast.
Mutiny! Lyrics by Richard Crane and David Essex. Music by David Essex, book by Richard Crane. London: Telstar 2261, 1985. Original London Cast.
Mutiny! Selections. Telstar Records 2261, 1983. Lyrics by Richard Crane and David Essex. Music by David Essex, book by Richard Crane. Original London Cast.
Mutiny on the Bounty. SLP 190. "Classics Story Teller" series from *Classics Illustrated* comic books. Packaged with a copy of the comic book.
Mutiny on the Bounty. Wonderland Golden Records LP-289, 1973. Adapted from the novel by Charles Nordhoff and James Norman Hall. *Great Movie Adventures in Sound and Story* series.
Mutiny on the Bounty. MGM Records 1E4, 1962. Soundtrack from *Mutiny on the Bounty* (1962), MGM. Score by Bronislau Kaper.
   Packaged in a box, with the souvenir book from the film. Also issued in other formats with original soundtracks from *How the West Was Won* and *Taras Bulba*.

Comic Books

"The Ghost of Captain Bligh." *True Comics*, October 1942, no. 17.
"Mutiny on the Bounty." *A Classic in Pictures*, no. 11, n.d. (1960).
"Mutiny on the Bounty." Poughkeepsie: K. K. Publications, in cooperation with Golden Press, Inc., 1962. "Gold Key" comic book, based on the 1962 film.
Pinkoski, Jim. *The New Illustrated Mutiny on the Bounty.* Altamont: Harvestime Books, 1991.

Appendix I: Selected Documentaries

Bounty's Heritage: The Legacy of Fletcher Christian (Video Book Series—1997). Pacific Visions, 1997. Produced and narrated by Jerry Miller. Twelve chapters, six 60-minute videotapes. Consists of 12 chapters presented on six one-hour videotapes. Covers the history of Pitcairn Island from the *Bounty* mutiny to the 1990 Bicentenary celebration.

Captain Bligh: Mutiny on the Bounty (1996—Television). A Satel Documentary Production for A&E Television Networks. Broadcast on *Biography*. Narrator: Mac MacDonald. A visually attractive program about Bligh's life told through a series of interviews. Unfortunately, it is not always historically accurate.

H.M.S. Pandora: In Pursuit of the Bounty (Television—1986). David Flatman Productions, Pty Ltd., Sydney, Australia. Broadcast on The Discovery Channel. Producer and Director: David Flatman. Written by David Flatman and David White. Narrator: David Attenborough. This excellent documentary features footage of divers raising *Pandora*'s artifacts to the surface, including a massive cannon and Surgeon George Hamilton's delicate pocket watch. The diving segments alternate with scenes of museum conservators at work. The story of *Pandora* itself is accompanied by outstanding graphics.

Island of the Bounty (1984). Cochran Film Productions. Produced, written and directed by Ted Cochran. A beautifully photographed record of Glynn Christian's expedition to Pitcairn Island on the square-rigged brigantine *Taiyo*. Christian's investigations here were essential research for his book, *Fragile Paradise: The Discovery of Fletcher Christian, Bounty Mutineer*. This video captures day to day life on Pitcairn as Christian and his travel companions explore the entire island, including the underwater remnants of *Bounty*.

The Log of the Bounty (Television—1994). Terra X/The Discovery Channel. Produced by Gottfried Kirchner. Written and directed by Hartmel Schoen. Narrator: Hal Douglas. Early in this program, the narrator states, "The idea that Bligh was some kind of monster simply has no basis in fact." *The Log of the Bounty* does a good job of defending Bligh's reputation, but its presentation of the mutiny is weak, attributing it simply to the crew's desire to return to Tahiti. It also is silent on the fate of the mutineers who remained on Tahiti, and Bligh's later career. It does include some visual treats, such as footage of "Bligh's Cave" on Tofua, Irma Christian working at Pitcairn's radio station and a brief discussion with Tom Christian on the future of Pitcairn Island.

The Real Captain Bligh (Television—2002). October Films. Broadcast on A&E Television Networks. Producer and Director: Chris Wilkinson. Narrator: Greg Stebner. Original Narrator: Tom Wilkinson. One of the better documentaries on Bligh and *Bounty*, *The Real Captain Bligh* features interviews with Caroline Alexander, Glynn Christian and Greg Dening. It is far more accurate and engaging than *Captain Bligh: Mutiny on the Bounty*. Examines Bligh's entire career, and features clips from the 1935 MGM film *Mutiny on the Bounty*.

The True Story of Mutiny on the Bounty (Television — 2001). *History's Mysteries*. Produced by MPH Entertainment for The History Channel. Directed by Jim Milio. Historical Consultant: Glynn Christian. Narrator: David Ackroyd. Written by Robert Goubeaux. This is the most authoritative program available on the *Bounty* mutiny, offering perceptive comments from Glynn Christian, Gavin Kennedy, Roy Maloney and Sven Wahlroos. They emphasize aspects of Fletcher Christian that have been discussed primarily in books, including his family background, personality, social position, financial debts to Bligh and meeting with Charles Christian just before the *Bounty* voyage.

Voyage on the Bounty. Camera and editing by Charles Ayer. An Airborne Video Production. Lifestyle Home Video, 1986. This program follows a group of trainees learning to sail a square-rigged ship: the *Bounty* replica constructed for the 1984 film. Most of it consists of interviews with the crew as they voyage from Sydney to Freemantle. There is some excellent footage of *Bounty* in rough seas, but very little of historical interest. The program does provide a good idea of what it must have been like to sail *Bounty* on the open sea.

Appendix II:
Selected Web Sites

Beshero-Bondar, Elisa E. "Romantic Women Bards and Revolutionary Epic Heroines: The International Diplomacy of Feminine Desire"; *http://mendota.english.wisc.edu/~BWWC/Panels.html.* Discusses Mary Russell Mitford's *Christina, the Maid of the South Seas.* Presented at 10th Annual 18th- and 19th-Century British Women Writers Conference: "Evolving Domains of Knowledge and Representation," April 19–21, 2002 at the University of Wisconsin-Madison.

Buckley, Anthony. *The Man Who Met Raymond Longford; http://www.screensound.gov.au/ Screensound/Screenso. nsf/AllDocs/97BB720E0A526F2ECA256E830020119F?OpenDocument.* This lecture on the pioneering filmmaker also discusses the first film treatment of the *Bounty* mutiny. The Inaugural Longford Lyell Lecture was presented May 12, 2001, by ScreenSound Australia, the National Screen and Sound Archive.

Bury, John M. "Redefining the Romantic Bower: Virtual Space in Byron's Poetry"; *http:// prometheus.cc.emory.edu/panels/3A/J.Bury.html.* John Bury suggests that *The Island, or Christian and His Comrades* is Lord Byron's "most fully developed" treatment of the "bower," where "fallen man," i.e., Fletcher Christian and the mutineers, can escape society to explore his definition of self and his relationship with others."

"Charles Chauvel (1897–1959.") *Tribute to Great Australians of Screen and Sound;* http:// www.screensound.gov.au/. This site features an illustrated biography of the great Australian filmmaker who produced and directed *In the Wake of The Bounty.*

Fulford, Tim. "Poetic Hells and Pacific Edens." *Romanticism on the Net* 32 – 33 (November 2003 – February 2004): 1–16; *http://www.erudit.org/revue/ron/2003/v/n32–33/009259ar.html.* Tim Fulford's discussion of *The Island, or Christian and His Comrades* places it in context with a public feud that Lord Byron had with Robert Southey over the poetic representation of South Pacific native peoples.

HMS *Pandora; http://www.qm.qld.gov.au/features/pandora/pandora.asp.* For those interested in the marine excavation of the *Pandora* wreck, this site provides background history and regular updates.

"The Mutiny of the Bounty 1916"; http://www.screensound.gov.au/pdf/photoplayartiste_ reel2.pdf. This site has a downloadable PDF that features the screenplay, photo stills and production details of Raymond Longford's silent film treatment of the *Bounty* mutiny.

Mutiny on the H.M.S. Bounty; *www.lareau.org/bounty.html.* Includes a large number of topics and links, accompanied by graphics and photos. Features the "Pitcairn Island Home Page," "The Story of the Bounty Chronometer," "The Bounty's Acting Crew" and "Mutiny! A Tribute to Mutiny! The David Essex Musical," and H. L. Kerr's *The Bibliography of Literature Regarding HMS Bounty, William Bligh and Pitcairn Island.*

Appendix II: Selected Websites

Pitcairn Islands Study Group; http://www.pisg.net/. Devoted primarily to Pitcairn Island's philatelic history, this site also focuses on the cultural aspects of Pitcairn and its people. Publishes a quarterly magazine, *The Pitcairn Log*.

Pitcairn Island Study Group, UK; *www.pitcairnstudygroup.co.uk/*. The Pitcairn Island Study Group, UK is devoted to Pitcairn Island history, its people and the *Bounty* Saga in general. People who are interested in the island's philatelic history will find the site particularly informative. Publishes *The UK Log*, a magazine.

Pitcairn Islands Study Center; library.puc.edu/pitcairn/studycenter. A museum and research facility at Pacific Union College in Angwin, California, the Pitcairn Islands Study Center holds one of the world's largest collections of materials relating to the mutiny, Bligh, H.M.S. *Bounty*, and Pitcairn and Norfolk Islands. Herbert Ford, one of the world's foremost authorities on the history and culture of Pitcairn Island, from its beginnings to the present, serves as director.

Tallshipbounty.org: Official Site of the H.M.S. Bounty; *www.tallshipbounty.org*. Devoted to the ongoing activities and voyages of the *Bounty* replica constructed for the 1962 film *Mutiny on the Bounty*.

References

Alexander, Caroline. *The* Bounty*: The True Story of the Mutiny on the* Bounty. New York: Viking Press, 2003.
Allen, Douglas, and Allen Douglas, Jr. *N. C. Wyeth: The Collected Paintings, Illustrations and Murals.* New York: Bonanza Books, 1972.
Barrow, Sir John. *The Mutiny and Piratical Seizure of H.M.S. Bounty.* With an Introduction by Admiral Sir Cyprian Bridge. London: Oxford University Press, 1914. Oxford World's Classics edition.
Bligh, William, and Edward Christian. *The Bounty Mutiny.* Introduction by R. D. Madison. New York: Penguin Books, 2001. Penguin Classics edition.
Bibliography of the Golden Cockerel Press, 1921—1949. San Francisco: Alan Wofsy Fine Arts, 1975.
Bold, Alan. *George Mackay Brown.* New York: Harper and Row, 1978.
Bowker, R.M., and Lt. William Bligh, R.N., in his official log. *Mutiny!! Aboard H. M. Armed Transport 'Bounty,' in 1789.* Old Bosham, Sussex, England: Bowker and Bertram, 1978.
Briand, Jr., Paul L. *In Search of Paradise; The Nordhoff-Hall Story.* New York: Duell, Sloan and Pearce, 1966.
Buckley, Anthony. *The Man Who Met Raymond Longford*; http://www.screensound.gov.au/Screensound/Screenso.nsf/AllDocs/97BB720E0A526F2ECA256E830020119F?OpenDocument
Carpenter, Humphrey and Mari Prichard. *The Oxford Companion to Children's Literature.* Oxford: Oxford University Press, 1984.
Cave, Roderick, and Sarah Manson. *A History of the Golden Cockerel Press, 1920-1960.* London and New Castle: The British Library and Oak Knoll Press, 2002.
Christensen, Alta Hilliard. *Heirs of Exile: the Story of Pitcairn Island, Paradise of the Pacific.* Washington, D.C.: Review and Herald Publishing Association, 1955.
Claver, Scott. *Under the Lash: A History of Corporal Punishment in the British Armed Forces.* London: Torchstream Books, 1954.
Clement, Russell T. *Mutiny on the Bounty. An Exhibition Commemorating the Two-Hundredth Anniversary of the Mutiny.* Introduction by Russell T. Clement. Provo, Utah: Friends of the Brigham Young University Library, 1989.
Coleridge, Ernest Hartley, ed. *The Works of Lord Byron.* Poetry, Vol. 5. London: John Murray, 1905. Second edition.
Curry, Kenneth, ed. *New Letters of Robert Southey: Volume One: 1792—1810.* New York and London: Columbia University Press, 1965.
Darton, F. J. Harvey. *Children's Books in England; Five Centuries of Social Life.* Cambridge: Cambridge University Press, 1960. Second edition.
_____. *Children's Books in England; Five Centuries of Social Life.* Revised by Brian Alderson. Cambridge: Cambridge University Press, 1982. Third edition.
Day, A. Grove. *Jack London in the South Seas.* New York: Four Winds Press, 1971.
_____. *Louis Becke.* New York: Twayne Publishers, 1966.
_____. *Pacific Islands Literature: One Hundred Basic Books.* Honolulu: University Press of Hawaii, 1971.

Dictionary of Canadian Biography Online; www.biographi.ca/EN/ShowBio.asp?BioId=37895
Doyle, Brian, ed. *The Who's Who of Children's Literature.* New York: Schocken Books, 1974.
Du Rietz, Rolf. *Thoughts on the Present State of Bligh Scholarship. Banksia 1.* Uppsala: Dahlia Books, 1979. Limited edition of 250 copies.
_____. *Fresh Light on John Fryer of the "Bounty." Banksia,* Vol. 2. Uppsala: Dahlia Books, 1981.
Ebersole, Barbara. *Fletcher Martin.* Gainesville: University of Florida Press, 1954.
Érudit: Promovoir et diffuser de la recherche universitaire. www.erudit.org
Essex, David. *A Charmed Life: The Autobiography of David Essex.* London: Orion, 2002.
Ford, Herbert. *Pitcairn — Port of Call.* Angwin: Hawser Titles, 1996.
Fraser, George MacDonald. *The Hollywood History of the World.* London: Michael Joseph, 1988.
Gleckner, Robert F. *Byron and the Ruins of Paradise.* Baltimore: Johns Hopkins Press, 1967.
Green, Roger Lancelyn. *Tellers of Tales; Children's Books and Their Authors from 1800 to 1968.* London: Kaye and Ward, 1969. Revised and enlarged edition.
Guide to Pitcairn. Auckland: Pitcairn Island Administration, 1999.
Hill, Kenneth E. *The Hill Collection of Pacific Voyages at the University of California, San Diego.* New Haven and Sydney: William Reese Co. and Hordern House, 2004. Second edition, revised and enlarged.
Houfe, Simon. *The Dictionary of British Book Illustrators and Caricaturists, 1800–1914.* Woodbridge, Suffolk: Antique Collectors' Club, 1981. Revised edition.
Hromatko, Wesley. "Dickens and Denominational Christianity." Unitarian Universalist Historical Society. www.uua.org/uuhs/duub/articles/charlesdickens.html
Kerr, H. L. *The Bibliography of Literature Regarding HMS Bounty, William Bligh and Pitcairn Island.* http://www.lareau.org/mainpagebb.html
Labor, Earle, Robert C. Leitz, III, and I. Milo Shepard, eds. *The Letters of Jack London, Vol. 2: 1906–1912.* Stanford: Stanford University Press, 1988.
Leask, Nigel. "Resolving *The Corsair: Lara* and *The Island." Byron.* Edited by Jane Stabler. London: Addison Wesley Longman, 1998.
Lloyd, Christopher. *Mr. Barrow of the Admiralty; A Life of Sir John Barrow 1764–1848.* London: Collins, 1970.
London, Charmian. *The Book of Jack London.* New York: Century, 1921.
_____. *The Log of the Snark.* New York: Macmillan, 1915.
Lowes, John Livingston. *The Road to Xanadu: A Study in the Ways of the Imagination.* Boston and New York: Houghton Mifflin, 1927.
Lucas, Sir Charles, ed. *The Pitcairn Island Register Book.* Introduction by Sir Charles Lucas. New York and Toronto: Macmillan, 1929.
Mackaness, George. *The Art of Book-Collecting in Australia.* Sydney: Angus and Robertson, 1956. Limited to 300 signed and numbered copies.
_____. *The Life of Vice-Admiral William Bligh RN, FRS.* Sydney: Angus and Robertson, 1951. New and revised edition.
Marshall, John. *Royal Naval Biography.* 12 vols. London: Longman, Hurst, Rees, Orme, and Brown, 1823–35.
Maude, H. E. *Of Islands and Men: Studies in Pacific History.* London: Oxford University Press, 1968.
McClintock, James I. *White Logic: Jack London's Short Stories.* Grand Rapids: Wolf House Books, 1975.
Meigs, Cornelia, Anne Thaxter Eaton, Elizabeth Nesbitt, and Ruth Hill Viguers. *A Critical History of Children's Literature.* London: Macmillan, 1969. Revised edition.
Murray, Rowena, and Brian Murray. *Interrogation of Silence: The Writings of George Mackay Brown.* London: John Murray, 2004.
Mutiny on the Bounty: An English Graphical Bibliography. http://larryvoyer.com/MutinyOnTheBounty/BOUNTY.htm
Nineteenth Century Reader's Guide to Periodical Literature. New York: H.W. Wilson Co., n.d.
Pitcairn Islands Office. www.government.pn/
Pitcairn Islands Study Center. http://library.puc.edu/pitcairn/index.shtml
Poole, William Frederick, et al., eds. *Poole's Index to Periodical Literature.* Gloucester, MA: P. Smith, 1963.
Prothero, Roland E. *The Works of Lord Byron: Letters and Journals.* London: John Murray, 1898–1901.
Quayle, Eric. *Ballantyne the Brave: A Victorian Writer and his Family.* London: Rupert Hart-Davis, 1967.

Reardon, Ed. "Captain Bligh in Film." *Films about Polynesia: Scholarly Interpretations.* http://www.fiu.edu/~harveyb/filmsx2.html

Roselle, Daniel. *Samuel Griswold Goodrich, Creator of Peter Parley: A Study of his Life and Work.* Albany: State University of New York Press, 1968.

Selborne, Joanna. *British Wood-Engraved Book Illustration, 1904—1940.* Oxford: Clarendon Press, 1998.

Silverman, David. *Pitcairn Island.* Foreword by Luis Marden. New York: World Publishing, 1967.

Southworth, Dr. Rufus. *A Doctor's Letters from Pitcairn, 1937.* Wenham, Mass.: privately printed, 2003. Limited to 500 copies.

Townsend, John Rowe. *Written for Children: An Outline of English-language Children's Literature.* New York: J. B. Lippincott, 1983. New Edition.

Turner, Adrian. *Robert Bolt: Scenes from Two Lives.* London: Hutchinson, 1998.

Van der Voort, P. J. *The Pen and the Quarter-Deck: A Study of the Life and Works of Captain Frederick Chamier, R.N.* Leiden: Leiden University Press, 1972.

Wahlroos, Sven. *Mutiny and Romance in the South Seas; A Companion to the Bounty Adventure.* Topsfield: Salem House Publishers, 1989.

_____. *Mutiny and Romance in the South Seas; A Companion to the Bounty Adventure.* Lincoln: iUniverse.com, 2001. Revised edition.

Watson, Vera. *Mary Russell Mitford.* London: Evans Brothers, n.d.

(William Reese Company). Catalogue Two Hundred Forty, *Travels and Voyages.* New Haven: William Reese, n.d.

Woodbridge, Hensley C., John London, and George H. Tweney. *Jack London: A Bibliography.* Georgetown: Talisman Press, 1966.

Woodson, Thomas, et al., eds. *The Centenary Edition of the Works of Nathaniel Hawthorne.* Vol. 23, miscellaneous prose and verse. Columbus: Ohio State University Press, 1994.

Index

Numbers in *italics* indicate pages with illustrations. Numbers in **bold** indicate pages with main entries.

Academy Awards 204, 211, 217
An Account of the Natives of the Tonga Islands, in the South Pacific Ocean (Mariner) 133, 163
An Account of the Voyages Undertaken by the Order of His Present Majesty for Making Discoveries in the Southern Hemisphere (Hawkesworth) 103
Ackroyd, David 232
Acquit or Hang! (Miller) 130
ACT (container ship) 89
Adams, Hannah *32*
Adams, John: in Ballantyne's story 140, *141*; in Barbary's novel 154–55; Barrow's account of 30, 193; in Becke and Jeffery's novel 143; Beechey's account of 29–30, *29*, 41, 43, 168; Belcher's account of 41–42; in *Blackwood's Edinburgh Magazine* 43; Bligh's account of 170; in *Cassell's Family Magazine* 43, 44; in *Classics Illustrated* **214**; conversion of 40, 43, 44, 203; death of 47, 60; and death of Christian 143; Delano's account of 27–28, 43; in Edmonds' novel 154; films about 207, 210, 216–17, 219; Folger's account of 24, 48; grave of *44*, 210; in *A Guide to Pitcairn* 91; in Lang's stories 140; Lummis' account of 93–94; in Mitford's poem 131; in *Mutiny!* (musical) 221, 223–24; in Nordhoff and Hall's novels 148, 151–52; in Peter Parley stories *137*; and *Pitcairn Island Register Book* 60;
Robert Brown's account of 43, 44; role in Pitcairn Island massacres 93; in *Sailors' Magazine* 40; Shillibeer's account of 24–25; Wahlroos' account of 48, 87; Wilkinson's account of 69; in Wilson's novel 130, 160; Young's account of 45
Adams of the Bounty (Wilson) 130, 160
Adamstown 25, 210
Addison, Catherine, "Gender and Race in Byron's *The Island* and Mitford's *Christina*" 162
Admiralty: and Barrow 31, *33*; and Beechey 28; and Bligh 8, 10, 12, 96, 164, 179, 224; and Edwards 18, 56–57, 73; and Staines 25
Adventist Heritage 56
Adventure Bay 96, 167, 190, *190*
"Adventures of Captain Bligh" (Hack) **135–36**
Adventures of Robin Hood (film) 210
Alaska 143
alcohol use 39–40, 82, 93, 96, 103, 148, 155–56, 181
Alexander, Caroline 40–41, 231; *The Bounty: The True Story of the Mutiny on the Bounty* 30, 40, 56, 82, **94–97**, *95*, 190, 224; "Wreck of the *Pandora*: The Fate of the Men Sent to Hunt Down the *Bounty* Mutineers" 94, *95*, 201
Allen, Kenneth S., *That Bounty Bastard* 55, 97
Allward, Maurice, *Pitcairn Island: Refuge of the Bounty Mutineers* 56, 97

American Museum of Natural History 90
American Neptune 56
American Revolution 223
American Sunday-School Union 38
Amis, Peter, "The 'Bounty' Timekeeper" 102
Andersen, Roy 169, 198
Anderson, David, *The Mutiny on the Bounty* 225–26
An Answer to Certain Assertions Contained in the Appendix to a Pamphlet (Bligh) **11–12**, 15, 17, 67
Anthony, Irvin, *The Saga of the Bounty* 97, 193
Appendix to Minutes of the Proceedings of the Court-Martial see *Minutes of the Proceedings...* (Barney and Christian)
"Armed Services Editions" 151
The Armed Transport Bounty (McKay) 99
Armstrong, Richard, *The Mutineers* 161
Arrenberg, Gerard Abraham *168*
Assistant, H.M.S. 58–59, *100*
asthma 94
Atlantic Monthly 99, 169, 224–25, *225*
Attenborough, David 231
Aubrey/Maturin novels 130
Australasian Record 56
Australia 56, 59, 63, 98–99, 205, 207
Australian Historical Society 64, 207
Australian National Library 85
Awake, Bold Bligh! William Bligh! (Brunton, ed.) 55, 98

239

Axon, Tim: "The 'Bounty' Re-experienced" 227; "Brief History of 'The Bounty'" 227
Ayer, Charles 232

Bacchus, Dr. *see* Huggan, Thomas
Bach, John, ed., *The Bligh Notebook* 55, **85–86**, 167, *197*
Ball, Alec 198, *199*
Ball, Ian M., *Pitcairn: Children of Mutiny* 56, **80–82**, *81*, 93
Ballantyne, R.M. 43; biography of 160; The Coral Island 138; The Lonely Island, or the Refuge of the Mutineers 129, **138**, **140**, **141**; *Young Fur Traders* 140
Ballantyne the Brave: A Victorian Writer and His Family (Quayle) 160
"Ballyhoo and Bali'Hai: Hollywood's Love Affairs with the South Seas" *(Islands)* 227
Banks, Sir Joseph 10, 174, 205, 207, 210
Banksia 2 (Fryer) 56
Barbary, James, *The Boy Mutineer* 130, **154–55**
Barker-Mill, Peter 169, 181, *182*
Barney, Stephen: Minutes of the Proceedings of the Court-Martial...with an Appendix **11–12**, **14**, 15, 17–18, 20, 101, 102; *On Ten Persons Charged with Mutiny on Board His Majesty's Ship the Bounty with an Appendix* 55, 67
Barrow, Sir John 30, *33*, 36, 63; *Description of Pitcairn Island and Its Inhabitants: With an Authentic Account of the Mutiny of the Ship Bounty* 31; *Eventful History of the Mutiny and Piratical Seizure of H.M.S.* Bounty see *Eventful History...* (Barrow); *The Mutiny of the "Bounty"* 198
Barry, Mrs. 156
Batavia 59, 73, 87, 171, 174, 181
Batty, Lieut.-Colonel 30, 197
Beaglehole, J.C., *Captain Cook and William Bligh* 97
Beard, William, *Valiant Martinet* 160
Becke, Louis 99, 158; *The Mutineer: A Romance of Pitcairn Island* 129–30, **143**, 157
Beechey, Frederick W. 29, *29*, 45, 50, 76–77, 79, 167–68; *Narrative of a Voyage to the Pacific and Beerings Strait*, 23, 25, **28–30**, *29*, 41–42, *42*, 43, 97, 102, 168
Begum's Fortune: With an Account of The Mutineers of the "Bounty" (Verne) **200**, 201
Belcher, Lady Diana Jolliffe 40, 63, 173; *The Mutineers of the Bounty and Their Descendants in Pitcairn and Norfolk Islands* 23, **40–42**, *42*, 43, 146, 156, 173
Belcher, Edward 30
Bellarosa, James M., "Odyssey for Survival: The Wreck of the 'Wild Wave'" 162
Belle Isle (Lake Windermere) 193, *195*
"Benito Cereno" (Melville) 27
Bennett, Frederick Debell, *Narrative of a Whaling Voyage Round the Globe* 47
Bennett, Jack, *The Lieutenant: An Epic Tale of Courage and Endurance on the High Seas* 157
Benton, Thomas Hart 185
Best South Sea Stories (Day and Stroven, eds.) 158
Bibles 39, 94, 138, 140, *141*
Billy Budd (Melville) 130
Bingley, Thomas, "Uncle Thomas Tells About the Mutiny of the Bounty" 161
Birkett, Edward 216
Blackwood's Edinburgh Magazine 42–43
Bligh (Kennedy) 55, 63, 99
Bligh, William: Adams' account of 29–30; alcohol use of 103, 155; Alexander's account of 94–97, *95*; as artist 167; Ball's account of 80–81; in Barbary's novel 154; Barrow's account of 31–33, 43; Beechey's account of 29–30; Belcher's account of 41–42, 43; biographies of 55, 61–65, *62*, 73, 97, 99, 101–4, 162; Bridge's account of 32–33, 47; Buckley's article on 224–25, *225*; in Byron's poem 133; character of 15, 17, 38, 64–66, 71, 73, 75, 89, 99, 101, 105, 140, 146, 154–55, 160, 163, 188, 190, 195, 207, 211, 215; "cheese incident" 32, 210, 222; in Chodes' play 162, *163*; in *Chronicles of the Sea* 36; in Collett's novel 157; conspiracy theory of 32, 36, 80; and Cook 77, 97, 131, 155; court-martial of 8, 10, 95–96; in Crane's play *165*; Danielsson's account of 73; Darby's account of 75; death of 23, 157, 185; Dening's account of 98; discipline by 64, 95–96, 140, 146, 152, 173, 175, 183, 210–11, 215, *216*, 217, 221–22; dispatch to Admiralty 164; documentaries about 231–32; in Edmonds' novel 152, 154; films about 50, 65–66, 96, 204–5, 207, *208*, 210–11, 215–17, *218*, 219, *220*, 221, 228; Ford's account of 82, 103; in George Mackay Brown's story 155–57; Gibbings' wood engravings of 171; Glynn Christian's account of 84–85; as governor-general of Australia 99, 158; Hall's account of 99; Hough's account of 77–80, *78*; in Ingleton's illustrations 191, *192*; journals of 10, 99, 182–83; Kennedy's account of 55, 65, 99; Lacy's account of 103–4; Lambourne's drawings of 198; in Lang's stories 140; Lee's account of 57–59; Leslie's account of 47; letters of 55, 67, 98, 174; logs of 19–20, 31, *34*, 55, 63, 71, 80, 85–86, 149, 169, 170, 178–82, 191, 193–95, 207, 224, 231; McFarland's account of 48; McKee's account of 71; Michener and Day's account of 99; in Mitford's poem 131; in Morrison's journal 173, 190; Murray's account of 38; and music/dancing 174–76, *176*; and mutiny *see* mutiny, *Bounty*; in *Mutiny!* (musical) 221–22, *223*; in Nordhoff and Hall's novels 146, 148–49, 163, 185; open-boat voyage of *see* open-boat voyage; in Pearl's story 215, *216*; portraits of 102; relationship with Christian 10, 12, *14*, 15, 17, 32, 40, 65, 75, 77–79, *78*, 86–87, 89, 93, 103, 105, 158, 207, 221–22, 224; "Relics" of *39*; reputation of 8, 12, *14*, 41–42, 58, 63, 80, 85, 96, 97, 133, 152, 154, 170, 178–79, 203, 224, 231; Robert Brown's account of 43; Rutter's account of 65–66; in *Sailors' Magazine* 40; seamanship of 86, 135–36, 140, 149, 170, 179, 188, 215, 221; second breadfruit voyage of 10, 12, 57–59, 63–64, 75, 87, 89, 95–96, 99, *100*, 102 (see also *Providence,* H.M.S.); in Shillibeer's account 25; Smyth's account of 50; and social class 162, *163*; and

"Sourabaya incident" 181; storytelling gifts of 10–11; television series about 227; Wahlroos' account of 87, 89, 105
Bligh, William, works of 23; *An Answer to Certain Assertions Contained in the Appendix to a Pamphlet* 11–12, 15, 17, 67; *Awake, Bold Bligh! William Bligh!* 98; *Bligh and the "Bounty"* 174–76, *176*, *177*; *The Bligh Notebook* 55, **85–86**, 167, *197*; *Bligh's Voyage in the Resource* 181–83, *182*; *A Book of the "Bounty"* 8, 11, 15, 18, 47, 55, 67, **68**; *Dangerous Voyage of Captain Bligh, in an Open Boat* 7, 198; "Despatch to the Admiralty" 169–71, *171*; *Journal of Bligh's Voyage to England* 182–83; *Log of HMS Bounty 1787–89*, 181; *The Log of the Bounty* 178–81, *179*, *180*; *Mutiny! Aboard H.M. Armed Transport "Bounty" in 1789* 181; *A Narrative of the Mutiny on Board His Majesty's Ship Bounty* 7–**10**, *9*, 11, 17, 20, 31–32, 133, 167, *168*, 170, 179, 205; "Remarks on Morrison's Journal" 173, 182; *The Voyage of the Bounty's Launch as Related in William Bligh's Despatch to the Admiralty and the Journal of John Fryer* 21, **169–71**, *171*; *A Voyage to the South Sea* 7, **10–11**, *12*, 17, 20, 27, 55, 67, 131, 135, 146, 149, 155, 169, 174–76, 179, 181, **188**, **190–92**, *190*, *191*, *192*, 195
Bligh: A True Account of Mutiny Aboard His Majesty's Ship Bounty (McKinney) 198
Bligh and the "Bounty" 102, 169, 174–76, *176*, *177*
"Bligh Is Cast Adrift" (artwork) *13*
The Bligh Notebook (Bach, ed.) 55, **85–86**, 167, *197*
"Bligh of the 'Bounty'" (Johnston) 198, *199*
Bligh of the "Bounty" (Rawson) 55, 73
"Bligh Relics" *39*
"Bligh's Disciple: Matthew Flinders' Journals of HMS Providence (Darby) 102
Bligh's Voyage in the Resource (Bligh) 181–83, *182*
blind fiddler *see* Byrne, Michael
Blossom, H.M.S. 25, 28–30, 45, 167–68, 198
Bolt, Robert 80, 219, 227

Bond, John, and Francis Godolphin, letters of *62*, 64–65, 67, 99
Bond, Thomas 64
Bonner Smith, D.: "More Light on Bligh and the Bounty" 102; "Some Remarks about the Mutiny of the Bounty" 102
A Book of the "Bounty" (Mackaness, ed.) 11, 18, 47, 55, **67**, **68**, 87; Kennedy's introduction to 8, 15, 17, 64–65
Book of the Month Club 177
Book TV (C-Span) 94
Booklist 155
Bora Bora 219
Boston Globe 96
Botany Bay 73
Bounty, H.M.S.: Barrow's account of 31; Beechey's account of 28–29; Bligh's account of 8, 10–11, *12*, 15, 188 (see also *A Voyage to the South Sea*); Buckley's article on 224; in *Chronicles of the Sea* 36; chronometer of 38, 48, 102; crew of 15, 19, 59, 64, 73, 75, 81–82, 84; dancing/music on 174–75, *176*; Delano's account of 23, 26–28; destruction of 60, 231; documentaries about 232; explosion of gun from 45; films about 211, 217, 219, 221, 227–28; Ford's account of 89; in George Mackay Brown's story 155–56; Gibbings' wood engravings of *172*, 173; Hough's account of 77–79, *78*; Lamb's wood engravings of *179*; launch, voyage of *see* open-boat voyage; log of 19–20, 31, *34*, 63; Lummis' account of 91; Mackaness' account of 63–64; Mansir's illustrations of 194–95; Marden's account of 104; Maude's account of 104; McKay's account of 99; Murray's account of 38; in *Mutiny!* (musical) 222–23; mutiny on *see* mutineers; mutiny, *Bounty*; in Pearl's story 215; Shillibeer's account of 24; Silverman's account of 76; Wahlroos' account of 87, *88*; websites 234; Young's account of 45
The Bounty (film, 1984) 66, 77, 80, *88*, 162, 204, 215, **219–21**, **220**, 222, 227–28, 232
The Bounty (Hough) 77, 80, 226
"The Bounty Again!" (Smyth) 50
Bounty Bay (Pitcairn Island) *42*, 82, 136, 168, 226

A Bounty Boy (Bullen) 157
"Bounty Descendants Live of Remote Norfolk Island" (Roughley) 104
The Bounty Mutiny (Penguin Classics, 2001) 11, *13*, 18, 20
"The *Bounty* Mutiny Remembered" (Menard) 163
"The 'Bounty' Re-experienced" (Axon) 227
"The 'Bounty' Sails On and On" (Clowes) 227
The Bounty: The True Story of the Mutiny on the Bounty (Alexander) 30, 40, 56, 82, **94–97**, *95*, 190, 224
"The 'Bounty' Timekeeper" (Amis) 102
The Bounty Trilogy (Nordhoff and Hall) 31, 33, 129–30, 143, **145–52**, 157, 160, 169, 201, 211
The Bounty's Boy (Edmonds) 130, **152**, **154**
Bounty's Heritage: The Legacy of Fletcher Christian (documentary) 231
Bourke, William 205
Bower, Tim *225*
Bowker, R.M. 181
The Boy Mutineer (Barbary) 130, **154–55**
Brando, Marlon 216–17, *218*, 219
"Brandywine School" of art 177
breadfruit 8, 10–12, 105, 174, 190, 217, 221
Briand, Paul L., Jr., *In Search of Paradise: The Nordhoff-Hall Story* 145–46, 157
Bridge, Andy *92*, 93
Bridge, Sir Cyprian 32–33, 47, 217
Bridger, Alan 165
"Brief History of 'The Bounty'" (Axon) 227
Brisco, James 155
British Academy of Composers and Songwriters 222
British Heritage 103
British Wood-Engraved Book Illustration, 1904–1940 (Selborne) 201
Briton, H.M.S. 24–26, 29, *137*, 140, 167, 205
Brodie, Walter, *Pitcairn's Island and the Islanders in 1850* 47, 151
Brown, George Mackay, "Lieutenant Bligh and Two Midshipmen" **155–57**, *156*
Brown, Robert, "The Pitcairn Islanders, and the Mutiny of the *Bounty*" 42–43, *44*

Brown, William 175, 216–17
Brunswick, H.M.S. 21
Brunton, Paul, *Awake, Bold Bligh! William Bligh!* 98, 227
Bryant, Mary 73
Bryant, William Cullen, "A Song of Pitcairn's Island" 129, 160–61
Bryce, Robert 144
Buckley, Christopher, "Scrutiny on the Bounty: Captain Bligh's Secret Logbook" **224–25**, *225*
Buffett, John 60
Building Fort George (painting) 198
Bullen, Frank T., *A Bounty Boy* 157
Burkett, Thomas 8, 21, 170, 205, 210, 222
Burney, James 10, 131, 181
Byam, Roger (fictional narrator) 148, 154, 185, *186*, *187*, 188, *189*, 210–11, 213, *214*, 227
Byrne, Michael 102, 174–76, *176*, 207, 210, 216, 219, 222
Byron, Lord George Noel Gordon: "The Death of Christian and the Mutineers" 161; *The Island, or Christian and His Comrades* 129, **133–35**, *134*, 157, 161–64, 205, 233
"Byron's Polynesian Fantasy" (Spence) 164

Cain's Birthday (Rutter) 65, 158, 160, 193
Callao 60
Callender, Geoffrey 102
Camperdown, Battle of 63
Cape Horn 11, 50, 57, 71, 179–80, 210, 215, 217, 221–22
Cape Town 151
"Capt. Beechey's Narrative" (Smyth) 50
Captain Bligh and Mr. Christian (Hough) 55, **77–80**, *78*, *79*, 87, 93, 103, 158, 219, *220*, 221, 226
"Capt. Bligh and the Mutiny of the Bounty" (Denman) 103
Captain Bligh: Mutiny on the Bounty (documentary) 231–32
"Captain Bligh of the *Bounty*" (Pearl) 215, *216*
Captain Bligh: The Man and his Mutinies (Kennedy) 55, 99
Captain Bligh's Second Voyage to the South Sea (Lee) **57–59**
Captain Blood (film) 210
Captain Cook and William Bligh (Beaglehole) 97
Captain William Bligh: An Illustrated History (Weare and Graham) 162
Carlsson, Susanne Chauvel, *Charles and Elsa Chauvel, Movie Pioneers* 226
carvings 91
Carysfort's Island 57
Cassell's Family Magazine 42–43, 44
The Causes of the Bounty Mutiny: Some Comments on a Book by Madge Darby (Du Rietz) 75–76
Cave, Roderick, *A History of the Golden Cockerel Press* 198
celibacy 75, 77
"Celluloid Bountys" (Solomon) 228
Century 144
Chamier, Frederick, *Jack Adams, the Mutineer* 129, 157, 160
The Charge of the Light Brigade (film) 210
Charles and Elsa Chauvel, Movie Pioneers (Carlsson) 226
A Charmed Life (Essex) 222
Chauvel, Charles 204, 207, *209*, 210, 233; *In the Wake of the Bounty* 226
Chauvel, Elsa 204; *My Life with Charles Chauvel* 226
"cheese incident" 32, 210, 222
Childe Byron (play, 1981) 223
children's books 23, 43, 129–30, 135–43, 152, 154–55, 161–62, 204, 226
Chodes, John L., *The Longboat* 130, 162, *163*, 217
Christensen, Alta Hilliard: *Heirs of Exile* 104; *The Story of Pitcairn Island* 104
Christian, Allan 210
Christian, Charles 84, 95–96, 232
Christian, Edward 63, 102, 158; *Minutes of the Proceedings of the Court-Martial...with an Appendix* **11–12**, *14*, 15, 17–18, 20, 101, 102; *On Ten Persons Charged with Mutiny on Board His Majesty's Ship the Bounty with an Appendix* 55, 67; *A Short Reply to Capt. William Bligh's Answer* 12, **17–18**, 20, 67
Christian, Eva 210
Christian, Fletcher: Adams' account of 29–30, 41–43; alcohol use of 40, 82, 96, 103; Alexander's account of 40, 82, 95–96, 190; as "Ancient Mariner" model 69, 161, 164; Anthony's account of 97; in Armstrong's novel 161; Bach's account of 86; in Ballantyne's story 140, *141*; Ball's account of 80, 82; in Barbary's novel 154–55; Barrow's account of 32, 67, 69; in Becke and Jeffery's novel 143; Beechey's account of 29–30, 41–42; Belcher's account of 41–42; biographies of 82–85, *83*; Bligh's account of 8, 10, 170; Buckley's article on 224; in Byron's poem 133, 135; in *Chronicles of the Sea* 36; Danielsson's account of 73; Darby's account of 75; daughter of 130, 162; death of 25, 27–28, 43, 87, 130–31, 142–43, 178, 193; Delano's account of 27–28; documentaries about 232; in Edmonds' novel 152, 154; family of 12, 15, 58, 63, 69, 79, 84, 89, 96, 162, 192, 203, 232; films about 50, 65, 204, 207, 210–11, 216–17, *218*, 219, *220*, 221, 228; Ford's account of 40, 82, 103; in George Mackay Brown's story 157; Glynn Christian's account of 84–85; grave of 84, 143; Hough's account of 77–80, *78*, *79*; Kennedy's account of 64–65; in Kinsolving's novel 158; in Lang's stories 142; Lee's account of 59; and letters hoax 67, 97, 160, 163–64, **192–93**, **194**, *195*, 203; Mackaness' account of 10, 64–65; in Maxwell's novel 130, 158; in Mitford's poem 130–31; Murray's account of 38; in *Mutiny!* (musical) 221–24, *223*; in Nordhoff and Hall's novels 146, 148, 151–52, 185, *187*; *Pandora's* search for 57, *58*, 73–74, *75*; in Pearl's story 215; on Pitcairn Island 25, 30, 76, 80, 140, *141*, 158; relationship with Bligh 10, 12, *14*, 15, 17, 32, 40, 65, 75, 77–79, *78*, 86–87, 89, 93, 103, 105, 158, 207, 221–22, 224; in Rinaldi's novel 162; as ringleader of mutiny 8, 10, 32, 64–65, 67, 75, 80, 84; Robert Brown's account of 43; rumors of return to England 33, 43, 67, 69, 82, 130, 154–55, 158, *159*, 164, 193, *195*; Rutter's writings about 65, 67, 160; in *Sailors' Magazine* 40; and sextant 86; in Shillibeer's account 25; in "The Ship and the Island" (anon.) 138, *139*; Silverman's account of 76; and social class 217, 232;

sons of 24–26, *26*, 140, *142*; in Stanley Miller's novel 158; on Tahiti 59, 75, 77, 81–82, 84–85; in Thrapp's novel 160; and Tubai settlement 84, 87, 154, 173; and venereal disease 191, *191*, 195; Wahlroos' account of 87, 89, 105; Wilkinson's account of 67, 69
Christian, Glynn, 143, 221–22, 226, 231–32; "Film-makers and *Bounty*" 211; *Fragile Paradise* 55, 69, **82–85**, *83*, 96, 143, 167, 231; "Pitcairn's Revolutionary Women" 102
Christian, Irma 231
Christian, Isabella 60
Christian, John 193, *195*
Christian, Mary Ann 130, 148, 162
Christian, Peggy 60
Christian, Thursday October 24–26, *26*, *142*, 167
Christian, Tom 231
Christian's Cave (Pitcairn Island) 140, *141*, 143, 148, 158, 210, 224
Christie's *39*
Christina, the Maid of the South Seas; A Poem (Mitford) 129, **130–33**, *132*, 162, 233
Chronicles of the Sea: Or, Fateful Narratives of Shipwrecks 36, *37*
chronometer 38, 48, 102
Churchill, Charles 73, 170, 210, 219
cinema *see* films
Clark, Mamo 210, *212*
Clarke, Peter, *Hell and Paradise: The Norfolk-Bounty-Pitcairn Saga* 98
A Classic in Pictures 213
Classics Illustrated **213–15**, *214*
Clowes, Peter, "The 'Bounty' Sails On and On" 227
Cochran, Ted 231
coconut husks 188
coconuts: Adams' account of 10, 30; Barrow's account of 32; Beechey's account of 30; Danielsson's account of 73; Edward Christian's account of 15; films about 207, 221; Ford's account of 82, 103; Lambourne's drawings of 198; Mackaness' account of 65; Morrison's account of 10; Schreiber's account of 101; Wahlroos' account of 105
Cole, William 10, 86, 149, 219, 221
Coleman, Joseph 17, 57, 102, 210
Coleman, Ron, *24-Gun Frigate Pandora* 99

Coleridge, Ernest Hartley, *The Works of Lord Byron* 133, 161
Coleridge, Samuel Taylor 131, 133, 135, 193; *Lyrical Ballads* 69; "The Rime of the Ancyent Marinere" 69, *70*, 129, 161–64
Collett, Bill, *The Last Mutiny: The Further Adventures of Captain Bligh* 130, 157, 167
comic books 213–15
communalism 94
compass 136
confidence artists 39
conspiracy theory 32, 36, 80
Cook, James: and Bligh 77, 97, 131, 155, 191, 222; and Burney 10, 131; in *Chronicles of the Sea* 36; death of 59; in George Mackay Brown's story 155; in Metcalfe's novel 158; on Tahiti 60; *Voyages* 18
Cooper, James Fenimore 157, 177, 213
The Coral Island (Ballantyne) 138
corn 89
Cornwallis, wreck of 45
Coupang 149, 151, 181, 194
The Course of the Wild Wave (Hurd) 162
The Court-Martial of the "Bounty" Mutineers (Rutter, ed.) 65, 101, 102
courts-martial 7, 15, 36, 50, 55, 73, 77, 101, 102, 157, 170, 203; in Barbary's novel 154; of Bligh 8, 10, 95–96; of Byrne 176; films about 211, 217, 219, 221; of Heywood 31, 33, 35–36, 38, 40, 59, 154, 173; in Miller's play 130; of Morrison 21, 173; in Nordhoff and Hall's novels 148; of Norman 217; of Purcell 181
cows 25
Crane, Richard: *Mutiny!* 205, **221–24**, *223*; *Mutiny on the Bounty—A Sea-Faring Show* 165, 193, 205
Cross, George 205, 207, *208*
Crown and Sceptre Inn (Greenwich) 15, 102
"The Crown and Sceptre Inn, Greenwich" (Darby) 102
The Crusoes of Pitcairn Island (Knowles) 162
Curacao, H.M.S. 60
Curry, John Steuart 185
Curwen, Isabella 130, 158, *159*, 193, *195*

DaBall, Raymond F., *A Dream, Which Happened to Peter Heywood* 161

Daily Express Award 77
Dangerous Voyage of Captain Bligh, in an Open Boat (Bligh) 7, 198
Danielsson, Bengt 226; *Forgotten Islands of the South Seas* 73; *Love in the South Seas* 73; *What Happened on the Bounty* 69, 71, *73*, 167
Darby, Madge: "Bligh's Disciple: Matthew Flinders' Journals of HMS *Providence* 102; "The Crown and Sceptre Inn, Greenwich" 102; "The Glorious First of June: An Account of the Battle by Peter Heywood" 102–3; *Who Caused the Mutiny on the Bounty?* 55, 69, **75–76**, 77, 79, 87, 93, 103
David, Andrew C.F. 104, 226
Day, A. Grove: *Best South Sea Stories* 158; *Louis Becke* 157; *Mad About Islands: Novelists of a Vanished Pacific* 158; *Rascals in Paradise* 99
Day-Lewis, Daniel 219
"The Death of Christian and the Mutineers" (Byron) 161
Delano, Amasa 23, *27*, 43, *49*, 76; *A Narrative of Voyages and Travels* 23, **26–28**, *27*, 47, 49
Delano's Voyages of Commerce and Discovery 49
De Laurentiis, Dino 219
Dening, Greg 231; *Mr. Bligh's Bad Language* 98, 205
Denman, Arthur, "Capt. Bligh and the Mutiny of the Bounty" 103
Dent, Hugh R. 67
Description of Pitcairn Island and Its Inhabitants: With an Authentic Account of the Mutiny of the Ship Bounty (Barrow) 31
Desolation Island (O'Brian) 130, 155
"Despatch to the Admiralty" (Bligh) **169–71**, *171*
Dibdin, Thomas John, *The Pirates: or, The Calamaties of Capt. Bligh* **204–5**, *206*
Dickens, Charles 35
didacticism *see* moral lessons
Dillon, Peter, "Pitcairn's Island— The *Bounty's* Crew" 48, 93
Discover (British vessel) 151
The Discoverers of the Fiji Islands (Henderson) 105
A Doctor's Letters from Pitcairn, 1937 (Southworth) 146
documentaries 231–32
Dodd, Robert *62*, 63, *83*, 167, *223*

dogs 25, *142*
Dolphin, H.M.S. 19
Donaldson, Roger 80, 219
Donohoe, Rob *163*
Douglas, Hal 231
A Dream, Which Happened to Peter Heywood (Heywood and DaBall) 161
Drée *200*, 201
Ducie Island 28, 57, 91
Dumas, Alexandre, *The Three Musketeers* 213
Dunston, Douglas A. 188
Du Rietz, Rolf 71, 73, 75–76, 97, 146; *Banksia 2*, 56; *Causes of the Bounty Mutiny: Reply to Mr. Rolf Du Rietz's Comments* 75–76; *The Causes of the Bounty Mutiny: Some Comments on a Book by Madge Darby* 75–76; *Mutiny and Romance in the South Seas*, foreword to 87; *Studia Bountyana* 56, 69, 75–76; "The Voyage of H.M.S. Pandora, 1790–1792: Some Remarks Upon Geoffrey Rawson's Book on the Subject" 103
Dutch East Indies 104, 188
dysentery 60

East India Company 84
Easter Island 90
Edgar, David *165*
Edgell, H.J.A. 179
Edmonds, I.G., *The Bounty's Boy* 130, **152**, 154
Edwards, Edward, 73, 75, 94, 155, 173–74; Alexander's account of 94; in Barbary's novel 154; Barrow's account of 33; Delano's account of 27–28; dinner service of 98–99; films about 211; Gesner's account of 98–99; Hamilton's account of *16*, 18–19, 21; journal of 7, 18, 27–28, 55; Lee's account of 59; log of 104; Maude's account of 104; McFarland's account of 48; and Morrison's journal 173–74; in O'Brian's novel 155; Rawson's account of 73, 75; Thomson's account of 18; *Voyage of H.M.S. "Pandora" Despatched to Arrest the Mutineers of the "Bounty" in the South Seas, 1790–1791* 18, 28, **56–57**, *58*; see also *Pandora*, H.M.S.
Edwards, Francis 56
"The Edwards Papers" (Maude) 104

Elizabeth Island *see* Henderson Island
Ellison, Thomas 21, 210–11, 219, 221
Elphinstone, William 149, 221
Encyclopaedia Britannica 103
Endeavour, H.M.S. 158
Engen, Sadie, *John Tay, Messenger to Pitcairn* 104
English/Tahitian dictionary 35
Ennerdale 46
Essex (American frigate) 24
Essex, David: *A Charmed Life* 222; *Mutiny!* 205, **221–24**, *223*
Eventful History of the Mutiny and Piratical Seizure of H.M.S. Bounty (Barrow) **30–33**, *32*, *34*, 43, 45, 46–47, 203; Beechey, critique of 29; Belcher's account compared to 41–42; in Bingley's story 161; Bonner Smith's account of 102; on Christian in England 67, 69, 193; Hamilton, critique of 18; Heywood's sketch of *Pandora* sinking 167; illustrations in 197–98; and *Journal of James Morrison* 36, 57, 173; Nordhoff and Hall influenced by 145–46; and social class 217; staying power of 23
executions 21, 96, 213

Faust (Goethe) 213
fever 57, 59, 64
"The Fifth Bounty Film (or Is It the Sixth?)" (Murray) 227
Fiji Islands 59, 170, 195, *197*
"Film-makers and *Bounty*" (Christian) 211
films 31, 56, 80, 82, 94, 96, 204–13, 216–19, 226–28; *see also* names of films
Finlay, Frank 221–22, *223*
Fischer, Anton Otto 169, 201
Fiske, Nathan Welby, *Story of Alec, or Pitcairn's Island* 23
Fitzmaurice, William 28
Flatman, David 231
"Fletcher Christian and the Rime of the Ancient Mariner" (Houston) 162
Flinders, Matthew 59, 102
flogging 43, 95–96, 210–11, 215, *216*, 217, 224
Flynn, Errol 207, 210, 226
Folger, Mayhew 24–29, 43, 50; log of 24, 48; in Mitford's poem 130 ;in Nordhoff and Hall's novels 148, 152; on Pitcairn Island 89, 130; in Silverman's account 76

Ford, Henry J. 140
Ford, Herbert: "The Mutiny's Cause: A New Analysis" 40, 82, 103; *Pitcairn — Port of Call* 56, **89–91**, *90*
"The 'Forgotten' *Bounty* Movie" (Murray) 227
Forgotten Islands of the South Seas (Danielsson) 73
Fort George, building of 84, 138, 198
The Fortunate Adversities of William Bligh (Schreiber) 55
Fragile Paradise (Christian) 55, 69, **82–85**, *83*, 96, 143, 167, 231
Franklin, John 28
Fraser, George MacDonald, *Hollywood History of the World* 204
French Revolution 223
Fresh Light on Bligh (Mackaness, ed.) **61–65**
Freudian psychology 75–76
The Friend 23, 42
Friendly Islands 133, 188; *see also* Tofoa
Fryer, John 7; Alexander's account of 95–96; Anthony's edited version of 97, 193; in *Appendix to the Proceedings* (Christian) 15, 17; Bach's account of 86, 197; in Crane's play *165*; daughter of 183, 185; death of 170, 185; Du Rietz's account of 56; in Edmonds' novel 152, 154; films about 210, 216, 219, 221; Ford's account of 103; Gamble's account of 183–85, *184*; journal of 71, 97, 103, 170, 195; Mackaness' account of 10; in *Mutiny!* (musical) 221; in Nordhoff and Hall's novels 149; on *Resource* 181; *The Voyage of the Bounty's Launch* 21, 65, **169–71**, *171*, 183
Furthman, Jules 210

Gable, Clark 65, 210–11, *212*, 221
Galapagos Islands 26
The Gam: Being a Group of Whaling Stories (Robbins) 61
Gamble, Mary Ann, *John Fryer of the Bounty* **183–85**, *184*
Gareloch (British vessel) 89
Gates, E.H. 45
gender war 93
General Evans 90
George, Fort 84, 138, 198
George III, King of England 12, 173, 205, 207

Gesner, Peter 21, 227; *Pandora: An Archaeological Perspective* 19, 98–99
Gibbings, Robert 169–70, *171*, *172*, 173, 201
Gibson, Mel 162, 219, *220*, 221–22
Gilberton Company 213
Gilbraltar 35
"The Glorious First of June: An Account of the Battle by Peter Heywood" (Darby) 102–3
Goethe, *Faust* 213
Golden Cockerel Press 20–21, 35, 65, 102–3, 169, *171*, 170–74, 178, 181, 183, *184*, 185, 198, 201, 211
Goodrich, Frank B., *Ocean's Story: or, Triumphs of Thirty Centuries* 161
Goodrich, Samuel Griswold *see* Parley, Peter
Gordon, George Noel *see* Byron, Lord George Noel Gordon
Goubeaux, Robert 232
Gouriet, Victor 207, 210
Graham, Caroline, *Captain William Bligh: An Illustrated History* 162
The Grave Tattoo (McDermid) 130
Great Barrier Reef 56–57, 59, 73, 85, 104, 191, 198, *199*
"The Great Breadfruit Scheme" (Oster and Oster) 105
Great Historical Mutinies (Herbert) 23–24
"The Great Revolution in Pitcairn" (Twain) 129, 160
Greece's war of independence 223
Greenland 31
Grossman, Eddie *163*
A Guide to Pitcairn 91
Gunn, Dr. 60
gunpowder 19

Hack, Maria 43, 136–37; "Adventures of Captain Bligh" **135–36**; *Winter Evenings, or Tales of Travellers* 129, 135, 140
"Hæva" (ceremonial dance) 18, 180
Hagan, John *13*
Haggard, H. Rider 142–43
Hale, Edward Everett, "Pitcairn's Island" 161
Hall, James Norman 56, 158; biography of 145–46, 157, 160; *The Bounty Trilogy* 31, 33, 129–30, 143, **145–52**, 157, 160, 169, 201, 211; *Classics Illustrated* **213–15**, *214*; *The Hurricane* 227; *Men Against the Sea* 130, **148–51**, *150*, 169, 201, 211, 213; *Mutiny on the Bounty* 47, 50, 101, 130, **145–48**, *147*, 154, 163, 169, **185–88**, *186*, *187*, *189*, 211, 213, 227; *My Island Home* 145–46; *Pitcairn's Island* 79, 130, 148, **151–52**, *153*, 169, 201, 213; *The Tale of a Shipwreck* 99, 157; "The True Story of Peter Heywood" 185, 188
Hall, Thomas 149
Hallett, John 17, 30, 205, 222
Hamilton, George 17, 18–19, 33, 55, 71, 99, 231; *Voyage of H.M.S. "Pandora" Despatched to Arrest the Mutineers of the "Bounty" in the South Seas, 1790-1791* 18, 28, **56–57**, *58*; *A Voyage Round the World in His Majesty's Frigate Pandora* 7, **16**, **18–19**, **21**, 57
Harold Clurman Theatre 130
Harper, Ethel, *Paths of the Sea* 130, 162, 193
Harper's New Monthly Magazine 23
Harper's Weekly 23, 42
Harris, Bruce, "Torment in Tofua" 227
Harris, Richard 216, 219
Harris, Rolf 227
Hawkesworth, John 103
Hawthorne, Elizabeth Manning 136
Hawthorne, Nathaniel 136–37
Hayward, Thomas 15, 30, 85, 210, 215
Hector, H.M.S. 96
Heirs of Exile (Christensen) 104
Hell and Paradise: The Norfolk-Bounty-Pitcairn Saga (Clarke) 98
Henderson, G.C., *The Discoverers of the Fiji Islands* 105
Henderson Island 28, 91
Herbert, David, *Great Historical Mutinies* 23–24
The Heritage of the Bounty (Shapiro) 38, 56, 76–77, 91, 101
Heydt, Bruce, "Mutiny!" 103
Heyerdahl, Thor 71
Heywood, Nessy 31, 205
Heywood, Peter: Alexander's account of 95–96, *95*; in Barbary's novel 154; Barrow's account of 23, 31, 33, 42, 57, 67, 69, 198; Belcher's account of 40–42; biographies of 33, 36, 185, 188; Bligh's account of 59; court-martial of 31, 33, 36, 40, 59, 154, 173; Darby's account of 102–3; daughter of 188; death of 33, 36, 40, 50; *A Dream, Which Happened to Peter Heywood* 161; Edward Christian's account of 15, 17; family of 12, 15, 21, 31, 38, 40, 58, 96, 161–62, 203, 207; films about 205, 207, 219; as friend of Stewart 30, 41; glimpsing Fletcher Christian in Plymouth 33, 43, 67, 69, 154, 193; in Hough's account 77, 79; and *Journal of James Morrison* 173; Kennedy's account of 65; Lee's account of 59; letters/diaries of 35, 38, 40, 57, 77, 79, 95, 102–4, 188, 228; Marshall's account of 33, 36, 48, 50; Murray's account of 38; in *Mutiny!* (musical) 221; in Nordhoff and Hall's novels 148, 185, 188; in O'Brian's novel 130, 155; pardon of 12, 21, 31, 40, 59, 96, 148, 154, 173, 207; in *Sailors' Magazine* 39–40, *41*; sketch of *Pandora* sinking 167; Smyth's account of 50; and social class 217; stepdaughter of 40–42, 173; in Stevens' article 228; Tagart's account of 33, 35–36, 50; on Tahiti 35, 59, 161; and venereal disease 188, 191, *191*; Wahlroos' account of 87; Wilkinson's account of 67, 69
Highgate (London, Eng.) 35–36
Hill, Joshua 47, 160
The Hill Collections of Pacific Voyages 17
Hillbrant, Henry 33, 222
Historical Records of New South Wales 170
A History of the Golden Cockerel Press (Cave and Manson) 198
H.M.S. Bounty (Maxwell) 130, 158, 193
H.M.S. Bounty: A True Account of the Famous Mutiny (McKee) 69, 71, *72*
"HMS *Bounty:* The Bloodless Mutiny" (Wahlroos) 105
H.M.S. Pandora: In Pursuit of the Bounty (documentary) 231
Hollywood History of the World (Fraser) 204
Holmes, Sherlock 198
The Home of the Mutineers (Murray) 38
homosexuality 75, 77, 79–81, 87, 93, 103, 158, 221
honor 89, 96, 105
Hood, Samuel, Lord 154, 210, 219

Hopkins, Anthony 66, 215, 219, *220*, 222
Hough, Richard 30; *The Bounty* 77, 80, 226; *Captain Bligh and Mr. Christian* 55, 77–80, *78, 79*, 87, 93, 103, 158, 219, *220*, 221, 226
Houston, Neal B., "Fletcher Christian and the Rime of the Ancient Mariner" 162
Howard, Ed, "Pitcairn and Norfolk: The Saga of Bounty's Children" 104
Howard, Trevor 215–17, *218*
Hoyts Street Theatre (Sydney) 205, 207, *209*
Huggan, Thomas 103, 148, 191, *191*, 210, 219
Hunt, Leigh 135
Hurd, Edith Thatcher, *The Course of the Wild Wave* 162
The Hurricane (Nordhoff and Hall) 227

"I Found the Bones of the Bounty" (Marden) 104
"I Survived the Savage Mutiny on the Bounty" (Steven) 228
illustrated books 136–37, 161–62, 167–201
The Illustrated London News 23, 42
Im Thurn, Sir Everard 61
"In *Bounty's* Wake: Finding the Wreck of H.M.S. *Pandora*" (Marden) 94, 169, 198
In Search of Paradise: The Nordhoff-Hall Story (Briand) 145–46, 157
In the Wake of the Bounty (Chauvel) 226
In the Wake of the Bounty (film, 1933) 204, 207–10, *209*, 226
influenza 60
Ingleton, Geoffrey C. 169, 188, 190–92, *190, 191, 192*
Interrogation of Silence: The Writings of George Mackay Brown (Murray and Murray) 155
Irving, Lawrence, *Bligh and the "Bounty"* 102, 169, 174–76, *176, 177*
Isabella, the Haunting Love Story of Fletcher Christian and Isabella Curwen (Mountain) 130, 158, *159*, 193
Island of Tears: John I. Tay (Shapiro) 91
Island of the Bounty (documentary) 231
The Island, or Christian and His Comrades (Byron) 129,
133–35, *134*, 157, 161–64, 205, 233
Islands 227
Isle of Man 162
Ivor Novell award 222

Jack Adams, the Mutineer (Chamier) 129, 157, 160
Jackson, Peter 204
James Norman Hall (Roulston) 160
Jeffery, Walter, *The Mutineer: A Romance of Pitcairn Island* 129–30, *143*, 157
Jennings, Talbot 210
Jenny 48, 93, 104
John Fryer of the Bounty (Gamble) 169, 183–85, *184*
John Tay, Messenger to Pitcairn (Engen) 104
Johnson, Irving and Electa: "Westward Bound in the Yankee" 103; "The Yankee's Wander-world" 103
Johnston, Sir Harry, "Bligh of the 'Bounty'" 198, *199*
Jolliffe, Diana *see* Belcher, Lady Diana Jolliffe
Jones, Jenkin 60
Journal and Proceedings of the Royal Australian Historical Society 64
Journal of Bligh's Voyage to England (Bligh) 182–83
The Journal of Bounty's Launch (Mansir) 169, 193–96, *196, 197*
Journal of James Morrison 7, 55, 170–74, *172, 175*, 182–83, *182*, 190; in Anthony's account 97; in Barbary's novel 154; in Belcher's account 41, 173; Bligh's account of 173, 182; in Bonner Smith's account 102; on coconuts 10; in Ford's account 103; and Ingleton's illustrations 190, *190*; Lacy's account of 103–4; Mackaness' omission of 67; in Maude's account 104; in McKee's account 71; on *Pandora's* voyage 57; on pumpkin episode 173; Rutter's publication of 65; on sextant 86; on stolen cheeses 32
Journal of Maritime Law & Commerce 228
Journal of Pacific History 56
Journal of the Polynesian Society 56
Juback, John 163

Kane, Herb Kawinui, *Voyagers: Words and Images* 198
Kantner, Albert 213
Kaper, Bronislau 219
keelhauling 211, 215, 217
Keller, Ronald 198
Kennedy, Gavin 226, 232; *Bligh* 55, 63, 99; *A Book of the "Bounty,"* introduction to 8, 15, 17, 64–65, *67, 68*; *Captain Bligh: The Man and His Mutinies* 55, 99; *Eventful History of the Mutiny and Piratical Seizure of H.M.S. Bounty*, introduction to 31, 47; *The Mutiny of the Bounty* 167
Kent, Rockwell 174
Khandeish, wreck of 46
Kinbrum, Arnie *165*
Kingston, W.H.G. 201
Kinsolving, William, *Mr. Christian: the Further Adventures of Fletcher Christian* 130, 158, 160, 193
Kirchner, Gottfried 231
Klinkenborg, Verlyn 94
Knight, C. 102
Knowles, Josiah N. 161–62; *The Crusoes of Pitcairn Island* 162
Knox, Thomas W. *The Young Nimrods Around the World* 162
Koerner, W.H.D. 169, 201
Kon-Tiki raft expedition 71

Lacy, Gavin de, "Plagiarism on the Bounty" 103–4
Lady Belcher and Her Friends (L'Estrange) 40, 48, 173
Lamb, Lynton *34*, 169, 178, *179, 180*
Lamb, Robert 219
Lambourne, Nigel 198
Lang, Andrew: "The Pitcairn Islanders" 140, 142–43, *142*; *The Red True Story Book* 140, 142–43, *142*; "A Wonderful Voyage" 140
The Last Mutiny: The Further Adventures of Captain Bligh (Collett) 130, 157, 167
Laughton, Charles 65, 146, 152, 210–11, *212*, 215, 224
launch, *Bounty's see* open-boat voyage
Lawbreakers (filmscript) 80, 219
Lean, David 80, 204, 219, 227
Learmonth, Larry *79*
Leask, Nigel, "Resolving *The Corsair, Lara* and *The Island*" 163
Lebogue, Lawrence 15, 17, 82, 102, 197, 222
Lederer, Charles 216
Ledward, Thomas 103, 149, 151, *163*
Lee, Ida, *Captain Bligh's Second*

Voyage to the South Sea 57–59
Leslie, Edward E. 47
Lester, Liz *165*
L'Estrange, A.G., *Lady Belcher and Her Friends* 40, 48, 173
Letters from Mr. Fletcher Christian 67, 97, 160, 163–64, 192–93, 203
The Letters of Fletcher Christian 192–93, *194*, *195*
The Lieutenant: An Epic Tale of Courage and Endurance on the High Seas (Bennett) 157
"Lieutenant Bligh and Two Midshipmen" (Brown) **155–57**, *156*
The Life of Vice-Admiral William Bligh (Mackaness) 41, 55, 61–65, *62*, 99, 146, 211
Lincoln, Margarette, *The Mutiny on the Bounty* 225–26
Linkletter, Peter 149
Linney, Romulus, *Childe Byron* 223
Littledale, Isaac 102–3
Lloyd, Frank 210–11
Locke, John 35
Log of HMS Bounty, 1787–89 (Bligh) 181
The Log of the Bounty (Bligh) **178–81**, *179*, *180*
The Log of the Bounty (documentary) 231
The Log of the Snark (London) 145
London, Charmian 144–45
London, Jack 158
"The Seed of McCoy" 129, **143–45**, *145*, 158
London Times 63
The Lonely Island, or the Refuge of the Mutineers (Ballantyne) 129, **138**, 140, *141*
The Long Arm (filmscript) 80, 219
The Longboat (Chodes) 130, *163*, 217
Longford, Raymond 205, 207, *208*, 227, 233
Lord Hood's Island 57
The Lord of the Rings (Tolkien) 204
The Lord Will Repay (Von Horn) 162
Louis Becke (Day) 157
Love in the South Seas (Danielsson) 73
Lowes, John Livingstone, *The Road to Xanadu* 69, 163
Lucas, Charles, Sir, *Pitcairn Island Register Book* 59–61, *61*

Lummis, Trevor, *Pitcairn Island: Life and Death in Eden* 56, **91–94**, *92*
Lyman, John, "*Pitcairn*, Missionary Packet" 104
Lynch, Brendan *216*
Lynton, Mayne 207, 210
Lyrical Ballads (Coleridge and Wordsworth) 69
Lytell, Lottie 205

Macdonald, C. Alister *150*, 151
Mackaness, George 8, 10, 97, 160; *A Book of the "Bounty"* 8, 11, 15, 17–18, 47, 55, 64–65, 67, *68*, 87; *Fresh Light on Bligh* 61–65, *62*; *The Life of Vice-Admiral William Bligh* 41, 55, 61–65, *62*, 99, 146, 211
Mackenzie-Grieve, Averil 169, 183, *184*, 185
Mad about Islands: Novelists of a Vanished Pacific (Day) 158
Mahina 143
Mahoo 81
Maimiti 151, 210, 216
malaria 59, 149
Maloney Roy, 232
Mangareva Island 90, 144
Mansir, A. Richard, *The Journal of Bounty's Launch* 169, 193–96, *196*, *197*
Manson, Sarah, *A History of the Golden Cockerel Press* 198
Marden, Luis 76; "I Found the Bones of the *Bounty*" 104; "In *Bounty's* Wake: Finding the Wreck of H.M.S. *Pandora*" 94, 169, 198; "Saga of a Ship, the *Yankee*" 103
Mariner, William, *An Account of the Natives of the Tonga Islands, in the South Pacific Ocean* 133, 163
Mariner's Mirror 56, 102, 104
Maritime Life and Traditions 56
Marriott, Charles Bruce, Mrs. *see* Lee, Ida
Marryat, Frederick 157
Marshall, John: "Peter Heywood, Esq." 33, 36, 48, 50; *Royal Naval Biography of Peter Heyward* 33, 36, 188
Martin, Fletcher 169, 185, *186*, *187*, 188, *189*, 198
Martin, Isaac **214**
"Mary" 59
Mason & Hamlin Organ Company 46
Massachusetts 26
Matavai Bay 57, *100*, 167

Matavy (rechristened *Resolution*) 104, 174
Mauatua 84, 158, 219
Maude, H.E.: "The Edwards Papers" 104; "The Voyage of Pandora's Tender" 104
Maxwell, John, *H.M.S. Bounty* 130, 158, 193
McClintock, James I., *White Logic: Jack London's Short Stories* 144, 158
McCoy, James Russell 144–45
McCoy, Matthew 45
McCoy, William 144, 210, 216, 222, 224
McDermid, Val, *The Grave Tattoo* 130
McFarland, Alfred, *Mutiny in the "Bounty" and Story of the Pitcairn Islanders* 48
McGilchrist, John, *The Mutineers* 129
McIntosh, Thomas 59
McKay, John: The Armed Transport Bounty 99; *24-Gun Frigate Pandora* 99
McKee, Alexander: *H.M.S. Bounty: A True Account of the Famous Mutiny* 69, 71, *72*; *The Truth about the Mutiny on the Bounty* 55, 167
McKinney, Sam: *Bligh: A True Account of Mutiny Aboard His Majesty's Ship Bounty* 198; *Mutiny on the Bounty* 198
McKoy, Daniel 25
McKoy, William 25, 93, 219
measles 19
Melville, Herman: "Benito Cereno" *27*; *Billy Budd* 130; *Moby-Dick* 130
Memoir of the Late Captain Peter Heywood, R.N. (Tagart) **33**, **35–36**, 50, 161
Men Against the Sea (Nordhoff and Hall) 130, **148–51**, *150*, 169, 201, 211, 213
Menard, Wilmon, "The *Bounty* Mutiny Remembered" 163
Mensforth, Charlotte 154
Mercury (brig) 73
Metcalfe, Rowan, *Transit of Venus* 158
MGM film (1935) *see Mutiny on the Bounty* (film, 1935)
MGM film (1962) *see Mutiny on the Bounty* (film, 1962)
Miamiti 222
Michener, James: "Mutiny" 158; *Rascals in Paradise* 99
Middlesex (East India Company merchant vessel) 84, 96

mildewed sails 10
Milestone, Lewis 216
Milio, Jim 232
Miller, Stanley: *Acquit or Hang!* 130; *Mr. Christian! The Journal of Fletcher Christian* 130, 158, 160, 193
Mills, Eliza 151
Mills, John 87, 93, 151, 175, 216–17, 219, 223
Millward, John 21, 222
Minarii 216
Minutes of the Proceedings of the Court-Martial...with an Appendix (Barney and Christian) **11–12**, *14*, 15, 17–18, 20, 101, 102
miro wood 91
missionaries 104, 157
Missionary Magazine 104
Mr. Bligh's Bad Language (Dening) 98, 205
Mr. Christian: The Further Adventures of Fletcher Christian (Kinsolving) 130, 158, 160, 193
Mr. Christian! The Journal of Fletcher Christian (Miller) 130, 158, 160, 193
Mitchell Library 63, 170, 173, 181–82, *182*, 207
Mitford, George 131
Mitford, Mary Russell: *Christina, the Maid of the South Seas; A Poem* 129, **130–33**, *132*, 162, 233; *Our Village* 133
Moby-Dick (Melville) 130
Molloy, W.F. 170
Montagu 35
Montgomerie, H.S.: *The Morrison Myth: Pendant to William Bligh of the Bounty in Fact and in Fable* 103–4; *William Bligh of the Bounty in Fact and in Fable* 55, 99, 103–4
Moore, Hamilton, *The Practical Navigator* 86
moral lessons 129, 136–38, 140, *141*, 157, 160; *see also* religious instruction
"More Light on Bligh and the Bounty" (Bonner Smith) 102
Morrison, James: Alexander's account of 95; in Barbary's novel 154; Barrow's account of 23, 33, 57; in *Chronicles of the Sea* 36; construction of *Resolution* 73, 104, 154, 174, *175*; court-martial of 21, 173; diary of 173; family of 21; films about 210, 216; journal of *see Journal of James Morrison*; pardon of 21, 173

The Morrison Myth: Pendant to William Bligh of the Bounty in Fact and in Fable (Montgomerie) 103–4
Moulter, William 75
Mountain, Fiona, *Isabella, the Haunting Love Story of Fletcher Christian and Isabella Curwen* 130, 158, *159*, 193
movies *see* films
Murray, John 31
Murray, Rowena and Brian, *Interrogation of Silence: The Writings of George Mackay Brown* 155
Murray, Spencer: "The Fifth Bounty Film (or Is It the Sixth?)" 227; "The 'Forgotten' Bounty Movie" 227; "Why Roger Byam?" 227
Murray, Thos. Boyles: *The Home of the Mutineers* 38; *Pitcairn: The Island, the People, and the Pastor* 23, **36**, **38–39**, *39*, 45, 60
Muspratt, William 210, 222
The Mutineer: A Romance of Pitcairn Island (Becke and Jeffery) 129–30, **143**, 157
mutineers: Alexander's account of 94–97, *95*; Belcher's account of 40–42, 63; in Byron's poem 133; in *Chronicles of the Sea* 36; Clarke's account of 98; construction of *Resolution* 73, 104; Delano's account of 23, 26–27; descendants of 38, 40–42, 48, 69, 82–85, 87, 91, 94, 98, 101, 144, 157–58, 160, 205; execution of 21, 96; in George Mackay Brown's story 155–57; Glynn Christian's account of 82–85, *83*, 102; Lee's account of 59; in London's story 144; Lummis' account of 91, 93–94; in Morrison's journal 173–74; Murray's account of 38; in Nordhoff and Hall's novels 151–52, *153*; *Pandora's* search for 57, *58*, 73–75, *74* (see also *Pandora*, H.M.S.); on Pitcairn Island 23–24, 26–28, 31; in *Sailors' Magazine* 40; Shillibeer's account of 24; in "The Ship and the Island" (anon.) 138, *139*; Silverman's account of 76; Smyth's account of 50; on Tahiti 19, 84–85; *see also* mutiny, *Bounty*; names of mutineers
The Mutineers (Armstrong) 161
The Mutineers (McGilchrist) 129

"The Mutineers of the *Bounty*" (Young) 45
The Mutineers of the Bounty and Their Descendants in Pitcairn and Norfolk Islands (Belcher) **40–42**, *42*, 43, 146, 156, 173
"Mutiny!" (Heydt) 103
"Mutiny" (Michener) 158
Mutiny! (musical) 130, 204–5, **221–24**, *223*, 233
Mutiny! Aboard H.M. Armed Transport "Bounty" in 1789 (Bligh) 181
mutiny, *Bounty* 55–56; Adams' account of 25, 29–30, 41–42; Alexander's account of 95–96; Bach's account of 86; in Ballantyne's story 138, 140; Ball's account of 80–82; in Barbary's novel 154; Barrow's account of 30–32; Belcher's account of 41–42; Bligh's account of 8, 32, 86, 170, 176, *177* (*see also* Bligh, William, works of); and Byrne 176; in *Chronicles of the Sea* 36; Danielsson's account of 71, 73; Darby's account of 75–77; Delano's account of 27–29; Dening's account of 98; documentaries about 231–32; Du Rietz's account of 76; films about 210–11, 217, 219, 221, 228; Ford's account of 82, 103; Fryer's account of 170; Gamble's account of 183; in George Mackay Brown's story 156–57; Gibbings' wood engravings of 169, 171; Glynn Christian's account of 84–85; in Goodrich's collection 161; Hough's account of 77, 79–80; in Ingleton's illustrations 190; in Lang's stories 140; Lee's account of 59; Lummis' account of 93; Mackaness' account of *62*, 63–64; Mansir's account of 195; McKee's account of 69, 71; in Mitford's poem 131; Murray's account of 38; in *Mutiny!* (musical) 222–23; in Nordhoff and Hall's novels 146, *147*, 149, 152, 185; in Peter Parley stories 136; Rawson's account of 73; Robert Brown's account of 43; Rutter's account of 65–67, *66*; in *Sailors' Magazine* 40; Smyth's account of 50; and social class 162, *163*; in Stevens' article 228; Tagart's account of 35; Wahlroos' account of 87, 89, 105; Wilkinson's account of 67,

69; Williams' illustrations of *194*; Young's account of 45
mutiny, *Middlesex* 84, 96
mutiny, Nore 63
Mutiny and Romance in the South Seas (Wahlroos) 25, 48, **86–89**, *88*, 93, 105
Mutiny in the "Bounty" and Story of the Pitcairn Islanders (McFarland) 48
Mutiny of the "Bounty" (Barrow) 198
"Mutiny of the Bounty" *(Chronicles of the Sea)* **36**, *37*
The Mutiny of the Bounty (Kennedy) 167
"The Mutiny of the Bounty" (Oulton) 129
Mutiny of the Bounty and Story of Pitcairn Island (Young) 24, *43*, **45–46**, *46*, 151
The Mutiny on the Bounty (Anderson and Lincoln) 225–26
The Mutiny on the Bounty (film, 1916) **205**, **207**, ***208***
"Mutiny on the Bounty (ex–Bethia)" (Pew) 227–28
Mutiny on the Bounty (film, 1935) 50, 65, 94, 146, 152, 204, 208, **210–13**, *212*, 215, 227–28, 232
Mutiny on the Bounty (film, 1962) 97, 215, **216–19**, *218*, 226–28
Mutiny on the Bounty (McKinney) 198
Mutiny on the Bounty (Nordhoff and Hall) 47, 50, 101, 130, **145–48**, *147*, 154, 163, 169, **185–88**, *186*, *187*, *189*, 211, 213, 227
Mutiny on the Bounty (Vicary) 162
Mutiny on the Bounty, or, the Traitor's Doom! (play) 205
Mutiny on the Bounty, 1789–1989 (exhibition guide) 204, 226–27
Mutiny on the Bounty—A Sea-Faring Show (Crane) *165*, 193, 205, **221–24**, *223*
Mutiny on the Bounty: The Story of Captain William Bligh, Seaman, Navigator, Surveyor and of the Bounty Mutineers (illustrated catalog) 227
"The Mutiny's Cause: A New Analysis" (Ford) 40, 82, 103
Mutiny's Curse (Thrapp) 130, 160, 193
Mutiny's Daughter (Rinaldi) 130, 162, 193
My Island Home (Hall) 145–46

Narrative of a Voyage to the Pacific and Beerings Strait (Beechey) 23, 25, **28–30**, *29*, 41–42, *42*, 97, 102, 168
Narrative of a Whaling Voyage Round the Globe (Bennett) 47
A Narrative of the Briton's Voyage to Pitcairn Island (Shillibeer) **24–26**, *26*
A Narrative of the Mutiny on Board His Majesty's Ship Bounty (Bligh) **7–10**, *9*, 11, 17, 20, 31–32, 133, 167, *168*, 170, 179, 205
A Narrative of Voyages and Travels (Delano) 23, **26–28**, *27*, 47, 49
Nash, Brian 90
National Geographic Magazine 94, 104, 169
National Maritime Museum (Greenwich) 8, 170, 204, 226–27
Naval Military Magazine 23
Nelson, David 219
Nelson, R.A. 183
New Romantick Operatick Ballet Spectacle (play) 205
New South Wales Rebellion 63
New York Times 94, 216
New Yorker 94, *95*, 169, 224
New Zealand 82, 207, 219
Newbold, Jackie *165*
Nobbs, George H. 38–39, 50, 60
Nordhoff, Charles 56, 158; biography of 145–46, 157; *The Bounty Trilogy* 31, 33, 129–30, 143, **145–52**, 157, 160, 169, 177–78, *178*, 201, 211; *Classics Illustrated* 213–15, *214*; *The Hurricane* 227; *Men Against the Sea* 130, **148–51**, *150*, 169, 201, 211, 213; *Mutiny on the Bounty* 47, 50, 101, 130, **145–48**, *147*, 154, 163, 169, **185–88**, *186*, *187*, *189*, 211, 213, 227; *Pitcairn's Island* 79, 130, 148, **151–52**, *153*, 169, 201, 213; "The True Story of Peter Heywood" 185, 188
Nore mutiny 63
Norfolk Island 38, 60, 91, 98, 101, 104, 157, 161, 207
Norman, Charles 217
Norton, John 149, *171*, 219

O'Brian, Patrick, *Desolation Island* 130, 155
Ocean's Story: or, Triumphs of Thirty Centuries (Goodrich) 161
"Odyssey for Survival: The Wreck of the 'Wild Wave'" (Bellarosa) 162
Oeno Island 91
Oliver, Douglas, *Return to Tahiti: Bligh's Second Breadfruit Voyage* 99, *100*, 167
Olivier, Laurence 219
On Ten Persons Charged with Mutiny on Board His Majesty's Ship the Bounty With an Appendix (Barney and Christian) 55, 67
Once a Week 42
open-boat voyage 8, 10–11, *39*, 40, 43, 73, 85–86, 167, *168*, 181; Alec Ball's illustrations of 198, *199*; in Barbary's novel 154; in Bennett's novel 157; and Bligh as artist 167; in Byron's poem 133; in Chodes' play 130, 162, *163*; in Crane's play *165*; in Dodd's painting *62*, 63, *83*, 167; films about 211, 217, 219; Fryer's account of 170, 183, 185; Gamble's account of 183, 185; Gibbings' wood engravings of 171, *171*; in Hack's stories 136; in Ingleton's illustrations 190–92, *192*; Lamb's wood engravings of *180*; in Lang's stories 140; Mansir's illustrations of 193–95, *196*, *197*; in Nordhoff and Hall's novels *147*, 149–51, *150*; of *Pandora's* men 18, 73, 75, 104, 154, 176; in Pearl's story 215; Wyeth's illustrations of *178*
organ 46
Orkney Islands 133, 155, *156*
Oster, Gerald and Semalree, "The Great Breadfruit Scheme" 105
Otaheite/Otaheitans *see* Tahiti/Tahitians
Oulton, Abraham, "The Mutiny of the Bounty" 129
Our Village (Mitford) 133
Overland Monthly 45
Oxford World's Classics 33, *34*, 47, 145
oysters 191–92, *192*, 198, *199*

Pacific Islands Monthly 56
Pacific Record 56
Pacific Union Recorder 104
Palais, Rudy 213
Pandora, H.M.S.: Alexander's account of 94–95, *95*; Andersen's illustrations of 198; in Barbary's novel 154; Barrow's account of 31, 33; in *Chronicles of the Sea* 36, *37*; Danielsson's

account of 73; Delano's account of 27–28; films about 211, 219, 221; Gesner's account of 19, 98–99; Heywood's account of 102–3; Heywood's sketch of 167; Lee's account of 59; map of voyage of *58*; Maude's account of 104; McFarland's account of 48; McKay and Coleman's account of 99; prisoners on 18, 33, 35, 57, 73, 75, 87, 154–55; Rawson's account of 73–75, *74*; in *Sailors' Magazine* 40; shipwreck of 18, 30, 33, 35, *37*, 41, 56–57, 59, 73, *74*, 98–99, 104, 133, 154–55, 157, 167, 173–74, 176, 188, 211, 227–28, 231, 233; Smyth's account of 50; in *Voyage of H.M.S. "Pandora"* (Edwards and Hamilton) 18, 28, 56–57, *58*; in *Voyage Round the World* (Hamilton) 7, *16*, 18–19, 21, 57; Wahlroos' account of 87

Pandora: An Archaeological Perspective (Gesner) 19, 98–99
"Pandora's Box" 18, 33, 57, 73, 75, 87, 154
Pandora's *Last Voyage* (Rawson) 69, **73–75**, *74*, 103, 167
paranoid delusions 75–76
Parley, Peter 43; *Peter Parley's Universal History on the Basis of Geography* 136–37; Tales About the Sea, and the Islands in the Pacific Ocean 129, **136–37**, *137*, 140
Parry, Edward 28
"Particulars of the Late Execution on Board the *Brunswick*" (*The Gentleman's Magazine*) 21
Paths of the Sea (Harper) 130, 162, 193
Pearl, Jack, "Captain Bligh of the *Bounty*" 215, *216*
Pearson, Roger *165*
"Peggy" 18, 133, 135, 157, 188
Pelican, H.M.S. 89
The Pen and the Quarter-Deck: A Study of the Life and Works of Captain Frederick Chamier, R.N. (Van der Voort) 160
People 224
"Peter Heywood, Esq." (Marshall) 33, 36, 48, 50
Petty, Thurman C., Jr., *Wreck of the Wild Wave: The Untold Saga of Captain Knowles and Pitcairn Island* 162
Pew, Curtis E., "Mutiny on the Bounty (ex-Bethia)" 227–28

Phoenix (American whaling ship) 60
Photoplay Magazine 207
Piccadilly Theatre (London) 222, *223*
Pilgrim (barque) 60
Pipon, Philip 24–30, 140, *142*, 205
The Pirates: or, The Calamaties of Capt. Bligh (Dibdin) 8, **204–5**, *206*
Pitcairn (Seventh-day Adventist Church schooner) 104
"Pitcairn and Norfolk: The Saga of Bounty's Children" (Howard) 104
Pitcairn: Children of Mutiny (Ball) 56, **80–82**, *81*, 93
Pitcairn Island: Anthony's account of 97; in Ballantyne's story 138, 140, *141*; Ball's account of 56, 80–82, *81*; Barrow's account of 31–32, *32*; in Becke and Jeffery's novel 143; Beechey's account of 28–29, *42*, 168; Belcher's account of 40–41, *42*; Brodie's account of 47; in Bryant's poem 160–61; in *Chronicles of the Sea* 36; church on 46; Clarke's account of 98; in *Classics Illustrated* *214*; Danielsson's account of 73; Darby's account of 76; Delano's account of 23, 26–27; discovery of 50; documentaries about 231; and emigration 38, 48, 77, 91, 161; films about 204, 207, 210, 219, 221, 226; Ford's account of 89–91, *90*; Glynn Christian's account of 84–85, 102; in Goodrich's collection 161; in *A Guide to Pitcairn* 91; Hall's account of 99; Hough's account of 77, 79–80; Jenny's account of 48; Johnsons' account of 103; in Knox's novel 162; in Lang's stories 140, 142–43, *142*; language of 101; in London's story 144–45; Lummis' account of 91–94; Lyman's account of 104; Marden's account of 104; massacres on 25, 28, 76, 80, 93–94, 131–32, 151–52, 158, 207; Maude's account of 104; Mitford's poem of 130–32; Murray's account of 38–39; in *Mutiny!* (musical) 223–24; in Nordhoff and Hall's novels 146, 148, 151–52, *153*; and *Pandora's* voyage 57, *58*; in Peter Parley stories 136; in *Pitcairn Island*

Register Book 60; plays about 204–5; religious instruction about *see* moral lessons; religious instruction; Robert Brown's account of 43; in *Sailors' Magazine* 40; seamanship of natives 42, 82, 136–37, 210; Shapiro's account of 38, 56, 76–77, 90–91, 101; Shillibeer's account of 24–26; in "The Ship and the Island" (anon.) 138; ships calling at 89, 210 (see also names of ships); Silverman's account of 56, 76–77; in Snow's story 160; in *Sunday at Home* 50; in Twain's story 129, 160; voting rights for women on 85, 102; Wahlroos' account of 87, 89; websites 234; Young's account of 24, 45–46

Pitcairn Island (Silverman) 56, 76–77, 93
Pitcairn Island: Life and Death in Eden (Lummis) 56, **91–94**, *92*
Pitcairn Island: Refuge of the Bounty Mutineers (Allward) 56, 97
Pitcairn Island Register Book (Lucas, ed.) **59–61**, *61*
"Pitcairn Island—The *Bounty's* Crew" (Dillon) 93
Pitcairn Island Today (short film) 208
"The Pitcairn Islanders" (Lang) 140, 142–43, *142*
"The Pitcairn Islanders, and the Mutiny of the *Bounty*" (Brown) **42–43**, *44*
Pitcairn Islands Administration (Auckland, N.Z.) 91
Pitcairn Log 56
"Pitcairn, Lone Rock of the Sea" (hymn) 45
Pitcairn Miscellany 91
"Pitcairn, Missionary Packet" (Lyman) 104
Pitcairn—Port of Call (Ford) 56, **89–91**, *90*
Pitcairn: The Island, the People, and the Pastor (Murray) 23, **36, 38–39**, *39*, 45, 60
Pitcairn: The Miscellany of Pitcairn's Islands (Shapiro) 91
The Pitcairnese Language (Ross) 101
"Pitcairn's Island" (Hale) 161
Pitcairn's Island (Nordhoff and Hall) 79, 130, 148, **151–52**, *153*, 169, 201, 213
Pitcairn's Island and the Islanders in 1850 (Brodie) 47, 151

"Pitcairn's Island — The Bounty's Crew" (Dillon) 48
"Pitcairn's Revolutionary Women" (Christian) 102
Pitz, Henry C. 146, *147*, 152, *153*, 177–78, *178*
"Plagiarism on the Bounty" (Lacy) 103–4
plays 8, 130, 162, *163*, *165*, 193, 204–5, 217
pneumonia 19
pocket watch 99, 231
poetry 69, *70*, 129–35, 160–61
polar expeditions 28
Popular Mechanics Magazine 228
Portlock, Nathaniel 12, 59
Power, Wilton 205, 207
The Practical Navigator (Moore) 86
prayers 25–26
Primitive Pitcairn (short film) 208
Prince Edward Theatre (Sydney) 207
Pro Patria (schooner) 99
prostitutes 39
Providence, H.M.S. 10, 12, 203, 211; Alexander's account of 95–96; Darby's account of 75–76, 102; Lebogue's account of 17; Lee's account of 58–59; log of 19, 58; Mackaness' account of 63–64; Oliver's account of 99, *100*, 167; Oster and Oster's account of 105; and Tobin as artist 59, 99, *100*, 167; used as "control group" 75–76; Wahlroos' account of 87, 89
psychoanalysis 75–76
psychological readings 87, 89, 105
psychotic disorder 85, 89, 105
Publishers Weekly 224
pulp magazines 215, *216*
pumpkin 32, 173, 222
Purcell, William: Alexander's account of 95–96; in *Appendix to the Proceedings* (Christian) 15; Ball's account of 82; on *Bounty* 181; in Chodes' play *163*; films about 210, 219; in Ingleton's illustrations 190, *192*; in Nordhoff and Hall's novels 149; on *Resource* 181
Pyle, Howard 177
Pyrennes (steel bark) 144

quadrant 136
Quarterly Review 23, 27–28, 50, 135
Quayle, Eric, *Ballantyne the Brave: A Victorian Writer and his Family* 160
Queen Victoria's birthday 45

Queensland Museum 98
Quintal, Arthur 151
Quintal, Matthew 76, 87, 93, 151, 154, 210, 213, 215–16, 219, 222, 224
Quintall, Edward 60

radio plays 130
Ramsden sextant 86
Raroronga 104
Rascals in Paradise (Michener and Day) 99
Ravilious, Eric 67, *68*
Rawson, Geoffrey: *Bligh of the "Bounty"* 55, 73; *Pandora's Last Voyage* 69, 73–75, *74*, 103, 167
The Real Captain Bligh (documentary) 231–32
Reardon, Ed, "Captain Bligh in Film" 211, 228
The Red True Story Book (Lang, ed.) **140, 142–43**, *142*
Regent's Park (London, Eng.) 35
Reid, Alan 104
religious instruction 38–40, 43, 93–94, 104, 162; *see also* moral lessons
"Remarks on Morrison's Journal" (Bligh) 173, 182
Renee, Sinitaa 222
Renouard, David T. 104
Resolution (schooner built by mutineers) 57, 73, 104, 154, 174, *175*
Resolution, H.M.S. (Cook's ship) 59, 155, 191
"Resolving *The Corsair, Lara* and *The Island*" (Leask) 163
Resource (schooner) 87, 181, *182*
Restoration Island 85–86, 149, 192, *192*
Return of the Bounty: Flagship of the Fleet (Sudbury, ed.) 227
Return to Tahiti: Bligh's Second Breadfruit Voyage (Oliver) 99, *100*, 167
Review and Herald 56, 104
Reynolds, N.C. 146
"The Rime of the Ancyent Marinere" (Coleridge) 69, *70*, 129, 161–64
Rinaldi, Ann, *Mutiny's Daughter* 130, 162, 193
The Road to Xanadu (Lowes) 69, 163
Robbins, Charles Henry, *The Gam: Being a Group of Whaling Stories* 61
Robert Bolt: Scenes from Two Lives (Turner) 227
Robinson Crusoe (Defoe) 162–63
Rogers, G.A. 105

Rogers, John 96
Romantic movement, 69, 133; *see also* names of Romantic poets
Roskill, Stephen 47
Ross, A.S.C., *The Pitcairnese Language* 101
Rotorua 207
Rotterdam Welfare 151
Roughley, T.C., "Bounty Descendants Live of Remote Norfolk Island" 104
Roulston, Robert, *James Norman Hall* 160
Round the World and Other Stories 129, **137–38**, *139*
Royal Geographical Society 84
Royal Naval Biography of Peter Heyward (Marshall) 33, 36, 188
Royal Navy: and Barrow 31; and Bligh 12, 15, 33, 96, 203; and Fryer 170, 183; and Heyward 30, 35, 40, 50, 65, 96, 102–3; in Nordhoff and Hall's novels 148; sodomy as capital offense in *79*; and Stewart 65; and Tinkler 65
Royalty Theatre 8, 204
rum 82, 185
Rum Rebellion 63
Rutter, Owen 97, 102, 103, 169, 170, 173–74, 178–79, 181–83, *182*, 185; *Cain's Birthday* 65, 158, 160, 193; *The Court-Martial of the "Bounty" Mutineers* 65, 101, 102; "The Travels of Fletcher Christian" 163; *The True Story of the Mutiny in the "Bounty"* 55, **65–67**, *66*; *Turbulent Journey: A Life of William Bligh* 55, 63, 65, 101; "The Vindication of Captain Bligh" 105

Sadler's Wells Theatre 205
"Saga of a Ship, the *Yankee*" (Marden) 103
The Saga of the Bounty (Anthony) 97, 193
Saga: The Magazine for Men **215**, *216*
The Sailors' Magazine: Containing the Life of Peter Heywood, Midshipman of the Bounty **39–40**, *41*
Samoan Islands 104
San Francisco Morning Call 104
Saturday Evening Post 169, 201
Schoen, Hartmel 231
Schreiber, Roy, *The Fortunate Adversities of William Bligh* 55
Scientific American 224

Scribner's Classics 177–78
Scribners Monthly 45
"Scrutiny on the Bounty: Captain Bligh's Secret Logbook" (Buckley) 224–25, **225**
Sea: Its Stirring Story of Adventure, Peril and Heroism (Whymper) 201
Seagrave, Eleanor Roosevelt 47
sealing 24
Seaman's Friend Society 39–40, 41
"Secrets of the Movie Ships" *(Popular Mechanics Magazine)* 228
"The Seed of McCoy" (London) 129, **143–45**, *145*, 158
Selborne, Joanna, *British Wood-Engraved Book Illustration, 1904–1940* 201
Seventh-day Adventists 45, 89–90, 104
sextant 86
Shapiro, Harry L. 90–91; *The Heritage of the Bounty* 38, 56, 76–77, 91, 101; *Island of Tears: John I. Tay* 91; *Pitcairn; The Miscellany of Pitcairn's Islands* 91
Shearer, Charles 156
Shillibeer, John J. 167; *A Narrative of the Briton's Voyage to Pitcairn Island* 23, **24–26**, *26*, 167
"The Ship and the Island" (anon.) **137–38**, *139*
A Short Reply to Capt. William Bligh's Answer (Christian) **12**, **17–18**, 20, 67
Siege of Quebec (play) 204
Silverman, David, *Pitcairn Island* 56, **76–77**, 93
Simpson, Francis 35, 40
"A Single Unlucky Imposter" (Snow) 160
Sir John Barrow Commemorative Expedition 84
"Sketch of the Career of the Late Captain Peter Heywood, R.N." (Smyth) 33, 50
Skinner, Richard 33
skulls 93
slave revolts 27
Smith, Alexander *see* Adams, John
Smith, Carl 74
Smith, John 17
Smyth, William Henry 31, 73; "The Bounty Again!" 50; "Capt. Beechey's Narrative" 50; "Sketch of the Career of the Late Captain Peter Heywood, R.N." 33, 50

Snark (yacht) 144–45
Snow, Philip, "A Single Unlucky Imposter" 160
social class 162, *163*, 217
Society for Promoting Christian Knowledge (SPCK) 38, 60
sodomy 79
Solomon, Jon, "Celluloid Bountys" 228
"Some Remarks about the Mutiny of the Bounty" (Bonner Smith) 102
"A Song of Pitcairn's Island" (Bryant) 129, 160–61
Sotheby's 170
"Sourabaya incident" 181
South Africa 31
South America 193
South Sea Tales (London) 129, **143–45**, *145*
Southey, Robert 69, 193, 233
Southworth, Rufus, *A Doctor's Letters from Pitcairn, 1937* 146
Spence, Gordon, "Byron's Polynesian Fantasy" 164
Spithead 84
Squire, John, "Was Fletcher Christian the Ancient Mariner?" 164
Staines, Sir Thomas 24–30, 137, 140, *142*, 205, 216
Stebner, Greg 231
Steven, Jack, "I Survived the Savage Mutiny on the Bounty" 228
Stevenson, Robert Louis 177, 213
Stewart, George 217; Adams' account of 30, 41–42, 50; in Barbary's novel 154; Beechey's account of 30; Belcher's account of 41–42; in Byron's poem 133, 135; Darby's account of 75; death of 33, 41, 59, 133, 155, 157; family of 155; films about 210; as friend of Heywood 30, 41; in George Mackay Brown's story 155–57; journal of 104; Kennedy's account of 65; role in mutiny 75; and social class 217; wife of 18, 133, 135, 157, 188
Stories of the Sea, Told by Sailors (Hale) 161
Story of Alec, or Pitcairn's Island (Fiske) 23
The Story of Pitcairn Island (Christensen) 104
Strand magazine 198
Stroven, Carl, *Best South Sea Stories* 158
Studia Bountyana 1 and 2 (Du Rietz) 56, 69, **75–76**

Sturma, Michael, "Women, the *Bounty*, the Movies" 228
Sudbury, Neil, ed., *Return of the Bounty: Flagship of the Fleet* 227
Sultan (whaling ship) 48
Sumner, John 33
Sunday at Home Magazine 23, 50
Swift (New Bedford whaling ship) 60

Tagart, Edward 35, 50; *Memoir of the Late Captain Peter Heywood, R.N.* 33, **35–36**, 50, 161
Tagus, H.M.S. 24, 26, 29, 136, *137*, 140, 205
Tahiti/Tahitians: Ball's account of 80–82; in Barbary's novel 154; in Becke and Jeffery's novel 143; Bligh's account of 8, 11, 59, 80–81, 180, 191; in Bryant's poem 160–61; and Danielsson 71; Darby's account of 75; Delano's account of 23, 27–28; documentaries about 231; and emigration 38, 48, 77, 91, 161; European contact, effects of 18–19; films about *209*, 210–11, *212*, 216, 219, 221, 226–28; and fishing techniques 11; and Fletcher Christian 59, 75, 77, 79, 84; in George Mackay Brown's story 157; Glynn Christian's account of 84–85, 102; Hamilton's account of 18–19; and Heywood 35, 50, 79, 161, 188; and homosexuality 80–81; Hough's account of 77; in Ingleton's illustrations 191–92, *191*; Johnsons' account of 103; language dictionary 35; Lee's account of 59; Lummis' account of 85, 93–94; Maude's account of 104; in Metcalfe's novel 158; in Mitford's poem 131; and Morrison's journal 173–74; Murray's account of 38; in *Mutiny!* (musical) 222; in Nordhoff and Hall's novels 146, 148, 151, *153*, 188, *189*; Oliver's account of 99; and *Pandora's* voyage 57, *58*, 59, 73; Rawson's account of 73; in "The Ship and the Island" (anon.) 138, *139*; Tagart's account of 35; and Tobin as artist 167; and venereal diseases 40; Wahlroos' account of 87, 93, 105; Wyeth's illustrations of 178
taio friendship 105

Taiya (square-rigged brigantine) 84, 231
The Tale of a Shipwreck (Hall) 99, 157
Tales About the Sea, and the Islands in the Pacific Ocean (Parley) 129, **136–37**, *137*, 140
tapa trees 45
Tapsell, Alan 71
Tasmania 59, 167, 190, *190*
tattooing 221
Tay, John I. 89–90, 104
Taylor, Fiona *165*
Taylor, Harold Midgely 169
Teehuteatuaonoa *see* Jenny
Tegg, Thomas 30, 137, 197
Tehani/Tehanni 188, 210
tetanus 45
That Bounty Bastard (Allen) 55, 97
Thompson, Matthew 73, 210
Thomson, Basil 18, 28, 56–57
Thrapp, Dan L., *Mutiny's Curse* 130, 160, 193
The Three Musketeers (Dumas) 213
Timor 26–27, 57, 86, 98, 104, 136, 149, 164, 170, 176, 181, 188, 215, 224
Tinkler, Robert 65, 96, 148, 152, 154, *163*, 185, *187*, 188, 210, 221
Tobin, George 59, 65, 99, *100*, 167
Tofoa 149, *171*, *180*, 188, 194, 231
Tolkien, J.R.R., *The Lord of the Rings* 204
Tone, Franchot 210–11, *212*
Topaz (American sealing ship) 24, 28–29, 89, 130, 148, 152
Topliff, Samuel 48
"Torment in Tofua" (Harris) 227
Torres Strait 59
tortoises 26
Townsend, John Rowe, *Written for Children* 140
"The Transformed Island" (*Sunday at Home*) 50
Transit of Venus (Metcalfe) 158
"The Travels of Fletcher Christian" (Rutter) 163–64
The Triumph of Liberty (play) 204
"The True Story of Peter Heywood" (Nordhoff and Hall) 185, 188
The True Story of the Mutiny in the "Bounty" (Rutter) 55, **65–67**, *66*
True Story of the Mutiny on the Bounty (documentary) 232
The Truth about the Mutiny on the Bounty (McKee) 55, 167
Tryal (Spanish ship) 27

Tubai/Tubuai/Toobouai 36, 50, 59, 84, 87, 104, 133, 135, 138, *139*, 154, 173, 198, 211
tuberculosis 45
Turbulent Journey: A Life of William Bligh (Rutter) 55, 63, 65, 101
Turner, Adrian 219; *Robert Bolt: Scenes from Two Lives* 227
"Turning Mutiny into a Legend" (Kennedy) 8
Twain, Mark 47, 158; "The Great Revolution in Pitcairn" 129, 160
24-Gun Frigate Pandora 1779 (McKay and Coleman) 99

UK Log 56
Ulriksen, Mark 94, *95*, 201
"Uncle Thomas Tells About the Mutiny of the Bounty" (Bingley) 161
Unitarian Church 33, 35, 50
United Service Journal 23, 25, 31, 33, 50, 73
USA Today 96, 224

Valentine, James 148, 219, 222
Valiant Martinet (Beard) 160
Van der Voort, P.J., *Pen and the Quarter-Deck: A Study of the Life and Works of The Captain Frederick Chamier, R.N.* 160
Van Diemen's Land *see* Tasmania
Vanjon, Governor 27
venereal diseases 19, 40, 188, 191, *191*, 194–95
Verne, Jules 177; *Begum's Fortune: With an Account of The Mutineers of the "Bounty"* 200, 201
Vicary, Tim, *Mutiny on the Bounty* 162
Victory, H.M.S. 154
Villiers, Alan 188, 190
"The Vindication of Captain Bligh" (Rutter) 105
Virago (steamship) 45
Vlydt (Dutch packet) 181–83, *182*
Von Horn, W.O., *The Lord Will Repay* 162
voting rights for women 85, 102
"The Voyage of H.M.S. Pandora, 1790–1792: Some Remarks Upon Geoffrey Rawson's Book on the Subject" (Du Rietz) 103
Voyage of H.M.S. "Pandora" Despatched to Arrest the Mutineers of the "Bounty" in the South Seas, 1790–1791 (Edwards and Hamilton) 18, 28, **56–57**, *58*
"The Voyage of Pandora's Tender" (Maude) 104

The Voyage of the Bounty's *Launch* (Fryer) 21, 65, 169, 183
The Voyage of the Bounty's Launch as Related in William Bligh's Despatch to the Admiralty and the Journal of John Fryer (Bligh and Fryer) 21, **169–71**, *171*
Voyage on the Bounty (documentary) 232
A Voyage Round the World in His Majesty's Frigate Pandora (Hamilton) 7, *16*, **18–19**, 21, 57
A Voyage to the South Sea (Bligh) 7, **10–11**, *12*, 17, 20, 55, 155, 181, **188**, **190–92**, *190*, *191*, *192*; in *A Book of the "Bounty"* 67; in Delano's account 27; and Hack's stories 135; and *The Log of the Bounty* 179; and Mansir's illustrations 195; and Mitford's poem 131; and Nordhoff and Hall's novels 146, 149, 169; unabridged edition of 174–76
Voyagers: Words and Images (Kane) 198
Voyages (Cook) 18

Wahlroos, Sven 85, 232; "HMS Bounty: The Bloodless Mutiny" 105; *Mutiny and Romance in the South Seas* 25, 48, **86–89**, *88*, 93, 105; "What Caused the Mutiny on the Bounty? Separating Fact from Speculation" 105
The Wake of the Bounty (Wilkinson) 67, **69**, *70*, 82, 129, 164, 193
Walch, James *163*
Waldinger, Morris 213
Wallis, Samuel 19
Walter, Frank 207
Walters, Stephen 192, 227
"Was Fletcher Christian the Ancient Mariner?" (Squire) 164
Weare, Philip, *Captain William Bligh: An Illustrated History* 162
Webber, John 152
websites 233–34
Wells-next-the-Sea (Norfolk) *184*, 185
"Westward Bound in the Yankee" (Johnson and Johnson) 103
Wewitzer, Ralph 205
"What Caused the Mutiny on the Bounty? Separating Fact From Speculation" (Wahlroos) 105
What Happened on the Bounty (Danielsson) 69, **71**, 73, 167

wheat 89
White, David 231
White Logic: Jack London's Short Stories (McClintock), 144, 158
Who Caused the Mutiny on the Bounty? (Darby) 55, 69, 75–76, 77, 79, 87, 93, 103
"Why Roger Byam?" (Murray) 227
Whymper, F., *Sea: Its Stirring Story of Adventure, Peril and Heroism* 201
Wild Wave (California clipper ship) 161–62
Wilkinson, Chris 231
Wilkinson, C.S., *The Wake of the Bounty* 67, **69**, *70*, 82, 129, 164, 193
Wilkinson, Tom 231
William Bligh of the Bounty in Fact and in Fable (Montgomerie) 55, 99, 103–4
Williams, John 216, 224
Williams, M.J. 91
Williams, Roy 192–93, *194*, *195*
Wilson, Carey 210
Wilson, Erle, *Adams of the Bounty* 130, 160
Winter Evenings, or Tales of Travellers (Hack) 129, 135, 140
Winter Tales (Brown) **155–57**, *156*
The Women of Pitcairn Island (film) 227
women, Tahitian/Polynesian: in Becke and Jeffery's novel 143; Bligh's account of 59; in Bryant's poem 160–61; and Fletcher Christian 59, 75, 77, 84; Glynn Christian's account of 85, 102; Darby's account of 75; Delano's account of 23, 27–28; films about *209*, 210, *212*, 221, 227–28; Hough's account of 77; Lummis' account of 93–94; in Metcalfe's novel 158; in Nordhoff and Hall's novels 151, *153*, 188, *189*; voting rights of 85, 102; Wahlroos' account of 93
"Women, the *Bounty*, the Movies" (Sturma) 228
"A Wonderful Voyage" (Lang) 140
Wood, Grant 185
Wordsworth, William 69, 164, 193
The Works of Lord Byron (Coleridge, ed.) 133, 161
"Wreck of the *Pandora*: The Fate of the Men Sent to Hunt Down the *Bounty* Mutineers" (Alexander) 94, *95*, 201
Wreck of the Wild Wave: The Untold Saga of Captain Knowles and Pitcairn Island (Petty) 162
Wright, David Curtis 224
Written for Children (Townsend) 140
Wyeth, N.C. 169, 177–78

Yankee (brigantine) 103
"The *Yankee*'s Wander-world" (Johnson and Johnson) 103
Young, Edward: Barrow's account of 30; in Becke and Jeffery's novel 143; as "*Bounty's* Iago" 30, 79; Darby's account of 75–76; death of 94; diary/journal of 29, 76; films about 210, 216, 219; Hough's account of 79; journal of 93; Lummis' account of 93–94; in *Mutiny!* (musical) 221, 223–24; in Nordhoff and Hall's novels 148; role in mutiny 30, 75–76, 79; role in Pitcairn Island massacres 76, 93; son of 25, 140, *142*; Wahlroos' account of 87
Young, Elizabeth 87
Young, Ethel 61
Young, George 25, *32*, *142*
Young, Rosalind Amelia: "The Mutineers of the *Bounty*" 45; *Mutiny of the Bounty and Story of Pitcairn Island* 24, **43**, **45–46**, *46*, 151
Young, Simon 45
Young Fur Traders (Ballantyne) 140
The Young Nimrods Around the World (Knox) 162
The Youth's Instructor 45

Zaca (schooner) 90

www.ingramcontent.com/pod-product-compliance
Lightning Source LLC
Chambersburg PA
CBHW081547300426
44116CB00015B/2791